Globalization, Philanthropy, and Civil Society

PHILANTHROPIC AND NONPROFIT STUDIES
Dwight F. Burlingame and David C. Hammack, editors

Globalization, Philanthropy, and Civil Society

PROJECTING INSTITUTIONAL LOGICS ABROAD

EDITED BY

DAVID C. HAMMACK

AND

STEVEN HEYDEMANN

Indiana University Press
Bloomington and Indianapolis

A project organized by the Social Science Research Council

This book is a publication of

Indiana University Press
601 North Morton Street
Bloomington, IN 47404-3797 USA

www.iupress.indiana.edu

Telephone orders	800-842-6796
Fax orders	812-855-7931
Orders by e-mail	iuporder@indiana.edu

♾ The paper used in this publication meets the minimum requirements of American National Standard for Information Sciences—Permanence of Paper for Printed Library Materials, ANSI Z39.48-1992.

Manufactured in the United States of America

LIBRARY OF CONGRESS CATALOGING-IN-PUBLICATION DATA

Globalization, philanthropy, and civil society : projecting institutional logics abroad / edited by David C. Hammack and Steven Heydemann.
    p. cm. — (Philanthropic and nonprofit studies)
  Includes bibliographical references and index.
  ISBN 978-0-253-35303-0 (cloth : alk. paper)
  1. Charities. 2. Endowments. 3. Globalization. 4. Civil society. I. Hammack, David C. II. Heydemann, Steven.
  HV40.G583 2009
  361.7'7—dc22   2008053534

1 2 3 4 5 14 13 12 11 10 09

Contents

Foreword

Social Science and Philanthropic Studies

←——————————————————————————————————————→

Analytically constructed studies of philanthropy are in short supply. The shelf of foundation books remains overly crowded with self-congratulatory, mostly boring, insider accounts; or with shrill denunciations by outsiders—mostly ill-informed if often entertaining in a gossipy sort of way. Having grown weary of those tracts, we are hungry for works that tell us where foundations actually fit into the political economy, and how and when, even if, they are consequential.

On such questions, historians have been more productive than social scientists. The reader familiar with writings by historians will know much of importance about how organized philanthropy has matured in the United States and in a few instances elsewhere—though comparative historiography is in short supply. But the reader new to this field will discover that social scientists more generally have been slow to grasp the potentially rich field of philanthropic studies, despite ambitious efforts to assemble relevant data sets and to map out taxonomies that can begin to organize research. The social science project of which this volume is an early and important expression is now beginning to show that when social scientists, often working with historians, bring theoretical inquiry to the growth, behavior, and impact of grant-making foundations, the payoff is high. In the present instance, exploring civil society in countries that formerly fell under the control of the Soviet Union, it is especially valuable that the institutionalists among social scientists and historians have been bold enough to move into the comparative arena.

The institutions that inhabit civil society, though outside the state and outside the market, are nevertheless state-like and market-like actors. They are state-like in their obligation to provide public goods, yet they have no coercive powers; they cannot tax, regulate, legislate, enforce, or perform any of the other functions assigned to the state. They are market-like in their intention to meet the needs of society by providing sought-after services, yet they offer no profits or return on investments; they cannot deploy the many tools available to the commercial and financial institutions of the market. To use psychological terms, two basic human emotions—fear and greed—are essentially unavailable to civil society institutions. How, then, are they to mobilize the resources and influence the behaviors that allow them to do what neither the state nor the market seems willing or able to do? They rely on charity, volunteerism, and individual or organized philanthropy.

It is organized philanthropy that sits at the center of the studies in this collection. The first large fact we take away is that organized philanthropy is not only in and of the civil society sector; it has a vital interest in expanding that sector. This is where philanthropy finds the institutions which, for their part, legitimate philanthropy by carrying out philanthropic missions. This is particularly evident when we turn attention to the American grant-making foundation. These institutions need client grantees as recipients to absorb obligatory spend-out funds, but more importantly as the real and the symbolic expressions of what philanthropy is supposed to represent—the attachment of private wealth to public purpose. In the absence of civil society institutions there is no philanthropy as we know it.

What, then, are foundations to do if their trustees instruct them to establish a program in countries that do not have much of a civil society, that is, do not have a network of NGOs able to implement the foundation's intent to bring democracy to those countries? If the foundations are large, rich, self-confident, and American, they will set out to create what they believe in and are familiar with in their home-based liberal democracy and market economy—a robust civil society with a dense array of institutional actors. With newly established grantee partners, they will advocate for a division of labor among state, market, and civil society that offers maximum maneuvering room for the latter. In the terms used by the editors, philanthropy will *project* its liberal ideas and institutional logics. This philanthropic project of projection is the natural consequence of exporting who and what they are, and foundations at times go so far as to use their endowments to endow fledging foundations abroad that themselves become grant-making institutions.

From a comparative perspective, helping to establish civil society institutions in Eastern Europe is particularly instructive. There were earlier efforts by the West to export what, in its view, was its more sophisticated culture, art, and science to the lands and peoples of Eastern Europe. But in the post-Soviet era, philanthropy found an unusual eagerness for Western models to replace the discredited, impoverished polities and economies imposed by Soviet communism.

Despite this unusually fertile ground, projecting the principles of liberalism in Eastern Europe has not been unproblematic. Institutional logics of the sort studied in these fascinating accounts were not uniformly welcome, and when accepted, were nearly always refashioned to serve local priorities. It should not surprise us that there is nothing straightforward about negotiating maneuvering space between the state and the market in countries that are reinventing the ground rules for polity and economy even as they are growing a civil society. But if not surprised, we benefit from the careful documentation of the many ways in which the contest over maneuvering room plays itself out.

Explanations of philanthropic institutional logics and their reception under varying conditions will be further advanced when the Eastern European experience is compared with, say, the earlier entry into the new nations of Africa by western philanthropy, particularly by the Ford and Rockefeller Foundations. While the Ford Foundation took up state-building projects such as civil service reform, the Rockefeller Foundation retreated to the safer ground of health and agricultural research. The fate of these different approaches can usefully be compared with the variety of programs attempted in Eastern Europe. Incidentally, some of the most telling tensions were intra-foundational, as officers in the field fought with the home office—the former more inclined to defer to local institutional logics and the latter fixed on headquarter priorities. Asked, repeatedly and then insistently, to fill out forms for his New York–based supervisors, Norman Borlaug, soon to be a Nobelist for his pioneering green revolution work in Mexico, finally cabled back: "Did you send me out here to grow paper or grow corn?" (If there was an answer from headquarters, I was unable to find it.)

A chief contribution of this volume lies in its examination of how projecting institutional logics unfolds when those logics are skeptically examined by the societies for which they are intended. The lessons we take away have bearing on any number of philanthropic projects around the world—for example, bringing clean energy policies to China or higher education reform to Africa. The studies here have the additional merit of being provocative. The volume will excite other scholars to set it straight, which of course is how knowledge advances.

KENNETH PREWITT

Acknowledgments

In the most general sense, this volume owes its existence to the conceptual ferment that accompanied three major intellectual departures of recent years: the new interest in globalization and civil society, the emergent field of nonprofit and philanthropic studies, and the rise of new approaches to organizational behavior in sociology and in economics. Marcel Mauss long ago emphasized that gifts ("philanthropic" or otherwise) are always embedded in relationships—relationships that express hierarchy, conflict, and negotiation. Nonprofit, nongovernmental organizations are also engaged in the exchange and subordination dynamics of the gift economy—but they are also embedded in the dynamics of market relationships and in the arrangements of state power structures.

Many recent writers have shaped the discussions that the essays in this book engage. Samuel Huntington, Arturo Escobar, Margaret E. Keck, Kathryn Sikkink, John Boli, George M. Thomas, John W. Meyer, and many others have defined the debate over globalization. The study of nonprofit and nongovernmental organizations, in the United States, internationally, and with respect to the globalization of civil society and nonprofit organizations, owes a great deal to the extraordinary data collection and policy analysis work of Lester Salamon and his many associates, to Walter W. Powell, and to numerous others. Meanwhile, the institutional approach of sociologists Walter Powell and Paul DiMaggio and the economic analyses of Burton Weisbrod, Kenneth Arrow, Henry Hansmann, and others brought important new perspectives to the analysis of organizations. Much of this work responds to the rapid international proliferation and growth of nonprofit and nongovernmental organizations and to the many efforts to reform them.

It was against the background of these intellectual and practical developments that Kenneth Prewitt, then president of the Social Science Research Council (SSRC), succeeded in launching a Committee on Philanthropy and the Nonprofit Sector. Prewitt recognized the need to strengthen connections between the core disciplines in the social sciences and the study of philanthropy and the nonprofit sector. The committee he created pursued this aim from 1999 to 2005. A substantial grant from the Atlantic Philanthropies to the SSRC made possible the committee's work. Through grants and workshops for dissertation writers, the committee supported much of the work that is included in this volume, as well as the culminating conference at which all of these chapters were first discussed.

As leaders of the SSRC, Kenneth Prewitt and Craig Calhoun provided indispensable support for the Committee on Philanthropy and the Nonprofit Sector. Ellen Condliffe Lagemann and Bert Weisbrod provided excellent leadership through their successive terms as chairs of the committee; Elisabeth Clemens, Charles Clotfelter, Paul DiMaggio, David C. Hammack, Michael Katz, Stanley N. Katz, Ellen Condliffe Lagemann, Lester Salamon, and Janet Weiss offered astute and timely contributions to the committee's discussions. Lis Clemens, David C. Hammack, Kirsten A. Grønbjerg, Francie Ostrower, and Richard Steinberg provided helpful guidance when they joined us at the program's annual workshops. Lis Clemens, Alice O'Connor, Kenneth Prewitt, and Doug Guthrie—like our contributors Akira Iriye, Michael Lounsbury, David Strang, John W. Slocum, and Ann Swidler—made valuable interventions at the final 2005 workshop at the La Pietra Conference Center of New York University in Florence, Italy. Lis Clemens and Doug Guthrie, who are editing a companion volume, provided important advice as we started work on this one. Through its location as a central node in diverse networks of creative researchers, the SSRC enabled Steven Heydemann both to broaden his interest in institutions and to raise many of the questions at the center of these papers in discussions with thoughtful and well-informed researchers. Participation in the workshops and conferences, and service as a member of the committee, allowed David C. Hammack both to benefit from the quality of this SSRC initiative and to explore with remarkable colleagues the possible uses of the historical perspective.

Each of the dissertation writers benefited from suggestions made by other fellows at workshops and at the final conference, so it is appropriate here to acknowledge all fellows. They include Sada Aksartova, Elizabeth Bloodgood, Dorothea Browder, Christopher Capozzola, Bin Chen, Enid Coleman, Sarah Deschenes, Keri-Nicole Dillman, Joseph Doyle, Omri Elisha, Nicole Esparza, James Evans, Erzsébet Fazekas, Pamela Freese, Alysha Galvez, Brendan Goff, Teresa Harrison, G. Mark Hendrickson, Daniel Hungerman, Michael Jo, Gabriel Kaplan, Rebecca Kissane, Caroline Lee, Simon Lee, Sandra Levitsky, Scott Lien, Heather MacIndoe, Cheryl McDonald, Michael McQuarrie, Thomas Medvetz, Jodi Melamed, Amanda Moniz, Sandra Moog, Bethany

Moreton, Johann Neem, Stephen Porter, Natalia Sarkisian, Philipp Schmidt-Dengler, Anke Schwittay, Tracey Steffes, Erika Summers-Effler, Jonathan VanAntwerpen, and Rohit Wadhwani. Still more influential for each fellow, of course, were their departments and especially their dissertation advisors.

At the SSRC, program coordinator Amy Withers as well as assistants Aaron Beebe, Holly Danzheisen, Alexa Dietrich, Mira Edmonds, and Heloisa Griggs provided excellent staff support. Rebecca Kinsey and Sarah Cross at Georgetown and Katie Gresham at the U.S. Institute of Peace helped get all the materials together. Elise Hagesfeld at Case Western Reserve University provided helpful assistance in the final editing, as did Robert Sloan and his associates at Indiana University Press.

PART 1.
Introduction

1. Philanthropic Projections
Sending Institutional Logics Abroad

←——————————————————————————————→

STEVEN HEYDEMANN and DAVID C. HAMMACK

Frameworks

Ideas move. How they move and what they carry along with them as they do have been central preoccupations for generations of scholars. Today, however, we approach these questions from a distinctive vantage point. Barriers to the flow of ideas have diminished. We are awash in evidence of their movement in everything from fashion, music, and design, to conceptions of childhood and the family, to models for the organization of states and markets. Not least, we see powerful flows among strong and often conflicting cultural movements, whether promoting individualism, the imagined restoration of one or another version of moral purity, or the expansion of the geographic areas under the sway of particular religious beliefs. Indeed, the prominence of flows and the possibilities for movement are more than just markers of contemporary globalization: they are defining elements of modern life.

Yet the flow of ideas has not acquired the naturalness or taken-for-granted quality that would mark movement itself as a hegemonic and legitimating condition of modernity. This should not surprise us: ideas have consequences, and new ideas are likely to upset established relationships and hierarchies. Ideas are today, as they have been throughout history, carriers of conflict, sources of social struggle, and objects of resistance. They are subject to incomplete accommodation between the local and the imported, and to the tensions and adaptations that such accommodations produce. As this suggests, ideas do not always move spontaneously. The role of coercion in the flow of ideas has changed over time, but can never be entirely absent. Indeed, the language of projection and diffusion we adopt in this volume acknowledges the role of ideas as carriers of political, social, cultural, and economic power of the most tangible kinds.

Moreover, despite much discussion about the deepening and the consequences of globalization, it is clear that ideas are not equally portable. On one hand, the global diffusion of similar institutional forms—whether associated

3

with capitalism and democracy, with modes of social advocacy, with nationalism, national security, religion, or philanthropy—suggests to many a widespread decline in the range of possibilities for how we organize our lives. Institutional forms and functions seem more and more alike, in a growing number of domains. If, in the twentieth century, we experienced the emergence of the state as a "mandatory political unit," and the disappearance of alternative political forms, we are now seeing the internal arrangements of states become more similar in areas ranging from social policy, education, and labor markets, to norms of environmental protection and human rights. Movement toward a global consensus on the rights of individuals is central to many recent discussions of the growth of "civil society" or the expansion of the "nonprofit sector."[1] In a recent paper, Alex Wendt argues for the inevitable emergence, within one hundred years, of a single "world state" providing a unitary global government.[2] Whether this prediction is accurate or not, the extent to which states and other organizational forms are converging around a narrower and narrower set of governing norms and practices seems incontestable.

Yet the appearance of increasing isomorphism is offset by persistent and deep divergences, even within societies, economies, and polities that evidence considerable similarity when viewed at a sufficient level of abstraction. The notion of deepening global isomorphism among states, societies, and non-profit sectors must contend with the reality that variety, division, and divergence are persistent qualities of the international system. Ideas have different consequences in different contexts, and they fit differently into varying institutional arrangements. Even where form and function seem to converge, content is often stubbornly resistant to change. We are hardly the first to point this out, but it emerges as a main theme of the essays in this book.

Global environmentalism, for example, co-exists with divergent national approaches to environmental protection.[3] The presence of a "world culture,"[4] diffused in part through the agency of international NGOs, overlaps with highly varied local cultures that bear the imprint of the global, but are not simple reflections of it. Indeed, local cultures still dominate many areas and marginalize the "global." The spread of market-based strategies for the provision of social services, for example, has not overcome national and sub-national variation in preferences about the limits of the market, the role of the state, or the appropriate allocation of tasks among the state, market, and nonprofit sector. And, of course, the notion of the "market" is by no means simple or unitary: markets are always shaped by local laws, customs, regulations, and tax systems—and by inequities in enforcement mechanisms and inequalities in access to knowledge.

Thus although the universe of available institutions seems to be narrower, local realities ensure that the content of institutions, the meaning of institutional practices, and the relations among institutions and actors remain richly diverse. And what looks like convergence from one perspective may in practice be *increasing* the range of institutions and institutional forms that are accessible to individuals. The diffusion of common notions of human rights, property rights, women's rights, and the rule of law may, in practice, expand the range of legal practices that are available to citizens who are, at the same time, members of clans, sectarian communities, or other identitarian categories that carry with them alternate conceptions of law and individual rights. The experience of diffusion is not one of crowding out, as the local is displaced by the global, but of absorption, integration, layering, and, no less often, resistance.

It is critical to acknowledge that flows work both ways. It is often assumed that the smaller, "peripheral" national states and local organizations are the objects of pressures that circulate at the level of the international system. It is assumed that pressures originate with the powerful and flow "downward" to the weak. We agree that outside influences transform practices and institutional arrangements within nations, and constrain the autonomy of national governments to act in ways that diverge from global norms. Yet the reverse is also the case. States—even small states—continue to exert enormous influence on the form and content of transnational flows, and on actors such as transnational NGOs. To get there from here, even anti-globalization anarchists need passports. Historical trajectories of state formation, for instance, bear heavily on local models for the governance of private wealth. Ideas about the organization of philanthropy, of civil society groups, and of nonprofit sectors cannot be detached from their national places of origin any more than other institutional forms that are now wending their way around the international system.

These tensions between the movement of ideas and the authority of states extend inward as well as outward. As Migdal and others have noted, states have rarely managed to impose uniform rules, norms, and practices on the territories they control.[5] Every state contends with the particular claims of regions; of distinct cultural, ethnic, and religious communities; of economic and professional interests; of families, clans, and other solidarity groups. Such forces also affect charitable practices, including conceptions of philanthropy. Similarly, no state controls its borders in such a way as entirely to isolate its territory from the influence of the many trans-state communities, ancient as well as new, that exert pressures of their own—through trade, family ties, religious study and practice, language, literary communication, and scientific exchange.

Diffusion thus goes hand in hand with—is inextricably bound up with— the process of reception. Yet here too diffusion does not define how reception plays out. In some instances, the two may co-exist in a tightly coupled system.

The movement of an idea may carry with it demands that an existing institutional form or set of principles—for example, strategies of corporate governance—be replicated around clearly defined practices. In others, however, the two may be far more loosely coupled.[6] As Ann Swidler shows in this volume, systems for the treatment and prevention of HIV infection in Africa are hybrid forms that reflect general medical principles for the prevention of disease and "Western" ideas about community action, as well as local conceptions of health and well-being, and local social and political contexts. Nonprofit organizations serve as agents of diffusion, but they also serve to mediate between the institutional logics that have shaped HIV/AIDS programs in the United States and local logics in the contexts into which they are being imported. In the following chapters, the contributors show how the relationship between diffusion and reception develops in the global movement of nonprofit organizations in particular.

There is also the question of agency. How much of what we call the projection of institutional logics can be seen as the intentional act of particular agents? The question speaks to a crucial distinction between two terms scholars have tended to elide: projection and diffusion. Diffusion suggests unmanaged, decentralized flows, movements that evoke an organic sense of voluntary adoption of new ideas and flexible adaptation by organizations. Projection hints at something that is not only intentional and managed, but potentially darker, perhaps menacing in its implications. Whether recalling the long history of invasions, religious struggles, civilizing missions, and imperial conquest, or, more recently, Fukuyama's claim that the imposition of liberal institutions is needed to address state failures in the developing world, the idea of projection connotes a very different view than the idea of diffusion about what convergence means and how it happens.[7]

To what extent, then, are the processes considered in this book the competitive response of organizational units to changes in a larger institutional environment? To what extent are they evolutionary? How much can be explained as the result of an endless process of mutual adaptation or competitive emulation among organizations, detached from any identifiable intentionality or design? To take an example that is all too ordinary, U.S. Agency for International Development regulations demand accounting procedures that reflect conditions set out in Office of Management and Budget Circular A-133 (of the U.S. federal government). This in turn requires grantees to adopt bookkeeping procedures that demand new skills from an organization's finance staff, which requires re-tooling on the part of staff accountants, which alters the content of local training programs, etc. All of which aggregates, seamlessly and by way of the invisible hand of the bureaucracy, toward an NGO sector whose financial management, staff training and credentials, reporting procedures, and other details now look familiar to the Agency for International Development auditor during her annual visit to the field. Under conditions such as these, it appears, projection happens.

Contrast this with the conceptions of an Enrique Escobar or James Ferguson (or Henrique Fernandez Cardoso in his earlier incarnation), for whom globalization, via the projection of development norms (again, in large measure through the agency of development institutions and NGOs), is inextricably linked to a broader "project": the intentional underdevelopment, subordination, and exploitation of the Global South by the Global North.[8] From this perspective, it is "hybridity," the capacity of local actors to appropriate global norms and endow them with local meaning and local agency, that holds out hope for taming the regressive effects of globalization.

But we need not adopt the critical perspectives of anti-globalization writers to see that projection does not simply happen, or that stories of diffusion need to be firmly anchored in causal mechanisms and a concern to establish the conditions under which diffusion is more or less likely. The chapters in this volume explore these conditions, identify causal mechanisms, and seek to chart variations in how ideas and practices are received.

Projecting Institutional Logics: Definitions and Rationale

In the following chapters, the contributors focus on what we are calling *the philanthropic projection of institutional logics abroad*. By philanthropic projection we mean the effort to spread organizational norms and practices by means of the donation of money, goods, human effort, and ideas. The particular form of projection we have in mind is the movement of models for the organization of activities such as medical care, education, advocacy, social improvement, conflict resolution, and cultural expression. By institutional logics we mean organizational arrangements for putting ideas into action and for sustaining patterns of social relationships. The idea of institutional logics deserves consideration. It expresses the understanding that ideas, organizational forms, and social contexts are linked in ways that have both internal and external effects. It indicates that organizational forms carry with them, both explicitly and implicitly, both intentionally and otherwise, attributes and qualities that bear the imprint of their place of origin. It permits us to think about organizations and organizational flows across national boundaries in ways that are, on one hand, patterned, but on the other hand, differ significantly from one particular organization and organizational sector to another. We can thus use the notion of institutional logics to tease out the particularities that create meaningful variation among otherwise general processes like the globalization of certain ways to organize civil society groups, humanitarian relief missions, or community foundations.

Organizations, in this sense, are the hermit crabs of globalization—flexible ideas that reside within portable structures. They scrabble across national borders and drop their shells in remote settings where local inhabitants may find entirely new uses for a familiar form. There is a logic to the structure of a shell, but the structure leaves open multiple possibilities for how it might be used. In the process, the hermit crab builds a home from locally available materials. How actors that create and inhabit organizations think about what they are doing, understand what constitutes the available set of acceptable or legitimate ways to organize an activity, and imagine what they are trying to accomplish are thus all components of an institutional logic.

Contributors to this volume employ variations on this way of thinking about institutional logics. Ann Swidler, for example, views institutional logics as the "practices that structure group life." As she wrote in a preliminary version of her chapter, "by this I mean the ways cooperation, authority, hierarchies of prestige and influence, and patterns of interdependence and exchange are organized. On the one hand such patterns are 'culturally unique.' A specific understanding of witchcraft, or of the dangers that come from violating taboos related to menstruation, or child-birth, or death will not be comparable from one small group to another. On the other hand, at a more general level these do amount to institutional logics, for example, the notion that individual misbehavior can contaminate a whole group or that authority emanates from the spiritual power of a central leader."

There are several other ways of thinking about institutional logics. One tradition, which owes much to Max Weber and Talcott Parsons, emphasizes the way an institution's purpose or mission can shape its operations and define the organizational challenges it must overcome. Penny Edgell Becker's *Congregations in Conflict* exemplifies this tradition by showing that the patterns of conflict in religious congregations can be explained by the ways they select among possible "religious" purposes, so that "communities of worship" have an easier time than congregations that emphasize a social mission, see themselves as "families," or see themselves as "communities."[9] Another way of thinking emphasizes organizational *form*, or sometimes the importance of a good fit between an organization's form and the spirit that animates its people.

The contributors to this volume are especially concerned with institutional logics that have to do with philanthropy and with nonprofit, nongovernmental organizations. Philanthropy is about gifts, and as Marcel Mauss long ago emphasized, gifts are always embedded in relationships—relationships that express hierarchy, conflict, and negotiation.[10] As we view them, nonprofit, nongovernmental organizations are engaged in the exchange and subordination dynamics of the gift economy. But of course nonprofit, nongovernmental organizations are also embedded in the dynamics of market relationships, and in the arrangements of state power structures.

As the chapters in this book make clear, the customs and rules that govern the creation, legitimate purposes, internal structures, funding, operations, and governance of nonprofit, nongovernmental organizations vary widely from place to place, and especially from nation to nation. The very nature of the resources critical to an organization's effectiveness themselves vary just as do the wealth and culture of regions. In the United States, nonprofits fit into a larger institutional context dominated by profit-seeking firms that operate in markets, and in which a wide variety of federal, state, and local governments also play key roles. American nonprofits take many forms, but in general must find their own income by selling services, by obtaining payments from government, and by obtaining donated funds. The governing board of an American nonprofit is legally responsible for the organization's financial health as well as for assuring that it keeps a focus on its mission, obeys the general laws, and is accountable to its funders and to the larger society. The leaders of an American nonprofit operate in the context of a legal system that supports non-profit autonomy, in the context of government policies that assume the existence of nonprofits and expect them to provide certain services for a fee, and in the context of well-established markets both for nonprofit services and for donations. American nonprofits encounter many frustrations and challenges but, ideally, the logics of their internal organization fit well with the logics of their external context. Given all these particularities, however, it is not easy to project the institutional logic of an American nonprofit into the very different legal, political, and social contexts that prevail outside the United States.

Global Transformations, National Contexts

Our topic has taken on much-increased significance in recent decades. Nongovernmental, nonprofit organizations are prominently associated with efforts to restore vital "civil society" to the nations of the former Soviet bloc. China has taken remarkable—though hotly debated and by some measures sharply limited—steps to expand the roles of NGOs in meeting the needs of its citizens. The United Nations gives formal recognition to international NGOs, recognizing their increasingly prominent contributions to disaster relief, conflict resolution, the protection of human rights, environmental protection, and economic development. Indeed, debates on economic development currently place great emphasis on the potential of civil society and of NGOs in particular.

It is clear that ideas associated with particular philanthropic practices, and with nonprofit, nongovernmental organizations, have spread rapidly in the past thirty or forty years. Nonprofit, self-directed organizations of many kinds have proliferated throughout the world. This is especially true in the United States, which has been changing at least as rapidly as any other part of the world in this respect.

The American nonprofit sector has undergone a quiet revolution in nonprofit, nongovernmental activity since the 1960s. As Norman Silber has shown, before the 1960s, Americans—especially women and people of color—encountered sharp limits in most states on their right to create or join a nonprofit organization.[11] In the early 1960s nonprofit organizations employed less than 3 percent of the U.S. labor force. The civil rights movement led to increased associational rights, and by 2000 nonprofits employed nearly 10 percent of American workers, and more than a fifth of the workforce in most large cities east of the Mississippi and north of the Ohio. As nonprofit employment tripled, donations remained at a traditional level (under 2 percent of disposable income), and new sources of income fueled nonprofit expansion. In 1960 many nonprofits drew half or more of their income from donations and most of the rest from the sale of services (tuition, hospital charges, admission fees, etc.). By 2000 donations accounted for less than 3 percent of the income of hospitals and clinics, and less than a fifth of the income of colleges and social service agencies. Government payments of many kinds (reimbursements for medical care, direct funding for Head Start programs and the care of the disabled, as well as food stamps, rent supplements, and social security) accounted for as much as a third of nonprofit revenue. And U.S. nonprofits continued to get much of their income—by now a full half—from the sale of services.[12]

In the United States, several factors account for the extraordinary recent growth of nonprofit activity: a remarkable increase in individual rights, including the lifting of restrictions on association and group action; the significant expansion in government spending for health, education, job training, and social services (and the decision to have nonprofits rather than government agencies or for-profit firms provide those services); and the strong increase in per capita income that allows more people to purchase more services. Underlying the nonprofit expansion in the United States was not just a movement away from direct reliance on government agencies—privatization and devolution—but a very longstanding commitment to the use of nonprofit organizations to accommodate America's enormously varied congeries of religions and cultures. Think, for example, of nineteenth-century hospitals and orphanages sponsored by Catholics, Jews, and many Protestant denominations, of ethnic community centers, of the growth of Catholic and Lutheran school systems, of the many hundreds of colleges sponsored by religious organizations, of the great private research universities, of progressive schools, and of alternative centers for the arts.

As is more generally recognized, since the 1960s there has also been a global diffusion of models for the organization of nonprofit, nongovernmental, and philanthropic affairs. Projection, in one form or another, surely accounts for much of this diffusion. To take an example from the Americas, CEMEFI, the Mexican Center for Philanthropy, was founded in 1988 to promote the development of a private, nonprofit philanthropic sector in Mexico. Yet this was far from a spontaneous act of institutional formation. Organizations based in the United States that are actively engaged in diffusing a particular theory about how philanthropy should be done, including the W. K. Kellogg Foundation, Synergos, the Ford Foundation, and the Inter-American Foundation, sponsor the Mexican Center. Across the Atlantic, the European Foundation Centre proudly notes that it was created by a consortium of European funders on the day the Berlin Wall fell. Its mission is, in part, "to nurture efforts aimed at supporting independent, accountable and sustainable funders throughout the 'New Europe,' *particularly when the right to associate private capital for public benefit needs fostering.*"[13] Both the European Foundation Centre and CEMEFI are members of WINGS—Worldwide Initiatives for Grantmaker Support—a transnational coalition of foundations, whose purpose is to "strengthen the institutional infrastructure of philanthropy worldwide," not least by proactively spreading distinctive conceptions of "best practice," accountability, ethics, and efficiency. The founding chair of WINGS is a former senior vice president of the Ford Foundation in New York. Diffusion does not just happen: it is often driven by the agency of specific actors and organizations.

Our intent is to focus attention on a rapidly globalizing but nonetheless understudied domain: philanthropy and the nonprofit sector. While there is considerable interest in the projection of ideas and models for the organization of social movements, firms, professional fields, or advocacy groups, the global diffusion of practices, norms, and institutions in the field of philanthropy and the nonprofit sector has received less attention.[14] In part, this reflects how the comparative study of nonprofit sectors itself has developed. Research in the field has devoted considerable attention, first, to establishing a common definition of the sector, and second, to inventorying the size and scope of the nonprofit sector in as many countries as possible. The result has been considerable progress in building the taxonomic and data infrastructure for cross-national comparison, but less in developing the analytic tools we need to understand processes of institutional change in the nonprofit sector, or in understanding how state-level distinctions are being challenged by transnational flows. Our contributors address these gaps and, at the same time, begin to strengthen links with research programs that focus on processes of projection, diffusion, and institutional change in the international system more broadly.

The payoffs from such a strategy are potentially quite promising. At the most fundamental level, the case for the presence of a private nonprofit sector—much less for private nonprofit foundations as a way to ensure the public use of private assets—is not in any sense self-evident. Nonprofit organizations and private foundations in the United States reflect fundamental conceptions of how civic life should be structured that are deeply embedded in American experiences of skepticism about the value of state action, volunteerism, self-reliance, pluralism, and market liberalism.[15] In the wake of World War II, France, Germany, and other European states expanded the legal rights of individuals to personal autonomy and to associate as they wish, and in 1948 the United Nations adopted the Universal Declaration of Human Rights.[16] The later decline of welfare, demographic changes, economic challenges, and the spread of market-based forms of capitalism have been accompanied by other expansions of individual rights and reforms of regulation—especially in Europe, both old and new. One result is a "liberalization" of legal frameworks for the establishment and operation of foundations along American lines, even while organizations like WINGS proactively advance the notion of universal standards in the governance and management of philanthropy.[17]

As a result of these processes, institutional models once seen as distinctive to the United States are taking root in new settings. Relatively autonomous nongovernmental organizations have, by some measures, grown as rapidly in parts of Western Europe since the 1960s as they have in the United States. The density and scale of private foundations in the United States still distinguishes American philanthropy from that of Europe—and will continue to do so. Yet this institutional form is nonetheless expanding, slowly and gradually, even in cases where private foundations have historically been scarce, and associations remain the dominant form for the organization of philanthropic activity.[18] NGOs have arguably increased in autonomy as well as in number and range of activities, even in countries such as China that might otherwise be seen as relatively inhospitable to civil society groups.[19]

The accelerating diffusion of nongovernmental, philanthropic, and non-profit activity reflects, in part, an increasing international consensus on the value of individual rights, citizen control, and organizational autonomy. The deepening of these processes also reflects the extent to which the idea that organized philanthropy plays a positive role in strengthening civil society has become global.[20] Yet whether these assumptions really travel well—are easily and smoothly exported to social and political contexts that express historical trajectories and social preferences very different from those of the United States—is an open question. To take account of these processes of diffusion this volume will focus in part on the scope, implications, and effects for democracy of the globalization of a distinctive form of philanthropic institution.

As scholars of nonprofit organizations in the United States have emphasized, nongovernmental entities that do not exist to earn a direct profit serve several functions. They help solve the "institutional failures" of business and government to provide public goods that are not sought by majorities of voters. They help overcome contract failure when the provider of a service has much more information than the consumer. They provide a means for the distribution of (often unacknowledged) government subsidies. They can give consumers a means of controlling the services they receive. Scholars of philanthropy in the United States have noted that one of the perceived advantages of private foundations is their capacity to engage in "positive discrimination," that is, to target the allocation of resources toward particularistic purposes, where the state's actions are constrained by the equality of citizens under law. Differing principles of inclusion and different criteria for access to funding permit private foundations to discriminate in their allocation of resources, thus avoiding conflicts that might result if public policies endorsed or permitted inequalities in the management of public funds. By comparison with state colleges, for example, private colleges can more freely emphasize "excellence"—or commitment to particular religious views.

In general, local ethnic or sectarian nonprofits can seek resources and provide services—and foundations can allocate resources—on identitarian grounds, while the state typically may not do so. Government agencies, especially those that must respect the views of the "median voter" and that claim devotion to principles of democracy and universal rights, necessarily develop elaborate uniform rules and bureaucracies to enforce the rules. These governmental processes of rule making and bureaucracy often conflict, sometimes sharply, with efforts to accommodate diverse traditions within a single nation. Apposite cases range from the Dutch system of "pillarization" through which the state funds sectarian institutions, to India's effort to counter caste discrimination through affirmative action, to America's continuing struggles over the relationship of church and state, struggles that re-emerged in response to the faith-based initiatives of the Bush administration.[21]

In the U.S. tradition, the capacity of private foundations and nonprofits to target resources to particularistic purposes has generally been seen as beneficial. Nongovernmental organizations provide alternative channels for the provision of services and for the accumulation and distribution of capital that can accommodate particularistic needs and preferences—outside the formal political arena. Over the course of U.S. history, the most important use of nonprofit organizations has been to make possible the separation of church and state, and hence the management of conflicts among competing religious groups. Through independent nongovernmental organizations, groups can seek resources outside government, avoiding direct conflict over the control of government with adherents of other religious communities. The regulation of nonprofit organizations and foundations in the United States is very largely a matter of state policy, and states have always varied widely in their tolerance toward nonprofit organizations. Through most of the nineteenth century New England and some of the Great Lakes states encouraged these institutions. New York strongly promoted nonprofits and foundations from the beginning of the twentieth century, but the states of the Old South discouraged them until after the civil rights movement of the 1960s.

Overall, the model that has shaped the perception of state-foundation relations is one of reciprocity and complementarity, although critics of private foundations question whether these forms of discrimination have been positive in their effects.[22] In contrast, Western and Northern Europe experienced competition and antagonism between the state and institutions that controlled private assets, in particular, the Catholic Church and, in Britain, endowed charities.[23] The autonomous standing of the church and of several British charities—with their substantial endowments and extensive roles in social service provision and charitable activity—was cast as antagonistic to the consolidation of state authority, and as inconsistent with the public management of welfare and service provision organized around egalitarian and inclusive conceptions of citizenship, rather than faith, as the basis for access to resources. As a result, states actively intervened to constrain the formation of private foundations, to more tightly regulate charitable institutions, and to centralize social service provision within encompassing welfare systems.[24]

Variations in national experience have enormous implications in considering possibilities for the diffusion of nongovernmental organizations as an institutional form. In Western and Northern Europe, the deregulation of private organizations and foundations invokes deep historical questions about the division of labor among state, society, and the third sector that continue to be hotly debated.[25] At the same time, however, the increasing heterogeneity of European populations suggests that new models for the management of particularisms will become increasingly attractive to European policy makers in coming years. In particular, demographic shifts as a result of migration (including, prominently, from the Muslim societies of the southern

Mediterranean) open up the possibility that private foundations will come to be seen as complements to state institutions that lack the capacity for "positive discrimination."

What are the longer-term implications of organizing service activities and philanthropy in transitional states—where societies and national identities are also being reshaped—around models that rest on an understanding of "private," autonomous, self-governing, nongovernmental organizations as a means for accommodating needs that states are unable or unwilling to address, or as a mechanism for "positive discrimination" in the allocation of resources? Is this deregulation of philanthropy simply a way for the state to retreat from the task of building political communities grounded in egalitarian conceptions of national identity and citizenship in the face of increasingly heterogeneous populations? Is it a way for the state to withdraw from the provision of welfare? What will be the consequences of introducing multiple norms of inclusion and participation in societies that have stressed the formal equality of citizens? Can nations protect the rights of distinctive populations (majority as well as minority) and at the same time assure equal access to education, health care, and cultural opportunities? Can communal conflicts be minimized or channeled into nonviolent directions by encouraging the creation of non-state institutions? Recent trends hold out the possibility that, together with the broader erosion of welfare regimes, Europe could be on the verge of a moment comparable to the American "philanthropic revolution" of the early twentieth century, signaling significant shifts in large-scale patterns of state-society relations.[26] The implications of these changes for social capital, norms of inclusion, and the encompassing conceptions of welfare that have been prominent in Europe remain to be seen, but cannot be assumed to be positive.

Such issues take on starker form once we move beyond the flow of ideas among industrialized democracies to consider how such flows operate between the Global North and the Global South—or between what was once described as the first and second worlds—societies undergoing transitions from communism to some form of democracy. Indeed, most of the chapters in this volume concern the movement of nonprofit organizations and ideas along a North-South or North-East axis. As such, they are especially useful in shedding light on diffusion dynamics in contexts like Africa, Eastern Europe, the former Soviet states, and elsewhere. By incorporating these chapters into a discussion that includes United States–Europe flows as well, our intent is twofold. We wish to underscore both the range and variety of flows that define processes of projection—the full scope of institutional logics at play in contemporary globalization—but also to highlight the general features of diffusion more broadly, and to tease out the patterns that make experiences of diffusion generalizable.

Themes and Debates

The chapters in this book engage these issues through a focus on three closely related and often overlapping themes. First is the relationship between organizational forms, on one hand, and modes of projection, on the other. This theme underscores the shared interest of contributors in the extent to which institutional variation infuses the projection of norms, practices, and organizational models with a diversity that belies claims of convergence and isomorphism. It provides an opportunity, as in Bloodgood's chapter, to challenge claims about the extent to which institutional forms constrain the capacity of some organizations to adapt their strategies of projection to different local contexts. At the same time it creates an opportunity to explore the patterns that exist within this variation, and the ways in which institutional points of origin matter in defining both the form and the content of ideas as they move through the international system.

The second main theme concerns the mechanics of projection itself. Virtually all of our contributors include attention to mechanics, yet they do so from a range of perspectives. In some instances, chapters focus on specific agents of projection—whether particular NGOs, foundations, or, in the case of Goff's chapter, specific individuals—to highlight how a given institutional logic moves from one setting to another, and how these flows can inform our understanding of the contemporary international system. In other chapters, authors explore the ways in which acts of projection advance broader processes of social change; how they support or challenge the distribution of power (and of inequality) in the international system; or, as in the chapter by Lounsbury and Strang, how they serve to diffuse norms and practices associated with such notions as social entrepreneurship. Our interest in the mechanics of projection also includes attention to the many ways that efforts to export particular models of philanthropy, entrepreneurialism, civic engagement, or health care become politicized and turn the projection of institutional logics into sources of political, social, economic, and cultural contestation.

As the following chapters demonstrate, strategies of diffusion may be more or less hierarchical and centralized. They may be more "supply driven" as is evident in Swidler's account of public health interventions in Africa, in Aksartova's chapter on the activities of U.S. civil society promotion programs in the former Soviet Union, or in Slocum's references to the effort of leading U.S. foundations to promote the community foundation as a model for the organization of local philanthropy, exporting it via their own grantmaking activities into settings in which community foundations had not previously existed. Strategies can also be more "demand driven" as seen in VanAntwerpen's account of the attempts by post-authoritarian, post-conflict governments to import models of truth and reconciliation commissions that drew on the experience of the South African Truth and Reconciliation Commission, a process South Africans themselves were quite willing to support.

Similarly, the projection of institutional logics may be direct or indirect, intentional or unintentional. It can occur as a byproduct of technology transfer, or, as Goff illustrates, conveyed via individuals such as Zenjuro Horikoshi, a founding member of the Rotary Club in Japan. As Lounsbury and Strang emphasize in their chapter on social entrepreneurship, individuals play a critical role in helping to diffuse the norms and ideas they acquire during formative socialization experiences in specific institutional settings. Yet the similarities between Horikoshi and his contemporary counterparts—evangels of social entrepreneurship such as Jeff Skoll—are nonetheless limited.

Modes of projection are both historically and geographically contingent. Ideas that valorized businessmen in the interwar period when the Rotary Club spread to Japan may appear to find their contemporary analogs in the businessmen and women who celebrate individual initiative at the start of the twenty-first century. Indeed, comparing the interwar diffusion of ideas about American-style market capitalism to the current globalization of social entrepreneurship evokes useful skepticism about the extent to which the latter is really as novel and innovative as its advocates claim.

Nonetheless, each of these ideas, and the frameworks of projection within which they are embedded, is very much a product of their time. They differ, not least, in the extent to which they are allied with or challenge existing political, social, and economic hierarchies. Social enterprise emerged as a critique of the model of capitalism that the Rotary Club represents, notably its norms of corporate conformity that extend into the social lives of members. Moreover, what it means to be an entrepreneur takes on a very different valence when inserted into the context of egalitarian, consultative European models of welfare capitalism than it does in the context of American-style market capitalism. While attentive to similarities, therefore, chapters in this volume are also attuned to the particularities that differentiate mechanisms of projection along a variety of axes.

The third main theme concerns reception and the processes through which institutional logics are transformed as they enter local contexts. Here, too, our contributors range widely, both thematically and geographically. Some consider how local actors responded to Western efforts to promote an independent foundation sector and the development of civil society in several different parts of the former Soviet Union. Others assess the work of international environmental organizations in the Amazon Basin or the local effects of interventions by international NGOs in response to the HIV/AIDS pandemic in Africa. The issue that links this diverse set of chapters while also connecting them to those in the first section of the volume is their concern with agency, and with the agency of local actors in particular. In contrast to work on globalization and the transnational flow of ideas and institutions that discounts processes of reception and the agency of local actors, the chapters in this volume reinforce and amplify ongoing efforts to bring these elements to the fore.

In addition, however, our contributors share a sense that the most effective way to achieve this aim is to move beyond frameworks that situate local actors and their international counterparts in neatly packaged zero-sum relationships. Processes of reception, as we view them, are not unambiguous expressions of subordination, resistance, assimilation, or hierarchy. They do not produce consistent coalitions of support and opposition, of altruism and opportunism. Nor do they permit us to draw generalizable conclusions about those aspects of projection that are more likely to "stick" than others. In VanAntwerpen's chapter, to cite just one example, the emergence of South Africa's Truth and Reconciliation Commission as a model for how post-conflict societies should attend to processes of reconciliation, the appearance of transnational coalitions supporting the export of this model to Latin America, and the contention that these efforts sparked in societies wrestling with their own post-conflict traumas, all serve as useful reminders that projection comes in many forms, has many points of origin, proceeds along widely varying pathways, and provokes highly divergent reactions.

Among scholars of projection one common response to this messiness and complexity has been to fall back on generic and increasingly overused concepts such as hybridity. Our contributors have pushed further and worked, instead, to develop analytically informed but also case-sensitive "narratives of reception." These chapters do justice to local complexities without losing sight of how widely shared an experience reception itself has become. To be the object of projection, or to find oneself a participant in processes of reception— whether passively or actively—is an identity that hundreds of millions of people now share, even if they have very little else in common. And as the following chapters underscore, the economics, politics, and cultures of reception have themselves become an increasingly global frame of reference for individuals and social groups struggling to define their responses to the globalization of ideas about the organization of civic life and philanthropy. It is an identity that does not (or does not yet) carry with it a globalized repertoire of norms and practices of the sort that we associate with established social movements, sectarian, ethnic, or other sources of identity around which collective action might mobilize. But local actors certainly draw on these and other identities to influence the forms of collective action that accompany efforts to export institutional logics into their midst.

In organizing the following chapters we have distinguished between those that focus on the projection end of the spectrum and those that focus on the reception end. Yet we would not want to exaggerate the differences. It is very difficult to say exactly where one point on the spectrum shades into another or is influenced by the pull of factors further up or down the spectrum. As will become evident, our contributors tend to deal in wholes, rather than detaching one part of the process from another.

Projecting, Contesting, Transversing Borders

Akira Iriye was an early and influential contributor to debates about the globalization of philanthropy, civic norms, and nonprofit institutions. It is appropriate, therefore, that we begin the volume with his autobiographical statement setting out one of the central positions in these debates. Iriye's personal experience of American philanthropic and nongovernmental efforts in postwar Japan gave him an early understanding of one sort of philanthropic projection. His conception is a benign one, in which the international activities of foundations contributed to the emergence of an alternative, non-state form of transnational community. As he writes, the Ford Foundation and other international nongovernmental organizations "were promoting an alternative world order, an international community where tolerance and understanding, rather than ideological conflict, would be the rule."

Later generations of scholars, including contributors to this volume, have challenged this position. They argue that American contributions to international "philanthropy" were often, in fact, government-directed and government-funded interventions in the Cold War.[27] In their conception, the subsequent role of foundations in the post–Cold War era has reproduced this relationship. Foundations are seen as having a darker, or at least more instrumental, aspect in which organized philanthropy, whether wittingly or not, operates as an element of American "soft power." The foundations that Iriye viewed as a source of transnational tolerance, an international community apart from the ideological conflicts of states, are seen instead as an extension of state interests. They are participants in the post–Cold War triumphalism that sought to remake the world in America's image, relying on modes of projection that DiMaggio and Powell might view as a coercive strategy of institutional isomorphism.[28] Democracy promotion and the development of civil society in Eastern Europe and elsewhere are not simply cases of "building local capacity" or of enhancing tolerance and understanding. Rather, they are examples of the exportation of organizational norms and practices that reflect distinctly American conceptions of what civil society is, the kind of institutions it needs, its roles, and its relationship to the state and the market. State actors in Russia, the Ukraine, Zimbabwe, and Egypt certainly seem to share this view of civil society, and have taken steps to suppress ties between local NGOs and their international counterparts as a result.

Despite this alternative view of the normative status of nonprofit organizations, Iriye's attention to the tensions that mark the relationship between states and third sectors; his awareness of the extent to which the autonomy of foundations, however contingent, creates scope for actions that express and project non-state ideologies; and his understanding of the possibilities that third sectors hold out for alternative forms of community remain influential. They are evident, for instance, in the sensibility that informs the influential series of Global Civil Society Yearbooks that Anheier and colleagues have co-edited since 2001.

Projecting Philanthropic Logics

Brendan Goff's chapter on the "institutional transference" of the Rotary Club of Dallas to Tokyo in the 1920s highlights these ambiguities. As the first of three papers that emphasize the active *projection* of institutional logics across borders, it reflects both aspects of the debate over communities of tolerance versus projections of state and economic power. Goff's wonderfully textured account captures the tensions that surrounded the internationalization of a peculiarly American conception of the role of the businessman in society during the interwar period. Japanese industrialists valued the Rotary Club's norms of egalitarianism and inclusion among members. Like their American counterparts, they responded to its emphasis on self-improvement, social harmony among classes, and the apolitical characterization of its work. These provided the essential elements of a transnational network of businessmen linked through their commitment to service and self-help. Yet as Goff notes, "the core devotion to individual moral character precluded any type of community service activity that challenged any political or social inequalities in any significant way . . . RI's middle-class philanthropy, once bleached of the political, could only reinforce rather than challenge power relations at any level of governance." What made Rotary International such an adaptive model was its acquiescence in and commitment to the social and political orders it encountered as it moved from one setting to another. It was the packaging of modern capitalism in a Progressive Era framework of individual service and egalitarian striving that helped Rotary International project itself successfully into Japan.

Yet in other respects the Rotary Club's presence in Japan was deeply enmeshed in politics. Japanese businessmen viewed their participation in Rotary International in terms of Japan's economic and political coming of age. The transnationalism of businessmen was thus one more indicator of Japan's global ascent and its growing acceptance by the West. Membership was a source of pride among Japanese industrialists for just this reason. Ultimately, however, the "community of tolerance" represented by the Rotary Club could not withstand the rise of Japanese militarism and its global consequences. Although Rotary members in Japan tried to insulate their clubs from the growing tensions between Japan and the United States, with the outbreak of war they were compelled to sever the ties between Japanese Rotary clubs and Rotary International.

Lounsbury and Strang also focus on the projection of an idealized conception of the modern capitalist. Yet their interest is less in how a particular organization and individuals actively sought to advance an innovation than in how a particular logic—in their case the logic of the social entrepreneur as a model for innovation, creativity, and socially aware or socially directed modes of commercial activity—is actually coming to be diffused around the world. Processes of diffusion are typically studied by taking stock of how widespread a particular practice is and by charting the growth or decline of cases that exhibit the practice in question. Scholars track the diffusion of a particular approach to management, for example, by noting the number of firms that practice it; they assess the diffusion of that approach by observing its movement across firms over time. What such approaches neglect, however, is what Lounsbury and Strang call "the forging of new logics." How does a new logic take hold? How is it projected into new settings?

According to Lounsbury and Strang, to account for the emergence of new logics we need to "turn the conventional diffusion approach on its head to probe how concrete instances of a set of activities become *discursive fodder*" (emphasis added). "Discursive fodder" in this case consists of a narrative genre that is increasingly widespread but little studied: the success story. Stories that highlight the efficacy and impact of individuals whose practices are framed as instances of social entrepreneurialism become "a key cultural currency." They are deployed by philanthropists, business elites, and others to promote the idea of the social entrepreneur, to enhance the normative value of the practices associated with this idea, and to institutionalize the logic of social entrepreneurialism as a model to be emulated. In this instance success stories serve as the narrative form that supports the projection of a particular kind of behavioral, but also institutional, logic. At the same time, and as we have stressed in this introduction, diffusion does not imply an emergent isomorphism in the field of social entrepreneurship. Quite the contrary. "Funders that recognize, celebrate, and support individual heroes help keep social entrepreneurship a diverse, locally rooted, and structurally non-isomorphic field." In this as in so many other instances, the presence of a category such as social entrepreneurship that is sufficiently flexible and adaptive to make it useful for a wide range of purposes is important for understanding both its vitality and its durability.

In exploring the "intellectual cottage industry" that has developed to promote truth and reconciliation in divided societies, VanAntwerpen describes a mode of projection that shares many of the attributes identified by Lounsbury and Strang. Anchored in the iconic experience of South Africa's Truth and Reconciliation Commission, and spread globally through the entrepreneurial activity of such charismatic figures as Bishop Desmond Tutu, the idea of reconciliation has become central to the rise and consolidation of transitional justice as a field. And even while the organizational and professional ecology of this field is distinctive in many respects, it exhibits a familiar set of dynamics when it comes to processes of projection and diffusion. This includes a constructive ambiguity about core terms. It also includes the growth of linkages across a range of professional communities—human rights, conflict resolution, rule of law, and others—such that each appropriates elements of truth and reconciliation discourse as the basis for diverse activities.

As VanAntwerpen notes, "the frequently ambiguous discourse of reconciliation, full of shifting meanings and multiple significations, has come to represent one of the most prolific traveling theories of our time." Yet these theories do more than travel, they also take root. They provide the impetus for organizations to form. The ideas of transitional justice, reconciliation, and truth telling have prompted the emergence of a growing transnational network of nonprofit organizations, as well as university-based research centers, governmental agencies, and a permanent place on the agenda of "world cultural institutions" such as the United Nations. This network, in turn, is sustained by agents of projection, those whom VanAntwerpen, borrowing from Keck and Sikkink, calls "global moral entrepreneurs." These are individuals who actively promote the globalization of truth and reconciliation commissions as a necessary component of post-conflict or post-authoritarian national reconstruction. And to complete the ensemble, the ideas that animate this network have, in turn, given rise to a full-blown critical response from those who do not view forgiveness and reconciliation, or the possibility it implies for achieving social harmony, as appropriate alternatives to the pursuit of justice for the perpetrators of torture, murder, and other crimes. Moreover, South Africa's Truth and Reconciliation Commission becomes the touchstone experience, the singular point of reference, to which many of these divergent communities refer and in relation to which they seek their own legitimacy and moral standing. Contrary to the assumptions of many critical theorists of globalization, therefore, projection in this case does not originate from the Global North and move outward to the global periphery. Students of institutional diffusion, VanAntwerpen reminds us, "need to attend . . . to the manner in which institutional borrowing occurs on a sometimes crowded two-way street." Projection not only sustains organizational diversity, but happens through processes that are multi-directional, decentralized, and non-hierarchical.

Contesting Logics

Shifting focus, the volume turns to the question of *contested* reception, to the processes through which organizational logics enter into, affect, and are themselves affected by, their encounters with local contexts. Few instances of contestation are as sweeping and dramatic as those that attended the collapse of the Soviet Union and the avalanche of democratic transitions that moved across Eastern Europe beginning in 1989. This period, the crest of Huntington's Third Wave, not only brought an end to the Cold War as an organizing principle of the international system, it also sparked a three-fold transformation in the structures of domestic life across the region. State, economy, and society were all reconfigured to reflect versions of a market-oriented electoral democracy containing active and independent civic spheres.[29] Some of the states affected, including most Eastern European countries, had their own interwar traditions of civic life and philanthropy on which to draw. Others, notably Russia, confronted the challenge of creating an autonomous civic sector and a private philanthropic sector almost entirely from scratch. These processes were profoundly influenced, moreover, by the deep ambivalence among Russia's new leaders about the virtues of civic autonomy, the legal protections that should be accorded to private wealth, and the influence of foreign actors in the building of civic and philanthropic sectors and in cultural life in general.

Across Eastern Europe, Central Asia, and Russia, this simultaneous, rapid formation of market societies, civil societies, and philanthropic sectors opened up a vast frontier for the projection of ideas about how the newly independent states should organize civic and philanthropic life, one that American and Western European foundations and democracy promotion organizations were eager to exploit. At the outset, these interventions were spurred on, in part, by the sense of American triumphalism and democracy's global ascendance that accompanied the fall of the Soviet Union. Yet even as triumphalism gave way during the 1990s and beyond to a keen appreciation of the complexities of post-socialism, and even as post-socialist states became more assertive in delimiting and constraining the role of Western organizations—the "backlash" against democracy promotion—the civic and philanthropic experiences of the United States remained an especially potent model for those actively engaged in the projection of organizational logics into Eastern Europe, Central Asia, and Russia.[30]

Two chapters in this volume, by Slocum and Aksartova, address different aspects of the contentious reception accorded to Western ideas about philanthropy and civil society in post-socialist states. Slocum's chapter focuses on the still tentative position of organized philanthropy in Russia, where the first private foundation, the Potanin Charitable Foundation, was established only in 1999. Over the past decade, and in part as a result of Western efforts, a philanthropic sector has begun to emerge in Russia. As Slocum notes, Western funding in support of this process "arguably represents an active projection of the institutional logics—organizational structures, norms, and operating procedures—associated with private foundations in both the United States and Western Europe." The result is a Russian philanthropic sector that clearly bears the institutional imprint of its Western counterparts. Yet this institutional isomorphism, Slocum argues, is the product of mimetic rather than coercive processes of diffusion, and it can sometimes work to the advantage of local philanthropists, helping to "boost their legitimacy within an uncertain Russian context."

Nonetheless, the growth of a foundation sector in Russia has provoked sharp disagreements about the legitimacy of private foundations between state elites and emergent philanthropists. These disagreements underscore the limits of isomorphism. Local logics of political and economic power impose themselves onto the globalized institutional logics of a modern, professional foundation sector. Organizational similarities cannot obscure differences in the degree of legitimacy foundations enjoy, the legal and regulatory frameworks that govern them, or the extent to which they are required to coordinate their activities with, and operate as subordinate partners to, state agencies that channel foundation activities into a delimited set of areas deemed noncontroversial by the Russian government. In the Russian case, therefore, reception is marked by this interplay of local and imported logics, and by the combination of mimetic isomorphism in the structure of foundations and the coercive isomorphism that state authorities impose on their activities.

For Aksartova, on the other hand, coercive isomorphism has played a more central role in the processes through which U.S. donors have sought to export models for the organization of nonprofit and civic sectors into the former

Soviet Union. She focuses on the construction of a "Western grant economy" through which access to material, professional, and reputational resources are contingent on the extent to which local NGOs take on the norms, practices, and procedures of their Western counterparts. Donor organizations, driven by budget imperatives to allocate their funds, require local NGO sectors capable of absorbing them. In this context, reception takes a distinctive form: the emergence of indigenous NGOs—often created by U.S. donors as vehicles to receive funds and undertake programs crafted in the United States—that are compelled to adopt particular institutional forms that validate their capacity to serve as viable partners. They acquire office space in modern buildings and fill it with the technologies that render local NGOs familiar to foreign donors. They learn English, adopt the vocabularies of their American counterparts, and attend workshops and training seminars that serve principally to socialize local actors into the norms and practices of the grant economy. They generate products intended in large part for the consumption of U.S. donors, and only secondarily for the local communities who are supposed to be the beneficiaries of their work. The diffusion of institutional logics is thus an instrumental process, marked by avid competition among newly created local NGOs, both for access to the funding streams provided by Western donors and to keep competing NGOs at bay.

The result, however, is a political economy of civic rent-seeking whose unintended effects undermine the intent of U.S. donors to create NGO sectors embedded within and indigenous to local societies. Instead, foreign assistance creates "civic enclaves"; NGO sectors tightly linked to foreign donors but with tenuous connections to their own societies. This political economy is marked by substantial disparities of wealth, on one hand between donors and grant recipients, and on the other hand between grant recipients and their local neighbors. Over time, moreover, the creation of local cohorts of civil society experts permits U.S. donors to shift more of the work of diffusion to "homegrown specialists" capable of serving as intermediaries between donors and local societies.

Aksartova stresses that this grant economy is not simply utilitarian or rent-seeking. She notes the underlying commitments to social change, reform, and development that are present among both U.S. and local participants in this economy. She also details the efforts of donors and local NGOs to raise public awareness of their work and break down the barriers that separate them from the societies in which they are active. Yet the overriding effects of this process are to create NGO sectors that have assimilated the institutional logics of their donors to an extent that distorts their relationship to local societies.

Contestation and the complexities of reception also inform Swidler's chapter on logics of accountability at the African AIDS-NGO interface. She explores how the work of international NGOs affects levels of social trust, social capital, and organizational capacity among local social institutions. Reinforcing our core themes, her intent is not simply to identify modes of diffusion or to present the projection of organizational logics as inducing a mechanical process of convergence in the content and practices of local institutions. Rather, through careful ethnographic work in Malawi, Swidler seeks to understand how the activities of international NGOs affect levels of social trust, social capital, and organizational capacity among local institutions. In the process, she maps the multiple disjunctures that limit the capacity of international NGOs to reshape local institutions. Local actors willingly appropriate the vocabularies, ideas, and practices that are often taken as indicators of the efficacy with which international NGOs insert themselves into local contexts. Yet local actors assimilate these new resources into existing sets of rules, authority relations, and practices of governance—notably the dense patron-client networks around which so much of economic, political, and social life are organized—that operate in ways quite at odds with the intentions of the international NGOs that promote their diffusion.

Swidler's findings are all the more striking in an African context, where state weakness, low capacity to regulate and discipline the work of international NGOs, and the sheer urgency of the HIV/AIDS pandemic combined to place international NGOs in positions of exceptional authority. As Swidler notes, "all the resources necessary to impose Western practices on the institutional order of the Global South are in place." Yet local people nonetheless are able to "resist or subvert donor intentions." Swidler describes in Malawi many of the same practices that Aksartova documents in the grant economy of Central Asia, including the importance of workshops and training activities as opportunities for local organizers to secure material benefits. Yet in Malawi these benefits hinge on a kind of social connectedness between those who service international NGOs and broader society that stands in sharp contrast to the social alienation of their counterparts in Russia and Central Asia. For local workshop organizers, training and other group activities offer opportunities to serve as gatekeepers, to shape the opportunity structures of others, thus enhancing their own networks of clients and their own standing as patrons. In this instance, as well, what appears to be the globalization of a very specific instrument of diffusion—the training workshop—takes on very different valences depending on the context in which it occurs. There is both more and less to the diffusion of institutional logics than meets the eye.

Contributors to this section of the volume share a productive skepticism about depictions of diffusion as a seamless process in which local actors possess relatively little agency.[31] In contrast, the insertion of institutional logics into local contexts, to use Swidler's phrase, is understood as creating new arenas of social, cultural, political, and economic contestation, with outcomes that rarely conform to the expectations of those who export such logics. In making this point, our contributors tend to focus on uncovering local agency and mapping its effects on the diffusion of institutional logics.

Transnational Logics

Our final section emphasizes what might be called *transnational* logics—the emergence of organizational forms that seek to operate simultaneously in several very different national states. In our penultimate chapter, Bloodgood directs her attention toward the international NGOs that serve as leading agents of diffusion, notably two transnational advocacy organizations, Greenpeace and Friends of the Earth. As she makes very clear, at this level, too, the picture is more complex than is often assumed. Assessing the relationship between organizational forms and modes of projection, Bloodgood finds that structures do not significantly inhibit the capacity of international NGOs to adapt to new contexts. Identifying Friends of the Earth as more conservative in its tactics, but also as more flexible and less rule-bound than Greenpeace in its internal governance, she finds that both have the capacity to adapt a limited repertoire of strategic options to the varied national contexts they are trying to influence. "I find little evidence," Bloodgood writes, "that NGOs become trapped by their organizing principles when they attempt to take a set of strategies designed for one institutional context into another context." The constraints that do arise are located not in the formal rules governing NGO activities, but in informal practices and customs shaping the relations between state and non-state actors. Variations in national systems of governance turn out to matter in shaping NGO tactics, but not in determining the overall capacity of an NGO to project its institutional logics.

In our final chapter, Moog brings us back around to our initial preoccupation with the differences in conditions in the United States and in Europe, and on the consequences of these different sites of origin for the effectiveness of NGOs that seek to engage problems abroad. Moog focuses on American and German efforts over the past quarter century to protect ecosystems and indigenous peoples in the Amazon Basin. She finds that NGOs of different national origins encourage different kinds of initiatives, and have engaged in very different ways with local forces in the Amazon. U.S. groups have directly promoted development and conservation projects, and they have worked effectively to consolidate the position of new NGOs in the region. U.S. environmentalists have often worked closely with business interests: these have provided substantial resources, but have also sometimes evoked considerable local resistance. German groups, by contrast, have allied themselves closely with Brazilian governments, local as well as national, and they have had considerable influence on Brazil's official policies toward development and toward the responsible use of its resources. As a result, she argues, Germany has made important contributions to the administrative (and enforcement) capacities of Amazon Basin governments. On the other hand, she concludes, "the German movement has not played nearly as strong a role in directly shaping the development of civil society organizations in the Amazon."

In presenting this array of perspectives about the projection and reception of institutional logics within the nonprofit and philanthropic sectors, our aim is to enrich debates about the globalization of particular models for the organization of civil society, foundations, advocacy, entrepreneurialism, and public health by drawing out the micro-dynamics that shed light on how these processes operate in concrete settings, from interwar Japan to post–Cold War Russia, to Malawi in the era of HIV/AIDS. Each of these case studies could stand on their own. Taken together, however, the whole is more than the sum of its parts. By aggregating these cases we are able to see that the themes and issues at the core of this volume are not artifacts of individual cases. They are general and generalizable. They define an experience—life as the object of projection and life within organizations that project—that has become a common denominator of life for hundreds of millions of people at the end of the twenty-first century. If the case studies presented here give us pause about imposing on these individuals assumptions about their lack of agency in responding to the forces that are shaping their lives; if they illuminate strategies that can be used to inform our understanding of the contentions that surround processes of projection; if they help us understand the possibilities and limits inherent in the effort of institutions to remake local contexts, it will have achieved our purposes.

Notes

1. Lester M. Salamon and Helmut K. Anheier, eds., *Defining the Nonprofit Sector: A Cross-National Analysis* (New York: Manchester University Press, 1997); David C. Hammack, ed., Symposium on "Growth, Transformation, and Quiet Revolution in the Nonprofit Sector Over Two Centuries," *Nonprofit and Voluntary Sector Quarterly* 30, no. 2 (2001): 157–73; and Lester M. Salamon et al., *Global Civil Society: Dimensions of the Nonprofit Sector* (Baltimore, Md.: The Johns Hopkins Center for Civil Society Studies, 1999.

2. Alexander Wendt, "Why a World State Is Inevitable," *European Journal of International Relations* 9, no. 4 (2003): 491–542.

3. David John Frank, Ann Hironaka, and Evan Schofer. "The Nation-State and the Natural Environment over the Twentieth Century," *American Sociological Review* 65, no. 1 (2000): 96–116.

4. John Boli and George Thomas, eds., *Constructing World Culture: International Nongovernmental Organizations Since 1875* (Stanford, Calif.: Stanford University Press, 1999).

5. Joel S. Migdal, *Strong Societies and Weak States: State-Society Relations and State Capabilities in the Third World* (Princeton, N.J.: Princeton University Press, 1988).

6. David Strang and John W. Meyer, "Institutional Conditions for Diffusion," *Theory and Society* 22, no. 4 (1993): 487–511.

7. Francis Fukuyama, "The Imperative of State-Building," *Journal of Democracy* 15, no. 2 (2004): 17–31, and *State-Building: Governance and World Order in the 21st Century* (Ithaca, N.Y.: Cornell University Press, 2004).

8. Arturo Escobar, *Encountering Development: The Making and Unmaking of the Third World* (Princeton, N.J.: Princeton University Press, 1994); James Ferguson, *Global Shadows: Africa in the Neoliberal World Order* (Durham, N.C.: Duke University Press, 2006); and Henrique Fernandez Cardoso and Enzo Faletto, *Dependency and Development in Latin America* Los Angeles and Berkeley: University of California Press, 1979.

9. Penny Edgell Becker, *Congregations in Conflict* (New York: Cambridge University Press, 1999).

10. Marcel Mauss, *The Gift: Forms and Functions of Exchange in Archaic Societies,* trans. Ian Cunnison (Glencoe, Ill.: Free Press, 1954).

11. Norman J. Silber, *A Corporate Form of Freedom: The Emergence of the Nonprofit Sector* (Boulder, Colo.: Westview, 2001).

12. David C. Hammack, "Nonprofit Organizations in American History: Research Opportunities and Sources," *American Behavioral Scientist* 45, no. 11 (2002): 1638–74.

13. John Richardson and Eric Kemp, "Case Studies of Grantmaker Associations around the World: European Foundation Centre," WINGS (2002), http://www.wings web.org/download/csv1_efc.pdf (accessed September 23, 2008).

14. For differing perspectives on the globalization of social movements, ideas, and nonprofit organizations, see Margaret E. Keck and Kathryn Sikkink, *Activists beyond Borders: Advocacy Networks in International Politics* (Ithaca, N.Y.: Cornell University Press, 1998); Nicolas Guilhot, *The Democracy Makers: Human Rights and International Order* (New York: Columbia University Press, 2005); Boli and Thomas, *Constructing World Culture*; Martin Albrow, et al., eds., *Global Civil Society Yearbook 2007/2008* (Thousand Oaks, Calif.: Sage Publications, 2007); and Lester M. Salamon and Wojciech Sokolowski, eds., *Global Civil Society: Dimensions of the Nonprofit Sector,* vol. 2 (Bloomfield, Conn.: Kumarian Press, 2004).

15. David C. Hammack, ed., *Making the Nonprofit Sector in the United States: A Reader* (Bloomington: Indiana University Press, 1998); and Kenneth Prewitt, "American Foundations: What Justifies Their Unique Privileges and Powers," in *The Legitimacy of Philanthropic Foundations : United States and European Perspectives,* ed. Kenneth Prewitt et al., 27–46 (New York: Russell Sage Foundation, 2006).

16. William Korey, *NGOs and the Universal Declaration of Human Rights* (New York: Palgrave Macmillan, 1998). For a critical perspective, see Kenneth Cmiel, "The Recent History of Human Rights," *American Historical Review* 109, no. 1 (2004): 117–35.

17. Hammack, ed., Symposium on "Growth, Transformation, and Quiet Revolution in the Nonprofit Sector Over Two Centuries."

18. See Kenneth Prewitt, Steven Heydemann, and Stefan Toepler, eds., *The Legitimacy of Philanthropic Foundations: United States and European Perspectives* (New York: Russell Sage Foundation, 2006); and Edith Archambault, "France," in *Foundations in Europe: Society, Management, and Law*, ed. Andreas Schluter, Volker Then, and Peter Walkenhorst (London: Directory of Social Change, 2001), 121.

19. Qiusha Ma, "To Serve the People: NGOs and the Development of Civil Society in China," Oral Testimony before the Congressional-Executive Commission on China, Washington, D.C., March 24, 2003. Available at http://www.cecc.gov/pages/roundtables/032403/Qiusha.php (accessed November 3, 2008).

20. Steven Heydemann, "Doing Democracy's Work? Studying the Transformation of Global Philanthropy in the Twentieth Century," *Democracy and Society* 2, no. 2 (2005): 5, 20–23. Available at http://www8.georgetown.edu/centers/cdacs/DemocracyAndSociety05.pdf (accessed November 3, 2008).

21. Ary Burger and Vic Veldheer, "The Growth of the Nonprofit Sector in the Netherlands," *Nonprofit and Voluntary Sector Quarterly* 30, no. 2 (2001): 221–46.

22. For recent critical accounts of private philanthropy in the United States, see Mark Dowie, *American Foundations: An Investigative History* (Cambridge, Mass.: MIT Press, 2001); and Joan Roelofs, *Foundations and Public Policy: The Mask of Pluralism* (Albany: SUNY Press, 2002).

23. David Owen, *English Philanthropy, 1660–1960* (Cambridge, Mass.: Harvard University Press, 1964); and Paul Slack, *Poverty and Policy in Tudor and Stuart England* (London: Longman, 1988).

24. The history of relations among the church, charities, and national states in Europe is complex and contested; see, for example, Sigrun Kahl, "The Religious Roots of Modern Poverty Policy: Catholic, Lutheran, and Reformed Protestant Traditions Compared," *European Journal of Sociology* 46, no. 1 (2005): 91–126; and Ole Peter Grell and Andrew Cunningham, eds. *Health Care and Poor Relief in Protestant Europe 1500–1700* (New York: Routledge, 1997).

25. Adalbert Evers and Jean-Louis Laville, eds., *The Third Sector in Europe* (Cheltenham: Edward Elgar, 2004).

26. The phrase is from James Allen Smith, "The Evolving American Foundation," in *Philanthropy and the Nonprofit Sector in a Changing America*, ed. Charles T. Clotfelter and Thomas Ehrlich (Bloomington: Indiana University Press, 1999), 36.

27. Robert F. Arnove, *Philanthropy and Cultural Imperialism: The Foundations at Home and Abroad* (Bloomington: Indiana University Press, 1980); Frances S. Saunders, *The Cultural Cold War: The CIA and the World of Arts and Letters* (New York: New Press, 2000); Ron Robin, *The Making of the Cold War Enemy: Culture and Politics in the Military-Intellectual Complex* (Princeton, N.J.: Princeton University Press, 2001); and

Hugh Wilford, *The CIA, the British Left and the Cold War: Calling the Tune?* (London: Frank Cass, 2003).

28. Paul J. DiMaggio and Walter W. Powell, "The Iron Cage Revisited: Institutional Isomorphism and Collective Rationality in Organizational Fields," *American Sociological Review* 48, no. 2 (1983): 147–60.

29. Samuel Huntington, *The Third Wave: Democratization in the Late Twentieth Century* (Norman: University of Oklahoma Press, 1991).

30. Carl Gershman and Michael Allen, "The Assault on Democracy Assistance," *Journal of Democracy* 17, no. 2 (2006): 36–51.

31. For an example of this perspective, see Escobar, *Encountering Development*.

2. Nongovernmental Organizations and the Making of the International Community

AKIRA IRIYE

As a historian of international relations, I have been struck by the increasingly active participation of nonprofit and nongovernmental organizations in world affairs. In this essay I shall try to describe briefly how the diffusion of these organizations (in particular, philanthropies) has contributed to reshaping the international community.

Before doing so, however, I would like to insert a personal story indicative of the ways in which I, as a young schoolboy in Japan after the Second World War, and later as a teenager in the United States, became aware of American nonprofit organizations. I was ten years old when the war ended and the U.S. occupation of the country began. Of course, the power of the United States, demonstrated by the authority of General Douglas MacArthur's command, was awesome, but what impressed me with equal force was the influence of individual Americans who represented private organizations and were not formally part of the occupation regime. Many of them were affiliated with church organizations. They held Christian services that we were invited to attend and came to our school to teach us Bible stories and hymns. We learned that many American missionaries who had been active in prewar Japanese education returned immediately after the war to re-establish contact. Although we did not know it then, church groups in the United States were establishing organizations (such as Church World Service and Catholic Charities) to collect and ship food to war-devastated countries throughout the world, including Japan. An organization of Quakers, the American Friends Service Committee, which had been created during the First World War, was particularly active in sponsoring international seminars and work camps to which young Japanese and Asians as well as Americans were invited. One Quaker woman, Elizabeth Gray Vining, was one of the most popular Americans at that time as she served as a tutor to the crown prince. She and her successor, Esther Rhodes, as well as countless others, were deeply engaged in promoting personal-level exchanges between Americans and Japanese, believing that this was the best way to promote the two countries' reconciliation. I became a beneficiary of such efforts when, shortly after the end of the occupation in 1952, a private foundation established by Americans and Japanese in honor of Joseph C. Grew, U.S. ambassador to Japan during the 1930s, gave me a scholarship to study in the United States. That the college to which they sent me (Haverford College) was a Quaker institution was a coincidence, but it served to connect me to one of the most enduring nongovernmental ties between the two countries. During my four years at Haverford (1953–1957), I was frequently invited by churches, families, and organizations promoting international exchanges to participate in religious, social, and intellectual gatherings to which they brought numerous foreign students. It is no exaggeration to say that "my" America during the 1950s was much less the nation driven by the Cold War and McCarthyism than a country consisting of hospitable and open-minded people and groups. To this day, both as a scholar and as an individual, my perspective on U.S.-Japanese relations has been marked by this dual dimension.

What such personal experiences suggest is that international relations may be considered to consist of many layers and that state-to-state interactions are only one part of the picture. Private-level encounters are just as productive of a certain definition of world affairs. To be sure, the activities by individual Americans representing private associations that I witnessed in the aftermath of the war can be seen as having been closely connected with the overall narrative, the emergence of the United States as the most powerful nation in the world. International affairs in the wake of the Second World War were being shaped by the nation's military force, economic resources, and ideological influence, and private individuals abroad could be said to have been doing their share in establishing American hegemony. Certainly, to school children of my generation, the postwar world was essentially a creation of the United States, and we did not clearly differentiate between the action and motivations of the U.S. government, on one hand, and of individual Americans, on the other. Nevertheless, in retrospect it is clear that the world order the United States was promoting then (and since) consisted of different layers that were not always identical or interchangeable. There was, first, the world defined by military power and geopolitical calculations, one that came to be exemplified by the Cold War and in which the government pursued well-defined strategies. Second, there was an international economic order that connected various parts of the globe through the movement of goods, services, and capital. Here the major actors, as far as the United States was concerned, were not so much governmental agencies as business enterprises, merchants, and export-oriented farmers. Third, there was a world that reflected the ideas and visions of nongovernmental and nonprofit organizations that were deeply rooted in the nation's ideals but that were envisaged as universally valid. These three worlds, to which others could be added, were not identical, and there was significant tension among them. For instance, when Washington "reversed course" in Japan after 1947 and began pursuing a Cold War strategy of containment, including Japanese rearmament, it was not welcomed by many Americans in Japan who continued to help promote the vision of a pacifist Japan that would not embrace a domestic "reverse course." The world that these Americans were pursuing—a world that embodied moral cosmopolitanism, to use a phrase that has made its debut in the recent social scientific literature—was at variance with the strategy of containment that assumed the division of the globe into two halves; but both objectives represented the United States' approach to international affairs. While the containment strategy justified the policy of encouraging Japanese economic recovery and even resurgence, it was at odds with the economic transnationalism that would have entailed the creation of a unified global market.

Such considerations lead to the main purpose of this essay. In order to understand the role of nongovernmental and nonprofit organizations in international affairs, it will be helpful to differentiate between the world that they envision and try to bring into existence and the world order in which their nation interacts with other nations. The former is an imagined world, the latter the "real" world. The two may approximate one another, but they are never identical. One might call the world promoted by non-state actors the "international community" and contrast it to the real world. Some call the former "international civil society" and the latter the "international system." No matter by what name it is called, the community or society of nations and people that exists today would not have developed in the absence of nongovernmental and nonprofit organizations. In what follows, I shall try to summarize briefly the evolution of such a community with a view to highlighting the role of these organizations.

The Making of International Community

In *The Transformation of European Politics,* Paul Schroeder argues that the inter-state rivalries and conflict that had been endemic in Europe since the seventeenth century gave way to something different after the Napoleonic Wars.[1] Europe was changing, not because the states were altering their essential character—they remained fundamentally self-centered and self-interested—but because a transnational sensitivity was emerging that generated a sense of European community. The community was more than the sum of the states that existed in the same region but exemplified some shared values and common interests. These values, products of the Enlightenment such as freedom, justice, and human rights, defined modern European civilization and, it was widely believed, would usher in a new era of regional peace and prosperity.

Although such hopes proved premature, and while Schroeder does not give a detailed account of non-state actors, it is clear that Europe's shared values were most clearly expressed by some of the emerging nongovernmental and nonprofit organizations. Indeed, since most states were still in the business of looking after their respective interests, they were in no position to adhere to, let alone practice, universalistic principles. Governments might proclaim them, as the United States did in the Declaration of Independence and the Constitution, but the implementation and promotion of such principles were not the primary objectives of the states. Rather, it was private individuals and associations that sought to promote them and to bring the real world a step closer to those ideals. The most notable of such organizations were those that aimed at the abolition of slavery, but there were many others advocating various causes ranging from world peace to women's rights. What is particularly significant is that these nongovernmental organizations established contact with their counterparts abroad so that in effect they would become international movements. As Margaret Keck and Kathryn Sikkink have shown, already before the middle of the nineteenth century, there was a trans-Atlantic network of anti-slavery societies that provided a major force in support of emancipation.[2] There was, in other words, an international community of like-minded people who organized themselves at a different level from their governments.

The international order after the Napoleonic Wars is usually referred to as the Vienna system, after the Congress of Vienna of 1814–1815, and nineteenth-century European affairs tend to be analyzed in terms of such questions as what happened to that system, when it began to atrophy, and how it eventually collapsed. According to the usual interpretation, the Vienna order came to an end as a result of the Crimean War of the 1850s. That, however, is only one way of viewing the international order. If we bring nongovernmental organizations into the picture, we will not be able to say that the international system began to crumble by mid-century. On the contrary, the international community that consisted of non-state actors actually became strengthened in the middle decades of the century. Not only did the network of anti-slavery associations prove to be extremely successful, but the number of international nongovernmental organizations pursuing other objectives also began to increase. The International Committee of the Red Cross, established in 1863, is a good example. As F. L. S. Lyons shows in his seminal work, *Internationalism in Europe,* the last decades of the nineteenth century continued to give rise to private international associations that together served to promote internationalism.[3]

The international community, then, was defined, at one level, by sovereign states and at another by private organizations. The former busied themselves building up their military power and establishing overseas colonies, while the latter were concerned with philanthropic, humanitarian, and cultural pursuits. To ignore their role in the making of the international community is to distort history. The late nineteenth century was the age of globalization, when a new conception of time and space emerged thanks to technological breakthroughs in transportation and communication. Such developments facilitated the interaction of individuals and organizations across national boundaries, even as they also contributed to the making of new military strategies and colonial empires. Globalization thus had two faces: it enabled a number of states to aggrandize themselves, dividing up the world into a small number of empires and spheres of influence, while at the same time non-state actors generated a sense of transnational interdependence. The dialectic between the two was to define the nature of international relations for decades to come.

A Century of NGOs

One can clearly follow such a dialectic in the history of U.S. foreign affairs. I have elsewhere argued that the twentieth century was a century of NGOs and that this was particularly true of the United States.[4] Too often the international history of the twentieth century has been presented in terms of the emergence of the United States as a world power and ultimately as the world hegemon. But it would be misleading if world power, world hegemon, and the like were viewed simply in geopolitical terms. The United States certainly acted geopolitically and contributed to developing a world order on the basis of military arms, alliance systems, and economic resources. At the same time, however, the nation was also instrumental in developing an international community in which there grew interests and concerns across national boundaries. In this latter regard, the role of nongovernmental organizations was unmistakable. The so-called American century was not just a creation by the U.S. government and military, it was also a product of non-state actors. As Emily Rosenberg has noted in both *Spreading the American Dream* and *Financial Missionaries to the World,* non-state actors such as multinational business enterprises, religious institutions, and nongovernmental organizations spread American messages abroad, sometimes in conjunction with official policy but at other times independent of the government, and in so doing contributed to Americanizing the world.[5] But Americanization of the world did not just mean transforming other countries in the image of the United States; it also entailed globalization of the United States in that the nation became more and more closely integrated into the rest of the world. Nowhere could this phenomenon be seen more clearly than in the activities of nongovernmental and nonprofit organizations. They were increasingly oriented toward international affairs, and they inevitably interacted with their counterparts elsewhere or established overseas branches and worked closely with local populations. Either way, such international activities often resulted in strengthening a sense of transnational consciousness.

I have cited some examples of international nongovernmental organizations in my book, *Global Community,* and categorized them in terms of their primary activities, of which six were particularly noteworthy after the Second World War.[6] These six were: humanitarian relief, peace and arms control, developmental assistance, educational and cultural exchange, environmentalism, and human rights. In all these activities, American nongovernmental organizations played crucial roles, especially in the years immediately following the Second World War.

These years are usually depicted in terms of the origins of the Cold War, but a different picture would emerge if we focused, not on the state, but on non-state actors. While at one level Cold War tensions were undeniably dividing the world into two camps, each seeking to destroy the other (and annihilate the whole world, should there be a third world war in which nuclear weapons were used), there was another story, that of increasing interconnectedness among all parts of the globe. Non-state actors were establishing networks of interdependence even as the Cold War was creating exclusionary alliance systems.

This can be seen in the activities of several American nongovernmental organizations that were created immediately after the Second World War. For instance, various church groups established organizations for international relief, such as Church World Service, Catholic Relief Services, and Lutheran World Relief. Of course, such bodies might not have come into existence if there had been no Second World War, and to that extent their activities were part of the geopolitical story. We should note, at the same time, that their founding had nothing to do with the Cold War. Their activities, moreover, were independent of any governmental agency, and they continued their work more or less autonomously in the subsequent decades. The world in which such private relief organizations operated was at a different level from the "real" world of nuclear armament and Cold War crises. Likewise, peace activists in the United States and elsewhere, unwilling to accept the emerging bipolar confrontation in the wake of the war, sought what some of them called "one world," a world of peace and interdependence, not of perpetual preparedness for the next war. Nongovernmental organizations such as the Federation of Atomic Scientists and the United World Federalists aimed at developing an international society free from nuclear fear and national egoisms.

That proved to be an extremely difficult goal to realize, not only because the superpowers kept on piling up nuclear weapons but also because many new nations that were created in the wake of the Second World War proved to be just as self-centered as the older, more established states. Decolonization and nation building are just as important themes in the history of the second half of the twentieth century as the Cold War, but here, too, the contrast between state and society, between government and nongovernmental organizations, is significant. If anything, because few of the new countries had developed a mature civil society—other than traditional institutions such as families, clans, tribes, and religious congregations—many of them tended to be dominated by the power of the state, especially the military whose support of any new regime was essential if it were to survive against both external enemies and domestic dissidents. Under the circumstances, the fostering of non-state actors became a very important objective if the postcolonial states were to develop as stable and viable communities.

Here again, American nongovernmental organizations actively involved themselves in the task. During the 1950s and the 1960s, when more than one hundred new countries were born out of the former colonies in Asia, Africa, and elsewhere, some of the humanitarian agencies in the United States, including the religious organizations mentioned above, began to interest themselves in developmental assistance. They, as well as nonsectarian and large philanthropic institutions such as the Ford and Rockefeller foundations, became deeply involved in helping the postcolonial societies develop an adequate infrastructure, an economic strategy, and a political system that would ensure their successful "modernization." These decades tend to be remembered for such Cold War landmarks as the Berlin and Cuban missile crises, but decolonization and nation building were even more critical features of international relations. Actually, even the Korean and Vietnam wars, which are usually understood in the context of the Cold War, should more properly be considered aspects of the larger story of postcolonial development. And in Korea and Vietnam, too, American nongovernmental organizations were deeply involved in relief and reconstruction work. Some church groups even sent their missions to Vietnam while the war was going on, indicating that the military involvement by the United States was not the full story.

It would be too simplistic to argue, however, that nongovernmental organizations were always at loggerheads with, or able to maintain their distance from, the state. After all, they (both their headquarters and branches) were established within certain national jurisdictions, registering with their respective state agencies and conforming to the laws of these countries. When they operated overseas, they had to deal with governmental officials of the host countries. Even in the United States, with its traditionally vibrant civil society, nongovernmental organizations often cooperated with the government in carrying out their activities. Sometimes nongovernmental organizations sought the government's advice on policy formulation and implementation, while at other times federal agencies turned to them for input into official policy. There were also occasions when the government refused to endorse programs being planned by nonprofit organizations or even condemned some non-state initiatives.

In humanitarian relief activities, for instance, the U.S. government turned to CARE (Cooperative for American Remittances to Europe), a nongovernmental, nonreligious organization, to help distribute packages collected within the United States for distribution to Europe. Governmental and nongovernmental personnel worked closely to achieve the objective. Such collaboration showed that the two could sometimes work successfully together. For that very reason, perhaps, the governments of Bulgaria and Romania drove out representatives of CARE and other humanitarian organizations, accusing them of being agents of the U.S. government. The line between state and non-state actors was even more blurred in the area of developmental assistance. Federal agencies often contributed funds to nongovernmental organizations and turned to them for the implementation of developmental projects abroad. In the 1960s, when the Agency for International Development was established, it frequently sought out organizations oriented toward developmental assistance in order to persuade them to undertake projects that were not part of official aid programs. Of necessity, official aid had to be channeled through recognized governments overseas, but this could, and did, encourage nepotism, favoritism, and official corruption, resulting in a growing cleavage between the state and the rest of the population in aid-receiving countries. Because fostering civil society was considered an important objective of U.S. policy, it made sense to turn to private organizations for help. They would be in a much better position to contact non-state individuals and groups in aid-receiving countries. Sometimes, however, the growth of civil society could encourage dissent, to the detriment of local political order. If Washington were committed to the survival of the existing regime, such a development could prove embarrassing. Nongovernmental aid organizations, on the other hand, might be more interested in the growth of democracy than in regime stability. For this reason, in countries such as Pakistan, South Africa, Guatemala, and Nicaragua, official and nongovernmental aid policies frequently came into conflict.

The intricate relationship between governmental and nongovernmental organizations in the international arena can perhaps be most clearly seen in cultural exchange programs. In the United States, cultural exchange was traditionally an almost exclusive domain of private activities. Foundations, educational institutions, and religious organizations took the initiative in inviting foreign scholars and students to study in American educational and research institutions, and they also sent American scientists, artists, and others on exchange missions. In the late 1930s, however, the State Department became interested in cultural exchange, especially with Latin American countries, as an aspect of foreign policy, and after 1945 other offices, notably the Central Intelligence Agency, took an active interest in these activities. Governmental officials frequently met with executives and program officers of foundations and other nongovernmental organizations engaged in educational and cultural exchanges so as to make use of them in waging what was called "ideological warfare" with communist countries. Even when not engaging so explicitly in such warfare, Washington developed official exchange programs, as best exemplified by the Fulbright program and the American cultural centers (such as Amerika Haus in German cities), for both of which the United States Information Agency served as the umbrella agency.

This does not mean, however, that private organizations meekly accepted governmental direction and initiatives. A fascinating example of this intricate relationship may be seen in the ways in which foundations that were engaged in international exchange programs coped with the pressures and demands of the federal government. "What has been imagined as a program for the Government can be done, to a lesser extent, by the Carnegie Corporation," stated a paper submitted for consideration by the Carnegie Corporation's board of trustees in March 1946. The memorandum stressed close cooperation between the government and "all the non-governmental agencies working in the foreign relations field" in order to achieve "total peace."[7] Such cooperation, however, did not mean that this or other foundations stopped being non-state actors. An internal memorandum written in 1949 for the Ford Foundation insisted that "the greatest contribution which the Ford Foundation could make to human welfare would be to assist in efforts to avoid war and to construct the foundations of permanent peace." The paper suggested that the foundation establish committees on basic human rights, the humanities, fine arts and music, and other subjects with a view to furthering such objectives as "understanding and good will, or at least mutual tolerance among peoples of differing religious beliefs, racial origin or economic status."[8] These were admirable objectives for which nongovernmental organizations were well suited as they expanded exchange programs with other countries. Reading this and other memoranda around that time, one would not know that geopolitical tensions were growing. Within a few months, however, the language of geopolitics was seeping into foundation documents.

In 1951 Paul Hoffman, president of the Ford Foundation at the time, argued that "the threat of war is so great that the United States and the free peoples of the world must mobilize their economic and human resources to restrain aggression, to achieve peace, and to assure victory in case of war."[9] This was Cold War language expressing a willingness to define the foundation's programs in the framework of the government's strategies to wage what Hoffman called "the ideological conflict." But his tenure in the Ford Foundation was short lived, and his successor, Rowan Gaither, was willing to reorient the organization's tasks back to broader, more idealistic concerns—in his words, to "conditions of peace" that included "minimum levels of economic well-being and health, enhanced world understanding, and a world order of law and justice."[10]

To the extent that the Ford Foundation and other nongovernmental, nonprofit organizations conducted their activities in accordance with such a vision, they were promoting an alternative world order, an international community where tolerance and understanding, rather than an ideological conflict, would be the rule. The state and non-state actors, it is true, did share many ideas and ideals. After all, the U.S. government espoused such principles as democracy, freedom, and justice, and believed that they comprised the basic ideology in terms of which it would combat totalitarian, communist influences emanating from the Soviet Union. Nevertheless, in waging the Cold War, the state was far more interested in establishing a network of military bases and friendly regimes than in promoting transnational ties of interdependence and mutual understanding. It was the task of nongovernmental organizations to concentrate their resources on the latter objective.

The Twenty-First Century Outlook

I have argued that inter-state relations and international affairs are not always identical, and that while governments focus on issues of national security and interests, nongovernmental and nonprofit organizations reach beyond the state apparatus and establish transnational connections throughout the globe. To the extent that visions of an interdependent international community persist, and that they have been translated at least into a partial reality, due credit must be given to such organizations.

In the wake of the terrorist attacks on the United States on September 11, 2001, it is true, the power of the state seems to have been enhanced. Not just in the United States but in many countries, governmental agencies have been augmented and their authority expanded so as to cope with the threat of terrorism. But this has not meant the diminution of activities by nonprofit and nongovernmental organizations. If anything, because the state has had to earmark larger portions of its resources to waging war against terrorists—"a new kind of war," as Presidents Ronald Reagan and George W. Bush have both called it—the role of private associations to provide for people's well-being may have been enlarged. The successful activities by the Red Cross and other organizations to raise money from private sources to help the victims of Hurricane Katrina in 2005 is a good example. The apparent rise in the influence of religion in the contemporary United States may also fit into the picture. Christian organizations have been seeking to make a greater input into such issues as birth control and the teaching of evolutionary biology, thereby blurring the boundaries between church and state. To the extent that the nation state comes to be seen as a moral entity, the influence of religion may be expected to grow. Just as likely, at the same time, would be the involvement of non-religious organizations in these controversies. In either case, it is doubtful that the authority of the state will remain undiminished. The nation may become an arena for the contention of different religious communities as well as nongovernmental organizations representing divergent ideologies and orientations. Many legal experts seem to believe that in the process the constitutional principle of the separation of church and state may become increasingly difficult to maintain. Be that as it may, the nation state as a secular, independent, and sovereign entity, the locus of identity and loyalty, will erode.

In the international realm, too, contradictory tendencies appear to have developed. On one hand, the rise of nationalism in the wake of the ending of the Cold War has been notable. International relations have seemed to revert to old-fashioned power politics; the United States is said to be the hegemonic power that faces the challenge of would-be superpowers such as China and India. There is nothing new about this sort of power game. At the same time, however, regional communities such as the European Union, the North America Free Trade Area, and the Association of Southeast Asian Nations have retained their vigor, and others, notably an East Asian order, seem about to make their appearance. In all such regional entities, the old-fashioned state sovereignty would have to be moderated.

Even more crucial have been the activities of such transnational non-state actors as religions, civilizations, multinational enterprises, and nongovernmental organizations. Their presence ensures that the world is not going to return either to the nineteenth century, the century of empires, or to the twentieth century, the century of inter-state clashes and totalitarian aggressions. It is far more likely that the state and non-state actors will share power and influence in determining the shape of the world.

International relations will continue to be concerned with three main objectives, in all of which nonprofit and nongovernmental organizations became active in the second half of the twentieth century: inter-state peace, global human well-being, and transnational, transcivilizational understanding. While peace is largely the responsibility of nations and international organizations, non-state actors may increase their influence in the attainment of the second and third objectives. Their activities in promoting global well-being in such areas as economic development, control of diseases, and the protection of the natural environment will be invaluable. Perhaps even more crucial will be their contribution to promoting dialogue among religions and civilizations. Peace in the coming decades is likely to lie as much in inter-religious and inter-civilizational relations as in inter-state relations. While intergovernmental organizations such as UNESCO can help promote communication among religions and civilizations, ultimately it must be nonprofit and nongovernmental organizations, including religious entities, that take the initiative to prevent a calamitous confrontation from developing. It is to be hoped that, as non-state actors develop transnational networks throughout the world, nongovernmental organizations will cooperate with each other, with states, with regional communities, and with international organizations in building a world order that will prove beneficial to future generations of humankind.

Notes

1. Paul W. Schroeder, *The Transformation of European Politics, 1763–1848* (New York: Oxford University Press, 1994).

2. Margaret E. Keck and Kathryn Sikkink, *Activists beyond Borders: Advocacy Networks in International Politics* (Ithaca, N.Y.: Cornell University Press, 1998).

3. F. S. L. Lyons, *Internationalism in Europe, 1815–1914* (Leiden, Neth.: A. W. Sythoff, 1963).

4. Akira Iriye, "A Century of NGOs," *Diplomatic History* 23, no. 3 (1999): 421–35.

5. Emily S. Rosenberg, *Spreading the American Dream: American Economic and Cultural Expansion, 1890–1945* (New York: Hill and Wang, 1982), and *Financial Missionaries to the World: The Politics and Culture of Dollar Diplomacy, 1900–1930* (Cambridge, Mass.: Harvard University Press, 1999).

6. Akira Iriye, *Global Community: The Role of International Organizations in the Making of the Contemporary World* (Berkeley and Los Angeles: University of California Press, 2002).

7. "International Relations and the Carnegie Corporation," March 1946, Carnegie Corporation Archives.

8. "Report of the Political Science Division," November 1949, Ford Foundation Archives.

9. Paul Hoffman, "Excerpt from Memorandum to the Board of Trustees," January 29, 1951, Ford Foundation Archives.

10. Rowan Gaither, "Summary of Memorandum on a Program for Peace," May 23, 1951, Ford Foundation Archives.

PART 2.
Projecting Logics

3. Philanthropy and the "Perfect Democracy" of Rotary International

← ─── →

The Dominion of Canada and the British Isles gave way to the crusaders' demands. Paris is ours and today the slogan is "On to Berlin, Vienna, then to the Antipodes." Like those of the Napoleonic forces, the ambitions of our conquest know no limitations save the limitations of the civilized world. Unlike the conquest of the Napoleonic forces, our conquest is, and will continue to be, in the interests of men and the principles which make for the practical idealization of trade. . . . Rotarianism thrives in all places where men think and where men's hearts are large enough to include the cares of others.

—PAUL P. HARRIS, FOUNDER OF ROTARY INTERNATIONAL,
ANNUAL PRESIDENT'S REPORT, 1912

"I think the President believes that one role of his is to be practical, realistic, and effective, but he also believes that he has a second, and maybe more important, role, to set out an ideal," said Gerson. "The President's view is that one of the great soft power advantages of the United States of America is that we can imagine a different and better world, that we are unique because we are not defined by race or tradition but by a set of universal ideals."

—MICHAEL GERSON, SPEECHWRITER
FOR PRESIDENT GEORGE W. BUSH, 2006

In 1919 the Japanese government sent Umekichi Yoneyama, then director of the Mitsui Trust Bank, on a "financial mission" with Baron Megata to the United States. On his return trip, Yoneyama spent New Year's Day 1920 in Dallas, Texas, where he met Kisoji Fukushima, assistant manager of the Mitsui Bussan Kaisha. Fukushima, who was living and working in Dallas as a wool exporter to Japan, used the opportunity to tell Yoneyama of his experience as a member of the Dallas Rotary Club. Known simply as Bill rather than Kisoji by his fellow Dallas Rotarians, Fukushima and his club made quite an impression on the commercial banker, as "he thought the principles of Rotary exactly coincided with his philosophy." Yoneyama returned to Tokyo and immediately set about organizing Tokyo's very own club. After months of discouraging results, Rotary's headquarters in Chicago appointed Walter L. Johnstone, agent for the Pacific Mail Steamship Company in Yokohama and an experienced Rotarian from California, to assist Yoneyama in creating one of the first Rotary clubs in East Asia. (Shanghai and Manila already had clubs in 1919 thanks to Roger D. Pinneo of the Seattle Rotary Club, who also worked in a similar capacity for the same steamship line.) With Johnstone's guidance, Yoneyama invited "several of his intimate friends to a dinner at the Bankers' Club," where he finally met with success. "Every one present was thoroughly convinced of the noble purpose of the Rotary club, as expounded by Mr. Yoneyama." He must have made quite an impression on his business counterparts. By November 1920 Yoneyama's Rotary club had seventeen members, all of whom were partners, presidents, managing directors, and/or owners of corporations in all varieties of Japanese industry and business.[1] With help from Dallas and Chicago, and from Bill Fukushima and Walter Johnstone, Yoneyama brought back a very unusual souvenir from his "financial mission" to the United States.

The nature of Rotary's institutional transference to Tokyo emerged from networks of global trade and transportation. At the Tokyo club's sixth meeting in June 1921, Zenjuro Horikoshi, senior partner of Horikoshi and Company, described his most recent business trip to the United States in some detail. As a silk exporter with branch offices in New York, London, Paris, and Sydney, Horikoshi had crossed the Pacific Ocean a remarkable fifty-two times. He was the all-star of globetrotters. This particular journey, he explained to his fellow Rotarians in Tokyo, was quite different for him:

> I have been to the United States many times, but this was the first trip I made as a member of a Rotary Club. I was treated very kindly by fellow Rotarians everywhere. When I arrived at Chicago, for example, they met me at the station with an automobile and took me to a Hotel. They did everything I wanted, in fact, they treated me as though I was their long-time friend. I attended the New York Club meeting several times. There were present at every meeting something like 500 members, consisting of various trades and professions. . . . The members are very friendly to each other and *perfect democracy* exists among them. [italics added][2]

Horikoshi's experience is instructive. The friendship, hospitality, and deference shown to him in Chicago and New York City contrasted with the nativism that drove the Emergency Quota Act through the U.S. Congress only a month earlier and with the Immigration Act of 1924, which formally blocked all

Japanese immigration to the United States. The growing anti-Japanese racism behind the Gentlemen's Agreement of 1907 and California's Alien Land Law of 1913 was baring its teeth by the time of Horikoshi's triumphant welcome into the inner sanctum of the Chicago and New York Rotary clubs. But Horikoshi was hardly moving in a social world of isolationists, nativists, and provincials. His rosy description of the Rotary clubs of Chicago and New York as a "perfect democracy" of trades, professions, and businesses was not entirely fanciful, just limited to his own experience with one type of Rotary club in one type of U.S. city—large, industrial, and international. While more elite clubs existed in cities such as Chicago and New York City, those cities' Rotary clubs were willing to accept Horikoshi as a full member from afar rather than as a dignified guest for the day. For someone like Horikoshi and his fellow Rotarians in Tokyo, this was a business opportunity that paralleled new diplomatic openings between the United States and Japan in the immediate wake of World War I.[3]

What Horikoshi meant by "perfect democracy" among Japanese and U.S. Rotarians, therefore, was crucial. The world of international business and its currency of transnational class identity made possible the transplanting of a Rotary club from the cotton belt of America to the imperial capital of Japan in the wake of World War I. Yoneyama's belief that the "principles of Rotary so coincided" with his own Japanese philosophy drove him to become the god-father of over forty Japanese Rotary clubs by 1940. Meanwhile, the royal treatment of Japanese businessmen such as Horikoshi while visiting the United States in a period of heightened nativism and isolationism expressed two countervailing trends in U.S. business and political cultures during the interwar years. The experiences of Horikoshi in Chicago and New York and the activities of Yoneyama, Fukushima, and Johnstone in Dallas and Tokyo were not historical anomalies, blips on the screen of American isolationism after the rejection of the League of Nations and the adoption of landmark anti-immigrant legislation. Rather, the activities of these men and their international organization were a sign of things to come. Not only did Rotary clubs thrive in East Asia and the Pacific Basin long before the outbreak of war between China and Japan in 1937, they were also cropping up in smaller and smaller towns and cities within the United States, Canada, Great Britain, and many European and Latin American countries as well.

But the particular success of Rotary clubs in Japan during the interwar period presents a special case. The activities, goals, and evolution of the Tokyo Rotary Club in response to massive changes during the Taishô Democracy and early Showa period reveal some important divergences as well as continuities in U.S.-Japanese relations before and after World War II.[4] Like the cultural influence of American baseball, the diplomatic and cultural contacts of the Institute of Pacific Relations, the cosmopolitan exchange through the U.S.-Japan Societies, and the presence of international organizations such as the YMCA and the Boy Scouts, the expansion of Rotary International (RI) into Japan during the interwar years fit within a greater pattern of international engagement. Within this context, RI made its own contributions. As a well-funded nonprofit, RI had a specific institutional focus driving its presence and growth—unlike baseball.[5] As a non-state actor, RI was not formally beholden to state sponsorship or any particular corporate foundations—unlike the Japan Council of the Institute of Pacific Relations.[6] As an international service club, RI was not limited to U.S.-Japanese relations—unlike the U.S.-Japan Societies.[7] And as a businessmen's luncheon club, RI drew upon the upper echelons of Japanese economic elites for its membership—unlike the YMCA and similar organizations.[8] But most importantly, the singular success of Rotary clubs in Japan before 1941 allowed one of the most familiar elements of Main Street to enter the everyday world of Japan's urban, industrial elites and offer itself as a normative model for social and business relations within the Japanese context. What did Horikoshi, his fellow Japanese Rotarians, and their counterparts in the United States and all around the world, believe RI's "perfect democracy" to mean? What were the consequences of that belief?

The Heartland Abroad

The summer of 1928 was a busy time for the Tokyo Rotary Club. At the June 27 weekly meeting, both the Marquis Tokugawa, longtime speaker of the House of Peers, and Ariyoshi, the mayor of Yokohama, entertained the eighty members in attendance. Speaking in English, the marquis spoke of the club's growing reputation in Tokyo and throughout Japan and joked about the need for such regimented time management in the House of Peers since every speaker before the club was strictly limited to five minutes by a large clock. Mayor Ariyoshi's comments, however, went much further. Quite the regular attendee at the Yokohama club's meetings, he was more than familiar with the practices, beliefs, and goals of the international service club. "He thought what churches had done for the advancement of the moral standard in the 19th century, Rotary [was] doing in the 20th century." Ariyoshi not only saw Rotary International as the vanguard of modern, international business standards, but also as a moral force for good in the world at large. But the global-ity of Ariyoshi's vision for Rotary's secular calling in the emerging world of international business was imbued with a strong sense of Japanese identity as well since "that patriotism which brought about the restoration of the Imperial Government at the beginning of the Meiji era was the same as this spirit of

Rotary. The idea of Rotary existed in Japan even then; but now it has become the prime factor in business morality, advocated by the influential business and professional men of the world." As such, it was imperative that the Yokohama and Tokyo Rotary clubs deepen their ties and co-operation in the future.[9] Indeed, only the week prior, Japan's seven clubs were granted formal district status within the international organization of Rotary by the headquarters in Chicago. The move reflected the emerging status of Japan as a central player not only in Rotary but in the world of international business and politics. The newly formed 70th international district, it turned out, also included clubs in Shanghai, Peking, Tientsin, and Nanking, as well as three up and coming in Manchuria (Mukden, Harbin, and Dairen), and one in Seoul. Moreover, the governor of the new district was none other than Yoneyama, now president of the Mitsui Trust Bank. The "father of Japanese Rotary" seemed the natural and unanimous choice.

As a result, Tokyo's hosting of the Second Pacific Rotary Conference in early October of 1928 would, in effect, be its coming out party as scores of delegates and VIPs from China, Korea, Australia, New Zealand, the Philippines, Hawaii, and the mainland United States were to attend. Not surprisingly, the sense of coming into their own pervades the club's records throughout the period. Maybe Mayor Ariyoshi's syncretism of Japanese nationalism and Rotary's principles of "business morality" was not that off the mark. In anticipation of the conference, however, classes in English, dance, and singing began the following week. The Japanese businessmen and their wives and children needed to learn very un-Japanese ways of social interaction in order to play host to so many Rotarian visitors from abroad. Ariyoshi's syncretism could only meld so much together at a time. One cannot afford to be too exotic after all.

Before the marquis and the mayor spoke, however, the meeting began with a small but revealing transaction. The club's board of directors had sent a "message of sympathy" to the Lima Rotary Club because of the recent "disastrous earthquake" in Chachapoyas, Peru. The club had just sent a donation of $250 to the relief fund to "loud applause." At first, the moment might seem as so much back-patting and self-congratulation. But there was a more important reason for the applause. On September 1, 1923, Tokyo experienced a massive earthquake resulting in tens of thousands of casualties. The fifty members of the relatively untried service club became a nexus point for receiving relief funds from fellow clubs in the Americas, Europe, and the Antipodes. In the end, over 73,000¥ was donated from 374 clubs in the United States and Canada, and from another ninety-two clubs mostly in Great Britain and Mexico. The Chicago office of RI also wired $25,000 in support within days of the catastrophe.

RI's philanthropic actions formed only a part of a broader relief effort as the U.S. fleet entered Yokohama with emergency provisions within the week. Yoneyama recounted how "the American government sent General McCoy with a Red Cross corps. Ship after ship came in from the States loaded with food, clothing, and building materials. When both General McCoy and Ambassador Wood were leaving Japan, old and young were seen lined up at the station to express their heartfelt thanks for the kindness of the American Government." In the midst of Tokyo's near destruction, the benevolent power of the United States became manifest in the two-pronged outreach of military support and private relief, of naval logistics and institutional charity. The grateful sentiments of the Japanese bidding farewell to McCoy and Wood paralleled those held by Yoneyama when he "showed the members [of the Tokyo club] a Rotary badge which was given to him by an American friend. It had been dug out of the ashes of his office and miraculously found to retain its original shape and color. In showing it he said, 'Like this little badge the Rotary spirit lives and shines through earthquake and fire.' He then urged the members to be more active and to show their appreciation of what the Rotarians have done for Japan in this time of great disaster." And they did just that: the club refurbished 188 schools throughout Japan and resupplied them with maps and blackboards over a period of several years, with the remainder going toward a charity hospital and an orphan asylum. The club was very careful to account for all expenses before their Rotarian brethren worldwide as proof of fulfillment of their fiduciary roles. The transparency of the club's actions and spending was central to forging its reputation within the "world fellowship of business and professional men." The Tokyo Rotary Club's first real step into philanthropic activity was quite literally a baptism by fire.[10]

There was another first for the club in the midst of that conflagration. The Tokyo club's first and only "alien" member at the time, Edward D. Berton, used his automobile as an ambulance without stop for days afterward, resulting in "high recognition both from his own Government and from ours." Ed Berton, a representative of U.S. Steel in Japan, joined the Tokyo club in March 1922 and was classified officially on the club register as working in "Steel-Distributing." In fact, his first speech to the club was on the history of U.S. Steel and its management practices. Berton also had the respect of the club as he "spared no pains in helping the needy and visiting the sick," leading to the creation of the club's Visiting Committee. Having introduced the club to singing as well, Berton was seen by his fellow Japanese Rotarians as the paradigmatic Rotarian—and he was their creation, their first "Japan-made Rotarian from America!" It was a sad day in late July 1928, therefore, as Berton prepared for his return to the United States because of a promotion within U.S. Steel. The club's sense of loss upon Ed's departure was sincere and heartfelt.

Nor was the sentiment unprecedented or felt only by the Japanese Rotarians. Ed's heroics in the aftermath of the 1923 earthquake were matched by one of his own fellow Rotarians in Tokyo. When Rotarian E. L. Irvine of Kalamazoo, Michigan, visited a few years after Berton's departure, he recounted how Watari "Kitty" Kitashima, stock broker and partner of Kitashima & Co., received a telegraph from the Kalamazoo club inquiring about the fate of their very own Mr. Williams and his wife, who had been in Yokohama at the time the devastating earthquake struck. Kitashima "actually walked to Yokohama and, after great difficulty, ascertained that both Mr. and Mrs. Williams had met death in the great disaster. This service of 'Kitty' which was so unselfishly rendered at a great sacrifice to himself, has created a deep feeling of affection in the hearts of all the members of the Rotary Club of Kalamazoo for Kitashima, and has bound the Rotary Club of Kalamazoo to the Rotary Club of Tokyo in an enduring manner."[11] It is not often that these two cities appear in the same sentence, let alone in such a tightly knit and personal way. The link was an international service club.

And international links were Kitty Kitashima's specialty. By 1930 Kitashima had become a veritable celebrity among the 153,000 Rotarians in 3,300 clubs spread throughout most of the Americas, Europe, East Asia, and the Antipodes. But not because of his service to Kalamazoo. Rather, as the club's secretary, he took it upon himself in 1923 to write up in English and then distribute the club's bulletins to all the clubs of the world. Club president Noboru Ohtani, for example, reported that, while attending the 1928 annual international convention in Minneapolis as Japan's representative, he "had the opportunity of talking with very many of the American delegates and I found them without exception keenly interested in Rotary in Japan and very sympathetic with our work."

Kitty's "Tokyo bulletin" was one of two reasons for such interest and curiosity on the part of Main Street's best known denizens.[12] The other was a book simply named *Japan*, published by the club in 1927, which took boosterism to a whole new level. When RI's Chicago office wrote the Tokyo club asking for a "pamphlet" that could be used by clubs in the United States and Canada for preparing "20 to 30 minute presentations" on Japan in their meetings, the Tokyo club instead produced a gem that far exceeded RI's rather pragmatic expectations. Replete with photos, printed in gorgeous text and colors, and distributed worldwide, *Japan* was the club's attempt to introduce and explain Japanese business, industry, culture, and history to all their Rotarian counterparts. It was the perfect marriage of business statistics and cultural representation. The beautiful, nuanced, ancient culture of Japan was also a wise place for investment and an emerging industrial power. The boys in Kalamazoo surely loved Japan.[13]

The Service Ideology

Bill Fukushima had already left the Tokyo club in early 1921 for the exact same reason Ed Berton was leaving seven years later: their companies were transferring them, one to Osaka, the other back to the United States. Bill and Ed, dutiful managers in their respective corporations, were very much in the same world of international business. Likewise, just as the Dallas Rotary Club, the 39th in Rotary's history, took pride in having created the first American-made Japanese Rotarian in Bill Fukushima, so the 855th club in Rotary's world-wide expansion trumpeted its responsibility for having returned the favor with the first Japanese-made American Rotarian in Ed Berton. One must note, however, that Kisoji became Bill in Dallas while Edward was just Ed in Tokyo; and that Kisoji believed he had so much to learn and imitate when in Dallas, while Ed instigated and propagated so many new practices within his home club of Tokyo. But the common ground between Bill and Ed encompassed more than their shared managerial identities within their transnational corporations and the intra-class intimacies of a men-only luncheon club. RI was (and is) an international nongovernmental organization (INGO) that served as the platform on which they could meet, socialize, and interact as professional and business peers, and as community leaders committed to what RI called "service."[14]

By the 1920s the core of RI's formal set of institutional objectives centered on the overarching theme of service. Although the original club in Chicago in 1905 made no secret of its focus on garnering business through networking with fellow club members, the club's rapid evolution into the National Association of Rotary Clubs in 1910 and then the International Association in 1912 reflected in many ways broad national trends in the growth and development of the corporate cultures of managerial liberalism and community activism of middle-class professionalism. This was most apparent in the emergence of RI's "ideal of service" or service ideology. At the heart of the transition from the fraternal lodges of the nineteenth century to the service clubs of the twentieth lay a deeper transition from the secrecy, ritual, fraternity, and egalitarianism of the lodge to an unambiguous middle-class identity couched in the language of community service, civic improvement, and professionalism. In need of greater legitimacy and public trust at the height of the Progressive Era, businessmen—particularly at the middle-class level—turned to the respectability of a professional identity and its formal dedication to public service.[15] At the first national convention of Rotary clubs in Chicago in 1910, "Rotarianism" was already being defined as "the new business conscience and progressive business methods. It brings together people who desire to deal honestly, and who would not otherwise meet. It is co-operation among gentlemen." Chesley Perry, one of the key Chicago founders of Rotary and its general secretary 1910–42, explained to the delegates from the twelve cities ranging from Boston to San Francisco: "We are here in all the vigor of our manhood ready to do our part of the world's work, anxious to have a share in the great civic uplift of our day and desirous of establishing and maintaining the highest business standards."[16] From the first days of its institutional inception, the Rotary Club was founded on a service ideology that merged classic elements of Progressive Era anti-corruption discourse with highly gendered concepts of marketplace identities and managerial authority.

The newfound professionalism of business, as a result, was only the beginning. Drawing on the success of women's clubs and driven always by a healthy dose of boosterism, the early Rotary clubs combined a newly masculinized version of civic activism with a businessman's particular emphasis on selective uses of state regulatory and fiscal powers to build up communications and transportation infrastructure. As with many other organizations and initiatives that emerged during the Progressive Era, Rotary clubs became useful vehicles in legitimizing the managerial authority of the middle class in state, economic, and local affairs.[17] The Rotary Club's claim to authority emanated from its members' status as "representative men of the community" who bore some mark of character and success in the marketplace. The development of a service ideology professional and dispassionate in tone yet humanitarian— even sentimental—in purpose was fundamental as Rotarians blended business, professionalism, sociability, and fraternity together in the name of civic uplift and the public interest. As such, it would be hard to overestimate the importance of the service ideology to RI. Simply put, the organization staked its claim on the credibility of its ever-expanding notion of "service" from its birth.[18] Insofar as a set of ideas and ideals could catalyze a loose association of businessmen into a formal organization devoted to the community, the construction and promulgation of RI's service ideology drove its organizational synthesis and evolution.

The various charitable projects and community activities taken on by local clubs and championed by RI, however, never had any particular plan or coherence. Given the relatively large degree of autonomy on the part of the local clubs, this was no surprise. Due to the broad range of projects and activities taken up by clubs, in fact, there was a push by World War I to distinguish acceptable community service activities from uncoordinated, ad hoc club activities done in the name of the public good.[19] All those activities had two common denominators. The first centered on charity and philanthropy. Clubs often involved themselves in fundraising for the community chest or "crippled children," building new playgrounds and parks, or else supporting and mentoring through the Boy Scouts, student loans, and 4-H clubs. Work with Boy Scouts had become one of the most common projects of Rotary clubs in the United States during the interwar period. This was according to plan. Clubs were supposed to forge this kind of interlocking relationship with other community organizations, both public and private, and meet social needs not met by any other group, organization, or agency. (The teeth on the outside of the gear shaft of Rotary's emblem are said to symbolize the interconnectivity of the club with all other community organizations such as those listed above.)

The other common theme centered on economic and civic improvements. Better traffic regulation, fire protection, and zoning laws were typical goals, as well as support for public works and the creation of chambers of commerce where none existed. Although not quite as common as charitable endeavors like fresh air camps and aid to underprivileged children, this latter type of community outreach emphasized a streamlined municipal government, more efficient management of public resources, improvement of public health facilities, and development of transportation and communications infrastructure.[20] They were typical Progressive Era projects in both form and rhetoric. But RI's reform efforts tended to focus on face-to-face charity projects and especially on developing boys into good adult male citizens; the construction of roads, parks, hospitals, swimming pools, and playgrounds were generally secondary priorities. Given their mixture of sociability, boosterism, and sentimentalism, Rotary clubs gravitated toward meeting social needs that were personal and local rather than political and systemic. Community service projects, in other words, tended to reflect the businessman's individualist ethos of self-reliance and vested interest in development of community infrastructure.

Despite the rhetorical emphasis on cooperation and community, the core devotion to individual moral character precluded any type of community service activity that challenged political or social inequalities in any significant way. This was by tacit design. As with many other measures put forth by progressives, the real objectives of reform were about the defense of what were seen as traditional middle-class values in the midst of rapid changes in social and economic conditions. The cooperative model of club sociability among business and professional equals privileged intra-class harmony over all else. As a result, community service could only be conceived of in apolitical terms. Moral uplift, individual charity, and civic improvement, not genuine civic and political reforms, pervaded club projects and rhetoric. RI's middle-class phi-lanthropy, once bleached of the political, could only reinforce rather than chal-lenge power relations at any level of governance. Particularly at the local level, this served many purposes. As a result, the reconstruction of the city of Tokyo in the wake of the 1923 earthquake was an ideal—although daunting—task for the Tokyo Rotarians. The same was true of the club's work with the three hundred children of the orphan asylum over many years. Horikoshi's "perfect democracy" could achieve easy consensus on such community and civic proj-ects. Meanwhile, Bill and Ed could find common ground in their comparable corporate roles—whether it be wool or steel—and in their civic projects and community service, whether they be in Dallas or Tokyo.

Augusta, Kansas (pop. 4000) meets Tokyo (pop. 2,000,000)

At the Tokyo club's luncheon that same day in late July 1928 was one Jesse C. Fisher of Augusta, Kansas (pop. 4,000), seated with his two nephews. Although it is unclear whether Fisher and Berton actually spoke with each other during or after the meeting, they would have addressed each other as Jesse and Ed—and in no other way. U.S. Steel's representative in Japan, along with some of Japan's most important businessmen, were Jesse Fisher's business and profes-sional peers during that luncheon, fellow members of the "parliament of busi-nessmen" brought together by the world of Rotary. Before introducing Fisher and the other visitors from Yokohama and Seoul, however, the club first wel-comed its newest member, Masakazu Takata, managing director of the Tokyo Gomu Kogyo K. K. Like all other new members since the club's inception, Mr. Takata had exactly five minutes to speak on his particular business classifica-tion within Rotary, which in Takata's case was "rubber goods manufacturing." He described the future prospects of the rubber industry as very bright "even if only in the making of auto tires, for the number of cars is being increased at a tremendous rate nowadays." Takata's reference to an increasing number of automobiles in Japan would undoubtedly have interested Jesse Fisher since his town of Augusta was labeled as "Oil Center" within Rotary's club reports and located near the oil boomtown of El Dorado, Kansas (which got its own Rotary club in 1919, a year after Augusta's).

But Jesse Fisher's reason for being in Tokyo with his nephews had noth-ing to do with tires, automobiles, petroleum, or commerce in any form. After his introduction and greetings to the Tokyo Rotarians on behalf of his fellow Rotarians of little Augusta, he remarked that, after only three days into his first visit to Japan, he "felt quite at home attending the Rotary meeting—just the same sort of meeting as they have in America—and after mentioning many things which seemed so familiar to his eyes, he said they did not have an automatic clock in his home club, but thought it was a fine thing and was thinking of taking one back with him." (Oddly enough, Jesse Fisher admired the same clock and strict time management as the Marquis Tokugawa.) He then turned to his nephews and explained that "he thought travelling and seeing the different countries the best education for everybody, and the first step in the realization of the Sixth Object."[21] Such a cosmopolitan view for a man from a decidedly provincial town in the middle of Kansas raises the questions: Why was Jesse Fisher of Augusta, Kansas, attending the Tokyo Rotary club's luncheon in July 1928 and explaining his presence in terms of Rotary's Sixth Object? What was the nature of this kind of contact and the meaning of his sense of being in a home away from home?

All members and visitors of the Tokyo club would have understood exactly what Fisher meant by RI's Sixth Object: "The advancement of understanding, good will, and international peace through a world fellowship of business and professional men united in the Rotary ideal of service." But the meaning and value of RI's Sixth Object depended greatly on its audience and location. Formally adopted at Rotary's annual international convention in Edinburgh, Scotland, in 1921, the Sixth Object was Rotary's particular commitment to the international expansion of the service club into all the "commercial centers of the world." Yet Augusta, Kansas, was hardly a commercial center of the world—not even in Kansas. Jesse Fisher was welcomed nonetheless as one of their own. In theory, he was. In theory, Augusta, Kansas, and Tokyo, Japan, were just different parts of an integrating, globalizing whole. Umekichi Yoneyama had come to know better. He wrote:

> In America, there seems to be more private business and professional men in the Rotary clubs than the executive officers of the leading firms and companies. In the small towns especially, grocers, shoemakers, etc. are found among the members. There, he said, is the Rotary spirit—the recognition of all useful occupations, and the dignifying by each Rotarian of his occupation as an opportunity to serve society. . . . All seemed to have fully absorbed the true meaning of Rotary. America being such a large country, however, in some of the smaller places he feared that they do not fully grasp the magnitude of the international nature of Rotary.[22]

In the language of Sinclair Lewis and U.S. culture since the 1920s, Yoneyama's observations would easily be understood as a description of Main Street's Babbitts, small-town boosters and provincials with little or no understanding or interest in anything outside their own line of business and city limits. By coincidence, Augusta, Kansas, in particular serves as an important marker of Rotary's trend toward smaller and smaller locales, and lower and lower levels of the managerial, business, and professional classes since it was one of the first cities with a population less than 5,000 to have a Rotary club.[23] Fisher's fascination with the Tokyo club's strict adherence to time limits and meeting agendas contrasted sharply with the biweekly club meetings in Augusta, which in the 1920s and 1930s often rolled lackadaisically from dinner time into the late evening. One visitor, in fact, described the Augusta meetings as "very much of a social affair as well as a Rotary club."[24] Fisher's and Tokugawa's oddly shared interest in the club's time management techniques reflected the two very different worlds in which they moved: a small service club in a small town in the oil and wheat fields of the Kansas prairie and Japan's House of Peers. Yet both addressed the Tokyo Rotary Club in the summer of 1928. Although most of the Augusta Rotarians were members of the local chamber of commerce and some members served as mayor and even in the Kansas legislature, they were hardly movers and shakers at the national level like their Japanese counterparts.[25]

This basic class difference revealed much about the fundamental contradictions behind Rotary's Sixth Object. The Tokyo club met for most of the 1920s in the very prestigious Bankers' Club. Given Yoneyama's own high status in Japanese banking, this was never questioned. Augusta, on the other hand, had hardly any hotels to accommodate the gatherings, resulting in club meals being served by local "ladies' organizations." Although the Tokyo Rotarians leaned heavily on their wives and daughters to make a success of their hosting the Second Rotary Pacific Conference in Tokyo in early October 1928, they did not count on their spouses to provide the club's meals as in Augusta. Rather than serving the food at the club meetings, the Japanese wives and daughters served as the embodiment of Japanese culture and dignity at important social events outside the club. Moreover, whereas the first major club project for Tokyo Rotarians centered on rebuilding the city in the wake of the 1923 earthquake, the Augusta Rotarians put all their effort into the Fourth Liberty Loan drive of southern Butler County in the summer of 1918. Philanthropy and patriotism, however, did often mix together in both clubs—especially by the end of the 1930s. But Yoneyama was right in his assessment. His fellow Rotarians in towns like Augusta were hardly living and breathing in anything like the regal, cosmopolitan airs of the Bankers' Club. In a club report from 1931 which asked how the Augusta club's "international service committee" was faring and whether the club was promoting RI's Sixth Object within the community, the response was unadorned: "We have made but little use of it. Our community is practically 100% white American so that our problem is one of education regarding other peoples." What was meant exactly by "other peoples" was unclear, except to say not white and very far away—at least in mind. One must wonder how the club would have received a visit from a fellow Rotarian from Japan. Would it have been anything remotely like Horikoshi's experiences in Chicago and New York City? The Augusta club was not even attempting to correspond with Rotarians in other countries, which most other clubs managed to do even in the heart of the Depression. Instead, the club's passion during the interwar years centered on helping the Boy Scouts of America and the 4-H clubs.[26] One could easily write off Augusta, Kansas, as the bastion of isolationism and provincialism that is so easy to mock—the perfect counterpoint to cosmopolitanism. And yet Jesse Fisher was in Tokyo with his two nephews citing RI's "Sixth Object" on international peace and understanding among the world's businessmen to a large and welcoming audience comprising Tokyo's commercial elites.

The Wichita Plan

Jesse Fisher's presence, in fact, was not a complete anomaly. Augusta got its very own club thanks to ten Rotarians from Wichita, Kansas. The extension of Rotary into a satellite of Wichita seemed a logical step because Augusta lacked any "commercial organization" and so the club sought to do "a considerable amount of commercial and civic work together with boys' work." The Wichita Rotarians also saw it as their duty to bring their business counterparts and fellow community leaders into the fold, no matter how small and provincial the town. Although Jesse Fisher's devotion to the internationalist vision of Rotary's "world fellowship of businessmen and professionals" may have stood out in the Augusta club, there were many in Wichita who were very much in accord with him. In 1925 the Wichita club sent a letter to all other Rotary clubs in the United States—about 1,600 in total—inviting them to support what soon became known as "The Wichita Plan." The Wichita club had divided its more than 200 members into groups of ten in order to study "some one foreign country along peace lines." After several months of study, each group was to report its findings to the club as a whole during one of their weekly luncheon meetings "either through pageantry, speeches, papers, or the spoken word of a native of the country where possible." The Wichita Plan was to examine as a club the twenty-eight countries where Rotary clubs had already been established as part of a "movement for World Peace, launched by Business and Professional men, who through their affiliation with Commerce and Science represent the great majority . . . free of sectarian or political complexities. . . ."[27] To that end, the Wichita club drafted a resolution for the coming international convention in Cleveland that called for RI to "inaugurate . . . a campaign of

Education for the definite study of International Peace" so that "Rotary may be of service to mankind in doing its part to bring about World Peace."[28]

The Wichita Rotarians were clearly thinking of themselves and their club in an international context. The club members' plans to educate themselves on the many countries where Rotary clubs already existed showed that they were expecting something more out of their local club and their fellow U.S. Rotarians than improving regional roads, mentoring local Boy Scouts, and collecting Christmas baskets. Although the club's resolution was ultimately withdrawn at the 1925 convention in favor of a broader resolution that included ethical business practices, boys' work in the community, and worldwide expansion of Rotary, RI's Committee on Extension and its board of directors both claimed total support for the "sentiment" and goals of the Wichita Plan and then proved it when RI highlighted the plan for its approximately 100,000 readers in its monthly magazine, *The Rotarian*.[29]

Nor was Wichita the only club acting on its internationalist aspirations. The following year the Whittier Rotary Club in California managed to get unanimous support from the delegates representing all 130 clubs in its district (mostly the state of California) on their proposed resolution that "provides for a committee to suggest the programs and the methods of education in international understanding for which so many clubs are asking." Recognizing that "other forces are working among women and children to improve international relations," the Whittier club argued that "Rotary speaks directly to the only power which can stop war and maintain peace, BUSINESS. Every week in all the principal cities of the United States and in many of those in 34 other nations Rotary mobilizes leading business and professional men."[30] The Whittier club saw its peace proposal as part of a general trend toward "bettering international relations," but more important was the club's belief that the solidarity within its expanding international network of business and professional peers was the key to world peace. In the world of RI, it seemed only natural to project its voluntary, associational model of governance and economic citizenship in the United States beyond its borders. The implied logic was simple: just as the competition of nations brought only war, so the marketplace—the world of business—could alone transcend national rivalry and provide enduring peace. The virtues of an international marketplace, not the vicissitudes of nation states, were the hope of future stability and cooperation in the world. The Wichita and Whittier clubs saw the Sixth Object of Rotary in a serious light. Members of such clubs may not have been the paragon of cosmopolitanism, but neither were they exactly small-town provincials. The key to understanding Jesse Fisher in Tokyo and the Wichita Plan, then, lies in RI's institutional expression of the philanthropic and managerial impulses of the new middle classes and in its ability to weave its notions of "perfect democracy" and "new business conscience" into the tapestry of America's favored national narrative as a global force for moral and civic uplift. In short, RI's creed of civic internationalism.

Conclusion: A New Order—of Business

In mid-June 1940 Rotarian Takashi Komatsu took the stage before more than 3,700 Rotarians and their guests as one of the featured speakers in an "international round table" at RI's annual international convention in Havana, Cuba. Mr. Komatsu, a member of the Tokyo Rotary Club since 1929, was a close friend and protégé of Umekichi Yoneyama. As a managing director of the Asano Shipbuilding Company and as a graduate of Monmouth College, a Scottish Presbyterian frontier college now surrounded by Illinois cornfields, Mr. Komatsu knew both America's heartland and the business world of Tokyo very well. But, with warfare breaking out in both Europe and East Asia, this was a delicate time for Rotary to hold a round table on international peace and understanding. And Komatsu knew it. Though there was a net gain of ninety-nine new clubs for RI in the previous year, over seventy-five clubs had been terminated as a result of political change, conflict, and conquest, most of them being in Spain or Czechoslovakia that particular year. Clubs in Germany, for example, had already been banished by the German government several years earlier.

The Rotary clubs in Japan, however, were still going strong in the summer of 1940. In fact, Mr. Komatsu explained that their old district within RI had grown so much that they had formed three new separate districts, with nineteen clubs in northeastern "Japan proper," nineteen in southwestern Japan, and eight clubs in Korea and Manchukuo (Manchuria). Moreover, the Japanese Rotarians had formed their own "Advisory Committee" for all those clubs— much as the Canadians and Europeans had done years before—and expected soon to have over one hundred clubs organized within those three districts.[31] Rotary clubs, in short, were flourishing within the Japanese Empire up to the summer of 1940.

Sporting a smile described as "supreme," Komatsu exuded confidence and good will as he described the "spirit of fellowship" among the five hundred Rotarians and families at his club's latest conference in Yokohama a month prior, the thirty to forty "overseas Rotarians" that visit his club each week in Tokyo, and the student exchanges run by the club with their counterparts in the United States. In a folksy and heartfelt way, Komatsu invited the Rotarians in the Havana audience, about two-thirds from the United States and Canada and about one-third from Cuba and Latin America, to visit the Tokyo club the way Jesse Fisher had in 1928:

When you reach our meeting place you will be welcomed by the members of our fellowship committee, and you will wonder whether you are really so many thousand miles away from home. Perhaps the only sense of strangeness will come to you when you notice that the people about you are talking in an unintelligible tongue. But in this you need have no anxiety, because you will soon be surrounded by many friends who will be able to speak to you in one of the languages familiar to you.[32]

There would not be any demands or expectations that the visitors speak Japanese, he further assured them. Indeed, the Tokyo club's meetings began with the singing of the national anthem and "a Rotary song," much like in the United States, Canada, and Great Britain. Although the Japanese were not known for their "community singing," he explained that "under the leadership of one of the American members [Ed Berton], we learned to sing some of the simpler songs in English." The club, in fact, had developed many of its own club songs in Japanese since Berton's departure on the day of Jesse Fisher's visit back in July 1928.

But the Rotary club stood for something more than lunchtime sociability and businessmen's camaraderie. Komatsu then reviewed the origins of the Tokyo orphanage and children's home started by his club:

At the time of the great earthquake of 1923, the Rotarians of the world showered upon us their deepest sympathy in the contributions which they sent. I am sure there must have been generous gifts from many of you present here today. You will be interested to know that a Rotary home was erected with this money, and our members have assumed the responsibility of maintaining and perpetuating it. In this home the young women who are brought up at the orphanage, before they are sent out to take their places in life, are given courses in domestic science, arts and crafts, and in cultural training such as flower arrangement, tea ceremony, music, painting, and so forth.[33]

The orphaned girls of Tokyo had a place to go, a roof over their head, and a way to become proper Japanese women thanks to the Tokyo Rotarians. The Tokyo club had found its own unique way of blending patriotism and philanthropy under RI's umbrella of international fellowship and good will. Their clubs, Komatsu announced, were expanding into Manchukuo—not Manchuria.

But the global tensions of 1940 could not be erased by the sunny disposition of Komatsu. That took some explaining. Komatsu spoke after Rotarian

Gardiner of Ceylon, who described himself as a "full-blooded Tamil" and then proudly explained how his name was a product of Portuguese traders and American missionaries, and before Rotarian Jorge Fidel Durón of Tegucigalpa, Honduras, who drew much applause for his comments on "American ideals of liberty and democracy" and how America—both North and South—was "the continent of the future." Komatsu therefore knew he was expected to provide his own insights into the meaning and direction of international relations in the near future. "Surely we are living today in a troubled world," he began, "but let us not be dismayed by the darkness of the hour, nor forget our responsibilities as Rotarians. . . . Let us avoid any action which might be interpreted as casting stones of blame. Let us not lose sight of the fact that the peoples of the world do not possess the same psychological approach to the problems of life. The nations are still far apart in their understanding of human needs and interests in their ideals and aspirations, and even in their conceptions of right and justice." In the summer of 1940 the nations indeed were "far apart," and in other ways too close together. The differences, however, were hardly limited to the "psychological." Komatsu then closed by turning to the future "task of preparing the soil of understanding in the minds of men by upholding firmly the ideal of service and fellowship so that in God's own good time, peace and security may be established on this earth." He returned to his seat on the platform to the sound of thundering applause.[34]

Exactly three months after Takashi Komatsu's uplifting speech in Havana, the Tokyo Rotary Club voted to disband, along with all other forty-five clubs that fell under Japan's "Advisory Committee." The dream of over one hundred Rotary clubs within the Japanese Empire within a year had quickly passed into memory. The last club meeting opened first with Rotarian Nagasaki's distribution of his pamphlet "on the petroleum in the Dutch-Indies, and the Industrial Alliance in Germany." The final order of business then came to the floor: the formal disbanding of the Tokyo club, only months shy of its twentieth anniversary. Confusion and regret hung over the final meeting's conversations and debates since the exact reason for the elimination of the clubs was not clear. Described as "a desperate situation" and "a painful experience," the club members voted unanimously to vote for disbanding in deference to their officers' advice. Only Umekichi Yoneyama's speech could provide any sense of closure as he "in distressing mood sadly dragged himself to the speakers' stand and said, 'In twenty years of Rotary this is the first time I have had to speak before you with such painful feelings. . . . I simply wish to express my heartfelt humble apology for not being able to save our club from such a fatal condition. However, we did not and could not sit idly looking on with folded arms at the changing current of the time.'" He then suggested the reorganization of the Japanese Rotary clubs as "a new association based upon national unit administration" with clubs calling themselves by the day of the week on which they met. Yoneyama stipulated only that "It is absolutely necessary to maintain the international spirit even in the new organization. Without the ideal of service, its application to our business and community lives would be meaningless." To the bitter end, Yoneyama wished to remain true to RI's "perfect democracy" and its creed of civic internationalism among the world's businessmen and professionals. Kitty Kitashima recorded the final words: "It is the earnest hope of all the members of the Tokyo Rotary Club that the time may come soon when we can peacefully join again in world fellowship for the advancement of the Rotary principles." The Tokyo Rotary Club thus renamed itself the Wednesday Club and continued meeting until Tokyo was destroyed in the firebombings of March 1945. In the 1923 conflagration, the club found its raison d'être, and in that of 1945 its demise.[35]

Or did it?

While returning from India in the fall of 1948 on official RI business, George Means stopped off in Japan to inform the de facto proconsul of the United States, General MacArthur, of his plans to re-establish the extensive network of prewar Rotary clubs of Japan. MacArthur told Means, later to become the third General Secretary of RI (1953–1972) and a critical figure in RI's postwar national and international expansion, that "Washington" would have to authorize his request. Means did not welcome this kind of intrusion into the doings of a private nongovernmental organization: "Rotary cannot operate if it must be subject to the authority of governments."[36] To RI's officers and approximately 250,000 members worldwide, such oversight would have been especially galling since nearly fifty Rotary clubs had spread throughout the Japanese Empire from 1920 until 1940 with little or no direct help from the U.S. or Japanese governments. General MacArthur was well aware of Rotary's prewar history because one of his top aides during the war, Carlos Romulo of the Philippines, had been a high-ranking international officer and very active Rotarian from Manila in the 1930s. Moreover, MacArthur was already an honorary member of the Rotary clubs of Milwaukee, Melbourne, and Manila.[37]

George Means soon got his "permission" without any formal approval from Washington. He then found the ideal translator for the task at hand—Mr. Takashi Komatsu. As Means's interpreter and guide, Komatsu was now speaking in places very different from the Centro Asturiano in Havana, and likely using terms such as "international peace" and "world fellowship" with different connotations. With help from Komatsu and because the clubs had continued through the war as "day-of-the-week" clubs, the re-organization of the Rotary clubs throughout Japan went forward with little difficulty. When the Tokyo club was formally reinstated into Rotary International in 1949, one of the Tokyo club's first honorary members was General MacArthur, who explained that Rotary was "sorely needed in this time of so much world unrest." Thirty-three other clubs also emerged from the rubble by 1950–1951, including Hiroshima and Nagasaki. As Means explained it, RI was "the first non-religious international organisation readmitted to Japan after the war."[38] Foreshadowing RI's extensive expansion into India and East Asia after 1960, Japan quickly became a major epicenter of growth for RI in the postwar era. According to RI's official directory, there were 156 Japanese clubs by 1956, while a decade later there were 711 clubs. By 1986 there were 1,652 clubs, and by 2006 approximately 2,339 Rotary clubs, throughout Japan. Bill Fukushima and Ed Berton, Umekichi Yoneyama and the Rotarians of Wichita and Dallas, Kitty Kitashima and the Kalamazoo club, Zenjuro Horikoshi and Jesse Fisher, all would have been proud of George and Takashi and their new order of business. Despite RI's not being "subject to the authority of governments," its institutional practices and ideological tenets helped prepare the way for and served well under U.S. hegemony in postwar Japan.

Notes

The first epigraph is from the Annual Report of President Paul P. Harris, *Rotarian* (September 1912): 19. The second epigraph is written as quoted in "The Believer: George W. Bush's loyal speechwriter," Jeffrey Goldberg, *New Yorker,* February 13 and 20, 2006, 60.

1. *The History of the Tokyo Rotary Club* (Tokyo: Tokyo Rotary Club, 1940), 1:1–7; *The Rotary Club of Dallas: Silver Anniversary, 1911–1936* (Dallas: Rotary Club of Dallas, 1936), 20.

2. *The History of the Tokyo Rotary Club,* 1:8.

3. For analysis of the transitional period and the diplomatic promise it seemed to hold for both nations, see Sadao Asada, "Between the Old Diplomacy and the New, 1918–1922: The Washington System and the Origins of Japanese-American Rapprochement," *Diplomatic History* 30, no. 2 (April 2006): 211–30.

4. The historiography on U.S.-Japanese relations is extensive. For a general view of U.S.-Japanese relations, see W. G. Beasley, *The Rise of Modern Japan,* 2nd ed. (London: Weidenfeld and Nicolson, 1995); Herbert P. Bix, *Hirohito and the Making of Modern Japan* (New York: Harper Collins, 2000); John W. Dower, *Japan in War and Peace* (New York: New Press, 1993); Richard B. Frank, *Downfall: The End of the Imperial Japanese Empire* (New York: Random House, 1999); and Ramon Myers, Mark R. Peattie, and Ching-chi Chen, *The Japanese Colonial Empire, 1895–1945* (Princeton: Princeton University Press, 1984). For analysis of postwar U.S.-Japanese relations and the central role of private and philanthropic institutions in making the transition possible, see Tadashi Yamamoto, Akira Iriye, and Makoto Iokibe, eds., *Philanthropy and Reconciliation: Rebuilding*

Postwar U.S.-Japan Relations (Tokyo: Japan Center for International Exchange, 2006), especially, with respect to this chapter, chapter 9, Kimura Masato, "U.S.-Japan Business Networks and Prewar Philanthropy: Implications for Postwar U.S.-Japan Relations," 279–312.

5. See Sayuri Guthrie-Shimizu, "For the Love of the Game: Baseball in Early U.S.-Japanese Encounters and the Rise of a Transnational Sporting Fraternity," *Diplomatic History* 28, no. 5 (November 2004): 637–62. Managers of U.S. baseball teams regularly visited the Tokyo Rotary Club, often because they were already Rotarians in the United States. See, for example, Rotarian Carl Zamloch, "athletic instructor" for U.C. Berkeley, "who came with the baseball team" to visit the Tokyo Rotary Club and Rotarian Baxter of Los Angeles, coach of the Southern Pacific University baseball team, *The History of the Tokyo Rotary Club*, June 1, 1927, 2:57, and May 31, 1928, 2:205 (respectively) and the visit of Ishii, captain of the Tokyo baseball team, introduced to the Tokyo club by Rotarian Hiranuma of Yokohama and president of that city's Athletic Association. Ishii told the Tokyo Rotarians that several of his men "have made visits to the United States on a baseball tour, and they were always honoured by being invited to the Rotary luncheon at various places"; ibid., August 13, 1930, 3:154.

6. For the best historical survey of the Institute of Pacific Relations, see Tomoko Akami, *Internationalizing the Pacific: The United States, Japan, and the Institute of Pacific Relations in War and Peace, 1919–1945* (London: Routledge, 2002).

7. See, for example, Makoto Iokibe, "U.S.-Japan Intellectual Exchange: The Relationship between Government and Private Foundations," chapter 3, in Tadashi et al., *Philanthropy and Reconciliation*, 61–100.

8. See Manako Ogawa, "The 'White Ribbons League of Nations' Meets Japan: The Trans-Pacific Activism of the Woman's Christian Temperance Union, 1906–1930," *Diplomatic History* 31, no. 1 (January 2007): 21–50.

9. *The History of the Tokyo Rotary Club*, 2:217–316, for June 20, 1928, through October 1928. Mayor Ariyoshi's speech can be found on page 226 of this volume.

10. Ibid., 1:24–43 and 2:241–45.

11. Ibid., 3:69–73.

12. Ibid., 2:239–44.

13. Lester B. Struthers, Assistant Secretary of RI, to Special Commissioner Isaka, October 13, 1926, reproduced in introduction to *Japan* (Tokyo: Tokyo Rotary Club, 1927).

14. Kisoji "Bill" Fukushima returned to the Tokyo Rotary Club in October 1931 and remained there until September 1940. His new classification in the club was "Capital Investment." *The History of the Tokyo Rotary Club*, Appendix: "List of Members . . ." 5:6.

15. This was a very common theme in Rotary publications out of Chicago and London. At the 1911 Portland national convention Arthur F. Sheldon first coined the motto "He profits most who serves best." On the origins of emphasis on service from Arthur F. Sheldon, see "Members, Sheldon Arthur F.," Box 73, folder 3, Chicago Rotary/One Archives, Chicago, Ill. There are numerous articles about this in *The Rotarian* from 1912

onward; in particular, see articles under the heading "Salesmanship—Science Plus Art," *Rotarian,* June 1915, 91–96. See also "The Philosophy and Ethics of Successful Business: An Extract from the Buffalo Convention Address," *Rotarian,* September 1913, 113, and "The Ideal of Service as the Basis of All Worthy Enterprise" and "Perpetuating the Ideal of Service to Humanity" in Central Files/Subject Files, Pamphlets, Rotary International Archives; Evanston, Illinois (hereafter, RI Archives). On service as a "profitless ideal," see William Leach, *Land of Desire: Merchants, Power, and the Rise of a New American Culture* (New York: Vintage, 1993), esp. chapter 5, and Emily S. Rosenberg, *Financial Missionaries to the World: The Politics and Culture of Dollar Diplomacy, 1900–1930* (Cambridge, Mass.: Harvard University Press, 1999). On the rise of salesmen as respectable professionals, see Walter A. Friedman, *Birth of a Salesman: The Transformation of Selling in America* (Cambridge, Mass.: Harvard University Press, 2004), esp. chap. 6; and on the cross-class nature of lodges and the transition to service clubs, see Mary Ann Clawson, *Constructing Brotherhood: Class, Gender, and Fraternalism* (Princeton, N.J.: Princeton University Press, 1989).

16. *Proceedings of the First National Convention of Rotary Clubs of America*; Chicago, Ill.; 15–17 August 1910; 40, 13, respectively.

17. The best academic analysis of service clubs in general is Jeffrey Charles, *Service Clubs in American Society: Rotary, Kiwanis, and Lions* (Urbana: University of Illinois Press, 1993), and for Rotary International as an instrument for U.S. cultural and economic power, Victoria de Grazia, *Irresistible Empire: America's Advance through 20th-Century Europe* (Cambridge, Mass.: Harvard University Press, 2005), chapter 1, "The Service Ethic," 15–74. See also, Clifford Putney, "Service over Secrecy: How Lodge-Style Fraternalism Yielded Popularity to Men's Service Clubs," *Journal of Popular Culture* 27, no. 1 (1993): 179–90, and Thomas A. Wikle, "International Expansion of the American-Style Service Club," *Journal of American Culture* 22, no. 2 (1999): 45–52. A classic synthesis of the major streams in the broad historiography of progressivism is Daniel T. Rodgers, "In Search of Progressivism," *Reviews in American History* 10, no. 4 (1982): 113–32, while both James T. Kloppenberg, *Uncertain Victory: Social Democracy and Progressivism in European and American Thought, 1870–1920* (New York: Oxford University Press, 1986), and Daniel T. Rodgers, *Atlantic Crossings: Social Politics in a Progressive Age* (Cambridge, Mass.: Harvard University Press, 1998), are notable for analyzing progressivism as a function of international exchange and shared dialogue rather than of specific national political systems and cultures. For an update and summation of Rodgers's positions, see his "An Age of Social Politics," in *Rethinking American History in a Global Age,* ed. Thomas Bender, 250–73 (Berkeley and Los Angeles: University of California Press, 2002). See also Robert Wiebe, *Businessmen and Reform: A Study of the Progressive Movement* (Cambridge, Mass.: Harvard University Press, 1962); Ellis Hawley, *The Great War and the Search for a Modern Order: A History of the American People and Their Institutions, 1917–1933* (New York: St. Martin's Press, 1979); Paul Boyer, *Urban Masses and Moral Order in America, 1820–1920* (Cambridge, Mass.: Harvard University Press, 1978); Joan Hoff Wilson, *American Business and Foreign Policy, 1920–1933* (Lexington; University Press of Kentucky, 1971); Samuel Haber, *Efficiency and Uplift:*

Scientific Management in the Progressive Era, 1890–1920 (Chicago: University of Chicago Press, 1964); and Michael McGerr, *A Fierce Discontent: The Rise and Fall of the Progressive Movement in America, 1870–1920* (New York: Free Press, 2003).

18. The centennial history of RI, for example, is entitled "A Century of Service."

19. University of Chicago, Social Science Survey Committee, *Rotary? A University Group Looks at the Rotary Club of Chicago* (Chicago: University of Chicago Press, 1934), chapter 10, "Civic Leadership," 221–47. See also, Resolution 34 from the St. Louis convention in 1923 and countless pamphlets published on "community service" after 1915 by Rotary's publishing arm.

20. Ibid., 224–25 in particular.

21. *The History of the Tokyo Rotary Club,* 2:241–45; *The Augusta Rotary Club since 1918* (Augusta, Kans.: Augusta Rotary Club, 1968).

22. *The History of the Tokyo Rotary Club,* 2:485–86.

23. *The Augusta Rotary Club since 1918,* n.p., "Notes on the Beginning."

24. District Governor's Report, September 30, 1929, Augusta, Kansas, Club File, RI Archives.

25. *The Augusta Rotary Club since 1918,* n.p.; *The History of the Tokyo Rotary Club,* 2:269–310, for detailed coverage of the Tokyo club's hosting of the Second Rotary Pacific Conference, Oct 1–4, 1928.

26. *The Augusta Rotary Club since 1918,* n.p.

27. Form letter of the Wichita Rotary Club to the Rotary Clubs of the United States, May 14, 1925, duplicated in the Wichita Rotary Club's publication, *Round and Round* 10, no. 20 (May 16, 1925). Guy Gundaker Papers; File: "Rotary General—Notes on Convention at Pittsburgh," RI Archives. See also, "Meeting of the Extension Committee, July 28–30, 1925, Chicago," File: "Committee—Extension—1925–29," RI Archives.

28. See *Convention Proceedings,* Sixteenth Annual Convention, Cleveland, Ohio, June 1925, Rotary International, Resolution # 19, and Wichita Rotary Club bulletin, *Round and Round,* May 16, 1925; Guy Gundaker Papers, RI Archives.

29. *Rotarian,* August 1925, 37.

30. John G. Swain, President, Whittier Rotary Club, to all U.S. Rotary clubs, May 12, 1926, Guy Gundaker Papers; File: "Rotary General—Notes on Convention at Pittsburgh," RI Archives. The real impetus behind the Whittier Club's emphasis on improving international relations seems to have been Herbert E. Harris, Professor of English at Whittier College, and chairman of the "Sixth Object Committee." RI's Sixth Object, first formally adopted in 1922 and later renamed the Fourth Object in 1936, was: "The advancement of understanding, good will, and international peace through a world fellowship of business and professional men united in the Rotary ideal of Service."

31. *Convention Proceedings of the Thirty-First Annual International Convention of Rotary International* (Chicago: Rotary International, 1940), 118–22.

32. Ibid.

33. Ibid.

34. Ibid.

35. *The History of the Tokyo Rotary Club,* 5:265–73.

36. "Reintroduction of Rotary into Japan and Korea: Report of Assistant Secretary George R. Means," 9 in box 149, file: [Special Service Support Committee], RI Archives. See also George R. Means, Gen. Sec., Rotary International (1953–72), "Rotary's Return to Japan," 27 in box 144, file: [Extension—General, 1969–75], RI Archives.

37. David Shelley Nicholl, *The Golden Wheel: The Story of Rotary 1905 to the Present* (Plymouth, UK: MacDonald and Evans, 1984), 377, 426–29; David C. Forward, *A Century of Service: The Story of Rotary International* (Evanston, Ill.: Rotary International, 2003), 209.

38. Means, "Rotary's Return to Japan," 27–28; Nicholl, *The Golden Wheel*, 428.

4. Social Entrepreneurship
Success Stories and Logic Construction

MICHAEL LOUNSBURY and DAVID STRANG

*It is not from the benevolence of the butcher, the brewer, or the baker that we
expect our dinner, but from their own interest. We address ourselves not to
their humanity, but to their self-love, and never talk to them of our own neces-
sities but of their advantages.*
— ADAM SMITH, *THE WEALTH OF NATIONS,* 1776

*I shall not today attempt further to define the kinds of material I understand
to be embraced within that shorthand description [pornography]; and perhaps
I could never succeed in intelligibly doing so. But I know it when I see it.*
— U.S. SUPREME COURT JUSTICE POTTER STEWART,
JACOBELLIS V. OHIO, 1964

In our brave new neoliberal world, market models and market metaphors
reign supreme. It is not surprising that "social entrepreneurship" and related
notions like "venture philanthropy" are increasingly prominent discursive focal
points for the marketization of the nonprofit or "third" sector. While a variety
of definitions abound, the idea of social entrepreneurship challenges the conventional social welfare logics that suggest top-down, policy-driven efforts to
ameliorate social problems. In contradistinction to various forms of structured
collective action, entrepreneurialism celebrates bold, individual initiative as
the engine of social change. Drawing on the prestige of business leaders and
cultural models of heroic action, social entrepreneurship has begun to emerge
as a new institutional logic to address social problems in ways that circumvent
longstanding bureaucratic approaches to social welfare.

While the sources of the social entrepreneurial logic are complex and multiple, it began as an American movement shaped by receding state resources
and commitments. It has concretely taken form in the United States as a way
to introduce business methods and entrepreneurial energy into the nonprofit
sector to address social problems in a bottom-up fashion, and also to guide

71

nonprofits towards self-sufficiency through revenue generation. These ideas and practices have been driven by a variety of actors including philanthropists, universities, and other key nonprofit leaders and organizations. Some of these same actors have also been active in promoting this logic internationally and they have gained the attention of central development organizations such as the World Bank and the United Nations as well as a variety of nongovernmental organizations (NGOs).

There is great ambiguity about what social entrepreneurship is and how it should be structured. Some have advocated it as a state policy, while others insist on grassroots activism as the key to its efficacy. Despite rapid growth in recognized exemplars within the United States and also globally, fundamental questions about the content of social entrepreneurship remain.

In this chapter, we explore the origins and international spread of the emergent social entrepreneurial logic. Organizational scholars in the institutional tradition have identified a wide variety of relevant mechanisms. DiMaggio and Powell (1983) identify coercive, mimetic, and normative sources of institutional isomorphism. Scott (1987) describes multiple forms of social transmission: the imposition of structure by powerful actors, the authorization of structure where local actors align their behavior with legitimating bodies, the inducement of structure via rewards and resource flows, and the imprinting of structure through low-level demographic processes and taken-for-granted assumptions. Strang and Soule (1998) emphasize the contrast between network-based models of diffusion (where direct or indirect ties serve as channels for information and influence) and generalized diffusion processes where professional change agents, the media, and emerging cultural discourses catalyze imitation and practice adoption.

As Ann Swidler's chapter about AIDS programs in sub-Saharan Africa in this volume shows, for example, NGOs can provide a vehicle for the spread of Western ideas about disease treatment and prevention by incorporating local actors in program activities and providing them with resources (Spicer 2002; Rao and Hirsch 2003). Logics can spread as a result of authoritative action backed by negative incentives or force, as exemplified by the current nation building project of the U.S. government in Iraq. And they may diffuse on a more voluntary basis as ideas are theorized and gain legitimacy in transnational forums, becoming more accessible and appropriate for adoption as a result (Strang and Meyer 1993; Meyer, Kamens, and Benavot 1992 [on education curricula]; Frank, Hironaka, and Schofer 2000 [on environmental policy]).

The empirical literature typically starts with a relatively durable object such as a longstanding logic or a well-theorized practice that can be traced in some concrete way across space and time. For example, conventional diffusion studies presume that comparable instances of a practice can be identified as present or absent across a defined population of cases over time. Little research focuses on the forging of new logics which may be interpenetrated with their spread.

To make sense of the generation of a new logic, one can usefully turn the conventional diffusion approach on its head to probe how concrete instances of a set of activities become discursive fodder. In this paper, the key empirical cases are the success stories of particular individuals and organizations around the world that are identified as "social entrepreneurs." While stories have been argued to be a crucial element in entrepreneurial efforts to gain legitimacy and garner resources (Lounsbury and Glynn 2001), we argue that success stories provide a key cultural currency for philanthropists and other actors who promote the further development of this logic and associated practices. We combine a description of the role of resource-rich actors who promote the broad frame of social entrepreneurship with an inspection of these individual exemplars. While at one level these individuals work in very different domains in unique ways, collectively they form an ensemble that motivates and structures the very notion of the social entrepreneur.

In a subsequent section, we examine the origins of social entrepreneurship in the United States, and then pursue its spread globally. In tracking the early stages of this phenomenon internationally, we highlight some of the institutional infrastructure and actors who are involved, as well as some of the individual success stories that have become focal points for the construction and advancement of this new logic. We conclude with a discussion of the role of success stories in the construction of logics, highlighting the need for closer attention to the earliest stages of diffusion that are often marked by the social movement activism of proponents of new practices and logics as well as a high degree of ambiguity.

Alternative Conceptions of Social Entrepreneurship

There is no unanimity in how to define social entrepreneurship, although many might concur with Justice Stewart that they know it when they see it. Two different conceptualizations occupy the field. One approach defines entrepreneurship around a broad notion of *innovativeness,* an idea often linked to the great Austrian economist Joseph Schumpeter's analysis of the businessman as an entrepreneur who calls forth creative "winds of destruction." Gregory Dees (2003) invokes this image in a forceful way:

Social entrepreneurs play the role of change agents in the social sector, by:

- Adopting a mission to create and sustain social value (not just private value),
- Recognizing and relentlessly pursuing new opportunities to serve that mission,
- Engaging in a process of continuous innovation, adaptation, and learning,
- Acting boldly without being limited by resources currently in hand, and
- Exhibiting a heightened sense of accountability to the constituencies served and for the outcomes created.

From this perspective social entrepreneurship is a mindset or ethos that concentrates attention on how to create value in the social sector.

An alternative usage emphasizes the *commercial sustainability* of a viable revenue-generating approach to social problems. For example, the Roberts Enterprise Development Fund (REDF) supports a variety of initiatives that draw employees from "challenged" and "challenging" populations like the homeless, the physically disabled, and the mentally ill. Similarly, others identify social entrepreneurship with market-based organizations that operate in disadvantaged communities or that serve as incubators for such businesses, that dedicate a portion of their profits to populations in need, or that sell products that provide the infrastructure with which such communities can better help themselves.

Both conceptual strategies are potentially problematic. The Schumpeterian image of the innovator may identify social entrepreneurship with activities that are structurally indistinguishable from the conventional nonprofit sector, like the efforts of famine relief programs or even missionaries. The notion of social entrepreneurship as "social sustainability through market means," conversely, may point to organizations that are structurally indistinguishable from conventional for-profit businesses.

A variety of conceptual resolutions of these issues can be imagined. The interesting empirical question, however, is what perspective and content is linked to social entrepreneurship within funding circles and other sponsoring communities. By attending to those who underwrite and sponsor particular projects, we can develop insight into how specific visions of social entrepreneurship become authorized by key nodes that are at the center of trying to define a social entrepreneurial logic. Since efforts to construct such a logic are contested, we focus on concrete activities and individuals, rather than on conceptual oppositions between abstract principles, to gain an understanding of how the world of social entrepreneurship is taking shape.

The Origins of Social Entrepreneurship: The U.S. Case

Over the course of the twentieth century, the state has assumed growing responsibility over social problems. But while the major pension and health care financing programs are highly institutionalized, Lyndon Johnson's vision of a "Great Society" provoked a substantial backlash. Scholars and policy analysts, often but not solely on the right, criticized Washington for creating an elaborate bureaucratic structure consisting of state agencies, nonprofits, and other actors that seemed more focused on their own perpetuation than on devising novel ways to address pressing social problems (Moynihan 1969). This critique helped generate a wave of reforms in the U.S. social sector as nonprofit organizations have come under increased scrutiny and pressure to account for how they allocate their scarce resources (Light 2000).

The demand for accountability coincided with the devolution of federal governmental responsibilities to states and localities, privatization of services at all levels of government, and a reduction in funding for some key social programs. The "conservative revolution" inaugurated by President Ronald Reagan, which continues to the present day, has seen tremendous expansion in the nonprofit sector as private service providers have increasingly taken over the work duties and responsibilities of governmental agencies. From 1982 to 1998, the number of nonprofit organizations grew by 38 percent to over 1.2 million and operating expenditures increased by over 200 percent to over $550 billion. Today, nonprofits comprise almost 6 percent of all organizations in the United States, constitute almost 7 percent of national income, and employ over 9 percent of the U.S. workforce (Weitzman 2002). However, the growth of the sector has led to greater visibility, helping to fuel even more reforms.

As a result, nonprofit funding became increasingly contingent upon each organization's ability to demonstrate the efficacy of its work. In addition, there were efforts to redesign state policies to break the "culture of dependency" among those being served by social programs. This sea change in U.S. policy was prominently signaled by the passage of the Personal Responsibility and Work Opportunity Reconciliation Act of 1996 under President Bill Clinton. This legislation encourages unemployed parents of dependent children to find work by limiting welfare support to five years and forcing welfare recipients to seek other means of survival.

The declining ambitions of government-directed public policy over the last two decades are paralleled by the growing prestige of "business" and "management." As Lowenthal (1944) pointed out long ago, perceptions of the businessman as a national hero wax and wane over time. In the 1980s celebration of management expertise and the genius of particular CEOs was once again on the rise, a move signaled particularly by the popular success of Thomas Peters and Robert Waterman's book, *In Search of Excellence,* and maintained in the rapt attention paid to such business leaders as Lee Iacocca, Donald Trump, and Jack Welch. While business appeared in the 1950s and 1960s as a featureless domain peopled by conformist "organization men," in the 1980s and 1990s it seemed a realm of fearless entrepreneurial activity.

Social entrepreneurship arises at the intersection of these paired shifts in American culture and organizational structure. Nonprofit and socially oriented organizations are encouraged to employ the tools and tropes of business to fashion novel approaches to social change. The U.S. manifestation encourages not only salesmanship by museums and universities but also bottom-up efforts by individual entrepreneurs armed with big ideas about how to use business models to address social problems and change.

Via a LexisNexis search, Lounsbury and Lee (2004) date the first appearance of the phrase "social entrepreneurship" to 1983, when it was used in a story about retired executives consulting for nonprofits in Chicago (and at almost the same time, in stories about the efforts of a Catholic nun working with businessmen in New York, and about United Way partnerships with local companies in Washington, D.C.). But the term only gained currency in the late 1990s, when it was actively promoted in elite circles and the media picked it up. Bill Strickland, founder of the Manchester Craftsmen's Guild, states, "I didn't know I was a social entrepreneur until I went up to Harvard" (quoted in Spinali and Mortimer 2001, 2).

The origins of social entrepreneurship are found in the broader growth of managerial approaches to the nonprofit sector, a movement whose roots lie in the academic community. In 1971 the Association of Voluntary Action Scholars and its journal, the *Journal of Voluntary Action Research,* were created by David Horton Smith, a sociologist interested in voluntarism and grassroots associations (Smith 2003). Through the 1970s this association remained small and tended to focus narrowly on issues having to do with voluntarism rather than nonprofits more generally.

Beginning in the later 1970s, however, a more formal academic community of nonprofit researchers and degree-granting programs began to emerge. This was spurred by the creation of the Program on NonProfit Organizations (PONPO) at Yale University in 1978, the first research center focused specifically on nonprofits. While PONPO helped to establish a nonprofit research community in academia, Yale also created a professional master's program in public and private management and encouraged the use of business, government, and nonprofit cases in their educational curriculum.

Other universities followed Yale's lead. The University of Missouri/Kansas

City, SUNY/Stony Brook, and Case Western Reserve University established research centers to understand the role, behavior, and management of nonprofit organizations. Other universities established research centers focused on philanthropy such as the City University of New York, Duke University, and Indiana University (Young 1988). Concomitant with the establishment of these research centers, Columbia University's School of Business established a certificate program in nonprofit management, the first of its kind. Established in the mid-1970s, the program provided leadership and management training to top managers in voluntary, human service agencies in New York City.

While only four similar programs were established before 1985, twenty-one came into existence between 1985 and 1990 (Young 1990). This myriad of programs included ones offering not-for-credit short courses, certificate programs, and a few master's degree programs at schools such as the University of Colorado/Denver, University of San Francisco, New School for Social Research, University of Missouri/Kansas City, SUNY/Stony Brook, and Case Western Reserve University. Business schools also increasingly began to develop nonprofit management specialties—Harvard, Stanford, Northwestern, University of Pennsylvania, and Cornell were reported in *US News and World Report* as "up and comers" in the field of nonprofit management by deans of business schools.

The increase in nonprofit certification and research programs, fostered by organizations such as Independent Sector and people affiliated with the PONPO center at Yale, facilitated a broadening of research on nonprofits. This led to a transformation in the Association of Voluntary Action Scholars, which had become the main venue for a growing cadre of nonprofit researchers from a variety of disciplinary backgrounds. Signaling this broadening beyond a focus on voluntarism, the *Journal of Voluntary Action Research* was renamed *Nonprofit and Voluntary Sector Quarterly* in 1989 and the Association of Voluntary Action Scholars changed its name to the Association for Research on Nonprofits and Voluntary Action in 1990.

Since 1990 the number and scope of nonprofit management programs in U.S. universities and colleges has increased dramatically. As of 2000 ninety-one universities and colleges offered graduate degree programs with a concentration in nonprofit management (Mirabella and Wish 2000); while 242 had such programs by 2003, an increase of some 250 percent. Similarly, annual meeting attendance and membership in the Association for Research on Nonprofits and Voluntary Action doubled in the late 1990s, reaching 554 and over 1,000, respectively, by 2000. There are now thirty-eight university nonprofit centers that are members of the Nonprofit Academic Centers Council created in 1995. In addition, there has been an associated rise in management support organizations and nonprofit consultants, including the entrance of prominent management consultants such as McKinsey and Bridgespan. Furthermore, nonprofit associations are creating standards of excellence (e.g., Maryland Association of Nonprofits) and codes of conduct (e.g., Minnesota Council of Nonprofits and, more recently, Independent Sector) to help nonprofits demonstrate accountability. Peter Drucker (1994), management guru and active promoter of managerial thinking and practice in the nonprofit sector, commented:

> we know that social-sector organizations need management. But what precisely management means for the social-sector organization is just beginning to be studied. With respect to the management of the nonprofit organization we are in many ways pretty much where we were fifty or sixty years ago with respect to the management of the business enterprise: the work is only beginning.

Social entrepreneurship emerged as a spin-off of this more general managerialization of the social sector. In the words of one of the most esteemed social entrepreneurs, Bill Strickland, CEO of the Manchester Craftsmen's Guild and the Bidwell Training Center, "nonprofits have to recognize that they're businesses, not just causes. There's a way to combine the very best of the not-for-profit, philanthropic world with the very best of the for-profit, enterprising world. This hybrid is the wave of the future for both profit and nonprofit companies" (Terry 1998). On the webpage of the Social Enterprise Alliance, the association at the fulcrum of this "revolutionary social and economic movement," Charles King, founding chairman of the Social Enterprise Alliance, sums up the movement:

> What we are about is the business of changing the entire paradigm by which not-for-profits operate and generate the capital they need to carry out their mission—a new paradigm based on sustainability and social entrepreneurship.

The movement is comprised of a wide variety of actors from prominent foundations to large corporations to established and nascent social entrepreneurs who are interested in using business ideas to develop self-sustaining nonprofits in the arts, education, healthcare, and human services, as well as to address social problems like homelessness, at-risk youth, and job training. Movement insiders tend to be young and enthusiastic, often infused with a religious-like zeal. In fact, there are many religious organizations that are active in the movement. At a recent national gathering of the Social Enterprise Alliance in San Francisco, the event that annually brings together social entrepreneurship enthusiasts, there was even a pre-conference workshop titled "Doing Faith and Enterprise." The program brochure says:

> Every social venture is an act of faith—faith in people, faith in a cause, and, for many of us, faith in a purpose that flows from the ideals of a religious tradition. Yet social entrepreneurs engage in a work for which our religious traditions generally lack a language or theological framework. The result is that there is a great hunger among leaders to talk about why they do the work they do, to explore the values that motivate them to risk and venture, and to articulate the connections between their work and their faith. Doing Faith and Enterprise will explore the religious ideals that compel growing numbers of leaders to do justice through business.

Over the past few years, articles on social entrepreneurship have been featured in the *Harvard Business Review,* the *Wall Street Journal,* the *New York Times, US News and World Report, Fast Company,* and the *Stanford Social Innovation Review.* In January 2004 *Fast Company* published the first ever Social Capitalist Awards issue that highlighted the accomplishments of a wide variety of social entrepreneurs. Business schools at Berkeley, Columbia, Cornell, Duke, Harvard, Oxford, Stanford, and the London Business School have all established social entrepreneurship courses and related initiatives for MBA and executive education students. Organizations that provide a supportive infrastructure include the Kauffman Foundation, Echoing Green, the Roberts Foundation, the Social Enterprise Alliance, the Institute for Social Entrepreneurship, New Profit, Social Venture Partners, and Venture Philanthropy Partners (as well as Ashoka, the Skoll Foundation, and the Schwab Foundation for Social Entrepreneurship, three organizations with a more global orientation discussed in detail below). There has also been dramatic growth in community development venture capital funds. According to the Community Development Venture Capital Alliance, there are currently eighty funds in operation in the United States that together manage $535 million in capital.

While the environment for social services has certainly undergone significant changes over the past two decades, leading to the growth in efforts by nonprofits to generate earned income and engage in more entrepreneurial business-oriented activities, the more proximate drivers of social entrepreneurship discourse and practice are rooted in the actions of a couple of key institutions that catalyzed attention among social sector elites and the media. In 1993 John Whitehead, former head of Goldman Sachs and senior officer in Reagan's State Department, funded the Social Enterprise Initiative at the Harvard Business School. As part of this initiative, Gregory Dees developed a course called "Entrepreneurship in the Social Sector" that provided a foundation for a core course for all first year MBA students. Given the prominence of the Harvard Business School, this new initiative received a great deal of attention in the business world and in business schools that began to create nonprofit programs and their own social enterprise courses.

Alongside these developments, philanthropists began to explore ways in which business models could be applied to social sector problems. One of the early instances of this was when the Roberts Enterprise Development Fund (REDF—formerly the Homeless Economic Development Fund) approached Jed Emerson in 1989 to conduct a feasibility study on how free enterprise could be leveraged to move homeless people out of poverty. Emerson, a former executive director of a homeless and runaway youth center in San Francisco, convinced REDF to pursue the funding of novel business approaches to deal with problems related to issues such as homelessness and at-risk youth. In 1990 the fund began to make grants to a handful of nonprofits to start business ventures, and by 1996 REDF had funded over forty nonprofits with grants totaling more than $6 million (Emerson and Tuan 1998).

Another key moment in the mobilization of the entrepreneurial model occurred in 1996 when Bill Shore, social entrepreneur and president of Share Our Strength, brought together approximately fifty social entrepreneur advocates in Washington, D.C., including Emerson, to discuss the concept of community wealth. This gave rise to a conference, the National Gathering of Social Entrepreneurs in Colorado Springs in 1998. The second national gathering took place two years later in Miami and led to the creation of a 501(c)(3) organization focused on information dissemination, education, and networking in the social enterprise field. At the third national gathering in Seattle in 2000, a multi-year business plan was created and the group's organizational structure was formalized by electing a coordinating committee, creating an executive board, and hiring a director and president. The next national gatherings took place in Minneapolis in 2002 and then in San Francisco in 2004. In 2002 the National Gathering of Social Entrepreneurs merged with SeaChange, an organization created to connect social investors with social entrepreneurs who need capital, creating the Social Enterprise Alliance. As a result the name of the national conference was changed to the Gathering of the Social Enterprise Alliance.

While the Social Enterprise Alliance is one of the grandest and most visible manifestations of the social entrepreneurial movement, a lot of excitement has also been created around social sector business plan competitions. For instance, a student-led initiative at the Haas School of Business spawned the National Social Venture Competition in 1999. In May 2001 Columbia Business School and the Goldman Sachs Foundation partnered with Haas to extend the reach of this competition and help grow a national platform for social ventures. The competition's mission is to catalyze and promote the creation of financially self-sufficient or profitable social ventures. To achieve this goal, plans are judged according to the feasibility of their business concepts, and the feasibility and potential impacts of the stated social and/or environmental goals. Another successful competition, the National Business Plan Competition for Nonprofit Organizations, was first held in 2003 by the Partnership on Nonprofit Ventures. The Partnership is comprised of the Yale School of Management, the Goldman Sachs Foundation, and the Pew Charitable Trusts, which joined together to create an opportunity for nonprofits seeking to start or expand successful profit-making ventures to compete for significant cash prizes and technical support.

Over the past few years, there have been a growing number of stories about individual social entrepreneurs and social enterprises that have also given life to the entrepreneurial model. For instance, the Harvard Business School has published numerous cases that provide a crucial foundation for social entrepreneurship courses around the country. Hollywood is also getting into the act. Ovation Entertainment, a partnership between Jeff Skoll and Trilogy co-founder Richard Lewis, is in the process of making a movie about Bill Strickland's career at the helm of the Manchester Craftsmen's Guild and the Bidwell Training Center in Pittsburgh. While this is still in the planning stages, there are rumors that Denzel Washington may play Strickland.

These accounts of social entrepreneurship draw heavily on American narratives of the extraordinary individual who dreams of and then effects change. The logic has a more mundane side as well, of course, envisaging the routine application of standard business management practices in nonprofits. But the cultural emphasis of social entrepreneurship is on bold vision and heroic action.

The International Spread of Social Entrepreneurship

While social entrepreneurship has developed in the United States to the point where it might be considered a standard part of the nonprofit toolkit, it has also expanded internationally. Given the strong organizational ties and cultural connections between the United States and the United Kingdom, it is not surprising that social entrepreneurship began to emerge in the latter nation in the late 1990s. This occurred initially via the support of various philanthropic organizations whose cultural values about social entrepreneurship reinforce those in the United States. For example, the Community Action Network, founded in 1998, claims that "social entrepreneurs are the equivalent of true business entrepreneurs but they operate in the social, not-for-profit sector building 'something from nothing' and seeking innovative solutions to social problems. Their aim is to build 'social capital' and 'social profit' to improve the quality of life in some of the most 'difficult' and 'excluded' communities" (http://www.can-online.org.uk/se/, June 28, 2005).

The British approach diverges from the American in the more active role envisaged for the state. Tony Blair's government initiated a review of the social sector around the turn of the century that has resulted in the creation of regional governmental units that aim to support local philanthropic efforts to grow social entrepreneurship as a way of ameliorating social problems in the most economically depressed areas. The British state thus actively promotes the logic of social entrepreneurship and provides it with an organizational infrastructure, while social entrepreneurship in the United States is more closely linked to the state's withdrawal from many social problem arenas.

Social entrepreneurship has also gained resonance as a logic across Europe, Africa, India, Asia, Latin America, and elsewhere. Bornstein (2003) suggests that the spread of this logic has been supported by a robust global citizen sector marked by the recent proliferation of NGOs and other citizen groups. Bornstein writes:

> In Bangladesh, most of the country's development work is handled by 20,000 NGOs; almost all of them were established in the past twenty-five years. India has well over a million citizen organizations . . . Between 1988 and 1995, 100,000 citizen groups opened shop in the former communist countries of Eastern Europe. In France, during the 1990s, an average of 70,000 new citizen groups were established each year . . . Finally, during the 1990s, the number of registered *international* citizen organizations increased from 6,000 to 26,000. (Bornstein 2003, 4–5)

While social entrepreneurship has become a component of World Bank and United Nations discourse, there is little systematic data on its global spread. In large part this is because the movement involves little formal organizational activity, in the sense of NGOs implementing social entrepreneurship programs around the world. Instead, consistent with the themes of the movement and its emergence in the United States and the United Kingdom, the work of individual social entrepreneurs is supported, celebrated, and broadcast.

International Organizations and the Success Story Model

We describe three organizations—Ashoka, the Skoll Foundation, and the Schwab Foundation for Social Entrepreneurship—that employ a "success story" model.[1] All three are focused on the promotion of social entrepreneur-ship worldwide. While their tactics differ somewhat, the three organizations adopt the same general strategy of recognizing and supporting specific indi-viduals and their projects. Their aim is to help these individuals expand their work, and thereby to inspire others to become social entrepreneurs as well.

Ashoka was created in 1978 by Bill Drayton, a former McKinsey consul-tant, administrator in the Environmental Protection Agency, and community organizer in India. The organization's mission is to "shape a citizen sector that is entrepreneurial, productive and globally integrated, and to develop the pro-fession of social entrepreneurship around the world." Ashoka recognizes and supports inspiring social entrepreneurs, over 1,500 of whom have been elected as Ashoka Fellows since 1981.

The Skoll Foundation was created by Jeff Skoll, a founder of eBay, to pro-mote social change. Skoll explains, "The idea is that a little bit of good can turn into a whole lot of good when fueled by the commitment of a social entre-preneur. We find the people with those world-changing ideas, and then we empower them—by investing in, connecting and celebrating them—to effect even greater impact." The foundation supports social entrepreneurs through the Skoll Awards for Social Entrepreneurship and the Skoll Social Sector Pro-gram. In 2003 the foundation also launched an international MBA program in social entrepreneurship at the Saïd Business School at Oxford University.

The Schwab Foundation for Social Entrepreneurship was formed in 1998 by Klaus and Hilde Schwab. Klaus Schwab, a former professor of business policy at the University of Geneva, is best known as the founder of the World Eco-nomic Forum and its Davos meetings. (The forum was founded in 1971 when Klaus Schwab brought together a number of European corporate leaders to discuss ways that businesses could collaborate to benefit the common good. The forum presently has some 1,000 corporations worldwide as members.) The foundation has a current network of eighty-four Schwab entrepreneurs, and in 2005 developed a contest to identify the social entrepreneur of the year in twenty-four countries.

Ashoka, Skoll, and Schwab define the qualities of social entrepreneurs in broad but parallel terms. Ashoka searches for "the new idea," "creativity," "entre-preneurial quality," "social impact of ideas," and "ethical fiber." The Skoll Founda-tion indicates that "social entrepreneurs act as the change agents for society, seiz-ing opportunities others miss and improving systems, inventing new approaches and creating sustainable solutions to change society for the better. However, unlike business entrepreneurs who are motivated by profits, social entrepreneurs are motivated to improve society." Schwab describes the social entrepreneur as "a pragmatic visionary who achieves large scale, systemic and sustainable social change through a new invention, a different approach, a more rigorous application of known technologies or strategies, or a combination of these."

The three organizations screen and select social entrepreneurs in similar ways. Initial nominations are drawn from multiple sources, with the central role played by leaders within national nonprofit and social innovation communities. For example, Ashoka has developed a global network of nominators who generate and review applications, which are reviewed in second and later stages by professional staff. Each organization inquires in detail into a potential fellow's activities, qualifications, and standing in the community. Formal control systems like governing boards tend to play a limited role. Schwab promulgates a code of conduct, for instance, that puts great emphasis on relative intangibles like a candidate's rectitude and interest in collaborating with others.

The three organizations differ significantly in the material support each provides social entrepreneurs. Ashoka gives its fellows a living stipend, typically for three years (the organization spends about $17 million annually on its fellowship program). The Skoll Foundation provides awards on the order of $500,000 to be used for both operating expenses and program expansion. By contrast, the Schwab Foundation provides no monetary support to the individuals it recognizes.

These different levels of support locate the three organizations in overlapping but distinct "market niches." Ashoka tends to develop relationships with younger individuals, and with projects that are more likely to be locally oriented and at an earlier stage in their development. Skoll supports larger-scale organizations, generally at a later point in their development. Schwab entrepreneurs stand in between.

By contrast, all three organizations put similar and great weight on assisting their fellows build social capital. Ashoka forms a global network of current and former fellows to support collaboration within the social entrepreneurship community. It also builds ties between social entrepreneurs and those in the management and consulting worlds through a partnership with McKinsey. Skoll convenes the Skoll World Forum on Social Entrepreneurship, an annual conference that connects its award recipients with other leading figures in the field of social entrepreneurship. Schwab links its social entrepreneurs to the World Economic Forum's global network of business leaders in a variety of ways, including inviting them to its annual Davos meetings.

Finally, the strongest demonstration of the parallels in the approach to social entrepreneurship of Ashoka, Skoll, and Schwab is the fact that they frequently support the same individuals and projects. Seven of the fifteen Skoll Awards in 2005 went to Schwab entrepreneurs. The degree of overlap is limited, not by differences in philosophy or conceptions of social entrepreneurship, but for practical reasons that are linked to each organization's approach toward material support. The Skoll-Schwab overlap is thus large relative to each organization's connection to Ashoka, since both Skoll and Schwab support fairly large-scale, mature projects.

What Do Social Entrepreneurs Do?

What sorts of individuals are recognized as inspiring social entrepreneurs, and what sorts of projects have they created? A few examples:

Rodrigo Baggio: Committee to Democratize Information Technology, Brazil.
Rodrigo Baggio seeks to provide economically disadvantaged youths in Rio de Janeiro with computer skills. The Committee to Democratize Information Technology has trained more than 60,000 students to use computers. With corporate partners, Baggio is opening one hundred computer training schools in Japan, Mexico, Colombia, and Uruguay.

Rodrigo Baggio is a past Ashoka fellow, receives a current Skoll Award, and is a Schwab entrepreneur.

Jeroo Billimoria: Childline, India
Jeroo launched Childline, a 24-hour emergency hotline for street children. The organization provides follow-up services including police assistance and health care. Childline has serviced more than 400,000 calls over the past two years and has spread to twenty cities in India. (Ashoka, Schwab)

Martin Fisher and Nick Moon: KickStart, Kenya
KickStart (previously Appropriate Technologies for Enterprise Creation/ApproTEC) introduced human-powered irrigation pumps that enable farmers to grow more crops and sell during the dry season. The organization has helped farmers start 36,000 new businesses that generate more than $38 million in new profits and wages per year. (Skoll, Schwab)

Takao Furuno: Duck Revolution, Japan
Takao Furuno, a Japanese farmer, has developed a rice farming method that uses ducks to fertilize rice seedlings and protect them from pests and weeds. Furuno's technique serves as a demonstration project for the potential of organic farming. He markets "duck rice" at a 20 to 30 percent premium above conventional rice, and describes his ideas (including recipes for duck) in bestselling books like *The Power of Duck*. More than 75,000 farmers in Asia have adopted Furuno's methods. (Schwab)

Paul Rice: TransFair, U.S.A.

TransFair certifies coffee, tea, cocoa, and fruits grown by family farmers. The organization testifies to good employment and environmental standards used in farms, and has signed agreements with over 300 importers of these products. TransFair plans to become self-supporting in the future through certification fees. (Ashoka, Skoll, Schwab)

Even this small sampling of social entrepreneurship points to some core themes within the field. First, a number of projects occur in the marketplace, where social entrepreneurs produce and sell goods and services. The "social" component of these market activities takes a wide variety of forms. They include:

1) Organizations that market products or services that provide infrastructure for economic activity in disadvantaged communities,
2) Organizations whose employees are drawn from challenged populations,
3) Organizations that provide a new model for economic success relevant to disadvantaged populations and/or linked to other social values, and
4) Organizations that help bring the products of disadvantaged communities to market.

KickStart's human-powered irrigation pumps and other technologies provide a good example of products designed and marketed to stimulate business growth. Similarly, FreePlay (formed by South Africans Rory Stear and Kristine Pearson) sells wind-up radios that can be used in the absence of an independent source of electricity. William Foote's Ecologic (Skoll) provides loans to small- and medium-sized businesses to transition to "green" technologies and environmental sustainability, while Martin Burt's Fundacion Paraguaya (Skoll, Schwab) provides credit for business startups that have created over 19,000 new jobs.

One example of a business that draws its employees from "challenged populations" is Australia's Furniture Resource Center, led by Father Nic Frances (a Schwab entrepreneur). The organization began as a system of distributing donated furniture, but Frances then decided to hire "unemployables" to make quality furniture. Takao Furuno, the duck rice farmer, provides a different sort of business model, one that links commercial success to environmental friendliness and organic farming. So too does Sekem, an organic and phytopharmaceutical producer founded by Dr. Ibrahim Abouleish, an Egyptian medical pharmacologist (Schwab).

Finally, a number of social entrepreneurs act as middlemen, either certifying products or bringing them to market. Certifiers include Paul Rice's Trans-Fair, and Rugmark (Skoll), which monitors factories, certifies rugs made without child labor, and rescues and educates child laborers. Marketers include firms like Novica.com, an "e-tailer" that provides marketing and distribution services for the sale of indigenous art and artifacts (Schwab).

Some of these social entrepreneurs are business entrepreneurs as well. Takao Furuno and Sekem fall into this category, as does Novica.com (while organizations like Fisher and Moon's KickStart and Paul Rice's TransFair are nonprofits). FreePlay consists of both a for-profit corporation, the FreePlay Energy Group, which sells wind-up radios to outdoor enthusiasts in Europe and the United States, and FreePlay Foundation, a nonprofit operating in Africa.

This combination of profit-neutral marketing and socially beneficial business raises provocative questions about definitions of social entrepreneurship. Orientation toward the common good appears a shaky guide, particularly when we recall that even conventional profit-making corporations describe their goals in terms of social benefit as well as private gain—for example, Du Pont's corporate mission is

> To be the world's most successful energy and chemistry-based company, dedicated to creating high quality, innovative materials that make people's lives easier and better.

While Merck's mission statement reads:

> To provide society with superior products and services—innovations and solutions that improve the quality of life and satisfy customer needs—to provide employees with meaningful work and advancement opportunities, and to provide investors with a superior rate of return.

Organizations like Ashoka, Skoll, and Schwab appear to apply Justice Stewart's "I know it when I see it" test. They emphasize the range and distinctiveness of socially valued ends that a social entrepreneur addresses, its total impact, and evidence of limits to self-interested action (Adam Smith notwithstanding). In the case of Novica.com, for example, these include the benefits to artists of gaining access to global markets, the firm's low mark-ups, the higher returns to the producer generated when one rather than many middlemen bring the product to the consumer, and the opportunities for artists to price and withdraw their products from sale. For Takao Furuno's rice farm, ecological benefits and active dissemination of the technology are central. Sekem appears not just as an innovator in biodynamic pharmaceuticals, but as a supporter of biodiversity and sustainable agriculture, a force for social and cultural integration in Egyptian villages, the source of a variety of initiatives in the arts, and the founder of a university.

The majority of the individuals supported by Ashoka, Skoll, and Schwab, however, are not directly focused on economic development, and do not buy and sell goods. In addition to its Full Economic Citizenship Program, Ashoka's initiatives are in the areas of human rights, civic participation, global health, education, and the environment. Skoll and Schwab recognize individuals addressing a wide variety of global challenges including environmental sustainability, health, education and job training, and human rights, as well as economic equality.

On the human rights front, for example, Witness (Skoll, Schwab) provides video equipment and training to groups seeking to document human rights abuses. Founded in 1992 by musician Peter Gabriel and the Reebok Foundation for Human Rights, Witness helped bring about the prosecution of murderers of human rights activists in the Philippines, and has sparked reform in the California juvenile detention system and mental health in Paraguay. In Colombia, Stella Cárdenas (Ashoka) has documented the sexual exploitation of children and forged an alliance of citizen's organizations to push for legal action and provide social services.

Health care is a second major focus for all three organizations. For example, one Schwab entrepreneur is Govindappa Venkataswamy, whose hospital provides eye care to 1.4 million Indians a year, two-thirds of whom receive services for free. Victoria Hale's Institute for OneWorld Health (Skoll) is a nonprofit that develops drugs and vaccines for diseases that primarily affect developing countries. And Garba Hamadoun Cissé (Ashoka) created Assistance Médicale Décentralisée in Mali to enlist specialized doctors on a voluntary basis to care for socially disadvantaged populations, such as women, children, the elderly, and those living in remote areas or in detention.

Finally, many social entrepreneurs are involved in education and job training. Bunker Roy's (Skoll, Schwab) "Barefoot College" provides often semiliterate villagers with the skills to become health workers, teachers, and engineers; they return to their villages to use this knowledge to improve the community. Andrea David's (Ashoka) Salva Vita Foundation in Hungary seeks to give those with mental disabilities a chance to create new, independent lives by helping them develop vocational and life skills.

While market-oriented social entrepreneurs raise questions about how to identify the "social," the innovators described above raise the converse issue: how do they differ from traditional nonprofit organizations? The accounts provided by Ashoka, Skoll, and Schwab hint at possible answers, either in noting ambitions to make the nonprofit economically sustainable or in emphasizing spillover effects promoting economic development. But the link between social entrepreneurship and traditional nonprofits is very strong, and the degree to which social entrepreneurship is simply "old wine in a new bottle" is correspondingly large.

Who Are the Social Entrepreneurs?

The individuals celebrated by Ashoka, Skoll, and Schwab hail from a wide variety of backgrounds. Some come from distinguished families, like Qing Wu, daughter of China's most celebrated female author and of one of China's first sociologists, who is a leader of the women's movement in her country, a legislator, and a Schwab entrepreneur. Others, like Raúl Abásolo, an Ashoka fellow who has devised a support and social integration system for marginalized youth in Chile, grew up in the same circumstances as the young people he seeks to help.

Despite this diversity, particular backgrounds and personal trajectories dominate the field of social entrepreneurship. Social entrepreneurs are well educated, whether they come from privileged or disadvantaged circumstances. Nearly all whose stories we have read possess university degrees, often received in the United States or Europe. These educational backgrounds seem fundamental to the activities of social entrepreneurs, both as the source of technical skills and due to the social and cultural capital they provide.

Social entrepreneurs also tend to have a professional or administrative background, rather than a business or commercial one. The twenty-three Schwab entrepreneurs based in Asia, for example, include four university professors, four NGO administrators, a civil servant, three doctors, and two engineers/urban planners. By contrast, only two of the twenty-three were drawn from the world of business.

The majority of social entrepreneurs are nationals working primarily in their native country. Among Schwab entrepreneurs, for example, we would place seventy-two of eighty-four in that category. Skoll award recipients are less likely to be nationals of the country they work in, since the foundation supports larger-scale and more established organizations that are more likely to operate in the West or on a global basis. Nine of Skoll's fifteen award recipients work in their own countries, and three of these are Americans working in the United States.

A substantial minority of social entrepreneurs, however, are Westerners working in or for the Global South. Schwab projects of this type include People

Tree (clothing retail), Novica.com (artisanal product retail), Endeavor Global (entrepreneur support), Fundacion Paraguaya (microcredit), OneWorld Health (vaccines), Project Impact (hearing aids), Rural Development Institute (land ownership), TransFair (certification), CAMBIA (biotechnology), Kick-Start (irrigation), Riders for Health (transportation), and Witness (videos). What stands out most in this group of projects is the central role played by technology and technology transfer. This theme appears in indigenous social entrepreneurship as well (including indigenous projects in the United States), but to a substantially lesser degree.

Discussion

Social entrepreneurship fits well, in many ways, into this volume's notion of the philanthropic projection of institutional logics abroad. As we document, the notion of social entrepreneurship and the social movement behind it was largely an American invention. It expressed characteristically American cultural archetypes—social entrepreneurs take their place alongside not just business heroes, but cowboy heroes alienated from society who save it anyway (Wright 1975). The British notion of social entrepreneurship as supported by the state and embedded in broader philanthropic efforts gives way to a more American celebration of the individual, attention to his or her personal development, and the replicability of his or her model. And in a more subtle way, social entrepreneurship evokes a characteristically American belief in the compatibility of private action and social interest.

Is social entrepreneurship an institutional logic? If we use the term in an organizational sense to understand the structure of individual projects, the answer is no. What does an e-tailer like Novica.com have in common with a duck farmer like Takano Furuno or a political activist like Stella Cárdenas? Certainly not "organizational arrangements for putting ideas into action and for sustaining patterns of social relationships," in Heydemann and Hammack's useful language (see chapter 1). The first has developed a global network of buyer relationships with artists and artisans and retails products on the internet; the second has pursued the ecological benefits of introducing ducks into rice farming; and the third has built a coalition of legal and children's organizations to protect children against sexual exploitation.

In a more abstract sense, however, we can speak of the institutional logic of social entrepreneurship. First, the notion of individual action unconstrained by structured social relationships, cultural categories, and by history, is itself an institutional pattern. It is one close to the self-understanding of the West, particularly Anglo-Saxon and American versions (Hofstede 1984; Meyer and

Frank 2002). As Robert Bellah and his colleagues (1985) make clear, individualism is not just a projection from elsewhere but a language that all sorts of people express and use to understand themselves as well as others. Social entrepreneurship seeks to reinforce and strengthen this pattern.

Social entrepreneurship also appears as an institutional logic in the more cultural sense of the values and meanings it carries. These include positive terms. For example, the logic of social entrepreneurship places great importance on newness and innovation, and little on the maintenance and expansion of existing ways of promoting the collective good. Substantive values like democracy and autonomy are emphasized in contrast to the implicit or explicit paternalism of much traditional nonprofit activity. The "social" is defined around a distinctive set of global challenges that include not only poverty, but the environment and human rights.

But social entrepreneurialism violates cultural categories more than it creates new ones. It crosses and recrosses the boundary between private and public motives, between self-interest and the collective interest. Inspiring success stories transcend these categories, and blur them in the process. Social entrepreneurs may be businessmen or businesswomen who define their ends in terms of the common good, and (contra Adam Smith) speak to us of humanity. Or they may be leaders of nonprofits who can define their strategy in terms of market penetration. Both gain prestige and resources as a result.

Finally, we have sought to trace the "success story" model adopted by Ashoka, Skoll, and Schwab as a mode of international projection and diffusion. This approach has the same core ingredients as other diffusion mechanisms: social networks, effectiveness, learning, and legitimacy. But it puts them together in a distinctive way. Social entrepreneurship would look quite different if it were promulgated as the World Bank's development strategy, or if it was a strategic innovation that lacked a professional and organizational base in Western academic, business, and philanthropic circles.

The success story model has important organizational advantages. Like the internet, it has a self-organizing quality, where existing social entrepreneurs are recognized rather than created or coordinated. The three organizations described here have little overhead, can shift the mix of their activities readily, and have much scope for expansion. They are also well positioned to accept, or indeed embrace, local differences and indigenous traditions. They are lighter on their feet than organizations that directly or indirectly provide social programming, and less likely to blindly impose an external model.

The success story model seems compatible with the connotations of both "projection" and "diffusion." Resource-rich actors such as Jeff Skoll clearly possess a philosophy which they believe in, and which they seek to disseminate.

But so do recipients at the other end of the exchange. It is not clear which side adjusts more—in many ways, the social entrepreneurs are the "stars" that funders link themselves to, rather than the other way around (recall that many are recognized by two or even three of the organizations discussed here, and have other "sponsors" and "partners" as well). We can speak most safely of the congruence between frames, not their imposition or authorization.

One core feature of this kind of projection/diffusion system is its elite and professional basis. The cultural congruence between funder and recipient is strongest where they are products of the same cultural system. It is thus not surprising that social entrepreneurs around the world are highly educated professionals (as they also are in the United States, where elite business schools are an incubator). These are the key actors, within the Global South and the Global North, who share the motives, sensibilities, and vocabulary of international funders.

While the logic of the social entrepreneur is not grounded in a model of the target community, the success story mode of transmission does depend upon a community of ties among social entrepreneurs and between social entrepreneurs and government, business, and NGOs. The existence of this community at the local or national level is central to the capacity to identify social entrepreneurs, particularly those who are not yet internationally known. And a core goal of funders is to help social entrepreneurs build social capital—not with the populations they serve, but with each other and with national and transnational elites. In this sense the success story model is as much about networks as are relational models of diffusion; but social relationships serve to build entrepreneurial identities and opportunities rather than linking adopters to non-adopters.

In tension with the elite and inward-looking character of social entrepreneurship, however, are ways in which the success story mode preserves its charismatic roots as a convention-challenging movement. Funders that recognize, celebrate, and support individual heroes help keep social entrepreneurship a diverse, locally rooted, and structurally non-isomorphic field. They give little scope to efforts to standardize the product in formalistic ways, for example, by identifying approved modes of governance or by applying routine business criteria to new ventures. The centrality of success stories as an organizing principle may help keep social entrepreneurship a deeply ambiguous but vibrant movement.

Acknowledgments
We want to thank Brandon Lee for his research assistance. Professor Lounsbury received support for this project from the Cornell University Entrepreneurship and Personal Enterprise Program through his J. Thomas Clark Professorship.

Note

1. Descriptions of the three organizations and the social entrepreneurs they support are drawn largely from each organization's website. See: http://www.ashoka.org/; http://www.skollfoundation.org/; and http://www.schwabfound.org/ (all accessed November 3, 2008).

References

Bellah, Robert N., Richard Madsen, William M. Sullivan, Ann Swidler, and Steven M. Tipton. 1985. *Habits of the Heart*. Berkeley and Los Angeles: University of California Press.

Bornstein, David. 2003. *How to Change the World: Social Entrepreneurs and the Power of New Ideas*. New York: Oxford University Press.

Dees, Gregory. 2003. "The Meaning of Social Entrepreneurship." Working Paper. Stanford, Calif.: Stanford University.

DiMaggio, Paul J., and Walter W. Powell. 1983. "The Iron Cage Revisited: Institutional Isomorphism and Collective Rationality in Organizational Fields." *American Sociological Review* 48: 147–60.

Drucker, Peter F. 1994. "The Age of Social Transformation." *Atlantic Monthly*, November.

Frank, David J., Ann Hironaka, and Evan Schofer. 2000. "The Nation-State and the Natural Environment over the Twentieth Century." *American Sociological Review* 65: 96–116.

Hofstede, Geert. 1980. *Culture's Consequences*. Beverly Hills, Calif.: Sage.

Kessler, Daniel P., Jed Emerson, and Melinda Tuan. 1998. "The Roberts Enterprise Development Fund: Implementing a Social Venture Capital Approach to Philanthropy." Stanford, Calif.: Graduate School of Business Stanford University.

Light, Paul C. 2000. *Making Nonprofits Work*. Washington, D.C.: Brookings Institution Press.

Lounsbury, Michael, and Mary Ann Glynn. 2001. "Cultural Entrepreneurship: Stories, Legitimacy and the Acquisition of Resources." *Strategic Management Journal* 22: 545–64.

Lounsbury, Michael, and Brandon Lee. 2004. "The Origins of Social Entrepreneurship." Working Paper, Dept. of Sociology. Ithaca, N.Y.: Cornell University.

Lowenthal, Leo. 1944. "Biographies in Popular Magazines." In *Radio Research 1942–43*, ed. P. F. Lazarsfeld and F. K. Stanton, 188–205. New York: Bureau of Applied Social Research, Columbia University.

Meyer, John W., and David J. Frank, 2002. "The Profusion of Individual Roles and Identities in the Postwar Period." *Sociological Theory* 20: 86–105.

Meyer, John W., David Kamens, and Aaron Benavot. 1992. *School Knowledge for the Masses*. London: Falmer Press.

Mirabella, Roseanne M., and Naomi B. Wish. 2000. "The 'Best Place' Debate: A Comparison of Graduate Education Programs for Nonprofit Managers." *Public Administration Review* 60: 219–29.

Moynihan, Daniel P., ed. 1969. *On Understanding Poverty: Perspectives from the Social Sciences*. New York: Basic Books.

Rao, Hayagreeva, and Paul M. Hirsch. 2003. "'Czechmate': The Old Banking Elite and the Construction of Investment Privatization Funds in the Czech Republic." *Socio-Economic Review* 1: 247–69.

Scott, W. Richard. 1987. "The Adolescence of Institutional Theory." *Administrative Science Quarterly* 32: 492–511.

Smith, Adam. 1991 [1776]. *The Wealth of Nations*. New York: Knopf.

Smith, David Horton. 2003. "A History of ARNOVA." *Nonprofit and Voluntary Sector Quarterly* 32: 458–72.

Spicer, Andrew. 2002. "Revolutionary Change and Organizational Form: The Politics of Investment Fund Organization in Russia, 1992–1997." *Research in the Sociology of Organizations* 19: 91–124.

Spinali, Lisa, and Hayley Mortimer. 2001. *A Scan of Not-For-Profit Entrepreneurship: Status of the Field and Recommendations for Action*. San Bruno, Calif.: Ripple Effect Consulting.

Stewart, Justice Potter. 1964. *Jacobellis v. Ohio*, 378 U.S. 184.

Strang, David, and John W. Meyer. 1993. "Institutional Conditions for Diffusion." *Theory and Society* 22: 487–512.

Strang, David, and Sarah A. Soule. 1998. "Diffusion in Organizations and Social Movements: From Hybrid Corn to Poison Pills." *Annual Review of Sociology* 24: 265–90.

Terry, Sara. 1998. "Genius at Work." *Fast Company*, August.

Weitzman, Murray S. 2002. *The New Nonprofit Almanac and Desk Reference*. New York: Jossey-Bass.

Wright, Will. 1975. *Sixguns and Society*. Berkeley and Los Angeles: University of California Press.

Young, Dennis R. 1988. "Nonprofit Studies in the University." *Nonprofit World* 6: 35–36.

———. 1990. "Nonprofit Management Education Comes of Age: A Progress Report." *Nonprofit World* 8: 17–19.

5. Moral Globalization and Discursive Struggle

*Reconciliation, Transitional Justice, and
Cosmopolitan Discourse*

←————————————————————————————→

JONATHAN VANANTWERPEN

Reconciliation as Cosmopolitan Discourse

When South Africa's Truth and Reconciliation Commission (TRC) set out to assess the politically motivated crimes of that nation's apartheid past, it did so under the rubric of "reconciliation through truth." Posters reflecting this relationship—figuring "truth" as "the road to reconciliation," or encouraging victim testimony with the suggestion that "revealing is healing"—were pasted up across the country, and the commission's charismatic leader, Archbishop Desmond Tutu, referred often to the important work of reconciliation that this quasi-judicial transitional body would enable. "We are a people who know," said the archbishop, in response to a confession offered before the TRC, "that when someone cannot be forgiven there is no future."[1] Tutu's *ubuntu* theology of reconciliation and forgiveness was resonant.[2] "The process is unthinkable without Tutu," wrote poet and journalist Antjie Krog of the TRC. "It is he who finds language for what is happening . . . and it is this language that drags people along with the process."[3]

Can the truth be expected to heal? Although Tutu and other TRC leaders were compelled, as the work of the TRC progressed, to temper outsized expectations of what the commission actually might be able to accomplish, there is no doubt that the TRC assumed a positive answer to this question. Linked to notions of confession and forgiveness, cathartic testimony, redeemed suffering, and healing truth, Christian language of "reconciliation" was conjoined with that of "human rights" to produce a distinctive model of transitional justice.

In the popular imagination, the TRC's dominant discourse of reconciliation—what anthropologist Richard Wilson has called its "religious-redemptive narrative"—has come to be closely associated with South Africa's "miraculous" political transition, an association even more pronounced among international observers of the South African saga. In the context of that transition, the nation's search for reconciliation has been tied not just to the individual stories of confession and forgiveness that became the basis of some of the TRC's most memorable public theater, but also to an innovative amnesty agreement that attempted to steer a middle course between the "blanket" amnesties associated with previous political transitions and the unimpeded pursuit of prosecution on the model of the Nuremberg trials. Many have claimed that without that agreement—which eventually resulted in the TRC's uniquely individualized "truth for amnesty" arrangement—South Africans would have lost the linchpin of their negotiated settlement, an essential element of their successful transition.

In the aftermath of the South African commission, the language of reconciliation has proliferated widely, and the TRC has repeatedly been touted as an innovative "model" that transitional states in Africa and elsewhere might emulate. There has been noteworthy emulation on the part of practitioners of "transitional justice" operating in other national locations, and perhaps even more international attention from a legion of academics, journalists, and transnational activists. In the late 1990s Antjie Krog complained publicly about the dozens of scholars who were flooding South Africa to study the TRC, providing material for the stereotypical image of the jet-setting international academic who flew in for a few days of TRC hearings, a visit with Archbishop Tutu, and a trip to Kruger National Park. In the years that followed, Desmond Tutu was to become a much sought after global prophet of reconciliation, and others associated with the TRC would travel the world to talk about their experiences with the commission and the various "lessons" it might afford.

The South African story is undeniably captivating, and there has been no shortage of potential audiences for it. The pursuit of reconciliation has been on the political agenda throughout Africa, Latin America, Eastern Europe, and Asia. Whether through the establishment of truth and reconciliation commissions (such as those in Peru, Sierra Leone, and elsewhere), through the formation of governmental ministries devoted to promoting reconciliation, or through other governmental and nongovernmental initiatives, reconciliation has become a nearly ubiquitous watchword for states and societies in transition.[4]

This specifically national and localized interest in the prospects and promises of reconciliation has been attended by the work of an increasingly vocal international audience of transnational activists and border-crossing academics, in whose hands the language of reconciliation has become a widely disseminated form of cosmopolitan discourse. In the small number of years since the first volumes of its report were published, the politics and presumptions of South Africa's TRC—and to a lesser extent the workings of the various truth commissions that both preceded and followed it—have been the subject of scores of books and articles, written by political theorists and moral philosophers, anthropologists and NGO specialists, scholars of international law and human rights activists, Christian theologians and critical intellectuals. At the same time as an intellectual cottage industry has grown up around the topic of "truth and reconciliation," an emerging field of transitional justice has expanded and come into its own. As a result of numerous conferences held throughout the world, scholars studying various processes of truth and reconciliation, in addition to other aspects of transitional justice—from reparations to international tribunals—have increasingly been linked with each other, as well as with practitioners of transitional justice and NGO professionals.

Thus, over the course of the last decade the language of reconciliation has become both the focus of a great deal of practical activity and the basis for no small amount of discourse, academic and otherwise. In the midst of the "flood of political transitions that has marked the turn of the twenty-first century," there has been an inundation of talk about reconciliation, and the language of reconciliation—if not its reality—has proliferated wildly.[5] Indeed, the frequently ambiguous discourse of reconciliation, full of shifting meanings and multiple significations, has come to represent one of the most prolific traveling theories of our time. Focusing on both the South African history of reconciliation discourse and various formulations and critiques of reconciliation that have emerged in recent years, this chapter is concerned with the different shapes that this discourse has taken in the course of its international travels. I am particularly concerned with conceptions and criticisms forwarded by both recently formed NGOs and university-based scholars as they have drawn on and diverged from the TRC's purported "model."

What should be made of the unprecedented international proliferation of discourses of reconciliation? While proposed answers to this question have been as diverse as the field of transitional justice itself, more than a few observers have complained that an increasing focus on reconciliation represents an unwelcome moralization of political conflict, and indeed such moralization may be seen as an important element of the broader "politics of regret" in which both the discourses of reconciliation and the practices of transitional justice participate. If those individuals and institutions mobilizing discourses of reconciliation have participated in the moralization of political conflict, however, it has not been a moralization of their own making. First, while the rise of reconciliation as a prominent political concept is a relatively recent phenomenon, the politics of regret has a much longer historical trajectory.[6] Second, and more specifically, the political and discursive frameworks for conceiving reconciliation and transitional justice have been substantially influenced and inflected by the broader movement for international human rights, a movement that provided the context in which those frameworks were initially articulated and developed. This movement itself represents a substantially moral enterprise, inhabited by the "global moral entrepreneurs" who have been responsible for the transnational spread of human rights discourse and practice.[7] In other words, while the proliferation of discourses of reconciliation may be seen as a powerful example of what Michael Ignatieff has called "moral globalization," it is important to recall that the paradigm case of such moral globalization for Ignatieff was in fact the global diffusion of "human rights" discourse.[8]

Not incidentally, then, it is within the field of international human rights that many of the vigorously contested debates over reconciliation have taken place. One prominent critic of reconciliation, for instance, has been Reed Brody, a lawyer with Human Rights Watch. Writing in *The Nation* magazine in 2001, Brody took aim at the rise of truth commissions, and particularly the workings and international effects of South Africa's TRC. As a result of the TRC's international acclaim, he wrote, the "international community" has become "blindly besotted with truth commissions." The international human rights movement, he argued, was facing a "South Africa problem," since the conditions that made the TRC a notable success were difficult to replicate elsewhere, though far too many were beginning to try. For Brody, as for countless other international human rights activists, the "heart of the matter" was "whether to prosecute those who have committed atrocities," and in that respect South Africa was far from the perfect model. Truth commissions, Brody worried, were too easily "seen by abusive governments as a soft option for avoiding justice." As for "reconciliation," it was at best an ambiguous concept, difficult to define, and "too contested an ideal on which to base policy." Yet international donors were attracted to the "feel-good idea" of reconciliation, an idea that Brody contrasted with "justice," which he characterized as "a potentially messy affair in which there are not only winners but losers."[9]

Has the "international community" really become "blindly besotted with truth commissions" and romanced by the "feel-good idea" of reconciliation, as Brody claimed in 2001? While it is important to distinguish between the diverse work of multiple truth commissions and the pursuit of reconciliation, the sharp debates and transnational struggles over reconciliation in recent years suggest a more complicated reality. There is indeed a certain appeal among many donors in the broadly hopeful discourse of reconciliation. Yet among the cosmopolitan activists and academics who have occupied positions in the emerging international field of transitional justice, there has also been no small amount of struggle over the meaning and appropriate usage of the term. Brody is not alone in his identification of a "South Africa problem," and his serious reservations regarding the concept of reconciliation are representative of widely held concerns among human rights activists, academic analysts, and others within this rapidly expanding interdisciplinary arena. Rather than adequately or fully representing the contours of an international love affair with "truth and reconciliation," then—to be fair, not his primary intention—Brody's critical remarks might better be viewed as a rhetorical intervention in an ongoing dialogue and wide-ranging debate over the appropriate place of conceptions of reconciliation within the political discourses and state-sponsored institutions that figure and enact the work of transitional justice.

This debate, and the various transformations of the concept of reconciliation that it has produced, is a significant part of the story of reconciliation's international proliferation. Attention to its dimensions suggests not simply a proliferation of reconciliation discourse, but in fact a profusion of competing, conflicting, and at times overlapping conceptions. Whether in the work of international NGOs or in the academic formulations of scholars across the humanities and social sciences, the language of reconciliation has been reworked and refigured in provocative and interesting ways. There is little consensus regarding the appropriateness of its place and uses in political life, and even less agreement regarding its meaning. It is rather a term whose vast proliferation is aided and abetted by its ambiguity and multiple significations.

In what follows, I begin by briefly considering a well-established framework in American sociology for explaining processes of transnational diffusion, suggesting that sociological treatments of "world culture" are broadly useful, although generally limited by an under-theorization of the importance of struggle and transformation and by a relative inattention to the critical agents who engage in the conflict and contestation that is a constitutive element of transnational activity in the field of transitional justice. I then turn to the historical genesis and transformation of the widely touted discourse of reconciliation that was associated with South Africa's TRC. This sets the stage for the consideration of a variety of post-TRC formulations of reconciliation that have appropriated and transformed the discourse of reconciliation in the midst of its increasing international circulation. Rather than attempt to be comprehensive, I focus in particular on the work of two recently established international NGOs, the International Center for Transitional Justice and the Institute for Justice and Reconciliation, and on the work of a small handful of academic theorists and critics of reconciliation whose work I take to be engaged with the discourse in ways that are representative of important dimensions of the contemporary struggle over reconciliation's meaning and mobilization.

From Moral Globalization to World Definitions

At first glance, the recent proliferation of discourses of reconciliation does appear to be a good example of what Ignatieff has called "moral globalization." Linked to practices of public confession and political forgiveness and to notions of cathartic testimony, redeemed suffering, and healing truth, a frequently Christian discourse of reconciliation has been conjoined with the language of human rights to produce a distinctive trope of transitional justice, a model that was consolidated and transformed by the work of South Africa's TRC. As political transitions have proliferated, this alternative approach to justice in transition, sometimes captured under the rubric of "restorative justice," has since been reproduced in multiple forms. Hybrid products of historical and political particularities, recent discourses of reconciliation in a variety of disparate locations and institutional contexts have nonetheless exhibited striking similarities.

In light of such semblance, the proliferation of "reconciliation" might be figured not simply as an instance of moral globalization, but as a function of what John Meyer and his colleagues call "world culture." With an emphasis on moral suasion rather than economic sanction, Meyer's reworking of world-systems theory sometimes looks a bit like an updated version of modernization theory—albeit shorn of its explicitly normative aspirations. If Michael Ignatieff is moral globalization's liberal prophet, then perhaps we may call John Meyer its subdued sociological analyst. In Meyer's theoretical register, global political culture is identified with a shared set of global rules. These global rules—"world definitions" Meyer once called them—are taken to have a powerful political and cultural effect. They also serve a useful explanatory purpose, accounting for the transnational diffusion of both ideas and institutional forms and explaining "isomorphic expansion" that crosses national borders.

Work in this broadly "institutionalist" mode has had a wide appeal in sociology, much of it frequently referencing DiMaggio and Powell's now-canonical article, "The Iron Cage Revisited." In this influential article, the authors made the explanation of "startling homogeneity," rather than variation, their aim, thus elucidating an agenda for research that would rely on "institutional isomorphism" as a "useful tool for understanding the politics and ceremony that pervade much modern organizational life."[10] Even as DiMaggio and Powell were helping to lay the groundwork for what would become an expansive form of organizational analysis, scholars concerned with the transnational diffusion of both ideas and institutional forms were already taking a keen interest in "isomorphic expansion" that crossed national boundaries. Borrowing the language of Wallerstein, these theorists identify national locations in both the "center" and "periphery" of the world system, seeking to explain the flow of cultural or institutional forms from the first to the second, the distribution or reproduction of the dominant forms of the center in various peripheral locations.[11] "The contemporary world is rife with modeling," write Meyer and his colleagues, the most prolific proponents of world-cultural theory. "The poor and weak and peripheral copy the rich and strong and central."[12]

While cast at the conceptual level of Wallerstein's world system, however, world-cultural explanations draw on a different sociological lineage, opposed both to their functionalist predecessors and to macrorealist explanations that adopt reductionist accounts of culture. Thus, Meyer—in an early, much-cited article—rejected theories that viewed world politics as "simply a direct reflection of world economic relations." Seeking to explain the puzzle of "a worldwide system of structurally similar nation-states," Meyer proposed instead the concept of a powerful "world polity," representing worldwide political culture as a "shared and binding set of rules exogenous to any given society."[13]

Operating at a relatively high level of abstraction, Meyer's argument was least developed, if still evocative, when he turned to the mechanisms of transmission that would explain international isomorphism. His explicitly brief notes on the topic did little more than provide a short laundry list of possible explanations, just as his closing consideration of "the elites of the world political culture"—those "modernizing intellectuals" he deemed the "clergy" of that culture—was sketchy, if suggestive. More than two decades later, and despite further elaboration and an outpouring of empirical work, the broad strokes of Meyer's approach have not significantly changed.[14] As a result, critics have continued to call for a clearer articulation of the "mechanisms" of transnational transmission and transformation. "What connects concrete organizations to international models?" asked Charles Tilly in response to Meyer's explanation of state transformation. "Meyer does not state a clear answer," wrote Tilly, and "his frequent resort to passive voice masks the critical agents and agency of the transformation."[15]

Alongside related forms of institutional analysis, and under the umbrella of the "new institutionalism," Meyer and his colleagues have generated an expansive theory of organizations and the world system. Yet, as Tilly's remark indicates, one of the limitations of world-cultural explanations derives from a relative shortage of detailed analyses of concrete conflicts and changes, struggles and transformations. Thus, political scientists and policy theorists concerned with the shape of global culture have criticized world-cultural sociologists for ignoring both the sources of "global cultural norms" and the processes through which such norms develop and change.[16] Likewise, sociologists have recognized the need for consideration of such sources and mechanisms, calling for further analysis of transnational networks and additional examination of the "genesis of legitimated models" and "the definition and elaboration of organizational fields."[17]

Such constructive criticisms notwithstanding, Meyer and his colleagues have developed a formidable approach to world culture. Pitching their explanations at the level of the planetary, and aiming to parse transnational patterns of convergence, they show an especially promising concern with global intellectuals and institutions. "Diffusion among nation-states is heavily mediated by scientists and professionals who define virtuous instances, formulate models, and actively support their adoption," they write, and "the models of national development or human rights carried by international associations have their roots in scientific and legal knowledge."[18]

This insight about the "roots" of transnational models seems to point in the direction that Tilly indicates, and indeed beyond—to further investigation of the connections between internationally powerful models and the concrete organizations that transmit them, and to the model producers and the historical practices behind and beneath their productions. "World definitions," Meyer and his colleagues argue, are located not only in the sentiments of individual global elites or powerful cosmopolitans; they are also lodged in and championed by world-cultural institutions such as the United Nations, and promoted by numerous international NGOs—the "carriers" and "enactors" of world culture.[19]

Indeed, it is notable that recent years have witnessed the establishment of international NGOs dedicated to the transnational promotion of truth and reconciliation—from New York City's International Center for Transitional Justice, which has been called "the world's first truth commission consulting firm,"[20] to smaller, regional organizations such as the Institute for Justice and Reconciliation in Cape Town, which seeks to be a "conduit" through which expertise about reconciliation can travel from South Africa to other parts of the continent. Like the establishment of truth commissions themselves, the birth of these international organizations—both founded by former staff members of South Africa's TRC—marks a shift within a transnational field devoted to the promotion and expansion of human rights. At the same time, these NGOs and other purveyors of reconciliation's incipient world definition have crafted significantly different conceptions of reconciliation, complicating any attempt to render reconciliation as a monolithic institutional logic that might be neatly packaged and sent abroad to various receiving organizations. Borrowing the ever more popular language of South Africa's TRC, and trading on its prominence in the cosmopolitan imaginary, they have nonetheless stepped away from the theological specificities of the TRC's "religious-redemptive narrative." Yet this stepping away, and the transformation of the institutional logic of reconciliation it has entailed, has itself been far from uniform, such that it is more appropriate to speak of multiple attempts to transform the logic of reconciliation, resulting in a plurality of would-be world definitions of the term. The most developed of these different and frequently competing definitions of reconciliation have their own specific historical trajectories, or are at the very least situated within relatively well articulated political and theoretical frameworks. Yet given the international acclaim that has been visited upon South Africa's TRC, nearly all of them make substantial reference to that commission's theological conception of reconciliation, if only for the purposes of differentiation and distinction from it. To grapple with the contemporary proliferation of discourses of reconciliation, therefore, we must situate it within a historical context substantially influenced by the South African commission and its international reception.

Truth and Reconciliation in South Africa

While the South African TRC was a site of political and cultural contestation, and thus shot through with multiple and at times conflicting conceptions of reconciliation, it was Archbishop Desmond Tutu's substantially theological rendering of reconciliation that came to be most prominently associated with the commission, both nationally and internationally.[21] Tutu's emphasis on the importance of forgiveness for reconciliation—indeed his tendency to at times equate the two—was and continues to be controversial among South Africans. Yet when the Institute for Justice and Reconciliation, a Cape Town–based organization devoted to promoting reconciliation in post-apartheid South Africa, surveyed perceptions of the meaning of the word "reconciliation," "forgiveness" topped the list of responses—a fact that may have as much to do with South Africa's long history of theological politics, in which debates over reconciliation have figured prominently, and with its robustly religious culture as with the TRC's success in communicating Tutu's Christian vision of reconciliation to the South African public.[22]

A central theme in Paul's *Second Epistle to the Corinthians,* the discourse of reconciliation has long had distinctly Christian overtones and implications. A recurrent topic in modern European theology and philosophy—Karl Barth devoted four large tomes to the subject,[23] and it was one of Hegel's significant preoccupations—discourses of reconciliation have figured prominently in the historical contexts that gave rise to the first truth and reconciliation commissions. Catholic bishops in Chile called publicly for social reconciliation only one year after a coup that toppled the socialist Salvador Allende and brought

General Augusto Pinochet to power, and more than a decade and a half prior to the formation of that nation's Truth and Reconciliation Commission.

In South Africa, discourses of reconciliation also extend further back than many commentators on the TRC have acknowledged. During the years of struggle against apartheid, activist church leaders and South African theologians regularly debated the meanings and prerequisites of Christian reconciliation. As state repression intensified and religious leaders were dragged further and further into the anti-apartheid struggle, calls for reconciliation became more controversial. In the years just prior to South Africa's political transition, debates over reconciliation culminated in 1985 in the publication of the *Kairos Document,* a theological intervention in the South African public sphere that critiqued both conservative and liberal invocations of reconciliation.

Thus, the language of reconciliation and forgiveness—embodied so powerfully and persuasively by Tutu, but certainly not limited to him—has had a distinctive, contentious, and complicated history in South Africa, a history at once theological and political. Indeed, politics and theology in South Africa have been importantly and at times inextricably intertwined, especially in the years prior to apartheid's demise. Literary critic Susan Gallagher makes this point well in the course of discussing the significant theological disputes and South African "confessional discourse" of the 1980s:

> Secular observers may find such theological battles esoteric and peripheral. However, because theological paradigms have been repeatedly employed to validate apartheid, and because the political struggles of South Africa are so deeply implicated in religious beliefs and Church politics, anti-apartheid confessional discourse was a much more visible and significant aspect of South African life than similar movements in other countries. . . . [I]n South Africa, theological debates about confession have been conspicuous, consequential, and continual, forming a prominent social discourse.[24]

The extent to which theological paradigms were "employed to validate apartheid" was significant enough to lead the authors of the *Kairos Document* to refer to a "State Theology,"[25] and a story recounted by Pumla Gobodo-Madikizela puts flesh on the concept of an apartheid state that fell back on theology for its justification. Bibles distributed to soldiers of the South African Defense Force included both "the gold star-shaped army insignia embossed on the maroon front cover" and an inscription on the first page, in Afrikaans, from State President P. W. Botha. "Even this tampering with the book that many Christians consider sacred," Gobodo-Madikizela writes, "was not enough to provide the condemnation it deserved from the church: the Afrikaans Church stood by silently and watched apartheid's murderous plan unfold."[26]

If the discourse of the apartheid state was theological, so also was the discourse of much of the resistance to that state, which emerged in direct and conscious response to the South African political context. Thus the rise of both black theology—"the theological reflection of black Christians on the situation in which they live and on their struggle for liberation"[27]—and after it contextual theology, grounded "a new language of protest."[28] Spearheaded by figures such as Desmond Tutu, Beyers Naudé, Denis Hurley, Allan Boesak, Smangaliso Mkhatshwa, and Frank Chikane, these theological movements evolved in the midst of an increasing "spiral of involvement" in the liberation struggle on the part of South African churches.[29] The result was not only a closer relationship between religious communities and the liberation movement, but also a series of documents, declarations, and other publications that produced and promoted new discourses of liberation, justice, and reconciliation.[30]

Products of South African political struggle, these new theologies were influenced intellectually by U.S. black theology, Latin American liberation theology, and European political theology. Like their Latin American counterparts—contextual theology, which according to one scholar replaced black theology and thereby shifted the emphasis from "race" to "class,"[31] may be seen as a particular incarnation of liberation theology—South African theologies of liberation have continuously invoked notions of "real reconciliation." The *Kairos Document,* for instance, which has been "recognized as the definitive statement of contextual theology in South Africa,"[32] critiqued not only the "State Theology" of apartheid, but also a "Church Theology" that emphasized mediation and liberal reform.[33] As Tristan Borer writes, "For the Kairos theologians, reconciliation through compromise could never be made into an absolute principle that must be applied in all cases of conflict. . . . In contrast to reconciliation, the *Kairos Document* challenged churches to respond with a theology of confrontation and resistance."[34] The "Prophetic Theology" promoted by the *Kairos Document* did not, however, reject the language of reconciliation altogether. Rather, like liberationists in Chile and elsewhere, the authors made "true reconciliation" contingent on liberation from unjust and oppressive social structures upheld by a tyrannical regime: "There can be no doubt that our Christian faith commits us to work for *true* reconciliation and *genuine* peace. But as so many people, including Christians, have pointed out, there can be no true reconciliation and no genuine peace *without justice.* Any form of peace or reconciliation that allows the sin of injustice and oppression to continue is a *false* peace and a *counterfeit* reconciliation."[35] While the publication of the *Kairos Document* was a significant step in the development of contextual theology, earlier South African references to reconciliation also emphasized its social and material conditions.[36] In an open letter to Prime Minister John Vorster written in May 1976 (a month before the Soweto uprising), Desmond Tutu noted that "a people made desperate by despair, injustice and oppression will use desperate means" and worried about "a point of no return, when events will generate a momentum of their own" and about a "bloody denouement." In this context, Tutu introduced the language and possibility of real reconciliation. "I am deeply committed to real reconciliation with justice for all," he wrote, "and to peaceful change to a more just and open South African society in which the wonderful riches and wealth of our country will be shared more equitably."[37] Tutu thus closely linked reconciliation both with a dream of distributive justice and with the specter of a "bloody denouement," a vision to which he would return upon the submission of the final volume of the TRC's report in March 2003. Reminding President Thabo Mbeki of a proposal to impose a new tax on businesses in order to raise millions of dollars for reparations, Tutu argued that it was in the interest of the business community to make such contributions. "It is not altruistic," he said. "It is in their interest to help narrow the gap between the rich and the poor." "Can you explain," Tutu continued, "how a black person wakes up in a squalid ghetto today, almost 10 years after freedom? Then he goes to work in town, which is still largely white, in palatial homes. And at the end of the day, he goes back home to squalor? I don't know why those people don't just say, 'To hell with peace. To hell with Tutu and the truth commission.'"[38] Without substantial reparations, Tutu implied, real reconciliation—and the peaceful and just society it promised— would not be possible.

Representing Reconciliation: The Report of the South African TRC

Tutu's emphasis on the connection between reconciliation and reparations was written into the TRC report itself, which relied on a conception of "restorative justice" that linked the concepts of reparation and restoration. With a certain affinity to the vision of moral reconstruction proffered by Chilean human rights lawyer José Zalaquett, the emphasis of restorative justice in the TRC was on "restoring the human and civil dignity of victims."[39] Tutu would regularly invoke the concept of restorative justice when faced with criticisms that the TRC had sacrificed justice in favor of a weak reconciliation and a partial truth. Yet as the commissioners themselves realized, there were limits to the TRC's political power to enact the reparation it envisioned. While providing the public, quasi-legal, and indeed sacramental space in which representative acts of reconciliation and forgiveness might be performed and symbolized, the TRC could not simply legislate its vision of economic reparations, however radical it might have been to do so.

Not to be confused with—although importantly related to—any actually existing processes of reconciliation worked by the TRC or other agencies within South Africa, "reconciliation" in the TRC report nonetheless retained a fairly robust set of meanings. If the report of the Chilean truth commission had provided a relatively under-theorized conception of reconciliation, the report of the South African TRC gave a much more elaborated account. Describing reconciliation as "both a goal and a process," the report's first volume characterized the "different levels" on which reconciliation might operate, discussing such themes as "coming to terms with painful truth," "reconciliation between victims and perpetrators," "reconciliation at a community level," "promoting national unity and reconciliation," and "reconciliation and redistribution."[40] Discussing the all-important relationship between truth and reconciliation, the commissioners wrote: "There can be little doubt that gross violations of human rights and other similar abuses during the past few decades left indelible scars on the collective South African consciousness. These scars often concealed festering wounds that needed to be opened up to allow for the cleansing and eventual healing of the body politic."[41] While the truth telling of the TRC process would facilitate such healing, the report was quick to indicate that the commission itself could not "be expected to accomplish all the healing that was required,"[42] a sentiment Desmond Tutu would return to time and again in his public statements about the TRC.

What did the commission do, and what did its report say? As an institutional animal, the TRC was in many ways unlike any other. Differences when compared with commissions that preceded it included: the power to grant amnesty to individual perpetrators; much stronger powers of subpoena, search, and seizure; public process and testimony; institutional and special hearings which "allowed for direct contributions by NGOs and those who were involved in specific areas of activism, policy proposals and monitoring in the past"; a witness protection program; and larger size of staff and budget.[43] Furthermore, as Priscilla Hayner notes, "the degree of reconciliation as a goal of truth-seeking has varied greatly between commissions," and while reconciliation was a major theme in South Africa and Chile, in other contexts it was rarely invoked at all.[44] Made up of three committees—the Human Rights Violations Committee, the Amnesty Committee, and the Reparations and Rehabilitation Committee—the commission took testimony from over 21,000 victims and witnesses, 2,000 of whom were selected to appear in public hearings. Media coverage of the commission was massive, from newspapers to radio to television, and extended not just nationally but internationally.[45]

Notably, the commission's discussion of truth and reconciliation moved almost seamlessly back and forth between references to "reconciliation" and references to "forgiveness," at times apparently treating the two as if they were inextricably intertwined. Citing a "remarkable magnanimity and generosity of spirit" on the part of those who had "suffered gross violations of their human rights," the commissioners located such generosity not only in the willingness of victims and survivors to "display their pain to the world," but also in a "willingness to forgive."[46] Indeed, a substantial segment of the report's chapter on "reconciliation"—included in volume 5—involved "remarkable evidence" of this "willingness to forgive,"[47] while another section of the reconciliation chapter was devoted to "apologies and acknowledgements."[48]

While TRC commissioners closely associated forgiveness and reconciliation, and emphasized the stories of apology and forgiveness that became a part of its process, the TRC report also warned that forgiveness and reconciliation should not simply be conflated. "It is also crucial not to fall into the error of equating forgiveness with reconciliation," wrote the commissioners. "The road to reconciliation requires more than forgiveness and respectful remembrance."[49] Indeed, forgiveness itself should not be misunderstood. In response to calls to "close the book on the past"—and perhaps in response to criticisms of its constitution of anti-apartheid activists as "victims"—the commission warned that forgiveness could not be about "forgetting." It was rather a matter of "seeking to forego bitterness, renouncing resentment, moving past old hurt, and becoming a survivor rather than a passive victim."[50]

Given the TRC's robustly public quality, its report was not its only substantial "product." Its operation "in the full glare of publicity," as Tutu put it in his foreword to the TRC report,[51] was one of the unique features that set the South African commission apart from preceding commissions.[52] Since the commission did more than produce a report, this also meant that the TRC's public renderings of reconciliation and forgiveness were not simply matters of textual representation. Stories of its public processes of truth and reconciliation—along with the stories of apology and forgiveness that sometimes attended those processes—circulated widely. Here, for example, is one of those stories.

In September 1992 members of the African National Congress (ANC) marched through the streets of Bisho, a town in the Eastern Cape, to highlight their campaign for free political activity. Local Defense Force soldiers fired on the demonstrators, and twenty-eight of them were killed. During the early 1990s, when the collapse of apartheid seemed imminent, this sort of political violence was on the rise in South Africa. The killings in Bisho became known as the Bisho Massacre, and testimony was taken regarding it in front of the TRC.

What happened when the TRC received testimony regarding the Bisho Massacre was remarkable, and most would later emphasize that it was also somewhat unique. In a tension-filled hall, packed with local spectators who had been on the ANC's march or who had lost family members killed that day, a white officer, Colonel Schobesberger of the local Defense Force, asked for forgiveness:

> I say we are sorry. I say the burden of the Bisho massacre will be on our shoulders for the rest of our lives. We cannot wish it away. It happened. But please, I ask specifically the victims not to forget, I cannot ask this, but to forgive us, to get the soldiers back into the community, to accept them fully, to try to understand also the pressure they were under then. This is all I can do. I'm sorry, this I can say, I'm sorry.

In response to this plea and apology, another extraordinary thing happened. The people in the audience applauded. Then Tutu, making the link between confession and catharsis, acknowledgement and reconciliation, forgiveness and healing truth, said:

> Can we just keep a moment's silence, please, because we are dealing with things that are very, very deep. It isn't easy, as we all know, to ask for forgiveness and it's also not easy to forgive, but we are a people who know that when someone cannot be forgiven there is no future.

In the months that followed, the details of this event quickly became a success story for the TRC, taken to demonstrate that "reconciliation through truth" was a real possibility. Tutu would go on to recount this story in his own book on the TRC process, as would others.[53]

Such narratives indicate the TRC's fundamentally public character—marking a significant shift in the institutional form of the truth commission, and one that set South Africa's TRC apart from the Chilean commission, and others that preceded it. They also clearly demonstrate the robustly religious language that helped to constitute the TRC process, an orientation that again sets the TRC's volumes apart from other truth commission reports, including the one produced in Chile. Tutu, wrote Antjie Krog, "unambiguously mantled the commission in Christian language," even despite the opposition of some commissioners.[54] Along with reconciliation, both *ubuntu* and "restorative justice" were given a prominent place in the TRC report's discussion of the key "concepts and principles underlying the Commission's work."[55]

This unambiguous mantling of the TRC in Christian language has received a good deal of attention in South Africa and beyond.[56] Not all of it has been positive. In the words of political theorist André du Toit: "As religious leaders and churches became increasingly involved in the commission's work, the influence of religious style and symbolism supplanted political and human rights concerns."[57] In the international realm, academics such as Harvard political philosopher Dennis Thompson also took issue with the TRC's "theological rhetoric." Participating in a discussion of truth commissions that also involved du Toit, Thompson worried that truth commissions adopting such rhetoric might get "bogged down in . . . the therapy of forgiveness."[58] And indeed, the South African TRC had gone deeply into a theologically motivated quest for forgiveness and healing, producing in the process not simply the "intangible sacrament" recommended by Chilean human rights lawyer José Zalaquett, but a novel institutional form, a new global technology of truth and reconciliation.[59]

Reconciliation after the South African TRC

What has happened subsequently to the logic of reconciliation? In the wake of the South African TRC, how have conceptions of reconciliation been reconceived and reconfigured? Because of the TRC, and its close association with the so-called South African miracle, a distinctly South African discourse, significantly rooted in contextual and liberation theologies, has captured international attention. As a tool and goal of transitional justice, reconciliation has gone global. In the course of this transformation, new proponents and opponents, practitioners and critics, participants and observers, have joined the conversation about reconciliation. As the discourse has proliferated, the terms of debate have changed.

To best understand the competing conceptions of reconciliation currently vying for attention in South Africa and abroad, we must take stock of this change without losing sight of the theological dimensions of both reconciliation's history and its most prominent contemporary manifestations. Having opened with an assessment of reconciliation as a distinctly South African political theology, I now want to consider the various ways that alternative conceptions of reconciliation have reproduced or reworked, recycled or revised, redirected or resisted that theological discourse. This approach makes particular sense because a great many contemporary conceptions of reconciliation are in some way or another inspired by or parasitic on the work of the South African TRC, in which theological renderings of reconciliation figured prominently.

The terms of debate over reconciliation have changed. But how? Perhaps most significantly, reconciliation's reach has become increasingly global. The conception of reconciliation that emphasizes forgiveness, claims South African poet Antjie Krog, is "not easily grasped by the Western mind." Embedded in an understanding of humanity which is based on the notion of *ubuntu,* Krog sees South African reconciliation—including both amnesty and forgiveness—as "one of the biggest moral contributions of the 20th century." But "Westerners," as the subtitle to her *Sunday Times* editorial suggests, view this sort of reconciliation as an "unnatural aberration."[60]

This contrast—between (South) African conceptions of reconciliation and justice and those of "the West"—is not new. During the TRC, Archbishop Tutu made similar comparisons as he defended a vision of reconciliation and restorative justice against outside critics calling for prosecution and retribution. What is new is the intensity of an international debate—a global battle over reconciliation and forgiveness, justice, truth, and amnesty—transformed, if not inaugurated, by the worldwide attention lavished on the work of the South African TRC.

The development of truth commissions has involved what André du Toit calls an "international learning process," as previous commissions become models (positive or negative) for those that follow. Thus South Africa's TRC was established in the context of conferences that drew on the expertise of international figures, perhaps most notably those associated with the Chilean TRC. And most recent TRCs have looked to and been deeply influenced by the South African model, now seen as the exemplar against which new commissions will be matched. Through the international proliferation of truth commissions, discourses of reconciliation—if not the reality they seek to bring into being—have spread across the globe.

As I indicated above, human rights theorist Michael Ignatieff has referred to the worldwide proliferation of human rights discourse as an instance of "moral globalization."[61] While the term "globalization" is at once loaded and ambiguous, the spread of reconciliation—importantly connected to, but not limited to, the work of truth commissions—might be productively construed as a process of moral globalization. Especially as a result of the South African TRC, the issue of reconciliation is now debated in many countries throughout Africa. Drawn in part from the experience of the Chileans, South African conceptions and practices of truth and reconciliation have also traveled back to Latin America, where they influenced the work of the Peruvian TRC. Reconciliation has become a keyword in Northern Ireland and Australia (where reconciliation processes, guided by non-state actors, pre-date the South African TRC), and in East Timor and Burma. It has been pursued, in different ways, in Eastern Europe. It has even taken hold, albeit at a specific and local level, in the United States. And significantly, reconciliation has entered the lexicon of—and become a topic of shifting debates within—prominent international human rights organizations. It has also become an intense subject of academic study, propelling individual careers and generating conferences, seminars, courses, journal articles, and university press books.

The quest for reconciliation has also become a key frame through which international journalists measure the success of political transition or post-conflict peace making. From the perspective of the United Nations and other powerful international organizations and bodies, institutions and state-sponsored processes devoted to the promotion of reconciliation are now seen as an integral element of the so-called transitional justice package. Post-TRC organizations such as the Institute for Justice and Reconciliation in Cape Town, and the International Center for Transitional Justice in New York City, have contributed to the increasing dissemination, reproduction, and international prominence of reconciliation discourse. Promoted and contested worldwide, reconciliation is now substantially embedded in global moral and political vocabularies.

Entrepreneurs of Reconciliation and Retrospective Justice

A significant part of the explanation for reconciliation's substantial discursive dissemination has to do with the controversial proliferation of truth commissions themselves, a proliferation aided and abetted, as well as opposed, by the cosmopolitan global moral entrepreneurs who constitute the transnational field of human rights and the emergent and burgeoning field of transitional justice.[62] As an institutional tool of transitional justice, the truth commission has in recent years come into its own. Truth commissions, wrote scholar and consultant Priscilla Hayner, as the South African TRC was still wrapping up its work, "have caught the wind of popularity" and are "fast becoming a staple in the transitional justice menu of options."[63] The last few years have only served to reinforce her point, as truth commissions have been formed in transitional societies from Ghana to East Timor and Sierra Leone to Peru. Strikingly, while a number of early truth commissions were known officially as "commissions of inquiry," most recent commissions have borrowed their name, if not their precise structure and scope, from South Africa's TRC. Thus, along with the recent wave of truth commissions, the language of reconciliation has proliferated.

As with other forms of globalization, the globalization of truth and reconciliation has had both its proponents and its detractors. Here again, South Africa figures prominently, although South African voices critical of the TRC—those that might provide a substantial challenge to the sometimes oversimplified perceptions of observers—have often gotten lost in the midst of the commission's celebrated international reception. Especially in the international media, the TRC has too often been seen as simply another uplifting element of the

"South African miracle." Closer to the ground, South Africans know that the TRC was no unqualified or uncontroversial success. "The world," as Frederick Van Zyl Slabbert puts it, "is much more fascinated and impressed by the TRC than people in South Africa are." Referring to Alex Boraine's move from Cape Town to New York City, once his work as the deputy chair of South Africa's TRC had been completed, Slabbert sees the controversial Boraine's departure from South Africa and his subsequently generous reception in New York as "a case of the prophet not being honoured in his own country."[64]

If Boraine does represent a South African prophet not honored in his own country, he has certainly found an ample audience elsewhere for his vision of truth commissions and transitional justice. If one were to compile a list of prominent global moral entrepreneurs responsible for the transnational spread of truth and reconciliation processes, Alex Boraine's name would inevitably fall very near the top. Initially moving to New York City for a stint as visiting professor at New York University, Boraine soon co-founded the International Center for Transitional Justice (ICTJ). Headquartered in a metropolitan hub of international human rights activism, ICTJ is a powerful, well-funded international organization that signifies the rising prominence of truth commissions and transitional justice on the international scene.

Widely recognized proponents of the view that standard forms of prosecutorial justice are often not sufficient for grappling with difficult histories of violence, repression, and human rights abuse, Boraine and his staff at ICTJ have consulted with recent truth commissions in countries such as Ghana, Sierra Leone, and Peru, in addition to assisting various transitional justice efforts in more than twenty countries throughout the world. The work of ICTJ, like that of South Africa's TRC itself, has certainly influenced the shape and structure of contemporary truth commissions, and Boraine's prominence as a leading truth commissioner doubtlessly contributed to ICTJ's high international profile, though he was recently succeeded as president of ICTJ by the well-known Argentine human rights activist Juan E. Méndez.

Under the leadership of both Boraine and Méndez, the staff of ICTJ has been adamant that there is no single blueprint for transitional justice. South Africa's unique experiment with truth and reconciliation, they argue, should not just be uncritically replicated elsewhere. Indeed, internal dialogues over reconciliation at ICTJ have been marked by substantial disagreement over what the concept of "reconciliation" can and should mean in the context of transitional justice, a fact that has inhibited the robust operationalization of reconciliation as a working principle of the organization (despite the fact that it stands as one of the five original "pillars" of ICTJ's work). Thus, while ICTJ's consulting work has sought to ensure that countries interested in establishing truth commissions and working to implement other mechanisms of transitional justice will not have to "reinvent the wheel," the Center regularly suggests that each transitional situation must be seen as unique, and transitional justice mechanisms developed accordingly. ICTJ is not an entirely uncritical proponent of a singular "truth and reconciliation" model, and as such does not promote truth commissions at the expense of other mechanisms of transitional justice, including prosecutions. Indeed, while Boraine and ICTJ were initially viewed in some international human rights circles as soft on the so-called duty to prosecute perpetrators of past abuses, certain advocates of reconciliation and restorative justice have noted an opposite inclination at the Center—a tendency to focus too heavily on prosecutions, at the possible expense of supporting broader processes of social and political reconciliation.

Lodged somewhere in between hard-nosed advocates of a universal duty to prosecute and prophets of social reconciliation who highlight the healing power of forgiveness, ICTJ has, in the words of one legal scholar, "cornered the international market" on truth commissions. Global moral entrepreneurs closely connected to the proliferation of truth and reconciliation commissions, Boraine and his ICTJ colleagues increasingly find themselves actively discouraging the premature or "uninformed" establishment of just such commissions. Thus, they might best be seen not as entrepreneurs of truth and reconciliation at any cost, but rather as influential global managers of the complex and often contentious national and international processes that give rise to truth commissions and other mechanisms of transitional justice.

Reconciliation as a Political Art and a Political Science

Alex Boraine and his colleagues at ICTJ in New York City are cosmopolitan moral entrepreneurs who conspicuously downplay the significance of their organization's national location. "We are based in New York," says Boraine, "but we are not an American organization. We are an international organization." Staff members at ICTJ's sister institution in Cape Town, the Institute for Justice and Reconciliation (IJR), take a very different tack, celebrating their status as members of a distinctly African organization. Thus, while the cosmopolitan elites at ICTJ bear a sometimes obscure relationship to "the social conditions of their own discourse," IJR's staffers are self-conscious examples of what Tarrow has referred to as "rooted cosmopolitans."[65] Linked to transnational networks, institutions, and discourses, they are nonetheless committed to remaining firmly embedded in the South African context.

Charles Villa-Vicencio, the founder and executive director of IJR, has long been involved in South African debates over reconciliation. Under

Villa-Vicencio's guidance, the Institute's Africa Program seeks to be a "conduit" through which strategies for effectively pursuing and promoting reconciliation can travel to other parts of the continent. Once part of the group of Kairos theologians who promoted a "prophetic theology" of justice and reconciliation, Villa-Vicencio recently has emphasized the need to temper such ambitious conceptions of reconciliation with a good dose of pragmatic realism. In this vein, he now promotes a vision that he has dubbed "political reconciliation." Distinguishing it from more robust theologies of reconciliation, Villa-Vicencio argues that "political reconciliation does not necessarily include forgiveness" since forgiveness is neither "a priority for nation building" nor "a political task of the state."[66]

Although "political reconciliation" is not a specifically theological conception of reconciliation, it is nonetheless marked by its engagement with contextual and liberation theologies. First, it is marked by its realism and its modesty, explicitly contrasted with "high definitions of reconciliation that involve romanticized notions of repentance, forgiveness and restitution." From the perspective of political reconciliation, these high definitions—it would not be unreasonable to assume that they are of a piece with what Richard Wilson has called "the religious-redemptive narrative" of reconciliation—are "politically unhelpful" and even "dangerous." Theologically, therefore, political reconciliation is marked by what it is not. It does not demand or emphasize the necessity of forgiveness, since forgiveness is neither "a priority for nation building" nor "a political task of the state."

Yet political reconciliation is marked not only by its modesty, its resistance to and wariness of theological models premised on repentance and forgiveness. It is also positively marked by the traces of its engagement with such models. Thus, forgiveness, when it does come, is not figured as politically or ethically suspect. Rather, says Villa-Vicencio, it is "a bonus"; it is "grace." Likewise, political reconciliation itself is characterized poetically, as "an art rather than a science." This vision of reconciliation looks at times like a post-Christian or humanist theology: "It is a celebration of the human spirit"; "It is about making what seems impossible possible"; "It is a glimpse of a new way of living." An inspired, expansive, capacious, and inclusive vision, Villa-Vicencio's conception of reconciliation draws on and overlaps with multiple discourses of reconciliation, even as it is rooted in the South African experience.

While Villa-Vicencio characterizes political reconciliation as "an art rather than a science," some academic analysts have sought to establish an explicitly scientific approach to the study of reconciliation. In *Overcoming Apartheid*, for instance, James Gibson seeks a scientific answer to the question begged by the TRC: does "truth" lead to "reconciliation"? A social scientist, Gibson sets about to systematically investigate this question, to treat "the various components of the truth and reconciliation process as hypotheses subject to confirmation or disconfirmation through rigorous social science methods." Gibson must therefore operationalize "reconciliation." While he realizes that "reconciliation" is "one of the most abused words in the lexicon of South Africa," Gibson nonetheless contends that truth and reconciliation are "concepts that can be (and should be) measured and assessed using rigorous and systematic social science methods." In order to do so, he sets out to award "reconciliation" and "truth" "concrete and unambiguous conceptual and operational meaning."[67]

Emphasizing policy making, legal theorist Erin Daly also argues for the importance of bestowing reconciliation with an unambiguous and definitive meaning:

> It is extremely important for policymakers and others involved in the reconciliation debate to define what they mean when they use the term in any given situation. Failure to define reconciliation has both theoretical and pragmatic consequences. The undefined use of such an amorphous term impedes the development of a theory of reconciliation because it makes every statement both true and untrue simultaneously. . . . A definitional quagmire is not conducive to good theory. The absence of precise definition also interferes with the effective promotion of reconciliation at a pragmatic level. If we do not know what a particular mechanism was intended to achieve, we can not know whether it was successful, or whether it should be copied or modified.[68]

Is reconciliation an art or a science? The debate will no doubt continue, spurred on by the contributions of both practitioners and academic observers such as rhetorical theorist Erik Doxtader, who has put forward one of the most sophisticated and historically specific academic conceptions of reconciliation to date. Doxtader's conception of reconciliation is firmly rooted in a substantive engagement with the rhetorical history of reconciliation in South Africa. Thus, unlike many commentators on contemporary reconciliation politics, Doxtader connects his consideration to the concept's complex theological history. Yet his understanding of reconciliation does not stop there. Doxtader also advances a positive and even poetic conception of reconciliation, as in this oft-cited rendering:

> When distanced from the divine, released from the notion that it is strictly a gift and action of God, the faith of reconciliation appears poetic. Reconciliation promises a beginning, the creation of that which we can neither

hold nor control. It is something that goads our imagination and extends our knowledge. We quantify reconciliation at the risk of rendering it banal.

While his intellectual sensibility sets him apart from the quantifiers—those who seek to establish a political science of reconciliation—Doxtader is equally aware of the "serious problems" that attend "ideal visions of reconciliation." He thus seeks a conception of reconciliation that will be neither "quasi-scientific" nor "idealistic," but will rather locate "the middle ground of reconciliation's meaning." Reconciliation, he argues, "is about turning historical animosity into relationships that contain the potential for peace"; it is "neither a reality nor an abstract promise."

Perhaps most importantly, Doxtader conceives of the work of defining reconciliation—and the dialogue that winds around such definitional debates—as part of the process of reconciliation itself. At the heart of this conception of reconciliation, to which Doxtader returns time and again in his essays on the topic, is a vision of reconciliation as mutual engagement and dialogic process, a vision rooted in reconciliation's long and contentious South African history.[69]

Reconciliation as a Potentially Illiberal Aim

To political conceptions of reconciliation—which seek to distance, if not detach, the discourse of reconciliation from its theological roots—we may add more specifically "liberal" critiques and conceptions of reconciliation, connected to and emanating from powerful paradigms of North American political theorizing. Political theorists Amy Gutmann and Dennis Thompson, for instance, critically consider both therapeutic and theological approaches to the understanding (and moral justification) of truth and reconciliation commissions, as well as their civic and seemingly more secular (and liberal) cousins.[70] They find each approach wanting.

According to Gutmann and Thompson, whose analysis—like so many others—takes South Africa's TRC as its main example, any amnesty-granting truth commission, since it sacrifices the pursuit of justice in the name of truth and reconciliation, "carries a heavy moral burden" (22). "In a democratic society," they write, "and especially in a society that is trying to overcome injustices of the past, trading criminal justice for a general social benefit such as social reconciliation requires a moral defense if it is to be acceptable" (22).

An adequate defense or justification of a justice-sacrificing truth commission will, according to these authors, be moral in three important respects. In keeping with a "consistent democratic perspective," it will be moral in principle, moral in perspective, and moral in practice. By *moral in principle*, the authors mean that the justification will "explicitly appeal to rights or goods that are moral and therefore are comparable to the justice that is being sacrificed." By *moral in perspective,* they mean that the reasons offered by such a justification ought to be "as far as possible broadly accessible and therefore inclusive of as many people as possible who seek moral terms of social cooperation." Given "the need for citizens of a morally pluralistic democracy to work together in seeking fair terms of social cooperation," this requirement of inclusiveness demands, ideally, a justification that "cannot reasonably be dismissed by people who seek moral terms of cooperation" (23). By *moral in practice,* the authors mean that the justification "should offer reasons that are to the extent possible embodied or exemplified by the commission's own proceedings" (23). Since the possibility of just punishment is sacrificed in order to create a truth commission, the commission itself—and not simply future government policies or programs—should involve compensating practices, practices which concretely justify the sacrifice of justice.

In addition to considering "realist" and "historicist" responses to the moral burden of truth and reconciliation commissions—which emphasize necessary political compromise on the one hand, and the establishment and acknowledgement of past wrongs on the other—Gutmann and Thompson also consider responses that emphasize reconciliation, restoration, and forgiveness. How well do these "compassionate" approaches to truth and reconciliation— theological, therapeutic, and civic—live up the moral burden imposed by the TRC's sacrifice of justice? As the theoretical umbrella of these various approaches, *restorative justice* "remains a relatively undeveloped conception of justice" (29). Yet, in the name of victims of historical injustice, it does offer an explicitly moral response to Gutmann and Thompson's burden, thus meeting their first challenge. Nonetheless, the authors question the extent to which truth and reconciliation commissions "actually serve the victims who testify before the commission as well as these justifications claim" (30). Citing reports from Cape Town's Trauma Center for Victims of Violence and Torture indicating that "50 to 60 percent of the victims they had seen suffered serious difficulties after giving testimony" (30), the authors suggest that claims regarding the promotion of individual healing need to be carefully considered, especially in light of the limited counseling resources the TRC employed.

The most demanding of Gutmann and Thompson's criticisms of the so-called compassionate approach, however, are reserved for "proponents of forgiveness" such as Archbishop Desmond Tutu. "The difficulty," they write, "is that many victims do not share Archbishop Tutu's Christian faith, and even those who do may hold a different view about the appropriateness of forgiveness in such situations" (30). To Tutu's spectacles of forgiveness and personal reconciliation, therefore, Gutmann and Thompson counterpose a South African story indicating the limits—and indeed, refusal—of forgiveness. Careful not to dismiss the goal of forgiveness out of hand, they nonetheless suggest that forgiveness is an aim that may be "reasonably" resisted, thus challenging its ability to meet the requirement of inclusiveness:

> Many citizens (including the victims themselves) may reasonably believe that it is morally inappropriate to forgive people who are unwilling to be punished for their crimes or unwilling to offer their victims restitution. Many may also reasonably think that although forgiving does not logically entail forgetting, it makes forgetting much easier, and the crimes of apartheid should not be made easier to forget (31).

Not only does restorative justice of the South African variety problematically emphasize forgiveness and therapy, it does so at the apparent expense of "establishing a more democratic society for all South Africans who are willing to recognize the reasonable demands of a democracy" (32). As such, it fails to be as inclusive as it might be.

This is an important and illuminating aspect of Gutmann and Thompson's critique, and thus deserves particular attention. If reconciliation is taken to mean "comprehensive social harmony," then the authors perceive it to be a profoundly *illiberal* idea. "Reconciliation," they write,

> is an illiberal aim if it means expecting an entire society to subscribe to a single comprehensive moral perspective. . . . Reconciliation of this comprehensive sort is also deeply undemocratic. A democratic society should still seek reconciliation on some fundamental matters of political morality . . . but a democratic society that strives for consensus on such fundamental matters of political morality must still recognize that moral conflicts in politics more generally cannot be overcome or avoided (32–33).

Reconciliation of this robust variety will thus be problematic for reasons particular to liberal or democratic political theory, reasons closely tied to what Gutmann and Thompson call the "requirement of inclusiveness" (23). If the project of reconciliation involves seeking "comprehensive social harmony," then it would fail to respect reasonable moral pluralism, a form of respect central to liberal democratic societies. Likewise, although Gutmann and Thompson do not make this point entirely clear, reconciliation-as-forgiveness would also be suspect for similar democratic or liberal reasons, since the concept of forgiveness is particular to a "single comprehensive moral perspective," or what the political philosopher John Rawls calls a "comprehensive doctrine." In the context of a truth commission—a public, state-sponsored institution that is one element of a transitional political project aimed at creating a more democratic society—the official invocation of forgiveness represents an unwelcome intrusion of religious discourse into the public, political sphere.

To what extent does this line of thought get at Dennis Thompson's earlier worries—articulated in the context of the 1997 roundtable discussion on truth commissions sponsored by the World Peace Foundation—that truth commissions under leaders like Tutu could get "bogged down in the therapy of forgiveness"? Such worries might be seen as of a piece with the liberal concern to keep the invocation of particularistic religious commitments out of public, political discourse. But they also might be taken to represent—at bottom—a more substantial antagonism toward the specific substance of Christian theologies of forgiveness. Gutmann and Thompson write: "If 'the healing of the nation' is taken to mean forgiveness by the victims and repentance by the perpetrators of apartheid crimes, it is a utopian aim, and not even a positive one" (32). (As some critics of liberalism would argue, this is not simply about keeping comprehensive moral perspectives from dominating political life—the dimension Gutmann and Thompson emphasize here—but rather about rejecting one comprehensive moral perspective in favor of another. Secular liberal theorists, naturally, reject the language and practice of forgiveness in favor of the language and practice of liberal justice.)

Thus, in their own outline of a possible justification for amnesty-granting truth commissions, Gutmann and Thompson approvingly cite Arendt's declaration that "only love has the power to forgive," and "love . . . is not only apolitical but antipolitical" (39). Their version of liberal democracy and disagreement would therefore require democratic citizens not to love, but rather to develop, in the name of reciprocity, some degree of respect for one another. Acting in accord with a principle of the "economy of moral disagreement," such citizens would "search for significant points of convergence between their own understanding and those of citizens whose positions, taken in their more comprehensive forms, they must reject" (38).

With this model of democratic deliberation and disagreement in sight, the discourses of reconciliation prominent in South Africa's TRC begin to look especially suspect. Although Gutmann and Thompson are at pains to emphasize the successes as well as the limitations of the South African model, it is hard to avoid the conclusion that their ideal truth commission would look quite different. In particular, it would resist demands for convergence around one particular rendering of a repressive history, and—in the name of inclusion and respect—also resist a discourse of reconciliation that emphasized public calls for forgiveness or aimed to produce psychological or spiritual redemption. In the context of such a commission, benevolent acts of forgiveness would be considered "supererogatory" and thus officially unexpected (42). "Reconciliation" would be refigured as a somewhat more mundane—as opposed to transcendent or transformational—task. It would be a matter not of absolution or admiration, but of "civic acknowledgment" and "recognition" (39). Thus, although critical of certain prominent renderings of reconciliation, Gutmann and Thompson do not reject the discourse outright, but rather seek to re-articulate it to fit their own democratic aims and liberal dispositions.

Reconciliation as an Ideological Accessory

Yet another perspective on reconciliation has been put forward by anthropologist Richard Wilson. "The most damaging outcome of truth commissions," writes Wilson, "is a result of their equating human rights with reconciliation and amnesty."[71] Wilson's *The Politics of Truth and Reconciliation in South Africa: Legitimizing the Post-Apartheid State* is one of the most systematically critical accounts of the TRC to emerge in the last few years, and—in the frenzy of current writing on truth commissions—perhaps one of the most overlooked. His critique of truth commissions, and specifically his vigorous critique of South Africa's TRC, shares with others an aversion to both the religious dimensions and the amnesty provisions of the TRC.[72]

Yet Wilson's work also adds another dimension to critical perspectives on the TRC, reading the commission's linking of "human rights" and "reconciliation" as part of "an elite project of nation-building" (230) that sought to "manufacture legitimacy"—not altogether successfully—for the new, post-apartheid South African state.[73] Conjoined with the language of human rights, reconciliation discourse represented "the discursive linchpin" of this project, and thus Wilson figures the TRC as "one effort on the part of the new government to formulate a moral leadership and to establish a unified and uncontested administrative authority" (128–29). The TRC's "weaving together of religion, liberation and reconciliation," he writes, "was central to the wider hegemonic project of the first post-apartheid regime" (131), a project for which "organized religion proved a reliable ideological accessory" (142). Thus, Wilson brings a critical sociological perspective to the liberal project of theorizing democratic transitions, with South Africa's TRC as his key empirical site.[74]

Relying on his own anthropological fieldwork, Wilson seeks to raise "a serious question mark over the TRC's motto of 'Reconciliation Through Truth'" (173). With this rhetoric of reconciliation in sight—he refers to TRC's "saccharin-coated invocations of reconciliation" (160)—Wilson's fieldwork focused on practices of vengeance, revenge, and retribution in the townships of the Vaal region to the south of Johannesburg. Locating a yawning gap between the TRC's rhetoric and the realities of South African popular justice, he hammers away at "the contradiction between national human rights talk about reconciliation and what happens in townships where there is no retributive justice, only unhindered revenge in a context of impunity" (182).[75]

From Wilson's perspective, truth commissions are best served when they stick mainly to historical recovery and truth telling. What truth commissions can "achieve well," he writes, "if carefully designed, is a sophisticated historical account of a violent past which integrates a structural analysis with the consciousness of those who lived through it" (228). He holds up the Guatemalan commission as a virtuous example, to be contrasted with South Africa's TRC (225–26), whose scripted "religious-redemptive" approach to truth and reconciliation set it apart from others. "More than any other truth commission before it," writes Wilson, "the TRC sought reconciliation as a basis of nation-building" (121).[76]

While unveiling the technological tricks of the TRC's "truth making machine," therefore, Wilson reserves his perhaps most severe criticisms for the commission's invocations of reconciliation and forgiveness. Of Tutu's beloved concept of *ubuntu,* he writes: "*Ubuntu* should be recognized for what it is: an ideological concept with multiple meanings which conjoins human rights, restorative justice, reconciliation and nation-building within the populist language of pan-Africanism. In post-apartheid South Africa, it became the Africanist wrapping used to sell a reconciliatory version of human rights talk to black South Africans" (13). Indeed, reconciliation as ideological cover is a recurrent theme for Wilson. New political leaders in South Africa, he writes later, "wrap their complicity with the sophistry of reconciliation talk" (97). "Reconciliation," he continues, altering the metaphor only slightly, "was the Trojan horse used to smuggle an unpleasant past (that is, impunity) into the present political order, to transform political compromises into transcendental moral principles" (97). Reconciliation, in other words, hides the plain fact of amnesty for apartheid-era violators of human rights.

Conclusion: Profusion, Hybridity, Transformation

Having opened with a consideration of reconciliation discourse in South Africa, both prior to and during that nation's Truth and Reconciliation Commission, I have attempted to identify various ways in which reconciliation discourse has been revised and reworked in the period following South Africa's TRC, with a particular emphasis on its critique and reformulation by academic theorists. Celebrated and critiqued by influential global moral entrepreneurs, reconciliation discourse has increasingly become an integral element of debates over transitional justice and human rights. With a substantial and contentious theological history, reconciliation has recently been figured as a more narrowly circumscribed political tool or goal, a scientifically specifiable aim of public policy and an art employed by practitioners of political transition. Given its robust theological significations, it has also been rendered as a potentially illiberal aim and, from a different perspective, as an ideological accessory to post-conflict nation-building strategies.

As reconciliation is increasingly embedded in far-reaching projects of moral globalization, the tendency to conceive of it in specifically liberal terms—such that it might articulate more smoothly the dominant norms of "world culture"—seems to be on the rise.[77] Gibson's definition of reconciliation, put forward in *Overcoming Apartheid*, provides a good example. In specifying the meaning of reconciliation, Gibson suggests that it "refers to at least four specific and perhaps even independent sub-concepts": *inter-racial reconciliation*, "defined as the willingness of people of different races to trust each other, to reject stereotypes about those of other races, and generally to get along with each other"; *political tolerance*, "the commitment of people to put up with each other, even those whose political ideas they thoroughly detest"; *support for* the principles (abstract and applied) of *human rights*, "including the strict application of the rule of law and commitment to legal universalism"; *legitimacy*, in particular the predisposition to recognize and accept "the authority of the major political institutions of the New South Africa." While this list may not exhaust the meanings of reconciliation, claims Gibson, these "particular dimensions" are "central to the concept." Thus, "a reconciled South African is one who respects and trusts those of other races, who is tolerant of those with different political views, who supports the extension of human rights to all South Africans, and who extends legitimacy and respect to the major governing institutions of South Africa's democracy." As opposed to the views of many South Africans—who, as the Institute for Justice and Reconciliation's *Reconciliation Barometer* indicates, continue to associate reconciliation with forgiveness—Gibson's is a thoroughly liberal and secular conception of reconciliation. It is also strikingly individualist, referring not to *processes* of reconciliation or even the reconciliation of *relationships*, but rather to potentially "reconciled" *individuals*.[78]

With the global proliferation of reconciliation and the expansion of its academic analysis, then, has come an impulse to distance the political theology of reconciliation from its religious roots. This is not an entirely novel phenomenon, as there were certainly both liberal and secular attempts to formulate conceptions of reconciliation prior to South Africa's TRC. But it is a dynamic that has taken a new shape subsequent to the TRC, as attempts to forward compelling "world definitions" of reconciliation have taken on new urgency and prominence, and as reconciliation has become an increasingly cosmopolitan form of discourse. Theological formulations of reconciliation, such as those frequently associated with the TRC, occupy an uneasy place within the cosmopolitan imaginary. Demands of forgiveness frequently offend the secular sensibilities of many academics and human rights activists—or so the proponents of reconciliation and forgiveness have suggested. Thus are the comprehensive moral goals associated with this robust conception of reconciliation characterized by Gutmann and Thompson as potentially "illiberal" aims. In this context, there has been an effort to shift—some theologians would say to distort or diminish—reconciliation discourse, in an effort to make it fit more consistently with the dominant (secular, liberal, cosmopolitan) presuppositions of a nascent transnational public sphere and, more specifically, an emergent field of transitional justice. In the wake of South Africa's TRC, conceptions of reconciliation have shifted from "thick" to "thin"—from robust, theological, and collectivist to narrow, secular, and individualist. What remains to be seen is to what extent these latter conceptions of reconciliation will hold sway in the national contexts in which new truth commissions and other processes aimed at promoting reconciliation are currently cropping up. As theories of "reconciliation" continue to challenge, and are adapted to suit, the dominant presuppositions of international justice and global political culture, how powerful will that "culture" prove to be? Put differently, will discourses of reconciliation—and the practices and institutions to which they are attached, or in which they are embedded—succeed in partially reshaping the face of cosmopolitan liberalism, or will cosmopolitan liberalism effectively reshape these discourses and practices in its own image?

Adopting the language of sociology's new institutionalism, we may ask: to what extent do the norms of world culture have the power to produce "isomorphism" in this field? What is striking about the transnational proliferation of "reconciliation," as a world-cultural phenomenon, is the extent to which it seems to reverse the spatial directionality sometimes implied by the most prominent theorists of "world culture." Recall the statement from John Meyer and his colleagues: "The contemporary world is rife with modeling. The poor and weak and peripheral copy the rich and strong and central."[79] Without oversimplifying, the recent history of "reconciliation" presents a distinct counterexample to this claim.

Thus, an assessment of the recent historical trajectory of "reconciliation" upsets commonly held perceptions regarding the standard origins of transnational institutional models. As in the short statement above from Meyer et al., such models are not infrequently held to emanate from global centers of power, subsequently being taken up and emulated by those at the margins. Yet institutions devoted to truth and reconciliation, and their attendant discourses, have largely sprung up outside these centers. In the realm of "reconciliation," invention and innovation have developed at the periphery and the semi-periphery of the contemporary world system. Rather than being produced through an attempted mimicry of the powerful, political technologies of truth and reconciliation have arisen and circulated extensively in the Global South, being taken more seriously by intellectuals and organizations in the North only after their adoption and adaptation in Latin America and Africa. In the context of truth commissions and transitional justice, the trajectory of "reconciliation" demonstrates that students of philanthropic organizations in the United States need to attend not only to the sending of institutional logics abroad, but also to the potentially transnational sources of those logics, and to the manner in which institutional borrowing occurs on a sometimes crowded two-way street.

If one conclusion to be drawn from attention to the transnational circulation of reconciliation discourse lies in this historical trajectory, a second is connected to reconciliation's contested meanings and multi-vocal character and to the struggle to define and delimit its scope and substance, especially as it has risen to global prominence. Given the emergent and interstitial nature of the field of transitional justice, in which logics and discourses of reconciliation have developed, we can most appropriately refer to both a proliferation and a *profusion* of hybrid discourses of reconciliation. In the hands of the prominent theorists and practitioners of reconciliation who have been its worldwide promoters and critics, the discourse has been altered and adapted to suit various political values, institutional purposes, and academic perspectives. Human rights activists, critical intellectuals, moral philosophers, political theorists, theologians, and NGO specialists—these are the agents who have attempted to shape and reshape, to transmit and transform, the cosmopolitan renderings of reconciliation that have animated international debate. All too frequently their own participation in constituting the field of transitional justice is overlooked, as transitions and truth commissions in the Global South are taken to represent the true sites of political urgency and the essential objects of academic analysis. Yet the analysts and transnational activists themselves have also contributed substantially to reconciliation's rise to global prominence. In doing so they have not only served to refine the theory and practice of reconciliation associated with truth commissions and other forms of transitional justice; they have also contributed to the crystallization of a distinctive and recognizable discursive formation, a constellation of competing discourses and overlapping practices within which reconciliation has been figured as both a goal and a process, a religious ideal and a political necessity, a moral prescription and a social scientific variable.

Attention to this aspect of the proliferation of reconciliation discourse highlights not only its reproduction in various specific locations, but also its hybridity, its multiple uses and formulations, and its contested transformations, as it travels from one context to another. The foregoing consideration of the differential appropriation of reconciliation discourse highlights the extent to which the transnational diffusion of reconciliation has involved both transmission and transformation, both reproduction and adaptation. In this light, "transnational diffusion" and "moral globalization" can be seen not simply as mimetic processes producing "startling homogeneity," but as processes involving "the production of identity and difference . . . homogenization and heterogenization."[80] A consideration of the proliferation of reconciliation discourses suggests that we ought to attend not only to the power and potentially isomorphism-producing character of "world definitions," but also to the discursive struggle over their meaning and use. As students of international exchanges within "global civil society,"[81] we have the task, therefore, to attend not only the diffusion of world-cultural forms and formulas, but also their contestation and significant transformation in various "local" contexts, and by specific actors and organizations. Sociological investigation of moral globalization and transnational activism, in other words, should be concerned not simply with "the struggle *for* global society,"[82] but with the struggle *over* and *within* the sphere that the concept of global civil society is intended to mark out.

Notes

1. Tutu (1999).

2. Minow (1998) takes the concept of *ubuntu* to mean "humanness, or an inclusive sense of community valuing everyone." The term itself has been much discussed. See, for example, Tutu (1999) and Bell (2002).

3. Krog (1998).

4. Sarkin and Daly (2004).

5. Sarkin and Daly (2004): 661.

6. Olick and Coughlin (2003).

7. Keck and Sikkink (1998).

8. Ignatieff (2001).

9. Brody (2001).

10. DiMaggio and Powell (1983, 148, 150).

11. Wallerstein (1974).

12. Meyer et al. (1997, 164).

13. Meyer (1980).

14. See for instance the programmatic statement in Meyer et al. (1997).

15. Tilly (1999).

16. Keck and Sikkink (1998); Khagram, Riker, and Sikkink (2002).

17. Evans (1999); DiMaggio and Powell (1983). Indeed, the concept of the "field," whose analytic utility is increasingly recognized in sociology, provides the material for a critical adaptation and extension of the world-cultural research program. I consider the project of field analysis below. On the concept of "field," see Bourdieu (1977); Bourdieu and Wacquant (1992); Dobbin (1994); Fligstein (2001).

18. Meyer et al. (1997); see also Boli and Thomas (1999).

19. Boli and Thomas (1999).

20. Tepperman (2002).

21. Wilson (2001).

22. *The SA Reconciliation Barometer* 1, no. 1 (April 2003).

23. Barth (1961).

24. Gallagher (2002, 44). Gallagher's invocation of "confession" is meant to extend not simply to the sorts of confessions made in front of the TRC, but rather to a "confessional mode" that includes, in this context, theological statements and declarations.

25. *The Kairos Document.*

26. Gobodo-Madikizela (2003, 53).

27. Allan Boesak, as cited in Borer (1998, 91).

28. Borer (1998, 91).

29. For an extensive discussion of this "spiral of involvement," and of the theological developments that accompanied it, see ibid.

30. For details, see ibid.

31. Ibid., 98–99.

32. Ibid., 108.

33. The TRC report would borrow this notion of "state theology" in its consideration of the role of "faith communities as agents of oppression." See *Truth and Reconciliation Commission of South Africa Report* (*TRC Report*) 1998, 4:69.

34. Borer (1998, 109).

35. See *The Kairos Document.* KAIROS may be considered a "time of opportunity," and the authors of the *Kairos Document* figured Prophetic Theology as a theology that "would include a reading of the signs of the times" (Brown 1990, 49). For a discussion of "Kairos," see Brown (1990, 1–14). On the *Kairos Document,* see also Borer (1998) (esp. 108–10), Doxtader (2001a), and Gallagher (2002).

36. "Reconciliation" undoubtedly has deeper roots in South Africa. I have not attempted to trace them here.

37. Bell (2002, 86).

38. Ginger Thompson, "South African Commission Ends Its Work," *New York Times,* March 22, 2003.

39. See Zalaquett's interview with N. Roht-Arriaza in Hesse and Post (1999); and the *TRC Report,* 1:125. Because of its dramatic public character, a brief reading of the TRC's report cannot exhaustively do justice to its working conception of reconciliation.

40. *TRC Report,* 1:106–10. The report also distinguished between four different notions of truth: factual or forensic truth; personal or narrative truth; social or "dialogue" truth; and healing and restorative truth. See ibid., 1:110–14.

41. Ibid., 1:115.

42. Ibid.

43. Ibid., 1:55.

44. Hayner (2000, 39–40).

45. Hayner (2001). For further discussion of these differences, see Hayner (2000). For more details on the South African commission, see Krog (1998); Minow (1998); Ross (1999); Boraine (2000); Villa-Vicencio and Verwoerd (2000).

46. *TRC Report,* 1:116.

47. Ibid., 5:371–82.

48. Ibid., 5:382–92.

49. Ibid., 1:117.

50. Ibid., 1:116. During a presentation at Berkeley, Pamela Reynolds reported that many of the South African youths she interviewed refused to take part in the TRC process, seeing themselves as activists and survivors rather than "victims." From yet another angle, in responding to those who recommended taking up a forgetful rendering of the past, the commissioners might just as well have been responding to sentiments similar to those voiced by TRC commissioner Wynand Malan. In his Minority Position (including in volume 5 of the TRC's report), Malan attempted to reframe the prerequisites of reconciliation this way: "If we can reframe our history to include both perpetrators and victims as victims of the ultimate perpetrator—namely, the conflict of the past, we will have fully achieved unity and reconciliation and an awareness of the real threat to our future—which is dogmatic or ideological division that polarises the nation instead of promoting genuine political activity." Ibid., 5:443.

51. Ibid., 1:1.

52. "The Latin American truth commissions heard testimony only in private, and information only emerged with the release of the final reports." Ibid., 1:54.

53. Tutu (1999). Colonel Schobesberger's testimony was reproduced in the report's section on "apologies and acknowledgements," which was part of the chapter on reconciliation in volume 5. *TRC Report,* 5:382.

54. Krog (1998, 202).

55. For the concepts and principles see *TRC Report,* vol. 1, chapter five. For *ubuntu* and restorative justice, see *TRC Report,* 1:125–31. On Tutu's *ubuntu* theology, see Battle (1997).

56. For examples of its international reception, see Minow 1998; Rotberg and Thompson (2000).

57. As quoted in Minow (1998, 55). For an account that emphasizes, alternatively, that "a day at the TRC does contain much religious symbolism and rhetoric," much of which "arises spontaneously from the victims," see Gallagher (2002, 118–19).

58. Steiner (1997).

59. Zalaquett emphasized the "sacramental value" of Chilean President Patricio Aylwin's public acknowledgement of the suffering and abuses documented in the Chilean TRC's report. Such acts, Zalaquett claims, "can become indelibly etched in the moral slate of the society and have a long-term effect." While artists and playwrights may also contribute to the important work of reconciliation, Zalaquett said in a 1995 interview,

"something has to be done in the civic temple itself. . . . And that's why President Aylwin's great intuition in presenting the Truth Commission's report publicly and personally was to give it a sacramental value. That intangible sacrament went farther to promote healing in Chile than practically anything else." See Zalaquett's Interview with N. Roht-Arriaza (206–207, 209) in Hesse and Post (1999).

60. Antjie Krog, "Embarrassed by Forgiveness," *Sunday Times,* February 29, 2004.

61. Ignatieff (2001).

62. For an extended discussion of global moral entrepreneurs, see Keck and Sikkink (1998).

63. Hayner (2001, 251).

64. Van Zyl Slabbert (2003, 321).

65. On the ways in which cosmopolitan elites often fail to recognize the social conditions of their own discourse, see Calhoun (2002) and (2003). On rooted cosmopolitans, see Tarrow (2005, chapter 3).

66. Villa-Vicencio (2003).

67. Gibson (2002).

68. See Erin Daly, "Reconciliation in Iraq."

69. Doxtader (2001b).

70. See Gutmann and Thompson (2000). Unless otherwise noted, all citations here are to this text.

71. See Wilson (2001, 228). Unless otherwise noted, all citations here are to this text.

72. In South Africa, critiques of reconciliation were regularly tied to the issue of amnesty. "They think justice is of less value than their reconciliation showbiz and avalanche of tears," said Lybon Mabaso, AZAPO Gauteng chair, at a 1997 Johannesburg news conference about the TRC (cited in Wilson, 167). AZAPO, a political party, was one of the TRC's chief critics, pressing the case made against the TRC's amnesty provisions by the families of Steve Biko and Griffiths Mxenge.

73. "The TRC's actual ability to generate legitimacy was questionable," writes Wilson (29). In any case, he clearly sees the TRC's approach as mistaken: "In an international context where the jurisdiction of human rights institutions is intensifying and broadening, it is misguided to delegitimize human rights at the national level by detaching them from a retributive understanding of justice and attaching them to a religious notion of reconciliation-forgiveness, a regrettable amnesty law and an elite project of nation-building" (230). Thus, behind Wilson's critique of the TRC is an incipient and ultimately democratic—if not necessarily "liberal"—program for human rights in political transition: "Turning human rights talk into a moral-theological treatise which extols forgiveness and reconciliation in an effort to forge a new moral vision of the nation in the end destroys the most important promise of human rights; that is, its possible contribution to a thoroughgoing transformation of an authoritarian criminal justice system and the construction of real and lasting democratic legitimacy" (230).

74. "The study of transitional truth and justice has been too dominated by philosophical discussions abstracted from specific contexts, and we should instead examine how the politics of punishment and the writing of a new official memory are central to

state strategies to create a new hegemony in the area of justice and construct the present moment as post-authoritarian when it includes many elements of the past" (xvi).

75. In another of Wilson's formulations, "contra the established view within the Truth and Reconciliation Commission, retributive understandings of justice are much more salient in South African society than versions emphasizing reconciliation as forgiveness" (27). Further, "the TRC's version of human rights as reconciliation did little to challenge the prevalence of revenge in the townships because it could not meaningfully engage with a punitive view of justice" (161).

76. See Hayner (2000) for a similar judgment regarding the unique strength—when compared with previous truth commissions—of the South African TRC's emphasis on "reconciliation."

77. On "world culture," see especially Meyer et al. 1997 and Boli and Thomas (1999).

78. Gibson (2003).

79. See Meyer et al. (1997).

80. Hardt and Negri (2000).

81. References to "global civil society" have grown dramatically in recent years, driven in part by scholarship on the topic. See, for example, Walzer (1995), Salamon et al. (1999), and the Global Civil Society yearbook produced by the Centre for the Study of Global Governance.

82. My emphasis. See Smith (2005).

References

Asmal, Kader, Louise Asmal, and Ronald Suresh Roberts. 1997. *Reconciliation through Truth: A Reckoning of Apartheid's Criminal Governance.* New York: St. Martin's Press.

Barth, Karl. 1961. *Church Dogmatics: The Doctrine of Reconciliation.* Edinburgh: T&T Clark.

Battle, Michael. 1997. *Reconciliation: The Ubuntu Theology of Desmond Tutu.* Cleveland, Ohio: Pilgrim Press.

Bell, Richard H. 2002. *Understanding African Philosophy: A Cross-Cultural Approach to Classical and Contemporary Issues.* New York: Routledge.

Boli, John and George M. Thomas. 1999. "INGOs and the Organization of World Culture." In *Constructing World Culture: International Nongovernmental Organizations since 1875,* ed. John Boli and George M. Thomas. Stanford, Calif.: Stanford University Press.

Boraine, Alex. 2000. *A Country Unmasked: Inside South Africa's Truth and Reconciliation Commission.* New York: Oxford University Press.

Boraine, Alex, and Janet Levy, eds. 1995. *The Healing of a Nation?* Cape Town: Justice in Transition.

Boraine, Alex, Janet Levy, and Ronel Scheffer. 1994. *Dealing with the Past: Truth and Reconciliation in South Africa.* Cape Town: IDASA.

Borer, Tristan. 1998. *Challenging the State: Churches as Political Actors in South Africa, 1980–1994.* Notre Dame, Ind.: University of Notre Dame Press.

Bourdieu, Pierre. 1977. *Outline of a Theory of Practice.* Cambridge: Cambridge University Press.

———. 1991. *Language and Symbolic Power.* Cambridge, Mass.: Harvard University Press.

Bourdieu, Pierre, and Loïc J. D. Wacquant. 1992. *An Invitation to Reflexive Sociology.* Chicago: University of Chicago Press.

Brody, Reed. 2001. "Justice: The First Casualty of Truth?" *Nation,* April 30.

Brown, Robert McAfee, ed. 1990. *Kairos: Three Prophetic Challenges to the Church.* Grand Rapids, Mich.: Eerdmans Publishing.

Burawoy, Michael. 2000. "Grounding Globalization." In *Global Ethnography,* ed. Burawoy et al. Berkeley and Los Angeles: University of California Press.

Calhoun, Craig, ed. 1992. *Habermas and the Public Sphere.* Cambridge, Mass.: MIT Press.

———. 2002. "The Class Consciousness of Frequent Travelers: Toward a Critique of Actually Existing Cosmopolitanism." *South Atlantic Quarterly* 101: 869–97.

———. 2003. "Belonging in the Cosmopolitan Imaginary." Unpublished paper.

Cassel, Douglas W., Jr. 1993. "International Truth Commissions and Justice." *Aspen Institute Quarterly* 5: 77–90.

Clemens, Elisabeth S. 2002. "Invention, Innovation, Proliferation: Explaining Organizational Genesis and Change." *Research in the Sociology of Organization* 19: 397–411.

Clemens, Elisabeth S., and James A. Cook. 1999. "Politics and Institutionalism: Explaining Durability and Change." *Annual Review of Sociology* 25: 441–66.

Cochrane, James, John de Gruchy, and Stephen Martin. 1999. *Facing the Truth: South African Faith Communities and the Truth and Reconciliation Commission.* Athens: Ohio University Press.

Correa, Jorge. 1992. "Dealing with Past Human Rights Violations: The Chilean Case after Dictatorship." *Notre Dame Law Review* 67: 1455–85.

Daly, Erin. "Reconciliation in Iraq." Unpublished paper.

DiMaggio, Paul J., and Helmut K. Anheier. 1990. "The Sociology of Nonprofit Organizations and Sectors." *Annual Review of Sociology* 16: 137–59.

DiMaggio, Paul J., and Walter W. Powell. 1983. "The Iron Cage Revisited: Institutional Isomorphism and Collective Rationality in Organizational Fields." *American Sociological Review* 48: 147–60.

Dobbin, Frank. 1994. *Forging Industrial Policy: The United States, Britain, and France in the Railway Age.* New York: Cambridge University Press.

Doxtader, Erik. 2001a. "In the Name of Reconciliation: The Faith and Works of Counterpublicity." In *Counterpublics and the State,* ed. Robert Asen and Daniel C. Brouwer. Albany: State University of New York Press.

———. 2001b. "Making History in a Time of Transition: The Rhetorical Occasion, Constitution, and Representation of South African Reconciliation." *Rhetoric and Public Affairs* 4: 223–60.

Doxtader, Erik, and Charles Villa-Vicencio. 2003. *Through Fire with Water: Violence, Transition, and the Potential for Reconciliation in Africa.* Cape Town: David Philip.

Ensalaco, Mark. 1994. "Truth Commissions for Chile and El Salvador: A Report and Assessment." *Human Rights Quarterly* 16: 656–75.

Evans, Peter. 1999. "Counter-Hegemonic Globalization: Transnational Networks as Political Tools for Fighting Marginalization." In *Producing Public Sociology,* ed. Michael Burawoy and Jonathan VanAntwerpen. Available at: http://sociology .berkeley.edu/public_sociology_pdf/evans.pdf (accessed November 3, 2008).

Fligstein, Neil. 2001. "Social Skill and the Theory of Fields." *Sociological Theory* 19: 105–25.

———. Forthcoming. "Organizations: Theoretical Debates and the Scope of Organizational Theory." In *Handbook of Sociology,* ed. Craig Calhoun, et al. Thousand Oaks, Calif.: Sage Press.

Fligstein, Neil, and Doug McAdam. 2003. *Politics, Culture, and Action: An Essay on Collective Strategic Action.* Unpublished manuscript.

Foucault, Michel. 1988. "The Political Technology of Individuals." In *Technologies of the Self: A Seminar with Michel Foucault,* ed. Luther H. Martin, Huck Gutman, and Patrick H. Hutton. Amherst: University of Massachusetts Press.

Gallagher, Susan VanZanten. 2002. *Truth and Reconciliation: The Confessional Mode in South African Literature.* Portsmouth, N.H.: Heinemann.

Gibson, James L. 2003. *Overcoming Apartheid: Can Truth Reconcile a Divided Nation?* Cape Town: Institute for Justice and Reconciliation.

Gobodo-Madikizela, Pumla. 2003. *A Human Being Died That Night: A South African Story of Forgiveness.* Boston: Houghton Mifflin.

Grewal, Inderpal, and Caren Kaplan, eds. 1994. *Scattered Hegemonies: Postmodernity and Transnational Feminist Practices.* Minneapolis: University of Minnesota Press.

Guidry, John A., Michael D. Kennedy, and Mayer N. Zald, eds. 2000. *Globalizations and Social Movements: Culture, Power, and the Transnational Public Sphere.* Ann Arbor: University of Michigan Press.

Gutmann, Amy, and Dennis Thompson. 2000. "The Moral Foundations of Truth Commissions." In *Truth v. Justice: The Morality of Truth Commissions,* ed. Robert I. Rotberg and Dennis Thompson. Princeton, N.J.: Princeton University Press.

Habermas, Jürgen. 1989. *The Structural Transformation of the Public Sphere.* Cambridge, Mass.: MIT Press.

Hardt, Michael, and Antonio Negri. 2000. *Empire.* New York: Cambridge University Press.

Hayner, Priscilla. 1994. "Fifteen Truth Commissions, 1974–1994: A Comparative Study." *Human Rights Quarterly* 16: 597–655.

———. 2000. "Same Species, Different Animal: How South Africa Compares to Truth Commissions Worldwide." In *Looking Back, Reaching Forward: Reflections on the Truth and Reconciliation Commission of South Africa,* ed. Charles Villa-Vicencio and Wilhelm Verwoerd. Cape Town: University of Cape Town Press.

———. 2001. *Unspeakable Truths: Confronting State Terror and Atrocity: How Truth Commissions around the World Are Challenging the Past and Shaping the Future.* New York: Routledge.

Hesse, Carla, and Robert Post, eds. 1999. *Human Rights in Political Transitions: Gettysburg to Bosnia*. New York: Zone Books

Ignatieff, Michael. 2001. *Human Rights as Politics and Idolatry*. Princeton, N.J.: Princeton University Press.

Kairos Theologians. 1985. *Challenge to the Church: A Theological Comment on the Political Crisis in South Africa: The Kairos Document*. Braamfontein: Kairos Theologians.

Keck, Margaret E., and Kathryn Sikkink. 1998. *Activists beyond Borders: Advocacy Networks in International Politics*. Ithaca, N.Y.: Cornell University Press.

Khagram, Sanjeev, James Riker, and Kathryn Sikkink. 2002. *Restructuring World Politics: Transnational Social Movements, Networks, and Norms*. Minneapolis: University of Minnesota Press.

Kritz, Neil, ed. 1995. *Transitional Justice: How Emerging Democracies Reckon with Former Regimes*. 3 vols. Washington: U.S. Institute of Peace Press.

Krog, Antjie. 1998. *Country of My Skull: Guilt, Sorrow, and the Limits of Forgiveness in the New South Africa*. Johannesburg: Random House.

Leebaw, Bronwyn. 2002. *Judging the Past: Truth, Justice, and Reconciliation from Nuremberg to South Africa*. Ph.D. diss., Department of Political Science, University of California, Berkeley.

McAdams, A. James, ed. 1997. *Transitional Justice and the Rule of Law in New Democracies*. Notre Dame, Ind.: University of Notre Dame Press.

Meyer, John W. 1980. "The World Polity and the Authority of the Nation-State." In *Studies of the Modern World-System*, ed. Albert J. Bergesen. New York: Academic Press.

Meyer, John W., John Boli, George M. Thomas, and Francisco O. Ramirez. 1997. "World Society and the Nation-State." *American Journal of Sociology* 103: 144–81.

Minow, Martha. 1998. *Between Vengeance and Forgiveness: Facing History after Genocide and Mass Violence*. Boston: Beacon Press.

Neier, Aryeh. 1998. *War Crimes: Brutality, Genocide, Terror, and the Struggle for Justice*. New York: Times Books.

Olick, Jeffrey K., and Brenda Coughlin. 2003. "The Politics of Regret: Analytical Frames." In *Politics and the Past: On Reporting Historical Injustices*, ed. John Torpey. New York: Rowman and Littlefield.

Powell, Walter W., and Paul J. DiMaggio, eds. 1991. *The New Institutionalism in Organizational Analysis*. Chicago: University of Chicago Press.

Roht-Arriaza, Naomi, ed. 1995. *Impunity and Human Rights in International Law and Practice*. New York: Oxford University Press.

Ross, Amy J. 1999. "The Body of the Truth: Truth Commissions in Guatemala and South Africa." Ph.D. diss., Department of Geography, University of California, Berkeley.

Rotberg, Robert I., and Dennis Thompson, eds. 2000. *Truth v. Justice: The Morality of Truth Commissions*. Princeton, N.J.: Princeton University Press.

Salamon, Lester M., Helmut K. Anheier, Regina List, Stefan Toepler, S. Wojciech, and Associates. 1999. *Global Civil Society: Dimensions of the Nonprofit Sector*. Baltimore: Johns Hopkins Center for Civil Society Studies.

Sarkin, Jeremy, and Erin Daly. 2004. "Too Many Questions, Too Few Answers:

Reconciliation in Transitional Societies." *Columbia Human Rights Law Review* 35: 661–728.

Sewell, William. 1996. "Historical Events as Transformations of Structures: Inventing Revolution at the Bastille." *Theory and Society* 25: 841–81.

Sieff, Michelle. 2002. "Reconciling Order and Justice? Dealing with the Past in Post-Conflict States." Ph.D. diss., Department of Political Science, Columbia University.

Smith, Jackie. 2005. "Response to Wallerstein: The Struggle for Global Society in a World System." *Social Forces* 83: 1279–85.

Steiner, Henry J., ed. 1997. *Truth Commissions: A Comparative Assessment.* Cambridge: World Peace Foundation.

Tarrow, Sidney. 2005. *The New Transnational Activism.* New York: Cambridge University Press.

Tavuchis, Nicholas. 1991. *Mea Culpa: A Sociology of Apology and Reconciliation.* Stanford, Calif.: Stanford University Press.

Tepperman, Jonathan. 2002. "Truth and Consequences." *Foreign Affairs* 81: 128–45.

Tilly, Charles. 1999. "Epilogue: Where Now?" In *State/Culture: State-Formation after the Cultural Turn,* ed. George Steinmetz. Ithaca: Cornell University Press.

Truth and Reconciliation Commission of South Africa Report. 1998. Cape Town: Juta.

Tutu, Desmond. 1999. *No Future without Forgiveness.* New York: Doubleday.

Van Syl Slabbert, Frederik. 2003. "Truth without Reconciliation, Reconciliation without Truth." In *The Provocations of Amnesty: Memory, Justice and Impunity,* ed. Charles Villa-Vicencio and Erik Doxtader. Cape Town: David Philip.

Villa-Vicencio, Charles. 2003. "The Politics of Reconciliation." Unpublished paper.

Villa-Vicencio, Charles, and Erik Doxtader, eds. 2003. *The Provocations of Amnesty: Memory, Justice and Impunity.* Cape Town: David Philip.

Villa-Vicencio, Charles, and Wilhelm Verwoerd, eds. 2000. *Looking Back, Reaching Forward: Reflections on the Truth and Reconciliation Commission of South Africa.* Cape Town: University of Cape Town Press.

Wallerstein, Immanuel. 1974. *The Modern World-System I: Capitalist Agriculture and the Origins of the European World-Economy in the Sixteenth Century.* New York: Academic Press.

Walzer, Michael, ed. 1995. *Toward a Global Civil Society.* Oxford: Berghahn Books.

Weschler, Lawrence. 1990. *A Miracle, A Universe: Settling Accounts with Torturers.* New York: Penguin Books.

Wilson, Richard A. 2001. *The Politics of Truth and Reconciliation in South Africa: Legitimizing the Post-Apartheid State.* Cambridge: Cambridge University Press.

Zalaquett, José. 1992. "Balancing Ethical Imperatives and Political Constraints: The Dilemma of New Democracies Confronting Past Human Rights Violations." *Hastings Law Journal* 43: 1425–38.

PART 3.
Contesting Logics

6. Philanthropic Foundations in Russia

Western Projection and Local Legitimacy

←————————————————————————————————————→

JOHN W. SLOCUM

If foundations are, first and foremost, part of the nonprofit sector (Prewitt 1999), how do philanthropic foundations come into existence and gain legitimacy in societies that, until relatively recently, had no *for*-profit sector? For nearly the entirety of its seventy-four-year existence, there were essentially no formal, non-state institutions devoted to charitable giving in the Soviet Union. Yet Russia now stands out among other former communist countries for the size and variety of its non-profit sector and for the number of firms and wealthy individuals that are turning their attention to philanthropy. Pre-1917 antecedents notwithstanding, both the foundation as an organizational form and philanthropy as an institutional field are both new to Russia. The existence of a philanthropic sector in Russia appears to support the institutionalist thesis of increasing global convergence around a relatively limited repertoire of organizational forms—an institutional isomorphism tempered by the specific influences of local environments (DiMaggio and Powell 1991; Meyer 1999).

In the present essay, I examine the emergence of philanthropic foundations in post-Soviet Russia with a view to addressing two questions: first, the extent to which their presence can be attributed to the intentional transnational activities of various Western actors, and second, the sources and strength of foundation legitimacy within the Russian context.[1] In the language of this volume, the first question is whether and to what extent the emergence of philanthropic foundations as an organizational form in Russia is a product of the active international projection—as opposed to passive diffusion—of specific institutional logics.[2] The legitimacy question leads to a consideration of the roles of Russia's homegrown foundations.

Foundations are a part of civil society. Most analysis to date of the development of post-Soviet civil society has focused on nongovernmental organizations (NGOs)—understood as entities that must themselves raise money to support their activities. Much of this literature has examined the extent to which Western donors, public and private, have concentrated their grantmaking almost exclusively on NGOs, resulting in the creation of an NGO sector that is overly dependent on Western funding, and whose priorities are poorly aligned with those of Russian society (see Aksartova, this volume). In writings on Russian civil society, very little attention has been paid to the emergence of local ("indigenous") philanthropic institutions—philanthropy *in* Russia, as opposed to philanthropy directed *toward* Russia.

As of late 2007 there are at least seventy-five private, corporate, and community foundations in Russia. Although the first of Russia's true foundations were established as recently as 1999, their cumulative giving already approaches or exceeds that of private Western donors active in Russia.[3] Western donors have played an important, but limited, role in this process. The specific forms and operating practices of Russian foundations have developed in part through philanthropic projection, the latter defined as "the effort to spread ideas and practices by means of the donation of money, goods, human effort, and ideas" (Heydemann and Hammack, this volume). But their emergence also owes a great deal to the diffusion to Russia of the idea, now prevalent in market-oriented polities, that private actors can and should play a role in the provision of certain classes of public goods. The rise of foundations in Russia is, in this sense, a marker of the spread of the institutions of contemporary capitalism into the former Soviet Union.

Foreign entities—private foundations in particular—helped import the foundation as an institutional form, but the Russian sociopolitical context has been a deciding factor influencing foundations' legitimacy and the roles they play in Russian society. The legitimacy of foundations is ultimately tied to the legitimacy of market mechanisms and private property in Russia; the relatively modest set of roles taken up by Russian foundations—certainly more circumscribed than those of their counterparts in the United States—reflects the post-Soviet evolution of state-society relations.

During the presidency of Vladimir Putin, much was made of trends toward re-consolidation of political and economic power in Russia, the installation of sitting cabinet ministers on the boards of major corporations, and the regime's efforts to control and co-opt civil society. At the same time, the Putin years also saw the emergence and growth of Russia's foundation sector, a process that in part reflects the co-optation of Russia's economic elite by a regime intent on spreading the wealth of Russia's so-called oligarchs, while preventing them from developing independent power bases. Yet the current trajectory of Russian law and practice nonetheless suggests that Russian foundations are becoming more legitimate, and, with time, may become increasingly more significant civil society actors, contributing to institutional pluralism within Russia.

The Emergence of Philanthropic Foundations in Russia

As organizations, philanthropic foundations form a tiny proportion of Russia's noncommercial sector. In 2006, Charities Aid Foundation reported that Russia had more than 600,000 registered noncommercial organizations. The majority of these—about 60 percent—are institutions (*uchrezhdeniia*), a category encompassing a range of nongovernmental cultural and social establishments. Another 35 percent (or 210,000) are social and religious organizations of various types, and foundations (*fondy*) make up about 4.2 percent, or just over 25,000 (Yezhov 2006a).[4] The same study suggests that of 600,000 noncommercial organizations existing on paper, perhaps 70,000 have an active existence. Applying this coefficient to the category of foundations leads to an estimate of perhaps 2,000 to 3,000 active *fondy* throughout Russia.

Most of the comparative literature emphasizes control over one's own funds as a defining characteristic of foundations.[5] Only a relative handful of Russian *fondy* have their own assets and thus meet this analytical definition of a "true" philanthropic foundation. According to this criterion, there are about thirty private foundations in Russia, at least twenty corporate foundations, and no fewer than twenty-five community foundations.[6]

Foundations are a new institutional form in Russia—they could not have existed under the Soviet system. They have emerged quite recently—somewhat later than NGOs themselves—and in discrete waves: a false start beginning in the late 1980s, a burst of activity in 1999–2001, and another boom that became evident in 2006–2007.[7]

Prior to the Soviet regime, imperial Russia had a philanthropic tradition, with its roots in the charitable activities of the Orthodox Christian church, local social welfare agencies, and aristocratic and royal patronage.[8] The early years of the twentieth century saw a significant upsurge in private philanthropy in Russia by the rising commercial and professional elite, particularly in the form of patronage (*metsenatsvto*) of the arts and cultural institutions.[9] But if the development of foundations in many countries of Western Europe was interrupted by authoritarian rule in the 1930s and 1940s (Dogan 2006), the early evolution of Russia's foundation culture was even more definitively closed off by the 1917 revolution and the subsequent consolidation of the Soviet regime, which had no place for private wealth and philanthropy, nor for the larger practice of "bourgeois charity."

The first stirrings of the revival of philanthropy in the Soviet Union began after Mikhail Gorbachev became general secretary of the Communist Party in 1985. Gorbachev's policy of *glasnost'* (openness) led to public acknowledgement of various social and environmental problems. By the late 1980s, the gradual opening of new spaces for associational life allowed for the formation of new charitable societies. Although some of these explicitly harkened back to prerevolutionary forebears (Lindenmeyr 1998), they were formed in a radically different institutional and cultural context.

Olga Alexeeva begins her account of Russian philanthropy with the story of the *Detskii fond* (Children's Fund), which was established in 1987 as the first charitable organization to operate in Russia since the 1920s—followed by an increasing number of other new charitable organizations in the late 1980s and early 1990s (see also White 1993). In its rather short existence, *Detskii fond* collected private donations totaling more than 350 million rubles for the needs of children living in poverty, before coming to a troubled end in 1990 amid accusations of improprieties—a failure that, according to Alexeeva, set back the development of Russian philanthropy for another decade (Alexeeva 2008, 12–14).

The early 1990s were for Russia a period of thorough institutional collapse—on the macro level, with the disappearance of the leading role of the Communist Party, the dismantling of the planned economy, and the dissolution of the Soviet federal state, and on the micro level, as household savings were wiped out by price liberalization and socioeconomic life lost its previous predictability. Those "New Russians" who found ways of amassing wealth in those years became the driving force in seeking to revive prerevolutionary traditions of *metsenatsvo* (sponsorship, or patronage) in post-Soviet Russia, lavishing huge sums of money on art, rebuilding of Orthodox churches, and other forms of conspicuous giving (Gambrell 2004).[10] But the "regulatory and legislative void" of the early 1990s also saw widespread scandals, as the story of the *Detskii fond* was followed up by revelations that many other *fondy* were "covers or umbrellas for shady business activities, money laundering, [and] currency operations," causing the Russian public at large to associate philanthropic foundations with graft and corruption (ibid., 22).

The first true private foundations were established only at the end of the 1990s, following the initial accumulation of wealth by their founders, subsequent to the laws that clarified the legal category of *fondy*, and after the sobering experience of Russia's 1998 financial crisis. The first and most prominent of Russia's private foundations is the Vladimir Potanin Charitable Foundation, established in 1999 by Vladimir Potanin, the president and chairman of the board of the Interros holding company. The foundation's activities—grants and foundation-operated programs combined—now total about $10 million annually.[11] The Potanin Foundation's focus is education and culture; its signature activity is a highly regarded program of scholarships for outstanding university students. In the first six years of its existence, the foundation's Federal Scholarship Program has awarded 7,450 scholarships to students at state universities throughout Russia. Potanin also provides targeted scholarships for military academy cadets, funds internship programs in television production and international relations, and supports a well-regarded program encouraging innovative museum projects.[12]

Potanin—"Russia's Rockefeller" (Alexeeva 2008, 186)—and his foundation have been leading players in shaping this new sector. In 2000, the Potanin Foundation became the first Russian donor institution to join the Russian Donors' Forum—at that time an informal gathering of foreign grantmakers working in Russia—and became a founding member of the Donors' Forum once it gained formal institutional status (as a "noncommercial partnership") in early 2002. In late 2005, Potanin was appointed to the Public Chamber (*Obshestvennaya Palata*). This new governmental advisory body has been widely criticized as a vehicle for the Russian state's co-optation of civil society, but Potanin has made effective use of his position of chair of the Chamber's Commission on Philanthropy, Charity, and Volunteerism. In 2006–2007, he helped to develop and promote a new Russian Federal Law on Endowments, and his commission has cooperated with the Charities Aid Foundation and the Donors' Forum on other projects aimed at strengthening the philanthropic sector.

Potanin's philanthropic activities also have an international dimension—he is a major donor to the Guggenheim Museum, which in January 2002 announced his appointment to their board of trustees. When asked whether, with his billion-dollar net worth and active role in philanthropy, he considers himself Russia's Bill Gates, Vladimir Potanin gently suggested that his own philanthropic path was the more challenging one. Gates began his donor activities within an already mature field of philanthropy, whereas Potanin and other new Russian donors launched their work in an institutional and cultural context where philanthropy was poorly accommodated and little understood (Alexeeva 2008, 179).

Potanin was very soon joined by several other new foundations. Two in particular deserve attention—the Dynasty Foundation, established in 2001 by Dmitri Zimin, the founding president of Vympelcom, one of Russia's largest mobile phone operators, and Open Russia. Dynasty qualifies as Russia's first family foundation (Dmitri Zimin's son Boris chairs its board of directors). It supports scientific research and education, especially in theoretical physics, where Dmitri Zimin spent a long and distinguished scientific career before going into business in the 1990s. The Dynasty Foundation also funds projects aimed at the popularization of science, as well as various platforms for discussions of democracy, market reforms, and journalism. Like the Potanin Foundation, Dynasty is a member of the Donors' Forum; its annual budget has grown from a few hundred thousand dollars at the outset to $7 million in 2007.[13]

The story of Open Russia is the great cautionary tale of modern Russian philanthropy. Founded in 2001 by Mikhail Khodorkovsky and other shareholders of the Yukos oil company, Open Russia was explicitly modeled on George Soros's Open Society Institute (active in Russia since 1986). Of all the major Russian foundations, Open Russia was closest to its Western counterparts in terms of its thematic emphases: it funded human rights projects, civic education, independent public policy institutes and advocacy groups—alongside the more politically acceptable educational and cultural projects. A statement from Khodorkovsky on Open Russia's (now defunct) website shows the organization's activist stance: "Our organization strives to be not just a 'donor', but also an 'incubator' of civil initiatives that could contribute to the social and economic progress of the country."[14] Russian civil society activist and analyst Alexander Auzan suggests that the years 2002–2003 marked a peak for Russian civil society and philanthropy in terms of the openness and range of activities undertaken (Alexeeva 2008, 118), and at this time, Open Russia was Russia's most active foundation, awarding grants worth about $15 million annually.

This first flowering of Russian foundations was punctuated by the so-called Yukos affair.[15] Mikhail Khodorkovsky was viewed by the Kremlin not only as a business leader with an interest in philanthropy, but as an economic (and potentially, political) rival to the Putin regime. The Yukos affair began with the July 2003 arrest of leading Yukos shareholder Platon Lebedev, reached a climax in October of that year with Khodorkovsky's own arrest on fraud tax evasion charges, and culminated with Siberian prison sentences for Khodorkovsky and Lebedev and the bankruptcy and dismantlement of Yukos (once Russia's second-largest oil company). In March 2006, the Russian government froze the accounts of Open Russia, effectively forcing the foundation out of business. His foundation's support for controversial projects probably had much less to do with Khodorkovsky's fall than did his financial support for opposition politicians, but the message to other business leaders was clear: stay out of politics and avoid those sorts of philanthropic activity—funding for human rights, the rule of law, media freedoms, and the like—that could be construed as political.[16]

As an organizational form, the Russian private foundation has survived the closure of Open Russia, its most locally controversial avatar,[17] and Russia's foundation sector continues to thrive and expand.[18] A number of institutions which (together with foundations) compose the institutional field of philanthropy in Russia, have been formed over the first fifteen years of the post-Soviet period.[19]

The first regular periodical publication on philanthropy in the post-Soviet period was *Vestnik blagotvoritel'nosti* (Bulletin of Philanthropy), published from 1992 to 2001, and revived in 2005.[20] One of the co-founders of *Vestnik blagotvoritel'nosti* is the Agency for Social Information, a Russian nonprofit that provides technical support to NGOs and publishes analysis of the nonprofit and philanthropic sectors. The Moscow office of the London-based Charities Aid Foundation (CAF) opened in 1993; not a true foundation in the sense of being self-funded, CAF has played a critical role in promoting philanthropy in Russia. In 1994, CAF-Russia began publishing *Dengi i blagotvoritel'nost'* (Money and Charity), a monthly journal concentrating on issues of corporate philanthropy. Another key institution, the Moscow-based Donors' Forum, has already been mentioned and will be discussed in more detail below; while it was not officially registered until 2002, its beginnings date back to 1996. A Union of Charitable Organizations of Russia was established in 2000 with 237 members—mostly small humanitarian NGOs, half in Moscow and half in other Russian towns and cities—and an Internet journal on philanthropy— *Metsenat*—began operations in 2002. By the middle of the present decade, a sizable number of Russian academic researchers were working on issues of philanthropy, civil society, and the non-profit sector, and gathering in numerous conferences and seminars.[21] All these elements—journals, associations, conferences, along with increasingly high levels of corporate charitable activity, mark the coalescence of Russia's philanthropic field.

The years 2006 and 2007 saw the promulgation of a controversial new Russian law on NGOs (see Bourjaily 2006) and increasing pressure on civil society in advance of Russia's 2008 presidential election. Yet this same period has been marked by a significant series of measures that could further enhance the long-term prospects for Russia's philanthropic sector. President Putin declared 2006 the "Year of Philanthropy" in Russia, an initiative promoted by several leading philanthropic sector institutions. A number of new charitable campaigns were rolled out under the Year of Philanthropy rubric, as were numerous public lectures and media stories. In 2007, a handful of prominent museums and institutions of higher education (both public and private) set up the first charitable endowments under the new Law on Endowments.

At the time of writing, Russian foundations have yet to establish endowments under the new law—instead of funding grants out of the earnings from endowment capital, the donors behind Russia's private foundations have simply allocated funds to their foundation's activities on an annual basis. The promoters of Russian philanthropy hope that Russian foundations will soon set up endowments (Alexeeva 2008). Vladimir Potanin, for his part, counsels patience. In a March 2007 interview in the newspaper *Kommersant*, he explained his decision to become a founding trustee of the new endowment fund for the Moscow State Institute of International Relations (MGIMO) by noting the importance of establishing a working model for endowments; he also stated that the Potanin Foundation was in no hurry to set up its own fund (and had no urgent need to do so), but he expected most large Russian foundations to establish endowments within a few years (Ambinder 2007).[22]

Russian Foundations as Western Project and Projection

The Russian foundation field has been established in part through the activities of foreign philanthropic foundations. The first of the major private Western donors—George Soros's Open Society Institute—opened a Russia office as early as 1986. Several others set up shop following the end of the Soviet regime in late 1991: the MacArthur Foundation in 1992, the Howard Hughes Medical Institute in 1994, the Ford Foundation in 1996. Other U.S. foundations—the Carnegie Corporation of New York, the Charles Stewart Mott Foundation, and the Henry M. Jackson Foundation—have been active in Russia without opening field offices there.

As private donors, Western foundations in Russia share some attributes in common with public donors, including bilateral aid agencies (USAID, the Canadian International Development Agency, and their European analogues) and multilateral donors (such as UN agencies and the European Commission). To reduce a plethora of funding approaches to a set of basic similarities, both public and private donors active in Russia (and elsewhere in Eastern Europe) make a prominent emphasis of their support for civil society and funding for NGOs as agents for the development of civil society.[23] There are commonalities in the topics supported as well—both public and private Western donors have focused a great deal of attention on a favored set of themes, including democratization, human rights, ecology, women's rights, civil society development, and AIDS.[24]

In addition to supporting Russian NGOs, some private Western donors have also shown an interest in encouraging the development of local philanthropic foundations, and have launched specific projects toward this goal. This arguably represents an active projection of the institutional logics—organizational structures, norms, and operating procedures—associated with the private foundations in both the United States and Western Europe.[25] Russian foundations are beginning to resemble Western foundations in some key respects—the hiring of professional staff, the use of grant competitions and expert advisory bodies for distributing funds, a growing emphasis on norms of transparency, and the use of a standard repertoire of public relations practices (including the publication of glossy annual reports), all justified by similar rhetoric regarding the role of philanthropy in nourishing civil society.

Local actors—Russian foundations as well as individual Russian nationals working for foreign donors—have been active partners in this process. Perhaps the most visible and obvious institutional manifestation of cooperation between Russian and Western foundations has been the Russian Donors' Forum.[26] This organization was originally dominated by representatives of Western foundations, who needed to keep abreast of the changing legal and tax situations, share strategies and information on current and prospective grantees, and, to the extent possible, ensure that their efforts were complementary, rather than duplicative. But over time, more and more Russian donors have joined, including private, corporate, and community foundations, as well as re-granting agencies. Russian organizations now make up over half of the Forum's more than forty participants (including full and associated members and "partner institutions"), and the Forum's governing council has been headed since 2005 by a representative of a Russian donor (Elena Chernyshkova, executive director of the Dynasty Foundation).[27]

The Donors' Forum defines its mission as "to facilitate more effective grantmaking activities directed toward the development of democracy and civil society in Russia."[28] The Forum has become a useful mechanism for sharing information on grantmaking priorities and activities, promulgating common standards, monitoring legislation, and promoting tax and regulatory policy that would improve the conditions for the development of philanthropy in Russia. Supported by members' grants and dues, the Forum conducts research on these topics, hosts a grant managers' group, and has developed a code of ethics. The Donors' Forum sponsors lectures and publications, and holds a yearly competition for best annual reports.

The Forum constitutes an arena of mutual socialization between Western and Russian organizations. The diffusion of norms and procedures is reinforced by the circulation of personnel through Western and Russian donor agencies and NGOs. Russian nationals make up the overwhelming majority of the staff in the Moscow offices of Western foundations, where they work side-by-side with foreign nationals (and are in continuous phone, fax, and email contact with foundation headquarters abroad). When Western foundations post job openings for professional staff positions, they attract a growing pool of qualified Russian candidates that includes veterans of USAID-funded projects, staff of foundations and re-granting agencies such as IREX (the International Research and Exchanges Board), and Russian citizens with Western MBAs and experience in finance or international trade.

Alongside the Donors' Forum, a broader but more sporadic platform for interaction between staff of Russian and Western foundations is the Brussels-based European Foundation Centre (EFC), established in 1989, which is the leading professional association of grantmakers in Europe. Three Russian foundations—the Potanin Foundation, the New Eurasia Foundation, and the Victoria Children Foundation—have EFC membership. Many more Russian donor organizations participate in one particular EFC project, the Grantmakers East Forum (GEF), which offers a platform for interaction of local and international donors active through in Central and Eastern Europe and the former Soviet Union. Founded in 1992 as the Grantmakers East Group (the name change came in 2007), the GEF's main activity is an annual meeting, held in a different European city in October of each year beginning in 1996.[29] The GEG/GEF has done much to build a common vocabulary and agenda among both foreign and indigenous donors; topics covered at the annual meetings include building the capacity of indigenous grantmakers, partnering among donors, and project evaluation, among others.

These meetings are typically hosted by the local (country-specific) donors' forum. The October 2002 GEG meeting in Moscow was hosted by the Russian Donors' Forum; its closing plenary featured a talk by Mikhail Khodorkovsky (almost a year to the day prior to his arrest) and the late Bill Maynes, then president of the (U.S.-based) Eurasia Foundation.[30]

Apart from the GEF, where participation by representatives of Russian donors has increased significantly over the present decade, personnel from the Russian foundation sector have also begun to take part in other programs of the European Foundation Centre, including its Annual General Assembly and its Community Philanthropy Initiative. The Russia-based donor community also interacts with the global philanthropic community through WINGS (Worldwide Initiatives for Grantmaker Support), a global network of grant-making professionals.[31]

Community foundations represent one of the most clear-cut instances of international philanthropic projection in the Russian foundation sector. As a distinct institutional form characterized by multiple donors and an explicitly local funding mandate, community foundations were originally developed in the United States, and have since spread to the United Kingdom, Germany, and other countries. Community foundations were introduced to Russia by the Charles Stewart Mott Foundation and the Charities Aid Foundation in the mid-1990s.[32] With funding from Mott, CAF-Russia has carried out a series of projects that included the establishment of Russia's first community foundation in the industrial city of Togliatti in 1998, the replication of this model in a number of other localities, and the establishment in 2003 of a new professional association, the Partnership of Russian Community Foundations.[33] The Partnership has defined its mission as "the development of civil society through improving the quality of life of local communities on the basis of development and advancement of technologies of social stability"; its strategic priorities include "the creation of a favorable legislative basis for the activities of community foundations" and "advancing the idea of the community foundation on a national level."[34]

There are at least twenty-five community foundations in Russia. Although this is a small number in comparison with the United States (which has more than seven hundred community foundations), among European countries only Germany and the United Kingdom have more foundations of this type (European Foundation Centre 2004). Russia's sector is still of very modest size in financial terms. In 2006 the seventeen most active community foundations gave project support with a cumulative total of less than $1 million, and only a handful of these foundations have assets exceeding $100,000. But there is rapid growth, with eleven new community foundations established in 2006 alone.[35] For businesses, which make up over 80 percent of all funding, involvement with the activities of community foundations helps them "to gain community support and better relations with the authorities" (Sacks 2005, 119). Russian community foundations make grants across a range of social issues, usually through competitive tenders. The development of the field of community foundations in Russia continues to be supported by the activities of CAF-Russia, as financed by the Mott Foundation.

A final example of the active projection of foundations in Russia involves the so-called indigenization of Western foundations through the establishment of a local, Russian foundation as part of an exit strategy. The Open Society Institute (OSI) has long had an explicit strategy of seeding indigenous grantmaking organizations in its countries of involvement, of which the Stefan Batory Foundation in Warsaw is perhaps the most prominent example. Typically, these successor institutions receive continued but declining support from OSI, while governance, administration, and grantmaking priorities become increasingly autonomous and locally directed. For a variety of reasons, George Soros has chosen not to leave behind an OSI-Russia.

A prominent attempt to leave a successor foundation in Russia involved the formation, in 2003–2004, of the New Eurasia Foundation, a three-way partnership between the Eurasia Foundation, the Brussels-based Madariaga European Foundation (headed by Javier Solana), and the Dynasty Foundation. While the Eurasia Foundation continues its own grantmaking activities in Russia, the New Eurasia Foundation was formed as a vehicle for concentrating new resources on social, human capital, and regional development.[36]

Isomorphism and the Limits of Russian Foundation Legitimacy

Within the Russian foundation sector, the influence of Western philanthropy may be seen as a source of institutional isomorphism—a convergence of organizational behaviors and structures around established dominant forms (DiMaggio and Powell 1991). Such isomorphism can come about through coercive pressures, or through less coercive processes of imitation (mimetic processes). Aksartova (this volume) argues that the institutional development patterns of NGOs in the former Soviet Union result from coercive isomorphism. Many local NGOs (leading Russian human rights groups prominent among them) are structurally dependent on Western sources of funding, and such dependence tends to foster the "[d]irect imposition of standard operating procedures and legitimated rules and structures" (DiMaggio and Powell 1991, 68) characteristic of coercive isomorphism. In addition, Aksartova argues that foreign funding of NGOs in the former Soviet Union imposes a set of institutional logics (including the choice of thematic emphases and a lexicon lifted from the U.S. nonprofit sector) that has the effect of isolating the NGO sectors in post-Soviet countries from the societies around them (see also Sundstrom 2006; Sundstrom and Henry 2006).

But foreign efforts aimed at the development of local *foundations* is a rather different sort of philanthropic projection than foreign support for local NGOs. If foundations are defined as self-funded entities, it follows logically that Russian foundations (unlike Russian NGOs) cannot be financially dependent on Western financing.[37] The evident organizational convergence between Russian and Western foundations may have come about in part through the intentional efforts on the part of latter; but (in the language of institutionalist analysis) the resulting isomorphism is more mimetic than coercive. If Russian foundations have acquired the familiar terminological, grantmaking, and public relations apparatus of their U.S. counterparts, it may be that associating themselves with "state-of the-art" international models helps boost their legitimacy within an uncertain Russian context.[38] And the quest for legitimacy extends both ways—a Western foundation may feel that its activities in Russia can gain more local legitimacy if Russian donors (including both state agencies and private foundations) can be acquired as active partners.[39]

If foundations derive their legitimacy from the functions they perform in a given society (Heydemann and Toepler 2006), Russian foundations do seem to have achieved a certain level of legitimacy based on carrying out a circumscribed set of roles. This legitimacy remains tenuous—conditioned by the overwhelming dominance of the Russian state in setting the bounds of the permissible for Russian foundation activity, and by widespread and lingering societal expectations that the state *ought* to be the dominant player, even in the nongovernmental sector.

Comparative foundation research has begun to look cross-nationally at the roles taken on by foundations in the United States and Europe. Anheier and Daly (2006) analyze the experience of European foundations with respect to a menu of seven possible roles: complementing the state, serving as a substitute for the state, helping preserve traditions and cultures, serving as agents of redistribution, fostering social and policy change, promoting pluralism, and fostering innovation. In their support for educational scholarships, Russian foundations complement state provision of higher education. And Russian foundations do perceive the need for philanthropy to take on tasks that government is no longer able and willing to perform—that is, to play a role in substituting for the state (Bakhmin 2004). But in Russia, as in Western Europe, the big foundations are less likely than their U.S. counterparts to see themselves as catalysts of social and policy change, particularly if this means promoting specific policy innovations. And some specific types of NGOs—human rights groups—are off limits.[40]

Even the tasks of complementing and substituting for the state (the two roles become difficult to distinguish in practice when the state sector is shrinking) are fraught with additional layers of coercive potential in Russia. The widespread celebration of corporate social responsibility in Russia reflects both the influence of a trendy import from the Western corporate world, and a statement of the fact that large industrial firms, upon privatization, inherited the responsibility for providing a wide array of social welfare supports in the company towns that dot the Russian hinterland.[41] In the aftermath of the Yukos affair, President Putin's calls for corporate social responsibility carried a message tinged with implied threat: business *must* serve social interests.

Given all this, it is unsurprising that private Russian foundations are very reluctant to take on a visible role as agents of social change. The technical apparatus of foundations—their organizational and grantmaking mechanisms and means of presenting themselves to the public—have taken hold in Russia in a remarkably brief period of time, marking a successful diffusion of a Western organizational form. Yet the local legitimacy of Russian foundations is circumscribed by a sort of coercive isomorphism, enforced by the state, which keeps most foundations engaged in arts, culture, education, and such "safe" social and humanitarian issues as homeless children.

In addition to overt or implied political pressure, constraints on Russian foundations' roles and legitimacy also derive from ideational or cultural factors, from beliefs and attitudes of the Russian public and the meanings attributed to foundations by elites and the general public. The legitimacy of any organization (and in this case, of foundations) is a function of the rules, requirements, and "generalized belief systems" of its operating environment (Scott and Meyer 1991, 123); the same can be said for foundations as a specific organizational type (Toepler 1998).

Research undertaken by the Russian Donors' Forum suggests that the Russian public and governing elites believe that foundations and philanthropy ought to play a limited role, and one subordinate to the state. The public at large continues to feel that the most proper function of private donors is to provide charitable assistance to disadvantaged groups, and government officials believe that the appropriate function for these institutions to carry out is fulfilling social welfare obligations that the state is no longer capable of meeting. These officials are firm, however, in their conviction that donor choices must be made in consultation with the government (Donors' Forum 2005).

In acknowledging the legitimacy of at least some limited role for foundations, Russian state actors have opened a path to the consolidation of Russian foundations' legitimacy and a potential increase over time in the range of functions and roles they are willing to embrace. The Law on Endowments and additional legislative changes under consideration will likely create a more propitious regulatory environment. Discussions within the foundation sector have long questioned the boundaries of acceptable grantmaking topics.[42]

Moreover, a growing role for philanthropy may well be inherent in the institutional logic of the transition from Soviet-style socialism to a market-oriented economy. Kenneth Prewitt argues that in the United States the legitimacy of foundations is not fundamentally under question. U.S. foundations represent a way of directing private wealth to the public good without the coercive role of the state—thereby resolving a paradox of liberal society: the desire to provide public goods while keeping the state small (Prewitt 2006). In Western Europe, foundations began taking on larger roles in the 1990s as welfare states began to shrink (Gemelli 2006). The Russian trajectory over the same decade has been far more abrupt and discontinuous: the collapse of the Soviet state was followed within a few short years by the rise of great private fortunes.

By mid-decade the new Russian state thoroughly lacked the capacity to provide public goods at previous levels, while at the same time private actors had come into possession of great wealth. Russia's first private foundation was formed in 1999, in the brief interval between the 1998 financial crisis and the beginning of Vladimir Putin's presidency. During the Putin years, a government intent on reining in sources of autonomous authority began to discipline and tame Russia's philanthropists. But far from cutting off the flows of private funds, the Putin administration has chosen instead to encourage philanthropic initiative, while channeling it into politically acceptable uses.

Conclusion

If foundations have become a taken-for-granted component of liberal society (Prewitt 2006), Russia is at a midpoint in terms of foundation legitimacy. To the extent that there will be an undersupply of public goods in a market economy, there is a potential role for private philanthropy. To the extent that a functioning market economy relies on the stable rule of law, the rise of market capitalism in Russia is creating the necessary conditions for the emergence of private foundations.[43] The appearance within the Russian institutional milieu of the private philanthropic foundation as a specific organizational form owes much to processes of mimetic isomorphism stimulated by the presence in Russia of Western philanthropic institutions. The range of substantive topics taken up by private Russian foundations is limited by the coercive isomorphism imposed by a political system that is not yet genuinely democratic. But their mere presence in the Russian institutional landscape suggests the possibility that foundations may become increasingly autonomous and influential as Russian society grows more complex and the Russian political system eventually evolves in the direction of greater pluralism.

Notes

1. This article draws on the author's ten years of Russia-related grantmaking experience with the John D. and Catherine T. MacArthur Foundation. The analysis provided here is solely my own and does not reflect the position of the MacArthur Foundation. Special thanks to Rachel Weber for her generous editorial suggestions and conceptual guidance.

2. Stephen Heydemann and David C. Hammack (chapter 1, this volume) define institutional logics as "organizational arrangements for putting ideas into action and for sustaining patterns of social relationships."

3. Russian foundations spent the equivalent of $60 million in 2005, which is about the same as the combined annual giving of the largest private Western foundations active in Russia. This is dwarfed in turn by total corporate philanthropy (most of which is not channeled through foundations); in 2005, charitable giving by the 23 largest Russian firms totaled an estimated $1.5 billion (hundred million) (Yezhov 2006b).

4. The Russian word *fond* [sing.; *fondy* is the plural form] can be translated as either "fund" or "foundation." As a legal category, *fondy* are defined by the Federal Law on Public Associations (of 1995) and the Federal Law on Non-Profit Organizations (of 1996) as public associations (or non-profit organizations; the two are separate legal forms) without membership, and with activities directed toward socially beneficial goals (see Bourtseva 2002). A Russian *fond* is not necessarily an asset-based entity.

5. To date, most comparative literature on foundations has been based on the experiences of the United States, considered the originator of the modern philanthropic

foundation, and Europe, where foundations of one sort or another have existed for at least a thousand years. Foundation laws and traditions vary considerably across Europe and between Europe and the United States. A recent definition, intended to be applicable to both the United States and Europe, holds that a foundation is an asset-based, private, self-governing, and non-profit-distributing entity which serves a public purpose (Anheier and Daly 2006, 295). See also Anheier and Toepler (1999) for a range of comparative perspectives.

6. Email correspondence with Maria Chertok, director of Charities Aid Foundation–Russia, October 17, 2007. Although these Russian foundations have assets provided to them by their founders, the use of endowments to ensure long-term preservation of foundation assets was only recently made legally possible in Russian and is not yet a part of Russian foundation practice (see discussion below on the Law on Endowments, which came into force in January 2007).

7. Olga Alexeeva, who headed the Russia office of Charities Aid Foundation from 1997 to 2005, has written the most comprehensive account of Russian philanthropy to date (Alexeeva 2008); this section draws heavily on her work. I am also indebted to Natalya Kaminarskaya, who has served since 2000 as secretary of the Russia Donors' Forum, for her insights into the development of Russia's foundation sector, and to Tatiana Zhdanova, my longtime colleague and founding director of the Moscow Office of the MacArthur Foundation.

8. See Dinello (1998). Hinterhuber and Rindt (2004, 87–92) also provide a useful brief treatment of the prerevolutionary history of Russian philanthropy.

9. See Norman (1991) for a discussion of Pavel Tretiakov, the best known of the "merchant-patrons" (*kuptsy-metsenaty*) of the arts in late nineteenth-century Russia.

10. Relations between the Russian officialdom and the Russian Orthodox Church warmed considerably over the course of the decade, and newly wealthy Russians contributed heavily to prestige projects such as the rebuilding of the massive Cathedral of Christ the Savior in central Moscow. The cathedral's official website includes a page devoted to its fundraising foundation, which gathered contributions from a total of "56 thousand organizations and 3.5 million private citizens," a number of the most prominent of which are named on the website (http://www.xxc.ru/reconst/particip/ffp.htm, accessed December 10, 2007).

11. Interros has business interests ranging across mining, agriculture, media, and financial services, but its key asset is Norilsk Nickel, the world's leading producer of platinum and palladium. See http://www.interros.ru/eng/about/ (accessed December 12, 2007).

12. Basic information on the Potanin Foundation is available in English on the foundation's website, http://eng.fund.potanin.ru/ (accessed December 12, 2007).

13. See the Dynasty website, especially http://www.dynastyfdn.com/about (accessed December 12, 2007).

14. http://en.openrussia.info/about_en/strategy_en/, accessed in early 2005.

15. See Konończuk (2006) for a general analysis of the Yukos Affair. For a pro-Khodorkovsky timeline of the affair, see the website of the press center for the defense

attorneys of Khodorkovsky and Lebedev, at http://www.khodorkovsky.info/timeline/ (accessed December 12, 2007).

16. *Washington Post* Moscow correspondent Peter Finn makes this case in an article titled "In Russia, Cautious Generosity," wherein he quotes Irina Yasina, the former head of Open Russia: "The Khodordovsky case was a very clear signal to everyone to stop this kind of activity. . . . Our authorities believe that supporting civil society is opposition activity" (*Washington Post,* September 22, 2006).

17. An even more controversial, albeit "off-shore," Russian philanthropist is exiled oligarch Boris Berezovsky, who has provided funding for dozens of Russian human rights groups (as well as explicitly political opposition activities) through his New York–based International Foundation for Civil Liberties. For a critical account of Berezovsky, see Freedman (2007).

18. As of late 2007, dozens of new Russian corporate foundations are in the planning stage (Natalya Kaminarskaya, conversation with author, November 17, 2007).

19. According to DiMaggio and Powell (1991), an institutional field is characterized by an increasing density of interactions, cross-organizational structures and coalitions, the rapid expansion of information resources, and a growing sense of common purpose; all of these factors are present in Russia's foundation sector.

20. For an overview of media devoted to philanthropy in Russia, see Levshina (n.d.).

21. For a sense of the scale of this research community, see the Likhachev Foundation's extensive Russian-language online library, "Research on Russian Philanthropy and the Noncommercial Sector," at http://bb.lfond.spb.ru/index.php (accessed December 12, 2007).

22. The Law on Endowments begins to address the lack of support for philanthropic initiative in Russian tax law. Currently, not only is there no deduction for charitable contributions, but there are circumstances under which a donation can represent a tax liability to both the donor and the recipient (Tolmasova 2004). But scholars of philanthropy have noted that a tax regime that rewards charitable donation is not a necessary condition for the flourishing of philanthropy; and the private foundations that have emerged in Russia to date have not depended on tax breaks for their development (Alexeeva 2008). Regulatory changes under consideration by the Russian parliament as of late 2007 may finally result in more favorable tax treatment of donations.

23. Although, as I have noted elsewhere, systematic differences may be observed between the activities of U.S. foundations in Russia and the foundations from Germany active there, with the latter less likely to fund Russian NGOs and more likely to support exchanges and scholarships (Slocum 2005).

24. Beyond this simple dichotomy between private and public donors, the full range of Western philanthropic activity in Russia also includes the charitable activities of hundreds of intermediary agencies (USAID contractors and others), corporations, and religious organizations. In addition, there are donors from beyond Europe and North America active in Russia, such as Muslim religious missions from the Middle East. The funding activities of Western donors, which include support for universities and

think tanks as well as traditional NGOs, have always had their controversial aspects. These include local suspicions over Western motives in funding Russian science and the charge that Western funding has distorted the priorities and developmental trajectory of Russian civil society organizations, creating a situation whereby Russian NGOs have become dependent on foreign donors. Apart from simply building relationships of dependence, some argue that foreign funding for advocacy NGOs can have a pernicious influence, underwriting relatively (by local standards) comfortable lifestyles (less true now than in the 1990s, prior to Russia's recent economic boom), and in some instances, facilitating active corruption—breeding suspicion, jealousy, and resentment on the part of officials, the general public, and other (non-funded) activists (see Wedel 1998; Carothers 1999; Ottaway and Carothers 2000; Henderson 2003; Hemment 2004; Sundstrom 2006).

25. Jamey Gambrell argues that "[f]oreign foundations—particularly private ones—provided both potential grantees and would-be Russian philanthropists with a model of philanthropic activity. It involved a transparent, egalitarian grantmaking process, in addition to financing hundreds of millions of dollars of projects over the first decade of post-Soviet Russia. The staff of these organizations, as well as the juries constituted to evaluate the grant applications, consisted largely of Russian citizens. Thus, the foreign foundations served as a training ground for future Russian-funded philanthropic activity. Grant-makers and grantees alike gained valuable experience—both philosophical and practical—in their contacts with foreign philanthropy" (Gambrell 2004, 23–24).

26. Local donors' fora are a fixture in the U.S. philanthropic community, and nearly all of the former socialist-bloc countries of Eastern Europe have a national-level donors' forum located in the capital. Among their many functions is that of making the local philanthropic community "legible" to international donor agencies and foundations.

27. As of late 2007, full members of the Donors' Forum include the New Eurasia Foundation, International Research and Exchanges Board (IREX), Interregional Siberian Center for Social Initiative Support, Open Society Institute, John D. and Catherine T. MacArthur Foundation, Charles Stewart Mott Foundation, Dynasty Foundation, Vladimir Potanin Charity Fund, American Jewish Joint Distribution Committee, Cadet Corps Charity Foundation named after Alexis Jordan, Volnoe Delo Foundation, Russian Teachers Support Fund, Ford Foundation, Wild Salmon Center, Charities Aid Foundation, Russian Olympians Foundation, and Victoria Children Foundation.

28. See http://www.donorsforum.ru/about/mission/ (accessed December 15, 2007); information on the Donors' Forum is drawn from their website and the author's experience on the staff of a member organization.

29. The GEG/GEF has met in Paris (1996), Brussels (1997), Turin (1998), Berlin (1999), Warsaw (2000), Bucharest (2001), Moscow (2002), Bratislava (2003), Sofia (2004), Kiev (2005), Belgrade (2006), and Tallinn (2007).

30. In his talk, Khodorkovsky decried the government-coerced, company-town model of corporate charity, and said that his philanthropy was aimed at the establishment of civil society (author's notes).

31. The Russian Donors' Forum and CAF-Russia are members of WINGS, as are

two other Russian organizations, the Partnership for Community Foundations and the Siberian Civic Initiatives Support Center. Natalya Kaminarskaya, executive secretary of the Donors' Forum, is a member of the WINGS Coordinating Committee (its governing body).

32. Only a few years earlier, in the late 1980s, Mott and the Charities Aid Foundation had brought the community foundation form to the United Kingdom (see Leat 2006; Sacks 2005).

33. As Eva Hinterhuber and Susanne Rindt point out, conscious acts of framing were part of this diffusion practice. Notably, the Russian language lacked an equivalent term for the English "community foundation," and Russian legislation doesn't specifically provide for this form of charitable organization. But eventually the Russian-language term *fond mestnogo soobshchestva* (lit. "foundation of the local community") was settled upon and entered common usage, not least through the Partnership's promulgation, at its founding conference, of a requirement that adoption of this term was a necessary prerequisite for membership in this new association (Hinterhuber and Rindt 2004, 101).

34. See http://www.cafcf.ru/russian_cfs_partnership.htm (accessed December 17, 2007).

35. The 2006 annual report of the Community Foundations Partnership is available at http://www.p-cf.org/index.php?lng=eng&a=show&idlink=7 (accessed December 17, 2007). See also Hinterhuber and Rindt (2004).

36. See http://www.neweurasia.ru/index.php?option=com_content&task=view&id =17&Itemid=45 (accessed December 15, 2007).

37. The research literature may exaggerate the degree to which the Russian NGO sector is dependent on Western funders by concentrating attention on precisely those types of NGOs favored by foreign donors. CAF-Russia estimates that the Russian non-commercial sector as a whole—which includes, as noted above, various autonomous cultural and training institutions, social and religious organizations, and consumer cooperatives—receives about 6.8 percent of its funding from foreign sources, versus 46.3 percent in donations from Russian legal entities (Yezhov 2006a).

38. DiMaggio and Powell assert that modeling is a "response to uncertainty," and they further hypothesize that "[t]he more ambiguous the goals of an organization, the greater the extent to which the organization will model itself after organizations that it perceives to be successful" (DiMaggio and Powell 1991; 69, 75). The larger Russian philanthropic organizations, like big foundations elsewhere, tend to pursue goals that are broad, arguably inherently (and often deliberately) ambiguous programmatic goals.

39. As with Western funding for Russian NGOs, Western support for the growth of indigenous Russian foundations proceeds from a mix of motivations. In large part, it stems from a genuine appreciation of the usefulness of foundations as a source of relatively flexible financing for socially beneficial activities. There is in addition a pragmatic need, one that becomes more pressing over time: foreign foundations that have been in Russia for over a decade may eventually turn their attention elsewhere; those NGOs, institutions, and projects that have been nourished with foreign funds will eventually

need to find local sources of support (the question of exit strategy). There are also more specifically self-interested motives, including a felt need on the part of Western foundations to find local counterparts—to have peer institutions to talk and partner with, but also to dampen and defuse actual or potential criticisms of their motives and their outsider status in Russia.

40. A 2005 study by CAF-Russia shows that Russian foundations are poorly informed about human rights activities, they fear coming into conflict with the authorities, and they hold negative stereotypes about human rights activists (Charities Aid Foundation 2005, 2–3).

41. Philanthropy that serves as a substitute for the former Soviet welfare state can at times be indistinguishable from "charitable blackmail"—mid-sized companies remain structurally dependent on local governments, who will commonly coerce companies "to donate money to charitable causes in the local region (and at the same time benefiting the local council budget) under the threat of bureaucratic and tax hurdles or the promise of certain facilitations" (Hinterhuber and Rindt 2004, 133).

42. The summary report of the October 2007 Grantmakers East Forum in Tallinn includes an assertion "that the grantmaking sector ought to be the pioneer of innovating, creating new practices. Grantmakers are a kind of social engineers wanting to change the people, the societies" (see http://www.gef.efc.be/forum/?p=21), and the 2007 annual conference of the Russian Donors' Forum included a session examining the lessons of social change philanthropy in Russia (http://donorsforum.ru/_files/11_686.doc).

43. Dogan (2006) suggests that the rule of law (but not necessarily democracy) must obtain in order for foundations to attain legitimacy within a given society.

References

Alexeeva, Olga. 2006. *Istoriia doveriia v nedoveritel'nye vremena. Sovremennaia rossiiskaia blagotvoritel'nost'*. Moscow: Eksmo.

Ambinder, Lev. 2007. "Pervyi blagotvoritel'nyi capital."*Kommersant,* March 30. Available at http://fund.potanin.ru/publish/2007/30mar.htm (accessed December 16, 2007).

Anheier, Helmut K., and Siobhan Daly. 2006. "Roles of Foundations in Europe: A Comparison." In *The Legitimacy of Philanthropic Foundations: United States and European Perspectives,* ed. Kenneth Prewitt, et al., 192–216. New York: Russell Sage Foundation.

Anheir, Helmut K., and Stefan Toepler, eds. 1999. *Public Funds, Private Purpose: Philanthropic Foundations in International Perspective.* New York: Kluwer Academic/Plenum Publishers.

Bakhmin, Vyacheslav. 2004. "Russian Donors and Civil Society." *CCSF Newsletter* (Canada Civil Society Fund), no. 2 (Spring): 4–6.

Bourjaily, Natalia. 2006. "Some Issues Related to Russia's New NGO Law." *International Journal of Not-for-Profit Law* 8, no. 3 (May). Available at: http://www.icnl.org/knowledge/ijnl/vo18iss3/special_1.htm (accessed December 17, 2007).

Bourtseva, Natasha. 2002. "Foundation Law in Russia." *SEAL* (Winter). Available at:

http://www.efc.be/cgi-bin/articlepublisher.pl?filename=NB-SE-01-02-1.html (accessed December 11, 2007).

Carothers, Thomas. 1999. *Aiding Democracy Abroad: The Learning Curve.* Washington, D.C.: Carnegie Endowment for International Peace.

Charities Aid Foundation. 2005. "Kratkii obzor rezul'tatov issledovaniia pozitsii chastnykh I semeinykh fondov po razvitiiu institutov grazhdanskago obshchestva i demokratii v Rossii." Manuscript.

DiMaggio, Paul J., and Walter W. Powell. 1991. "The Iron Cage Revisited: Institutional Isomorphism and Collective Rationality in Organization Fields." In *The New Institutionalism in Organizational Analysis,* ed. Walter W. Powell and Paul J. DiMaggio, 63–82. Chicago: University of Chicago Press.

Dinello, Natalia. 1998. "Elites and Philanthropy in Russia." *International Journal of Politics, Culture, and Society* 12, no 1: 109–33.

Dogan, Mattei. 2006. "In Search of Legitimacy: Similarities and Differences between the Continents." In *The Legitimacy of Philanthropic Foundations: United States and European Perspectives,* ed. Kenneth Prewitt, et al., 273–81. New York: Russell Sage Foundation.

Donors' Forum. 2005. *Donorskie I nekommercheskie organizatsii: Chto my o nykh znaem. Obzor materialov issledovanii.* Moscow: Donors Forum.

European Foundation Centre. 2004. *Community Philanthropy Watch: Europe 2004.* Brussels: European Foundation Centre.

Freedman, Michael. 2007. "Dark Force: Boris Berezovsky Is Giving Russian Democracy a Bad Name." *Forbes.com* (May 21). Availble at: http://www.forbes.com/business/global/2007/0521/046.html (accessed December 16, 2007).

Gambrell, Jamey. 2004. "Philanthropy in Russia: New Money Under Pressure." *Carnegie Reporter* 3, no. 1 (Fall): 20–33.

Gaonkar, Dilip Parameshwar. 2002. "Toward New Imaginaries: An Introduction." *Public Culture* 14, no. 1 (Winter): 1–19.

Gemelli, Giuliana. 2006. "Historical Changes in Foundation Functions and Legitimacy in Europe." In *The Legitimacy of Philanthropic Foundations: United States and European Perspectives,* ed. Kenneth Prewitt, et al., 177–91. New York: Russell Sage Foundation.

Hemment, Julie. 2004. "The Riddle of the Third Sector: Civil Society, International Aid, and NGOs in Russia." *Anthropological Quarterly* 77, no. 2 (Spring): 215–41.

Henderson, Sarah L. 2003. *Building Democracy in Contemporary Russia: Western Support for Grassroots Organizations.* Ithaca, N.Y.: Cornell University Press.

Heydemann, Steven, and Stefan Toepler. 2006. "Foundations and the Challenge of Legitimacy in Comparative Perspective." In *The Legitimacy of Philanthropic Foundations: United States and European Perspectives,* ed. Kenneth Prewitt, et al., 3–26. New York: Russell Sage Foundation.

Hinterhuber, Eva Maria, and Susanne Rindt. 2004. *Bürgerstiftungen in Russland: Philanthropie zwischen Tradition und Neubeginn. Community Foundations in Russia: Philanthropy between Tradition and Rebirth.* Berlin: Maecenata Verlag.

Kononczuk, Wojciech. 2006. *The "Yukos Affair": Its Motives and Implications.* CES Studies, no. 25 (Warsaw: Center for Eastern Studies). Available at: http://www.osw.waw.pl/files/PRACE_25.pdf (accessed December 17, 2007).

Leat, Diana. 2006. "Foundation Legitimacy at the Community Level in the United Kingdom." In *The Legitimacy of Philanthropic Foundations: United States and European Perspectives,* ed. Kenneth Prewitt, et al., 252–70. New York: Russell Sage Foundation.

Levshina, E[katerina]. n.d. *Problemy osveshcheniia blagotvoritel'nosti: mifi, istoriia I sovremmenost'.* Available at: http://www.donorsforum.ru/library/articles/ (accessed December 15, 2007).

Lindenmeyr, Adele. 1998. "From Repression to Revival: Philanthropy in Twentieth-Century Russia." In *Philanthropy in the World's Traditions,* ed. Warren F. Ilchman, Stanley N. Katz, and Edward L. Queen II, 309–331. Bloomington: Indiana University Press.

Meyer, J. W. 1999. "The Changing Cultural Content of the Nation-State: A World Society Perspective." In *State/Culture: State-Formation after the Cultural Turn,* ed. George Steinmetz, 123–43. Ithaca, N.Y.: Cornell University Press.

Norman, John O. 1991. "Pavel Tretiakov and Merchant Art Patronage, 1850–1900." In *Between Tsar and People: Educated Society and the Quest for Public Identity in Late Imperial Russia,* ed. Edith W. Clowes, Samuel D. Kassow, and James L. West, 93–107. Princeton, N.J.: Princeton University Press.

Ottaway, Marina, and Thomas Carothers, eds. 2000. *Funding Virtue: Civil Society Aid and Democracy Promotion.* Washington, D.C.: Carnegie Endowment for International Peace.

Prewitt, Kenneth. 1999. "The Importance of Foundations in an Open Society." In *The Future of Foundations in an Open Society,* ed. Bertelsmann Foundation, 17–29. Gütersloh: Bertelsmann Foundation Publishers.

——— 2006. "American Foundations: What Justifies Their Unique Privileges and Power." In *The Legitimacy of Philanthropic Foundations: United States and European Perspectives,* ed. Kenneth Prewitt, et al., 3–26. New York: Russell Sage Foundation.

Sacks, Eleanor W. 2005. *2005 Community Foundation Status Report.* Brussels: Worldwide Initiatives for Grantmaker Support-Community Foundations (WINGS-CF).

Scott, W. Richard, and John W. Meyer. 1991. "The Organization of Societal Sectors: Propositions and Early Evidence." In *The New Institutionalism in Organizational Analysis,* Walter W. Powell and Paul J. DiMaggio, 108–40. Chicago: University of Chicago Press.

Slocum, John W. 2005. "Philanthropy in Russia: The Activities of U.S. and German Foundations and the Development of a Local Philanthropic Sector." *Maecenata Aktuell,* no. 53 (August): 3–11.

Sundstrom, Lisa McIntosh. 2006. *Funding Civil Society: Foreign Assistance and NGO Development in Russia.* Stanford, Calif.: Stanford University Press.

Sundstrom, Lisa McIntosh, and Laura A. Henry. 2006. "Russian Civil Society: Tensions and Trajectories," in *Russian Civil Society: A Critical Assessment,* ed. Alfred B. Evans

Jr., Laura A. Henry, and Lisa McIntosh Sundstrom, 305–22. Armonk, N.Y.: M. E. Sharpe.

Toepler, Stefan. 1998. "Foundations and Their Institutional Context: Cross-Evaluating Evidence from Germany and the United States." *Voluntas: International Journal of Voluntary and Nonprofit Organizations* 9, no. 2: 153–70.

Tolmasova, A. K. 2004. *Zakonodatel'nye uslvoiia i gosudarstvennoe regulirovanie filantropicheskiou deiatel'nosti. Rezul'taty issledovaniia. Vtoroe izdaniie, obnovlennoe i dopolnennoe.* Moscow: Donors Forum.

Wedel, Janine. 1998. *Collusion and Collision: The Strange Case of Western Aid to Eastern Europe 1989–1998.* New York: St. Martin's Press.

White, Anne. 1993. "Charity, Self-Help and Politics in Russia, 1985–91." *Europe-Asia Studies* 45, no. 5: 787–810.

Yezhov, Kirill. 2006a. "Nekommercheskii sector: kokoi on?" *Den'gi i blagotvoritel'nost'* no. 1/62 (July): 8–9.

———. 2006b. "Blagotvoritel'nost' v Rossii." *Den'gi i blagotvoritel'nost'* no. 1/62 (July): 9–10.

7. Promoting Civil Society or Diffusing NGOs?

U.S. Donors in the Former Soviet Union

SADA AKSARTOVA

*A striking upsurge is under way around the globe in organized voluntary
activity and the creation of private, nonprofit or nongovernmental organizations. . . . The scope and scale of this phenomenon are immense. Indeed, we are
in the midst of a global "associational revolution."*
— LESTER SALAMON, *FOREIGN AFFAIRS,* 1994

The former Soviet Union is a region where Lester Salamon's prediction
seems to have come true—indeed, almost all post-Soviet countries have
seen an explosive growth in the number of nongovernmental organizations
(NGOs) since the early 1990s. However, this case also makes clear that the
rise of the post-Soviet nonprofit sector has been driven almost exclusively by
Western donors—with the most prominent role played by American foreign
aid and philanthropic foundations, which operationalized the promotion of
civil society as the promotion of NGOs. The proliferation of post-Soviet NGOs
is indeed part of a global process, but this global process is better characterized as organizational diffusion, not "associational revolution." Aid and philanthropic donors, not NGOs, are the engines of this process.

The list of American donors that have funded civil society programs in Russia and other post-Soviet states includes both the U.S. government and large
private foundations. The U.S. Agency for International Development (USAID)
is the main government agency responsible for American democracy and civil
society assistance. Since 1992, the U.S. government has spent more than a billion
dollars on promoting democracy and civil society in twelve post-Soviet states
(U.S. Department of State 1995–2006).[1] In addition, several private American
foundations have been actively promoting NGOs in the region. Chief among
them is the New York-based Open Society Institute (OSI) funded by the billionaire George Soros, who since the late 1980s has spent more than a billion
dollars on programs to stimulate the development of open society in Russia
alone and millions more in other post-Soviet countries. There is also the New

York-based Ford Foundation, whose programs focus on Russia, where it has spent upward of $120 million since 1996;[2] the Michigan-based Charles Stewart Mott Foundation, which in the 1990s ran a program supporting NGOs in Russia and Ukraine from its Prague office;[3] and the congressionally funded but privately managed Eurasia Foundation (EF).

In my contribution to this volume, I analyze the Western grant economy by which U.S. civil society assistance operates in post-Soviet Russia and Kyrgyzstan.[4] The Western grant economy involves material and cultural practices underlying the diffusion of NGOs as well as the interaction between donors and NGOs. I discuss three elements of this economy: (1) material resources that U.S. donors have deployed to diffuse the NGO as an institutional form in the former Soviet Union; (2) socializing rituals, or recurring institutional venues where locals are socialized into the donor-NGO universe; and (3) discursive practices, or the language that donors and NGOs speak.

I argue that the principal effect of fifteen years of the donor-driven NGO diffusion is the institutionalization of the notion of U.S. civil society assistance itself. By this I mean that American civil society donors have established a universe of post-Soviet NGOs clamoring for their continuing support. Meanwhile, the position of local NGOs in Russia and in Kyrgyzstan is far more tenuous, and the primary reason is that the professional NGO, although well known to American donors, represents a new organizational and cultural template that is unfamiliar to post-Soviet societies outside the donor-NGO universe.

Western Grants and the Disparity of Wealth

U.S. civil society assistance involves U.S. donors making grants to local recipients. Therefore, an analysis of how U.S. donors diffuse NGOs has to begin with the donors' material resources. The logic of foreign aid and international philanthropy rests on the assumption that the transfer of funds from rich to poor societies is a necessary condition for solving the problems of underdevelopment, economic or political. Because foreign aid donors always work in non-affluent countries, it follows that the Western grant economy always operates against the backdrop of a significant wealth disparity between the donor and recipient countries. The post-Soviet societies are no exception, and the attractive economic opportunities inherent in U.S. donors' grants are an important dimension in the donor-NGO interaction over the last fifteen years.

Analyses of U.S. civil society assistance tend to overestimate the extent to which U.S. donors' activities are driven by their declared goals (such as democratizing Russia) and to underestimate the organizational dynamics impelling the day-to-day operations of aid agencies and philanthropic foundations. The core organizational function of donor agencies is the transfer of money, and their practices are built around the necessity to move money from the point of origin to the point of destination. Money is also the principal measure of a donor organization's activities (Tendler 1975). Once a yearly foreign aid budget is set, the closer the spending is to the target level, the closer American foreign aid is to accomplishing its goals, be they privatization or democratization. The availability and size of an absorptive capacity for donors' funds in a host country is taken as a measure of a pro-reform, pro-Western constituency. Should the U.S. Agency for International Development fail to spend a significant amount of its annual budget in, say, Russia, the U.S. Congress will interpret it in terms of either Russia's unwillingness to reform or USAID's inability to foster reform. Either outcome is unwelcome from USAID's standpoint as it will likely involve cuts in the following year's budget. The necessity to move money is less urgent for private foundations only because they are free to set their own budgets and are not subject to the same degree of public oversight. Nevertheless, the availability of an absorptive capacity for foundation grants is the main yardstick by which a private donor organization measures social demand for its programs. For both public and private donors, the size of grantmaking is a critical measure of their commitment to a given cause and of the efficacy of their programs.

Foreign aid agencies' ability to expend a given amount of funds within a delimited period of time is heavily dependent on the host country's absorptive capacity. This is a particularly pressing concern when donors first arrive in a place untouched by aid, such as the former Soviet Union in the early 1990s. To gain a foothold in Russia and Central Asia—and to prove to the political audience back home that there was a demand and a constituency for the United States–guided reforms in the region—USAID had to find, in short order, existing institutions or establish new ones that could absorb its funds. The challenge was magnified by the agency's lack of knowledge of post-Soviet societies and the domestic political pressure to produce immediate positive results.[5]

When USAID first set foot in the former Soviet Union, it confronted the very nontrivial task of finding ways to commit billions of dollars in twelve months.[6] Although civil society assistance constituted a small piece of this pie,[7] the challenge of identifying recipients that could absorb civil society funds was no less acute. Economic aid could and did go to Russia's central government and affiliated entities that could absorb large amounts of money (Wedel 1998). By contrast, nongovernmental organizations can absorb much smaller amounts, and there were very few of them in Russia or Kyrgyzstan at the time. Private donors found themselves in the same predicament. The necessity to establish absorptive capacity and the difficulty of identifying worthy recipients in a new country within a short timeframe encouraged donors to give bigger grants for fewer projects. For example, in 1993, the first year of the Eurasia Foundation's operations in the former Soviet Union, the foundation awarded $1.5 million divided into thirty-one grants, the average grant being $48,000. By 2002, when there were plenty of organizations, including NGOs, capable of absorbing this kind of funding, the foundation's annual grantmaking grew to $13.3 million but its average grant shrank to $22,000 (EF 2003, 6).

How do these grants compare to local incomes? In 1993, the average monthly Russian wage, according to a *Financial Times* (1995) survey, was $114, and a typical monthly academic salary well below $50 (Viviano 1993). Foreign donors' entry into the former Soviet Union took place at the time of a deep economic crisis. In the early 1990s, "economic decline and price hikes . . . assumed disastrous proportions" (Bogomolov 1993). In 1992 alone, "consumer prices increased 26 fold, an inflation rate of 2,600 percent" (Hiatt 1993). In 1990 one ruble was worth $1.6; in late 1993 one dollar was worth over 1,000 rubles; in late 1994 3,000 rubles; and by late 1995 the dollar exceeded 4,500 rubles.[8] Although the inflation rate abated over time, real incomes remained very low. According to the panel data collected for the Russia Longitudinal Monitoring Survey, the average real monthly household income in Russia declined from 7,800 rubles in 1992 to 4,500 rubles in the fall of 1998, immediately after Russia's financial crisis, and increased to 7,400 rubles (about $230) in 2002 (Mroz et al. 2003). In Kyrgyzstan, the average monthly wage in 1999 was less than $30 (UN 2001). In other words, the disparity between the size of donors' grants and local incomes has changed little over time. Against this backdrop, Western donors' grants offer economic security that can be matched by few other opportunities; paid in dollars, they offer grantees protection from inflation and economic volatility.

Compared to the early 1990s, today there are many more NGOs capable of absorbing donors' funds in post-Soviet countries. Donors now have an easier time awarding big and small grants because they themselves have exerted a lot of effort to spawn an entire universe of recipients vying for them. However, today as in 1992, $25,000–$50,000 is a very large amount of money in Russia, and is even more in poorer Central Asia. Therefore, the economic opportunities inherent in the Western grant economy remain as attractive as they were a decade earlier.

The disparity of wealth between donors and the recipient society creates temptations for abuse. A topic that regularly comes up in donor-NGO discussions is that donors need to be vigilant in drawing distinction between real and fake NGOs. The latter are NGOs that exist "on paper" with the sole purpose of obtaining one or multiple Western donor grants. Donors themselves do not discuss this issue much in public, and details are scarce regarding either the numbers of fake NGOs or the amounts of the donors' money that such NGOs manage to obtain over time.[9]

The existence of such NGOs, however, is one reason why estimates for the size of the NGO sector vary so widely. In both Russia and Kyrgyzstan NGOs have to register with the state,[10] and the registration numbers serve as estimates of the size of these countries' NGO sectors. According to one study done by a Russian NGO, of the 275,000 nongovernmental organizations registered with Russia's Ministry of Justice by 2000, fewer than 45,000, or about 16 percent, were bona fide NGOs (Sevortyan 2000). According to another study, one half of the active NGOs existed on foreign support and the other half on local funding or a combination of foreign and local funding (Baranova et al. 2001). Similarly, it was estimated that of 3,200 NGOs registered in Kyrgyzstan in 2002, about 500, which also amounts to 16 percent, were actual NGOs (Krimsky 2002). As for the remaining registered but inactive NGOs, some might have shut down, others could be fronts for other activities, and still others might register with the sole purpose of trying to obtain a grant. Given the level of average incomes mentioned above, it is understandable why even one grant of a few thousand dollars would be very tempting.

What is of greater interest to my study than the misuse or pilfering of donors' funds are the implications of the wealth disparity for bona fide NGOs. All the NGOs I observed and interviewed belonged to this category. Their staff is deeply committed to their work and because of that received consistent support from American donors. As far as these NGOs are concerned, the significance of opportunities inherent in the Western grant economy is that they provide a particular style of work and life. Salaries measuring in the hundreds, not thousands, of dollars, although modest by Western standards, put employees of such NGOs in high income brackets locally. No less important are the physical surroundings afforded by Western grants, which include well-appointed office space in a nice location equipped with computers, faxes, photocopiers, and so on. As many of the interviews I conducted with NGO activists happened at their place of work, I visited numerous NGO offices. Although the latter would appear quite ordinary and modest by Western standards, they are frequently luxurious by local standards (this is particularly so in Bishkek, Kyrgyzstan's capital). In a way, that is precisely the point: NGO offices look both unassuming and recognizable, conforming to Western expectations of what an NGO office is supposed to be.[11] But they also look nothing like the drab and battered Soviet-era offices that still abound at numerous institutions unable to afford anything else and that conjure vivid images of Soviet backwardness. In other words, for both NGOs and their Western donors, NGOs' physical surroundings have as much to do with what both consider the minimum comfort necessary for NGO activities as with the symbolism of a modern, forward-looking, upwardly mobile work style.

An essential part of the work style of the NGO representatives I interviewed is commitment to their cause and the feeling of doing important and virtuous work. To a significant degree, this feeling is reinforced by the attention NGOs receive in the West. The leaders of these NGOs regularly travel abroad, present at important international venues, and are invited to brief the U.S. Congress, Western parliaments, the Organization for Security and Co-operation in Europe, or the United Nations. Because of Western attention, in recent years NGOs were given recognition, even if grudgingly, by their own governments. For instance, in November 2001 President Putin's administration convened and funded a national congress of Russian NGOs, Grazhdanskii forum (Civic Forum), in Moscow. Putin made an address at the opening session and dispatched government officials to discuss important social issues with the non-governmental representatives.[12] The Commission for Civil Society and Human Rights, established by the Russian government with the purpose of advising the president, includes leaders of the several most prominent NGOs. The government's cooperation with civil society is increasingly prominent in the World Bank's and IMF's lending requirements. Therefore, Kyrgyzstan's government is expected to consult with NGOs if it wants Kyrgyzstan to be eligible for Western loans.[13] This style of work is associated in the eyes of NGOs with what David Strang and John W. Meyer (1993) might call progressive modernity, and for that reason it is attractive to people who work at NGOs, and made possible by Western donors' grants.

The grant economy of U.S. civil society assistance in Russia and Kyrgyzstan operates within the larger context of post-Soviet involution.[14] When American donors initiated their programs in the early 1990s, both Russia and Kyrgyzstan were experiencing a staggering economic decline, contraction of welfare services, and a drastic drop in incomes and the quality of life for the overwhelming majority of people. For the educated elite, the loss of social status and, frequently, of steady employment carrying a living wage accompanied this economic upheaval. Among other things, the decline of the Soviet system, as Michael Kennedy pointed out, meant that

> [t]he material interests of the old communist-made intelligentsia *cannot*
> be satisfied with the new system. The old system produced too many engineers and probably too many humanists and historians and writers for the
> new system to absorb. It produced too many old-style managers. It did not
> produce the kind of professional needed today. A whole new expertise is

required for the new capitalist system in statu nascendi and only a small portion of the old intelligentsia will find a place.[15]

The new NGO activists cum professionals are in that small portion of the old intelligentsia that found a place in the opportunities created by Western donors. The Western grant economy offers its entrants a high income, a respectable and interesting job, participation in international events, a comfortable and modern work environment, and the moral satisfaction of being engaged in a socially useful activity. For people working at the most prominent and best funded NGOs, it has turned into stable and secure employment. The attractiveness of this kind of work—with its intellectual, organizational, and moral dimensions—combined with valuable resources (not just salary, but such perquisites as a nice office space, computers, equipment, trips abroad, conferences at expensive hotels, etc.) creates powerful incentives for NGOs to be oriented toward donors, prioritize the cultivation of their relations with the donors, and position themselves as gatekeepers to donors' resources.

The Western grant economy, embedded in context of the wealth disparity between the donor and recipient societies, places the donor-supported NGOs into a cocoon of relative affluence. Whereas in Western countries, people working at NGOs find themselves in the middle range of the professional class, in Russia and Kyrgyzstan people working for foreign donor–funded NGOs are lifted far above other professionals such as university professors or doctors. Once an NGO succeeds in winning a grant, it is understandably determined to continue obtaining more of them because few other opportunities in Moscow and especially in Bishkek guarantee similar levels of economic security combined with similar moral rewards. This is not to cast doubt on NGO activists' commitment to what they do or to overstate material benefits.[16] For the people I interviewed, personal enrichment was clearly not the motivating factor. Rather, the point is that the conception of what constitutes the NGO is wedded to a particular style of work that was made possible by—and, for the time being, would be impossible without—multi-thousand-dollar grants provided by Western foreign aid agencies and private foundations. Any other mode of functioning becomes unimaginable, and great effort is expended on cultivating relations with donors and assuring the NGOs' organizational survival. Because, as a new and unfamiliar organizational form, NGOs do not have a ready-made base of grassroots support and frequently receive hostile treatment from Russia's and Kyrgyzstan's governments, NGOs cannot imagine themselves existing without foreign aid and international philanthropy. And this, in turn, creates incentives for NGOs—especially the best funded and therefore the most prominent NGOs, such as the ones I studied—to orient themselves toward Western donors.

Socializing Rituals

Early in my research, I encountered a criticism common in analyses of U.S. democracy and civil society assistance, namely that training, roundtables, and seminars continue to consume a great deal of donor funding. If the emphasis on these events was justified in the early years of U.S. involvement when locals needed to be trained, now that there is a sizable post-Soviet NGO sector, scarce resources, as the argument goes, could be better spent on more substantive ways of promoting democracy. Indeed, donor-funded training events, seminars, and roundtables seem to be taking place all the time,[17] and I attended many in the course of my research in Moscow and Bishkek.

The presumed beneficiaries of these activities, NGOs themselves, echo the criticism. Once I started interviewing NGO activists in Moscow and Bishkek, I discovered that it was a common topic of discussion among them, too. "Why do American donors continue to spend so much money on seminars and roundtables," they wondered, "instead of giving us more money for our work?" NGO activists also noted that if one wanted to obtain a grant, proposing to organize a seminar or training for other less advanced NGOs was more likely to get funding than other types of activities. Here a human rights activist in Bishkek writing about seminars devoted to the topic of independent media in Kyrgyzstan summarizes the prevailing sentiment:

> It is hard to resist the feeling that the freedom of speech has become a popular topic for obtaining money from the donors. This must be one reason why over 50 seminars for mass media organizations were recently held in our small country. However, the results have not met the expectations. The mass production of countless seminars, which frequently duplicate one another, discredits the very idea of defending freedom of speech.
>
> We tried to calculate how much money was spent on such seminars and came up with a hefty figure. Assuming that one seminar costs about $10,000 (this is an average, some events are modest and some are more expensive affairs involving foreign participants), the estimate for one year is half a million US dollars. *On the one hand, this sum is not that huge that one should be very distressed; on the other, many of the people we talked to both in our country and abroad feel that it could be spent far more effectively.* [italics added][18]

Two things are notable about the last sentence. One is that $10,000 per event is indeed not out of the ordinary in the universe of activities and organizations spawned by foreign donors in a country with per capita GDP of $1,600 in 2002. The other is that although doubts about the seminars' effectiveness are common inside the donor-NGO community, it does not seem to reduce their number. What could be the reason?

Observers and NGOs themselves point out that the emphasis on such events and other quantifiable indicators (NGOs established, people trained, photocopying machines distributed, websites created, Internet accounts used, projects conducted, reports issued, etc.) endures because it is a function of donors' efforts to measure the results of their activities for their own use and for public presentation. The pressure for quantifying achievements is stronger for a public donor that has to justify its activities before the political audiences back home in the United States.[19] However, after observing numerous events of this kind, I suggest that their import goes far beyond the need to quantify results. U.S. democracy and civil society assistance presumes that locals, with no previous exposure to democratic values and practices, need to be inculcated into Western values. Training, seminars, and roundtables are venues where the inculcation takes place.

We can view these events as socializing rituals crucial for the operation of Western assistance. For this reason they are unlikely to fade away from the standard repertoire of donor practices. These events socialize local participants into the donor-recipient relationship and the donor worldview. They are venues where locals pick up rules of appropriate professional conduct, networking, and public presentation and learn to become conversant in the Western conceptual vocabulary of active citizenship, democracy, and civil society. Such rituals are by no means unique to civil society assistance or foreign aid more generally. A Western corporation operating abroad would rely on similar techniques to initiate locals into its business practices and organizational culture. It is through such socialization that the process of organizational diffusion occurs. Socializing rituals of this kind are "highly institutionalized and thus in some measure beyond the discretion of any individual participant or organization" (Meyer and Rowan 1991, 44).

Locals eagerly participate to gain access to donors. Being socialized into the donor worldview is indispensable for learning about funding opportunities and themes prioritized by donors as well as for obtaining skills for writing successful grant applications. These rituals can be seen as sites of mutual attraction where both sides get benefits. Donors construct and mold their institutional environment, that is, create a universe of organizations acting as receptacles for their funds and ideas. NGOs acquire socialization necessary for securing donors' grants.

The motivations and benefits both sides derive are not simply utilitarian.

Each side seeks out people "like us." Donors look for people and organizations that espouse modern values associated with Western democracy and behave in a manner comprehensible to Westerners. Post-Soviet NGOs, especially those working on politically controversial issues, such as human rights, see donors as carriers of democratic values, widely viewed today as the chief attribute of progressive modernity, that are lacking in their own societies. Besides, people working at donor and at recipient organizations are in many ways quite alike. Both groups come from the professional class in their respective countries. Although the United States and the Soviet Union each defined itself in opposition to one another ideologically, the Soviet Union attempted to create its own version of, not deviate from, modernity (Kotkin 1995; Scott 1998). Its educational system produced people who believed in progress and development and would therefore find much to agree about with people working at aid agencies and American foundations. Most of post-Soviet NGO activists come from a background in academia, research, and education.[20] While the collapse of the state's economic support in those areas foreclosed career opportunities carrying living wages for many people in the post-Soviet educated elite, the arrival of foreign aid created opportunities that some of them are able to take advantage of by, among other things, forming and working in NGOs. These were also the people most likely to speak English, an essential skill for gaining access to and establishing relations with American donors when they first set foot in Moscow and Bishkek.

The main change in the socializing rituals of foreign donors since the early 1990s is the gradual replacement of foreign experts with local NGO experts who have been initiated into the donor worldview. In the early days of U.S. civil society assistance when local NGOs were few and far between, the focus of the assistance was on training individuals identified as promising civic leaders in the basics of NGO management and the functioning of democracy. Thousands of American consultants were flown into all the countries of the former Soviet Union to teach locals how to run nonprofit organizations and conduct activism. Because of the pressure to find ways to spend foreign funding, discussed earlier, and the perceived urgency for transmitting American capitalist and democratic expertise to societies emerging from totalitarianism, many such consultants were deemed qualified simply because they were Americans, that is, natural-born carriers of American values with the instinctive understanding of the workings of democracy and ability to transmit these values and appropriate skills to the Russians or the Kyrgyz. This approach was deeply resented by more knowledgeable Westerners and by local participants and observers (Wedel 1998), all the more so because of the jarring contrast between the consultants' generous remuneration and post-Soviet economic hardship.[21] Its failings were also documented by the U.S. government's own watchdog agencies.[22]

As the post-Soviet NGO sector grew, so did local expertise. At the time of my research in 2002–2003, most tasks previously conducted by Western consultants—such as training in grant writing, NGO management, public and media strategy, or writing evaluations of individual NGO activities and reports on thematic issues (human/civil rights, environment, nonprofit legislation)—were done by homegrown specialists who had undergone the necessary schooling. The so-called NGO resource centers, established by American donors with the purpose of building up a nationwide NGO infrastructure, were almost entirely staffed by Russians (albeit under the supervision of their American funders) designated as NGO development and management experts. The latter provided informational and technical services on a regular basis to new provincial NGOs, eliminating the need for American donors to bring in U.S. consultants in large numbers. One of the most important functions of resource centers is to serve as intermediaries between provincial NGOs and American donors based in capital cities by acting as mini-donors through conducting the "training of trainers" and administering small-grant competitions locally.[23] The result is a further spread of the message and practices of civic professionalization first introduced by the U.S. donors in capital cities a decade earlier.

Several American donor organizations became similarly indigenized.[24] The Open Society Institute was a pioneer of this trend as its national foundations outside the United States were, with very few exceptions, staffed and headed by locals. By the end of the 1990s, other donor organizations put local personnel in most positions, including at the program officer level, in both Russia and Kyrgyzstan. In some cases, even the top executive position was filled by a local person: for example, by 2002 the Eurasia Foundation appointed a Kyrgyz national as director of EF-Kyrgyzstan, a Russian and an American co-directed the MacArthur Foundation's Moscow office, and Russians headed the Moscow offices of the important USAID contractor International Research and Exchanges Board (IREX) and of the British Charities Aid Foundation.

The gradual indigenization of the donor-NGO sector in both Russia and Kyrgyzstan has been greatly helped by U.S.-funded educational and cultural exchanges. Since the early 1990s, the U.S. government and the Open Society Institute have spent in excess of one billion dollars on cultural and educational exchanges in the twelve states of Eurasia. According to the U.S. Department of State (2003), in fiscal years 1993–2002 U.S. government–funded training and exchange programs brought over 53,000 persons from Russia and 2,350 from Kyrgyzstan for short-term professional and long-term academic training.[25] The exchange programs run the gamut from high-school exchanges bringing students from the post-Soviet countries to study at American high schools for a year to two-year master's-level studies in business administration, public policy, and nonprofit management at American universities to shorter apprenticeships at American businesses and nonprofits. The U.S. Congress funds the so-called Open World Program of cultural exchanges that is directed by the Librarian of Congress and dedicated to Russia. It brings Russian political, business, and civic leaders on study tours of the United States. Kyrgyzstan's capital, Bishkek, is the site of the American University of Central Asia funded by the U.S. State Department, OSI, and the Eurasia Foundation. The university graduated its first students in the summer of 1997. As the university's website notes with pride, "[f]or the ceremony, both graduates and faculty were dressed in American-style academic caps and gowns, which had never been seen in Central Asia before."[26] The university adopted a U.S.-style curriculum, and its courses are taught by Western as well as local instructors. Among the latter, many received master's degrees in the United States through the educational programs described above. After a decade and a half of U.S. assistance for educational and cultural exchanges, both Russia and Kyrgyzstan have a pool of people with good English language skills and familiarity with American society, with American notions of democracy and democracy promotion, and American approaches to nonprofit management. While this pool of people is not that large relative to the size of each country's population, it is considerable relative to the size of that country's NGO sector and supplies professional staff for both NGOs and donor organizations.

Donors and Western observers of foreign aid view the growth and indigenization of the post-Soviet NGO infrastructure as an unqualified success of Western civil society assistance. The donor literature as well as outside evaluations and analyses, even when they conclude that the post-Soviet NGO sector can hardly be characterized as a vibrant civil society (Henderson 2003; Mendelson and Glenn 2002), are full of celebratory statements in the genre of "nobody could have imagined fifteen years ago . . ." that have become the staple of Western aid rhetoric on the post-Soviet transition. Similarly, when I asked the representatives of both donor organizations and recipient NGOs in Moscow and Bishkek about the greatest accomplishments of U.S. civil society assistance, they without exception cited the existence of thousands of NGOs, "something that could hardly be imagined only fifteen years ago."

An entire organizational infrastructure comprising so many NGOs looms large in the eyes of American donors because they have labored hard to construct it, and because, as they see it, there was no "nongovernmental" activity under the totalitarian Soviet regime. The profusion of NGOs is something donors can unambiguously take credit for; it is a tangible, quantifiable achievement in an industry where few others exist. Because NGOs enjoy a wide legitimacy in Western societies and international development, the underlying assumption is that the virtues of NGOs are many and self-evident, and that the more NGOs the better the prospects for democracy in Russia or Central Asia. The U.S. donors' belief that had there been no NGOs (and no civil society assistance), Russia's or Kyrgyzstan's democratization would have been in a worse shape, is but a reflection of the far wider Western consensus on this issue. The NGOs I interviewed embrace this view as well, in large part as a result of the socialization that constantly goes on in the donor-funded universe.

The socializing rituals endure because they help donors institutionalize themselves in host societies and because they are very attractive to citizens of those societies. The rituals facilitate the diffusion of NGOs by initiating the uninitiated locals into what NGOs are and why donors fund them. In the second half of the 1990s, local experts largely took over from Westerners in performing this function (in other words, the diffusion further out from Moscow and Bishkek was performed by locals). Donors are also always on the lookout for new grantees as they cannot keep funding the same NGOs. Training events are venues where donors find promising and trustworthy local activists, who may one day become grantees. Trustworthiness developed from face-to-face interactions is particularly important given the attractiveness of donors' resources against the backdrop of the wealth disparity between the donor and recipient societies and the donors' desire to filter out opportunists trying their luck at getting a grant. In short, the socializing rituals have staying power because they serve as sites of institutional reproduction. Relations between the donors and the grantees, like any social relations, do not exist without effort. Seminars and conferences are venues where both sides perform the work of maintaining their relationship and affirming the value of one another's contributions to building civil society in Russia and in Kyrgyzstan.

The Language Donors and NGOs Speak

When Western donor organizations first arrived in post-Soviet countries, they rarely had employees who spoke Russian or knew much about local society, politics, or culture. As a result, they relied heavily on educated English-speaking locals, who served as the donors' conduits to the host societies. Many of these locals would later form the first NGOs and become influential players in the NGO world. In the early days, it paid off for locals seeking entry into the Western grant economy to acquire some English proficiency, as grant application materials and information about donors' activities was in English.

A decade later, many Western program officers at donor institutions spoke very good Russian. In addition, the share of Western expatriates in this field diminished as more locals assumed positions at American donor and contractor organizations, the number of NGO recipients grew, and the most prominent local NGOs started advising donors on civil society assistance. Donors' literature and materials are now produced in Russian. However, in spite of this ostensible Russification of the donor-recipient universe, English remains its dominant discursive form.

Although my interviews in Moscow and Bishkek were conducted in Russian (I am a native Russian speaker),[27] my interviewees' speech was peppered with English words, such as "grant" (*grant* in Russian), "advocacy" (*edvokasi*), "fundraising" (*fandraizing*), and "gender issues" (*gendernye problemy*). Even those interviewees who did not know English well spoke in this manner. In other words, NGOs were using the American discourse of the nonprofit sector. It was clear that the dissemination of this discourse was an important part of the socialization process I discussed earlier. As my interviewees themselves noted, an NGO's ability to write successful grant applications depends on fluency in the American donors' language and conceptual vocabulary. In the early 1990s, understanding the donor mindset and modus operandi required learning English. While U.S. donors are proud to point out that today the post-Soviet NGO sector has fewer expatriates and English is no longer the only means of communication, discursively NGOs' language mimics the Western donors' language. Donors and NGOs in Russia and Kyrgyzstan generate a large amount of printed and Internet-based materials. In a typical donor-NGO Russian-language publication, as I will demonstrate shortly, not only are concepts drawn from American institutional experience, but also the style of argumentation is American, many of the words used are neologisms, and even orthography and syntax often follow American rather than Russian conventions.

Even the terms for "NGO" and "civil society" are literal translations from English. Two terms are used interchangeably for NGO in Russian: the more common one is *nekommercheskaia organizatsia* (for non-commercial, or non-profit, organization), known by its acronym, NKO, and the other is *nepravitelstvennaia organizatsia* (nongovernmental organization), abbreviated into NPO. "Civil society" is translated as *grazhdanskoie obshchestvo*.

The main reason for these discursive practices is that the American-style professional NGO that the U.S. donors are diffusing in Russia and Kyrgyzstan represents an organizational and cultural template that is new to post-Soviet societies. A new organizational form cannot function until the world around it has been appropriately constructed (Friedland and Alford 1991), and this, in turn, is impossible without having a language, a "legitimating account"

(DiMaggio 1988), describing what NGOs are and what they do. This account must also describe an institutional environment and a symbolic universe that are NGOs' reference points (Berger and Luckmann 1966). Professional NGOs propagated by American donors are vehicles for specific conceptions of associationalism and state-society interaction for which there is often no pre-existing vocabulary and literal translation is impossible. Hence my NGO interviewees had to use English words in reference to, for instance, their organizations' attempts at advocacy vis-à-vis the government or fundraising from various sources because their identification as NGOs presupposes constructing the world around them in the image of the U.S. nonprofit sector. At the same time, the concepts that are the building blocks in this process of social construction denote institutional relations that do not exist locally.

And this, in turn, creates a dilemma: although adopting the U.S. donors' discursive practices is necessary for NGOs' successful entry into and functioning inside the Western grant economy, it in effect insulates the donor-NGO universe from the rest of post-Soviet society. Most people in Russia or Kyrgyzstan do not speak English, they have not traveled to the United States, and often they have difficulty understanding what U.S. civil society assistance is all about. In order to understand what a grant is, one has to know that it comes from a donor or a sponsor. But in societies with no living memory of charity or philanthropy, it is not entirely clear why some foreign government, a private organization, or a wealthy individual would give out large amounts of money for no obvious reason. Charity and philanthropy, a normal feature of capitalist societies, are predicated on the unequal distribution of wealth, something that most post-Soviet citizens who grew up under socialism continue to resent. "Aid" (*pomoshch*) sounds even worse because it is appropriate for developing countries, not citizens of the former superpower.[28] The very words for NGO are confusing. Asked in the fall of 2001, on the eve of the Kremlin-sponsored Civic Forum, by the Russian Public Opinion Foundation, "What do you think the *nekommercheskaia organizatsia* [nonprofit organization] is?" 55 percent of respondents had no answer, and the next largest group, or 25 percent, thought that it was a state-affiliated (*gosudarstvennaia*) organization (FOM 2001, 120).[29] Similarly, a study of public perceptions of NGOs in Kyrgyzstan conducted by a British foreign aid contractor, INTRAC, has found that few in Kyrgyzstan understand the concepts of civil society and of the NGO (Baimatov, Stakeeva, and Heap 2002).

The donors and NGOs themselves are quite aware of the challenge they face in communicating with the post-Soviet public. A study funded by the Ford Foundation estimates that only about 0.1 percent of the Russian population understands the meaning of the Russian terms for nongovernmental organization and nonprofit sector, and "practically nobody" knows what civil society (*grazhdanskoie obshchestvo*) is supposed to mean. The study's focus group respondents complain that NGOs appearing in mass media use too many "jargon" words and describe their activities in a language people do not understand. Furthermore, the study paints a vivid picture of the prevailing popular attitudes toward NGOs and foreign assistance. It finds that those few in the general public who have heard about NGOs distrust the idea that people working in such organizations are motivated by altruism. Moreover,

> [t]he public treats with suspicion the activities of international donors and organizations believing that they pursue their own mercenary or political self-interest in Russia. . . . The main reason for the suspicion is that the majority of the people participating in the surveys sincerely fail to understand why foreigners want to help Russia [and] see citizens of other countries almost like Martians [*pochti kak inoplanetian*], who have a different morality and different values and would not, like in Russia, help others out of pity. At the same time, paradoxically, many respondents remark that real charitable giving is possible only abroad, where charitable organizations do not steal but really help those in need and people donate for genuine reasons. But it can only happen in one's own country and toward one's own people (Baranova et al. 2001, 12).[30]

The study also finds that even NGO leaders do not place much faith in altruism as a basis for civic action. Concerning foreign funding, in the southern Russian city of Krasnodar NGO representatives themselves suspect international donors of engaging in espionage.

Some scholars treat these attitudes as reflections of Soviet legacy since under socialism membership in state-sponsored public organizations was "often forced, coerced, or undertaken for instrumental and careerist purposes" (Howard 2003, 105). In my view, these attitudes convey to a greater extent the particularistic mindset—that is, distrust of everyone and anyone outside an immediate circle of family and friends—that was heightened by the post-Soviet involution and is deployed especially in reference to the unfamiliar.

How do donors and NGOs deal with this challenging situation? Unfazed by such overwhelming odds, they are determined to educate and enlighten. To that end, donors produce Russian-language publications such as *Everything You Wanted to Know about the Nonprofit Sector but Were Afraid to Ask* (Dorosheva 2002) and *The Third Sector, or Charity for Dummies* (Alekseeva 1997).[31] As an American reader might expect, these affect an easy, conversational style characteristic of the "but were afraid to ask" and "for dummies" genre. The former title is a manual for journalists, for, as the author explains, even journalists do not understand the language NGOs speak, which holds them back from reporting on NGO activities and accounts for the general population's ignorance of NGOs. Three chapters are particularly interesting: one aims to dispel "common myths about NGOs," the second introduces the concept of three sectors of society, and the third advises journalists on how to deal with the problem of "NGO speak."

The first of the three chapters packages the popular negative conceptions of NGOs into six "common myths":[32]

1. All NGOs are beggars, frauds, thieves, and parasites (*poproshaiki, moshenniki, vory, darmoedy*). People working in them are unscrupulous (*nechistoplotnye*) types who benefit from other people's problems and use charitable aid for personal enrichment.

2. All NGOs are created with the purpose of money laundering and as fronts for profit-making activities.

3. Charity/philanthropy (*blagotvoritelnost*) is a way to avoid paying taxes.

4. One need not create an organization to help others. It is better to help a concrete person (*luchshe pomoch konkretnomu cheloveku*) and hand the donation directly to that person.

5. People working in NGOs should not receive a salary.

6. People working in NGOs are losers (*neudachniki*) or victims of a personal tragedy.

The manual assures the reader that all these myths are wrong and that NGOs are beneficial for Russia. It explains that nonprofit organizations "play a significant economic role" in advanced countries and that 51 percent of Britons and 99 percent of British businesses make charitable donations. To drive its points home, it asks: "What would you do—would you rather give someone a fish or a fishing rod? What will be the end result of your help—parasitism and dependence or personal responsibility? Many charitable organizations follow the principle—to help not those who are worst off but those who know best how to improve things."

The other two chapters demonstrate that donors and NGOs are fully aware that their way of speaking invites incomprehension and their responses to this problem. The chapter titled "The Language NGOs Speak" (*Na kakom iazyke govoriat nkoshniki*) opens with an admission that this language is unintelligible to the uninitiated. It continues:[33]

[T]he language of NGOs, like the language of bureaucrats or the language of businessmen, is quite different from how regular people talk in their kitchens. Unfortunately, NGO employees [*rabotniki NKO*] often doing very good deeds forget that they ultimately work for the people who are at any given moment making tea, taking children to school, or repairing their apartments. And that these people don't understand the NGOs' professional terminology. . . .

Given this situation, what is a journalist to do? Although one can hope that third sector professionals might start speaking a human language, one should not count on it [*upovat na eto ne stoit*]. Therefore we ask mass media for one thing—not to fear the NGO terminology and phraseology, but to try and find behind them the real deeds that bring real benefits to people. It is important to understand that . . . NGOs are not perfect and one should treat it as unavoidable. Perhaps, a bright future will come when NGOs won't need translation into a normal language. Perhaps, the population will even get used to some terms; after all, NGOs in Russia are only a decade old. . . .

Even today many large foundations and NGOs have public relations specialists working hard to promote their organizations. This is a fairly difficult task because they have to begin with introducing the masses [*im prikhoditsia prezhde vsego vnedriat v massy*] to the idea of the "third sector." And you cannot touch the "third sector" . . . with your hands [*rukami ne potrogaiesh*] for it is not a product, but a range of services for the population.

The NGO movement cannot develop fully [*polnotsenno*] without the journalists' help and participation. And the language barrier is one of the obvious obstacles on this path that we need to overcome.

The manual uses the terms "civil society" and "the third sector" interchangeably. However, the emphasis, as this excerpt illustrates, is on the third sector as a sector of professionals. The sector's nonpolitical nature is conveyed in its description as a provider of services. The manual articulates that although the NGO language is an obvious "barrier," NGOs will continue speaking it, and journalists and the rest of the population will have to make an effort to understand it.

Finally, this is how the manual's opening chapter explains the division of society into three sectors and introduces the notion of the third sector:[34]

The state is the first sector of society. It takes care of all of us, as a crowd or a mass, not paying attention to the hang-ups [*zamorochki*] of an individual citizen. . . . Business is the second sector of society which takes care of us when we pay our hard-earned rubles. What remains is the third sector.

What is it? It is associations of people coming together to help themselves and others without the goal of making a profit [*ne s tseliu izvlechenia pribyli*]. It is bee breeder associations and tourist clubs, charitable foundations and environmental groups. It consists of those who are not putting up with things as they are . . . Of those who come together to try changing their lives on their own. . . .

The nonprofit sector exists all over the world because it has found its own niche in the market, even if its peculiar niche is the market for social services. Russia's nonprofit sector faces many obstacles. The main obstacle is the unequal relationship with the authorities and business. And it slows down solving many of our problems and ultimately constrains the development of civil society in our country.

The donor-NGO output, of which this manual is a representative example, provides a good illustration of what sociological neo-institutionalists would call a new organizational form engaging in "institutional work to justify that form's public theory" (DiMaggio 1988: 25).[35] The institutional work in question involves third-sector organizational entrepreneurs advancing legitimating accounts about NGOs and the division of society into three sectors. This "public theory" is new in two respects in the context of post-Soviet societies: as cultural form, or genre, and as cultural content, or story and symbols (Adams 2005). Concerning the former, the manner of presentation is an explicit copy of a foreign genre whether it is the chatty title and style of *Everything You Wanted to Know about the Nonprofit Sector but Were Afraid to Ask* or the packaging of information into "common myths." The form is chosen deliberately—to signal NGOs' novelty because it is the novelty that supposedly makes NGOs interesting and attractive. The content, introducing the division of society into three sectors and preaching the virtue of self-reliance, is not only new but bound to find limited appeal in post-Soviet societies, which continue to mourn the passing of the Soviet paternalistic welfare state and believe that the state, not individuals, should be responsible for "taking care of us" (Pantin 2002; Gal and Kligman 2000). Although donors and NGOs seek to educate and to enlighten, they do so by using a message and a medium that are unfamiliar to the post-Soviet public.

U.S. Donors Are Institutionalized, but NGOs' Position Is Tenuous

So far I have analyzed three elements—material resources, socializing rituals, and discursive practices—of the Western grant economy set in motion by U.S. civil society assistance. Whereas analyses of post-Soviet NGOs commonly focus on issue areas (gender inequality, human rights, environmental protection),[36] I wanted to explore what the post-Soviet NGO is in sociological terms. I find that the post-Soviet NGO is defined by the people it employs (educated professionals), by the physical space it inhabits (Western-style office), and by the language it speaks (the language of three sectors). Whereas other scholars might view these features as self-evident—after all, that is what NGOs are in the West—I find them remarkable because Russia and Kyrgyzstan are not the West, and the NGO is a recent organizational and cultural species in the post-Soviet world. American public and private civil society assistance, which was the earliest and largest NGO-oriented assistance from the West, is the primary reason why post-Soviet NGOs appear to bear such a strong resemblance to their Western counterparts. This result is achieved through the socialization post-Soviet NGOs undergo by frequenting institutional venues, such as training and seminars, that are the centerpiece of the Western grant economy. The latter is the context in which foreign donors construct and interact with post-Soviet NGOs. The Western grant economy is both a site of mutual attraction where foreigners and locals come together and a site of institutional reproduction where foreigners and locals maintain their relationship.

The diffusion of NGOs over the last fifteen years has been motivated by foreign donors' desire to impose a familiar conceptual and institutional order, or legibility (Scott 1998), on unfamiliar and confusing post-Soviet terrain. I argue that U.S. donors have accomplished this task by building up the post-Soviet NGO sector. In so doing, the donors succeeded in institutionalizing themselves, having created a constituency vying for their funds and ideas. At the same time, the position of post-Soviet NGOs themselves is far more tenuous, precisely because the NGO "cultural schema" (Sewell 1992) familiar to the U.S. donors is unfamiliar to post-Soviet societies. By learning how to make themselves recognizable to Western donors—how to look like an NGO, talk like an NGO, and behave like an NGO—local actors who form NGOs simultaneously make themselves illegible to their own societies, where almost no one outside the donor-NGO circle understands what the words for NGOs and civil society mean.

Instead of helping NGOs to communicate with the larger public, the language that donors and NGOs speak serves to enhance the insularity of the donor-NGO universe because they use words that remain empty signifiers in the post-Soviet symbolic landscape. As Russian sociologist Vadim Volkov points out, this is an illustration of the concept of *grazhdanskoie obshchestvo,* literally, "turns near empty and devoid of history behind it." As he sees it, "this is not the problem of applicability, but rather that of cross-cultural translation. . . . To translate a concept across cultural boundaries would require a search for an indigenous concept of equal historical and practical significance" (Volkov 1996).[37]

The notion of *grazhdanskoie obshchestvo* first appeared in Soviet public life during Gorbachev's perestroika, reflecting its ascendancy in Eastern Europe and the West. It has since become a staple of the post-Soviet political and mass media discourse. NGOs born out of Western civil society assistance have greatly contributed to the ubiquity of the phrase. But even though U.S. donors have not been responsible for introducing *grazhdanskoie obshchestvo* to the former Soviet Union, their approach is the opposite of cross-cultural translation: the implicit and often explicit premise of U.S. and other Western assistance is that literal borrowing is desirable since ideal-typical Western institutional and cultural forms are seen as universally applicable.[38] In addition, local actors, the NGOs themselves, often embrace such a borrowing: they are attracted to Western concepts precisely because they associate progressive modernity with the West and because these concepts do not carry Soviet baggage. As anthropologist Julie Hemment shows, many NGO activists like the language of the "third sector" because it enables them to reclaim working for the public good from its old Soviet associations as an activity that appeared voluntary but was in fact coerced by the state and the Communist Party. The language of the third sector also allows them to make sense of the post-Soviet involution: NGO activists see the third sector as a "righteous," moral, and decent location, separate from the other two sectors, business and politics, that are widely viewed in contemporary Russia as immoral (Hemment 2004).

However, NGOs' socialization into the foreign grant economy simultaneously facilitates their interaction with Western donors and makes it difficult for them to step outside the donor-NGO universe. Scholars note that for the time being, post-Soviet NGOs' existence and survival depends on the continuing operation of foreign assistance, because there are no other sources of comparable economic support. What is less appreciated is that the institutional logic that comprises material and symbolic practices (Friedland and Alford 1991) operating inside the Western grant economy does not travel well outside it.

One good example is fundraising. American donors, including those I interviewed, frequently express concerns about NGO sustainability. Extending the institutional logic of the professional NGO from the United States, they define sustainability in terms of fundraising. In the absence of a sizable and affluent middle class willing to make sufficient donations to NGOs in either Russia or Kyrgyzstan, American donors have encouraged NGOs to cultivate local sources of funding in business and government.[39] This is bound to be problematic given the popular perception, which NGOs share, that these are spheres of dirty and immoral activities. Indeed, the study I referred to earlier that was funded by U.S. donors themselves confirms it (Baranova et al. 2001). For instance, when NGOs apply for funding or bid for social provision contracts from local governments, the latter often stipulate that the government must be the only source of funding and that those NGOs that have, for instance, applied for Soros grants, need not apply for government money. Confronting such attitudes from officials, NGOs that succeed in receiving government funding feel conflicted, fearing, justifiably, that they might lose their autonomy. When it comes to raising funds from Russian businesses, many NGO leaders say that fundraising is a "shameful" activity, that they feel embarrassed asking for businessmen's money, and that soliciting funds from sponsors is "a necessity we all condemn" (Baranova et al. 2001, 7). The situation is aggravated by the fact that few business people know what the third sector is as well as by economic instability (a business that did well last year and gave some money to NGOs may do poorly this year) and legal uncertainty surrounding charitable donations in Russia.

As these examples demonstrate, NGOs face numerous difficulties when attempting to deploy the skills they have learned to make themselves successful with foreign donors outside the immediate donor-NGO universe. Compared to asking for money from the Russian government or business, which NGOs find shameful and demeaning, getting U.S. donors' grants is empowering. For donors, NGOs' value to society is self-evident, whereas government officials and businessmen do not always view NGOs as legitimate. Besides, Western grants provide a dignified life and work style that neither government nor local private funding can match, and donors and NGOs speak the common language that others (the state, business, or the larger public) do not understand. It is not surprising then that NGOs orient themselves toward the donors.

The interaction between the U.S. donors and post-Soviet NGOs provides an on-the-ground view of structural isomorphism. U.S. civil society donors are "powerful organizations [that] force their immediate relational networks to adapt to their structures and relations" (Meyer and Rowan 1991, 49). Using Paul DiMaggio and Walter Powell's typology of isomorphic processes, I suggest that the variety of isomorphism we are observing here is coercive isomorphism, which involves "the direct and explicit imposition of organizational models on dependent organizations" as well as "more subtle and less explicit" pressures (DiMaggio and Powell 1991, 68).[40]

The isomorphic pressure, experienced by post-Soviet NGOs, comes in the form of elaborate requirements for writing grant applications, budgetary plans, accounting reports, and other documents that donors demand of their recipients. An NGO finds itself under the pressure to conform to donors' expectations even before it obtains its first grant, because the process of writing a grant application already requires it to mold itself according to the terms set by the donors. Since a successful post-Soviet NGO is an NGO that succeeds in winning Western grants repeatedly, its practices are thoroughly permeated by donor influence and constantly adapted to donors' programmatic and bureaucratic preferences.

The fact that local actors eagerly participate in this process and derive benefits from their association with the donors does not attenuate the coercive nature of the relationship. Local actors are such keen participants because the very post-Soviet society in which they live and which is riven by profound economic, social, and cultural involution makes the Western grant economy, in both its material and its symbolic dimensions, so attractive. This is not to say that NGOs are unaware of or entirely happy with the implications of their situation; they are quite aware, and they voice their concerns (Hemment 2004). In fact, coercive isomorphism is best glimpsed through NGOs' complaints. I will give two examples from my research. Acknowledging the donors' crucial role in supporting environmental NGOs, one environmental activist in Moscow suggests that the way grantmaking is structured often produces "destructive effects." He explains:

> Getting a grant depends on how well you write a grant application, not on how effective your organization is. As a consequence, a successful grant application can be used in Moscow and in Chukotka, although from the standpoint of nature protection these are very different regions. Because it is more difficult for provincial NGOs to obtain grants [since donors are located in Moscow], pursuing grants becomes even more of a priority for them. Grants stipulate rigid deadlines, which often don't correspond to the work that needs to be done. . . . If until recently environment was a priority for European donors and international organizations, in the last two years they all switched to poverty. But it means that all the money that had been spent on environmental programs earlier went to waste. Those NGOs that had worked consistently, produced good results, laid the foundations for productive work suddenly lost support. The donors did not allow for any transition from environment to poverty. But these things are inter-related; they could be related to one another if a more smooth transition had taken place.

A human rights activist at a leading Russian human rights NGO describes the rules of the game imposed by donors:

Most donors are interested only in separate projects. Very few have a global view. But the world is not made up of thousands of projects, as the donors seem to think. Projects are not necessarily steps toward something cumulative. . . . NGOs are inclined toward self-sufficiency, and they should be taught how to interact with others. Here, donors' support for Internet projects has played a very negative role; many put up a website and think that it's enough. But in a provincial Russian city, for instance, few people use Internet, so very few people really know about this NGO, and the project's significance is small . . .

Recently, a foreign donor came and said: we want to help you, what ideas do you have? I have this idea that we should connect NGOs and libraries, because libraries can provide a strategic and physical space while NGOs can provide ideas. I suggested a couple of things: one is a cooperative online catalogue of ten libraries and NGOs, the other one is to organize cooperation between regional libraries and regional NGOs. NGOs could organize human rights discussions, book exhibits (we could help them with materials from Moscow) devoted to prisoners, refugees, you name it. And this donor chose without blinking the Internet project, and gave substantial money, $25,000. It's a good idea, but a far less important one.

These two quotes convey well the donors' power to impose their authority on recipient NGOs. Although the latter might think that better alternatives are available, they have to conform to donors' programmatic choices. Perhaps even more vividly, these quotes illustrate how coercive isomorphism operates through the suppression of local knowledge, or what Scott (1998) calls *mētis*. Indeed, the legibility desired by the donors comes at the expense of NGO activists' local knowledge and practices.[41] The interviewees from donor organizations liked to tell me that as the post-Soviet NGO sector became more professionalized donors increasingly treated recipient NGOs as full-fledged partners and sought out their input (for instance, both NGO leaders quoted above sat on donors' advisory panels). However, in reality the NGOs' input into the donor-NGO interaction is immeasurably smaller than the donors'. Not all NGOs are upset about donors' lack of interest in local knowledge; many are content to keep organizing seminars and creating websites as long as donors readily fund these activities. The ones that are not content are those that aspire to have "a global view" and think of ways to compel the weak, apathetic, and disorganized post-Soviet public into a semblance of civic activities. And yet even as foreign donors complain of the severe lack of civic spirit in recipient societies, indigenous initiatives have a very hard time making their way into donor-funded programs.

Conclusion

The coercive isomorphism inherent in the Western grant economy and multiple implications of the newness of post-Soviet NGOs remain under-appreciated in the existing accounts of U.S. civil society assistance for post-socialist countries. U.S. civil society assistance operates by diffusing NGOs to receiving societies. I argue that the main effect of U.S. civil society assistance is that U.S. donors themselves have become institutionalized, whereas post-Soviet NGOs occupy a far more tenuous position. This is because NGOs represent an organizational and cultural form unfamiliar to post-Soviet societies and because NGOs' activities are largely determined by donors' preferences and priorities. In other words, the donor-driven NGO diffusion works through the exclusion of local knowledge and practices. Premised on the literal borrowing of Western cultural forms, the NGO diffusion orients recipient NGOs toward the donors by enhancing the insularity of the donor-NGO universe. It is therefore another iteration of development as a hegemonic form of social engineering (Scott 1998), where Western organizational and cultural models are assumed—by both diffusers (donors) and adopters (local NGO actors)—to be superior to local models.

Acknowledgments

I thank the following organizations for providing funding for this research: the International Research and Exchanges Board, the Social Science Research Council, the American Association for University Women, the Kennan Institute, and Princeton University. I am very grateful to Michèle Lamont, Miguel Centeno, Stephen Kotkin, Gilbert Rozman, and Robert Wuthnow for their comments on earlier drafts.

Notes

1. We do not know from publicly available data what proportion of that money is spent in receiving countries. Because USAID rarely administers aid directly, it means that programs to create and promote local NGOs are designed and implemented by USAID's American nonprofit contractors. Hence, the U.S. government's efforts to promote NGOs abroad also support an infrastructure of nonprofit contractors at home.

2. According to the information posted online at http://www.fordfound.org (accessed spring 2008).

3. Another major U.S. funder, the Chicago-based John D. and Catherine T. MacArthur Foundation, opened an office in Moscow in 1992. Although MacArthur occasionally gives grants to NGOs, its primary focus is on scientific research and education.

4. This chapter draws on interview-based research conducted in Moscow, Russia, and Bishkek, Kyrgyzstan, in 2002–2003.

5. For example, the Government Accountability Office notes that USAID's own inspector general reported in 1994 that in Russia the agency "lacked an information system with baseline data, targets, time frames, and quantifiable indicators by which to measure program progress and results." The GAO adds: "USAID's Bureau for Europe and the New Independent States was exempted from a new agencywide management system because the program was intended to be short term and regional rather than long term and country-specific. USAID officials said the pressure to provide assistance quickly meant forgoing . . . developing progress indicators" (GAO 1995, 11–12).

6. In 1994, when U.S. assistance for the post-Soviet transition was at its highest level, congressional appropriations for economic and political aid for Russia were $2.5 billion (U.S. Department of State 1995).

7. In 1992–2002, democracy and civil society assistance made up about 10 percent of all U.S. assistance for Eurasia (Aksartova 2005).

8. Kyrgyzstan was in the ruble zone until May 1993.

9. Abuse comes in many shapes. George Soros's Open Society Institute and USAID fell victim to more spectacular forms of fraud. In the early 1990s OSI's Russian employees used the foundation "as a cover for their own international business dealings. While the scope of these undertakings, all carried out without authorization, has never been fully determined, enough details have surfaced to suggest that the scams were broad and imaginative. For example, a fishing fleet operating off Nigeria had been using the foundation's name, credit, and, perhaps, its funds. Another venture involved the purchase of 110 thoroughbred horses and their sale in Italy. Three one-time directors of the foundation ended up establishing a department store. Cars meant for the use of the foundation ended up as private property" (Kaufman 2002, 226).
In 2004, a U.S. court ruled that two American advisers, Andrei Shleifer and Jonathan Hay, from the now defunct Harvard Institute for International Development, breached the terms of the federal contract while they led the largest USAID-funded program for economic reform in Russia in 1992–1997. The infraction involved making personal investments with the benefit of insider knowledge at the time when Shleifer and Hay were supposed to provide impartial advice to the Russian government on how to design its laws and regulatory institutions (Bombardieri 2004; Wedel 1998 and 2004).

10. An organization has to register in order to be able to open a bank account, engage in financial transactions, rent office space, and hire and pay employees.

11. In an article, "How to Obtain a Grant?" posted by the online Russian magazine *Russkii Zhurnal*, its author dispenses advice based on his own record of obtaining multiple grants from foreign donors in Russia. This is how he instructs grant seekers to present themselves so that foreign donors can recognize them as NGOs: "Your organization must have an office. The office should have a respectable, European look [*dolzhen smotretsia prilichno, po-ievropeiski*]. It must have a fax machine, Xerox, computers, Internet; it should be clean and comfortable, and you should treat visitors politely. In short, your office would resemble a business office but be a bit more modest. It is important not to overdo it" (Kordonskii 2003; translation is mine).

12. See Nikitin and Buchanan (2002) and Weigle (2002) for detailed accounts of the forum.

13. In 1999 the World Bank and IMF established new rules under which the heavily indebted poor countries, such as Kyrgyzstan, could apply for their concessional loans. According to these rules, Kyrgyzstan's government had to prepare a comprehensive strategy for poverty reduction, the so-called Poverty Reduction Strategy Paper (PRSP). The PRSP mechanism required Kyrgyzstan's government to consult with "external donors" and "domestic stakeholders," including NGOs, in the course of preparing the strategy. See the PRSP fact sheet online at http://www.imf.org (accessed November 3, 2008).

14. Michael Burawoy, who introduced the concept of involution into the analysis of post-Soviet society, describes the post-Soviet transition as the primitivization of economic, political, and social life. Economy "eats at its own foundations" (Burawoy 1996, 1105; see also Burawoy 2001) without rejuvenating production, politics is feudalized, life expectancy plummets, and informal networks proliferate.

15. Kennedy (1992, 65); emphasis in the original.

16. The NGO life and work style, however, establishes a benchmark so that NGO professionals, when they leave NGOs, look for economic opportunities that can match or exceed the material benefits to which they have become accustomed. The most common career advancement is to move on to donor agencies themselves or to international organizations (Mandel 2002).

17. U.S. government reporting on democracy and civil society promotion has a special category for training, and in 1992–2002 this category consumed one-fifth, or $200 million, of total U.S. bilateral civil society assistance to the former Soviet Union (U.S. Department of State 1995–2003).

18. See Ablova (2002); translation and italics are mine.

19. As Thomas Carothers (2002a, 2002b) points out and as I have found out, donors rarely, if ever, talk about failures, much less quantify them.

20. With one or two exceptions, my NGO interviewees were university graduates, and many held advanced degrees.

21. American journalist Matt Bivens's story in *Harper's Magazine* (1997) on his short-lived career as a private-sector consultant in Kazakhstan painted a particularly devastating picture of the follies of U.S. technical assistance in the former Soviet Union in the early 1990s.

22. "Many US officials, Russians, and [USAID] contractors said that relying on 'fly-through' consultants . . . was an ineffective approach" (GAO 1995, 7).

23. OSI-Russia was an exception to this rule with its network of about two dozen regional offices.

24. Several interviewees in Moscow noted that the 1998 Russian economic crisis accelerated this trend. After the crisis many donors and USAID contractors reduced expatriate salaries, which precipitated an exodus of Westerners paid on a Western scale and provided employers with an additional incentive to hire and promote Russians paid on a much lower local scale.

25. These figures underestimate the total number of beneficiaries of U.S.-funded educational programs, because they do not include alumni of OSI-funded exchange

programs or several hundred students and alumni of the American University in Kyrgyzstan.

26. Retrieved from http://www.auca.kg in the summer of 2005.

27. The Russian, not Kyrgyz, language is predominant among Bishkek's NGOs as well.

28. A Russian journalist writing about U.S. assistance captured well the prevailing attitudes: "What do Americans get out of this? Is the first question journalists always ask US Embassy representatives at opening ceremonies for the latest project built in Russia with American money? . . . As anyone knows, only your mother will love you and help you unselfishly. The image of expanding American imperialism is not yet banished from our minds, and it is being reinforced by a new post-perestroika skepticism toward the West. . . . [We] are a great power ourselves. Sarcasm and hurt feelings always crop up in our conversations about aid. . . . They treat us like an underdeveloped country! Some newspapers go as far as to portray all foreigners, particularly [advisers] to the State Property Committee, as spies. Why should they be helping to privatize our enterprises? That looks very suspicious, particularly if [your notions of how foreigners normally behave come from the American soap opera] *Santa Barbara* and all those action films" (Yemelyanov 1995; translated into English by the Foreign Broadcast Information Service).

29. The most likely reason is that Russians see NGOs as equivalent to the Soviet-era state-sponsored public institutions (*obshchestvennye organizatsii*), which also claimed to rely on volunteer work and advance the greater public good.

30. The study is based on surveys and focus groups of both general population and NGOs. It was conducted by a team of Russian sociologists in 1999 in eight Russian cities.

31. These publications were produced by the Moscow office of the British Charities Aid Foundation (CAF). CAF Russia was started with British funds in 1993 and has since received funding from U.S. foundations, including a $1 million endowment grant from the C. S. Mott Foundation. According to its website, http://www.cafrussia.ru, by the spring of 2008 it had spent more than $40 million on over 300 initiatives all across Russia. Located in Moscow, CAF Russia functions as a national resource center for NGOs and for budding Russian philanthropists.

32. Dorosheva (2002: 24–29). All translations from this publication are mine.

33. Ibid., 30–32.

34. Ibid., 10–11.

35. Cited in Friedland and Alford (1991, 246).

36. See, for instance, Evans, Henry and Sundstrom (2005), Henderson (2003), Mendelson and Glenn (2002), Sperling (1999), Sundstrom (2006).

37. Relevant page reference is missing in the original document.

38. See Peter Evans (2004) on "institutional monocropping" in international development.

39. They also encourage NGOs to seek funding from other international donors—especially in Kyrgyzstan, where there is not much private wealth and the state itself is

indigent—as the latter followed in recent years in American donors' footsteps and initiated civil society assistance.

40. DiMaggio and Powell (1991) distinguish between three types of structural isomorphism: coercive (imposed by authority), mimetic (produced by uncertainty), and normative (stemming from professionalization).

41. Describing her experience of serving on the board of a USAID-funded project "to fund local NGOs and train potential NGO workers in the requisite techniques for forming them" in Kazakhstan, anthropologist Ruth Mandel reports that "[p]roposals that remained unfunded were those to which the Western funders could not relate. They were, in a sense, 'too' local" (Mandel 2002, 285–86).

References

Ablova, Natalia. 2002. "Vseobshchaia seminarizatsia SMI i eio rezultaty" [Seminarization of the Media and Its Results]. Unpublished paper. Bishkek, Kyrgyzstan.

Adams, Laura. 2005. "Modernity, Post-Colonialism, and Theatrical Form in Uzbekistan." *Slavic Review* 64, no. 2: 333–54.

Aksartova, Sada. 2005. "Civil Society from Abroad: U.S. Donors in the Former Soviet Union." Ph.D. dissertation, Department of Sociology, Princeton University.

Alekseeva, Olga. 1997. *Tretii sektor, ili Blagotvoritelnost dlia "chainikov"* [The Third Sector, or Charity for Dummies]. Moscow: BBC MPM.

Baimatov, Bakyt, Bermet Stakeeva, and Simon Heap. 2002. "'From My Private House to the White House': Civil Society in the Kyrgyz Republic." Bishkek, Kyrgyzstan: International NGO Training and Research Center (INTRAC).

Baranova, Irina, et al. 2001. *Otnoshenie naselenia k blagotvoritelnosti v Rossii* [Popular Attitudes to Charity/Philanthropy in Russia]. Moscow: Charities Aid Foundation.

Berger, Peter L., and Thomas Luckmann. 1966. *The Social Construction of Reality: A Treatise in the Sociology of Knowledge.* Garden City: Doubleday.

Bivens, Matt. 1997. "Aboard the Gravy Train: In Kazakhstan, the Farce That Is US Foreign Aid." *Harper's Magazine* (August): 69–76.

Bogomolov, Oleg. 1993. "Why Russia Is Counting the Cost after Falling off the Tightrope." *Guardian,* March 10.

Bombardieri, Marcella. 2004. "Harvard Professor, Employee Liable in Fraud Case." *Boston Globe,* June 29.

Burawoy, Michael. 1996. "The State and Economic Involution: Russia through a China Lens." *World Development* 24, no. 6: 1105–17.

———. 2001. "Transition without Transformation: Russia's Involutionary Road to Capitalism." *East European Politics and Societies* 15, no. 2: 269–90.

Carothers, Thomas. 2002a. "The End of the Transition Paradigm." *Journal of Democracy* 13, no. 1: 5–21.

———. 2002b. "A Reply to My Critics." *Journal of Democracy* 13, no. 3: 33–38.

DiMaggio, Paul J. 1988. "Interest and Agency in Institutional Theory." In *Institutional Patterns and Organizations,* ed. Lynne G. Zucker, 3–22. Cambridge, Mass.: Ballinger.

DiMaggio, Paul J., and Walter W. Powell. 1991 [1983]. "The Iron Cage Revisited: Institutional Isomorphism and Collective Rationality in Organizational Field." In *The New Institutionalism in Organizational Analysis,* ed. Walter W. Powell and Paul J. DiMaggio, 63–82. Chicago: University of Chicago Press.

Dorosheva, Natalia. 2002. *Vsio, shto Vy khoteli znat o nekommercheskom sektore, no boialis sprosit: Posobie dlia zhurnalistov* [Everything You Wanted to Know about the Nonprofit Sector but Were Afraid to Ask: A Manual for Journalists]. Moscow: Gendalf.

Eurasia Foundation (EF). 2003. "Fiscal Year 2002 Year End Report. Presented to the US Agency for International Development." Washington, D.C.

Evans, Alfred B., Laura A. Henry, and Lisa McIntosh Sundstrom, eds. 2005. *Russian Civil Society: A Critical Assessment.* Armonk, N.Y.: M. E. Sharpe.

Evans, Peter. 2004. "Development as Institutional Change: The Pitfalls of Monocropping and the Potentials of Deliberation." *Studies in Comparative International Development* 38, no. 4: 30–52.

The Financial Times. 1995. "Survey of Russia." April 10.

Fond "Obshchestvennoie mnenie" (FOM). 2001. *Pogovorim o grazhdanskom obshchestve* [Let's Talk about Civil Society]. Moscow: Institut FOM.

Friedland, Roger, and Robert A. Alford. 1991. "Bringing Society Back In: Symbols, Practices, and Institutional Contradictions." In *The New Institutionalism in Organizational Analysis,* ed. Walter W. Powell and Paul J. DiMaggio, 232–63. Chicago: University of Chicago Press.

Gal, Susan, and Gail Kligman. 2000. *The Politics of Gender after Postsocialism: A Comparative-Historical Essay.* Princeton, N.J.: Princeton University Press.

Government Accountability Office (GAO). 1995. "Foreign Assistance: Assessment of Selected USAID Projects in Russia" (GAO-NSIAD-95-156). Washington, D.C.

Hemment, Julie. 2004. "The Riddle of the Third Sector: Civil Society, International Aid, and NGOs in Russia." *Anthropological Quarterly* 77, no. 2: 215–41.

Henderson, Sarah L. 2003. *Building Democracy in Contemporary Russia: Western Support for Grassroots Organizations.* Ithaca, N.Y.: Cornell University Press.

Hiatt, Fred. 1993. "On Brink of Promise—or Peril; Inflation Could Collapse Russia's Newly Privatized Economy." *Washington Post,* February 4.

Howard, Marc Morjé. 2003. *The Weakness of Civil Society in Post-Communist Europe.* Cambridge: Cambridge University Press.

International Research and Exchanges Board (IREX). 2001 "Promoting and Strengthening Russian NGO Development Program." Washington, D.C.

Kaufman, Michael T. 2002. *Soros: The Life and Times of a Messianic Billionaire.* New York: Alfred A. Knopf.

Kennedy, Michael D. 1992. "The Intelligentsia in the Constitution of Civil Societies and Post-Communist Regimes in Hungary and Poland." *Theory and Society* 21, no. 1: 29–76.

Koestler, Arthur. 1972. *The Call Girls: A Tragicomedy with Prologue and Epilogue.* London: Hutchinson.

Kordonskii, Mikhail. 2003. "Kak poluchit grant?" [How to Obtain a Grant?]. *Russkii Zhurnal.* Available at: http://old.russ.ru/ist_sour/20030117_mk.html, January 17. Accessed September 2008.

Kotkin, Stephen. 1995. *Magnetic Mountain: Stalinism as a Civilization.* Berkeley and Los Angeles: University of California Press.

Krimsky, George A. 2002. "Struggle and Promise: The Independent Press of Central Asia, Kyrgyzstan." Almaty, Kazakhstan: International Center for Journalists.

Mandel, Ruth. 2002. "Seeding Civil Society." In *Postsocialism: Ideas, Ideologies and Practices in Eurasia,* ed. C. M. Hann, 279–96. London: Routledge.

Mendelson, Sarah E., and John K. Glenn, eds. 2002. *The Power and Limits of NGOs: A Critical Look at Building Democracy in Eastern Europe and Eurasia.* New York: Columbia University Press.

Meyer, John W., and Brian Rowan. 1991 [1977]. "Institutionalized Organizations: Formal Structure as Myth and Ceremony." In *The New Institutionalism in Organizational Analysis,* ed. Walter W. Powell and Paul J. DiMaggio, 41–62. Chicago: University of Chicago Press.

Mroz, Thomas A., et al. 2003. "Monitoring Economic Conditions in the Russian Federation: The Russia Longitudinal Monitoring Survey 1992–2002." Report submitted to the U.S. Agency for International Development. Chapel Hill, N.C.: Carolina Population Center.

Nikitin, Alexander, and Jane Buchanan. 2002. "The Kremlin's Civic Forum: Cooperation or Co-optation for Civil Society in Russia?" *Demokratizatsiya* 10, no. 2: 147–65.

Pantin, V. I., ed. 2002. *Zapad i zapadnyie tsennosti v rossiiskom obshchestvennom soznanii* [The West and Western Values in Russian Public Consciousness]. Moscow: IMEMO RAN.

Salamon, Lester M. 1994. "The Rise of the Nonprofit Sector." *Foreign Affairs* 73, no. 4: 109–22.

Scott, James C. 1998. *Seeing Like a State: How Certain Schemes to Improve the Human Condition Have Failed.* New Haven, Conn.: Yale University Press.

Sevortyan, Anna, ed. 2000. *Doklad o sostoianii nekommercheskogo sektora v Rossii i ego vklade v sotsialno-ekonomicheskoie razvitie strany* [Report on the State of the Nonprofit Sector in Russia and Its Contribution to the Country's Socio-economic Development]. Moscow: Center for the Development of Democracy and Human Rights.

Sewell, William H., Jr. 1992. "A Theory of Structure: Duality, Agency, and Transformation." *American Journal of Sociology* 98, no. 1: 1–29.

Sperling, Valerie. 1999. *Organizing Women in Contemporary Russia: Engendering Transition.* Cambridge: Cambridge University Press.

Strang, David, and John W. Meyer. 1993. "Institutional Conditions for Diffusion." *Theory and Society* 22, no. 4: 487–511.

Sundstrom, Lisa McIntosh. 2006. *Funding Civil Society: Foreign Assistance and NGO Development in Russia.* Stanford, Calif.: Stanford University Press.

Tendler, Judith. 1975. *Inside Foreign Aid.* Baltimore: Johns Hopkins University Press.

United Nations (UN). 2001. "Kyrgyzstan: Common Country Assessment." Prepared by Anara Tabyshalieva in cooperation with the National Statistics Committee of Kyrgyzstan. Bishkek, Kyrgyzstan.

U.S. Department of State. 1995–2006. "US Government Assistance to and Cooperative Activities with Eurasia." Fiscal Years 1994–2006. Prepared annually by the Office of the Coordinator of U.S. Assistance to Europe and Eurasia. Washington, D.C.: Bureau of European and Eurasian Affairs.

Viviano, Frank. 1993. "Russia Tries to Combat Black Market." *San Francisco Chronicle*, October 16.

Volkov, Vadim. 1996. "Obshchestvennost: An Indigenous Concept of Civil Society." In *Civil Society in Northern Europe in Theory and Practice*, ed. Elena Zdravomyslova and Kaija Heikkinen. St. Petersburg: Centre for Independent Social Research.

Wedel, Janine. 1998. *Collision and Collusion: The Strange Case of Western Aid to Eastern Europe, 1989–1998*. New York: St. Martin's Press.

———. 2004. "Danger of Private Agendas in Foreign Policy." *Financial Times*, August 11.

Weigle, Marcia A. 2002. "On the Road to the Civic Forum: State and Civil Society from Yeltsin to Putin." *Demokratizatsiya* 10, 2: 117–46.

Yemelyanov, Petr. 1995. "US Aid Programs in Russia Praised." *Ekho Planety*, May 5.

8. Dialectics of Patronage

Logics of Accountability at the African AIDS-NGO Interface

← ──────────────────────────────── →

ANN SWIDLER

The AIDS catastrophe has justified huge projections of Northern philanthropy, power, and resources into the Global South. I focus here on both the influence and the limits of that power; by looking at the influx of AIDS organizations in sub-Saharan Africa, I examine how differing institutional logics interact. Using evidence from a larger study of responses to AIDS in sub-Saharan Africa, I ask how NGO interventions in Africa are inserted into existing patterns of social and institutional life.

The dominant form of political accountability in Africa is not universalistic bureaucratic rule, but personalistic patron-client ties (Chabal and Daloz 1999). We can understand the institutional consequences of NGO interventions first by understanding their effects upon—and their frequent incorporation within—these patron-client relationships. More broadly, we can think about the institutional effects of international interventions into African societies by asking when those interventions make such traditional forms of power more responsive and accountable, versus more exclusionary, divisive, and irresponsible. I also suggest ways of thinking about how NGO interventions might increase or decrease social trust, social capital, and the capacity of local social institutions.

AIDS in Sub-Saharan Africa

The AIDS crisis in Africa is an ideal laboratory for analyzing the insertion of institutional logics from abroad. First, the financial and organizational resources committed to preventing and treating HIV/AIDS in Africa have been growing dramatically since the mid-1990s (UNFPA n.d.). AIDS was already a high-profile disease with a voluble and politically effective constituency (Epstein 1996) when, after the mid-1990s, the enormity of the global pandemic produced a torrent of organizational activity and an ever-widening flow of resources, much of it channeled through (or originating in) the NGO sector.[1] According to the United Nations Resource Flows Project, which tracks funding for population activities, since 1995 AIDS funding increased from 9 percent to 43 percent of population funding with more than 400 percent increases in resources for sub-Saharan Africa, and with an estimated 57 percent of population assistance flowing through NGOs (Resource Flows Project 2004).

Second, most African states are so poor that they may have little bargaining leverage when it comes to negotiations with international donors (Shiffman 2008). Some scholars have argued that African states may trade on the misery of their own people, with suffering their best "export" (Bayart 1993). But Africa's poverty and its weakness in governance mean that outside donors are often providing a substantial share of a country's AIDS health budget, and as much as 90 percent of its budget for AIDS activities (see, e.g., Allen and Heald 2004).

That many African states are deviant with respect to world models of the nation state provides another reason to look at how they respond to philanthropic interventions. Just as commercial interactions with Western firms are transforming China's institutional culture (Guthrie 1999), in Africa the bevy of international NGOs, often performing governmental or quasi-governmental functions, are the main transmission belts for globally validated institutional models. African states—corrupt rather than transparent; riven by internal conflict rather than stable and unified; exercising only partial sovereignty over the territory they supposedly govern (Herbst 2000)—are the "bad boys" of the global institutional system. They are then ideal candidates for the instant makeover the international system aspires to provide.

There are additional reasons why AIDS and the organizations that have rushed in to deal with it provide such an interesting site for analysis of contending cultural logics. The biomedical peculiarity of AIDS itself creates unusual interdependencies between global and local actors (see Heimer 2007). AIDS presents itself as a distinctive illness only when defined and named by international medical authorities. Its biological distinctiveness—the long time between infection and visible illness, the fact that someone who looks and feels healthy can infect others, and AIDS's manifestation as an array of other illnesses rather than a single, distinctive syndrome—make the entire illness itself, from definition to prevention to treatment, especially dependent on the intersection of local and international actors. On the other hand, because in Africa HIV is transmitted primarily through sexual contact, dealing with HIV and AIDS has not been purely, or even primarily, a medical matter. The well-worn techniques of international public health—vaccinations, clinics, visiting nurses, even sanitation and such amenities as wells, latrines, and nutrition—are largely irrelevant. Like family planning but more so, AIDS prevention seems to require changes in some of the deepest, most intimate, and least understood aspects of human behavior.[2]

Finally, the AIDS crisis is distinctive precisely because it is a "crisis." (Malawians again and again refer to AIDS as *mulili,* a word used for the devastation of the biblical plagues.) Even with the advent of antiretroviral drugs, it is fair to say that there is no effective, agreed-upon technology against AIDS. Yet there is a remarkable global consensus that AIDS is a devastating crisis to which the world must respond. Reports detailing the millions infected (whether the more than 33 million estimate of today or the 42 million of several years ago [UNAIDS/WHO 2002, 2004, 2007]), the millions newly infected each year, the millions of deaths, the orphans, devastated households, blasted economies— all create an insistent chorus.[3]

An urgent crisis without a clear technical fix has generated a remarkable proliferation of organizational effort. While UNAIDS and the Global Fund (GFATM) have begun to try to coordinate some of the major international efforts, imposing a few standard formulae (such as "multisectoral response" [see Putzel 2004]), the AIDS universe contains an astounding variety of international organizational actors, from the World Bank, UN agencies, and major bilateral donors such as USAID, NORAD (Norwegian), CIDA (Canadian), and the EU HIV/AIDS Programme to independent foundations such as the Gates Foundation, the Kaiser Family Foundation, and the Rockefeller Foundation; universities (Harvard, Johns Hopkins, Tulane, University of Washington, Baylor, and many others); and the enormous array of organizations that get contracts from the big funders to carry out actual AIDS projects on the ground—organizations such as Population Services International (PSI), Family Health International (FHI), John Snow Inc., Humana People to People, or Abt Associates.

In addition to these more or less mainstream players, there is an array of other organizations, from large, established philanthropic and development organizations such as World Vision, CARE, the Peace Corps, and Save the Children, to missionaries and activists from a variety of religious denominations (both those, like the Catholic Church and the Seventh-day Adventists, who have long had a presence running hospitals and clinics in Africa and those Pentecostal and Evangelical missionaries who are often drawn to AIDS work by an individual calling). And then, if one is "on the ground" even briefly in one of the AIDS-affected countries, one will quickly come across spontaneous individual enterprises such as the Canadian undergraduates whose professor wanted them to have an experience working with AIDS orphans in Botswana; the Baptist church members from Arkansas who arrived in Malawi and set about finding villages for which they could dig boreholes (wells deep enough to have clean water); and the many other "mom-and-pop" charitable groups that are seeking a way to link up with local people to whom they can offer funding, projects, or volunteer labor. Nonetheless, despite a dizzying array of new actors (the Clinton Foundation), new initiatives (PMTCT+) and even new approaches ("routinizing" HIV testing), on the ground many of these international organizations end up doing, or trying to do, many of the same things.

Isomorphism the Easy Way: Buzz Words and Slogans

In a classic article, Paul DiMaggio and Walter Powell (1983) analyze the forces that produce "isomorphism" among organizations, making a set of organizations more and more alike. John Meyer and his students have shown across a wide variety of organizational types—corporations, American municipal governments (Tolbert and Zucker 1983), and nation states (Meyer 1983, 1987)—how shared images about what constitutes and/or legitimates a particular kind of organization drive organizations to adopt similar structures and purposes. Organizations may conform to dominant models because their personnel are selected from a common pool trained in similar ways, because their environment "selects for" organizations of a single type, or because, in a process DiMaggio and Powell call "mimetic isomorphism," organizations see themselves as members of a common type and adjust their structures, personnel, and policies accordingly. The question these institutionalists rarely raise is: how do institutions actually function when world-legitimated forms are imposed on top of (and often in conflict with) indigenous models.

At least in theory, all the resources necessary to impose Western practices and forms on the institutional order of the Global South are in place. International donors have the expertise; they often work through country staff educated in and oriented to Western nations. They provide the financial resources (see Luke and Watkins 2002), and both donors and recipients take for granted the right of donors to monitor how their resources are spent. And, finally, international staff and their views of legitimate practices often have considerable cachet.

Despite these advantages, I argue, the "success" of the Global North's attempts to impose its forms and principles has been remarkably limited. The one area in which global models have penetrated, however, is at the level of rhetoric and ideology. Some of this influence is direct: local people discover that they increase their chances of jobs or funding if they say the right things. But a great deal more of it comes from the earnest belief that, at least in some respects, the Western view is the prestigious, legitimate, "correct" view, which any right-thinking person would share. In Malawi, a young employee of the motel where I stayed told me that local "customs"—such as the taboo on sexual intercourse during the latter months of pregnancy and for several months after giving birth—are an important cause of AIDS. Many people told us either that they had been "sensitized" (or that others needed to be sensitized) on issues such as gender or stigma. When, during a 2004 survey project in rural Malawi,[4] the Malawian supervisors had the job of selecting forty interviewers from the 150 or so who had applied, their chosen method was to give each applicant a questionnaire designed to ferret out how many of the "misconceptions" about AIDS that health surveys track the local applicants still held (reducing these misconceptions is among the UN's Millennium Development Goals). They regarded being able to name five NGOs working on AIDS in Malawi as another important marker (though the AIDS NGOs might be alarmed to know that many of the local English-speaking high school graduates who applied for interviewer positions could name none of the international organizations, such as Save the Children, World Vision, or CARE, doing AIDS work in Malawi).

Vinh-Kim Nguyen's (2005a) research on a community of men in Côte d'Ivoire shows how Western understandings of self, disease, identity, and the body are enacted as Ivorian men who are part of an underground group of men who have sex with men recast themselves as "gay" men with the rights of "therapeutic citizenship." As Nguyen summarizes his argument:

> Spurred by funding from development organizations and other international donors with AIDS prevention on their agenda, local community groups began to proliferate from 1994. Drawing on health education approaches honed in AIDS prevention campaigns in the West, these community groups were vehicles for disseminating AIDS prevention messages that encoded normative, biologized notions of sexuality. . . . [T]he social technologies imported by international NGOs to prevent HIV/AIDS furnished an opportunity for Abidjan's homosocial communities to re-define themselves in light of the "new facts of life."
>
> Transnational and transcultural negotiations were used to adapt social practices imported by AIDS NGOs to local circumstances, helping to reshape the cultural geography of same-sex relations. These practices advocated sexual openness such as frank depictions of sexual activity in order to foster the adoption of safer sexual practices such as condom use during penetration. They also sought to "give a face" to the epidemic by using confessional technologies (techniques used in workshops such as role playing, using open-ended questions, and so on) to encourage

Africans diagnosed with HIV to "come out" about their illness and testify. Together, these practices worked to link dissident performances of gender to notions of sexual orientation. (246–47)

In a study of the responses of developing-country elites to the 1994 "Cairo" reorientation of population policies, Luke and Watkins (2002, 727) found that "[e]nthusiasm was most evident in rhetoric," but they also "found limits to the control exerted by global agencies." National elites used their control over policy implementation to "pick and choose among the items on the Cairo agenda," supporting "family planning and maternal health programs, programs that had long been promoted by the international community and had become domesticated, familiar items in the health services landscape" (728), but ignoring such priorities as domestic violence or treatment of STIs. Luke and Watkins also note the importance to local actors of "realist" concerns, the awareness of both NGOs and government officials that donors provide the money and expect some control. Those working for NGOs were more uniformly enthusiastic about the Cairo agenda, perhaps because NGOs (and the relatively higher salaries foreign-funded NGOs offer) are directly dependent on donor funds, and even on enthusiasm for donors' priorities.

Despite the enormous leverage that donors can exercise over those they fund, it is surprising how often—on the ground—local people resist or subvert donor intentions. Indeed, the AIDS fight has already expended enormous resources with, to date, relatively little effect.

Difficult Isomorphism: Affecting Actual Governance

Despite donors' prestige and financial heft, they have more difficulty penetrating and altering local patterns of governance than one might expect. Many kinds of institutional imageries, ideologies, and buzz words are embraced with great enthusiasm by those whom NGOs and other international organizations seek to transform. But what donor organizations offer is received (or seized) within a different social organization, where intended and actual effects differ. In order to understand the penetration of new models of governance, it is important to know how governance actually operates on the ground— what power, influence, and administrative authority actually consist of. Only attention to the actual characteristics of African systems of governance can help us understand why some NGO interventions take root and thrive, while others fail to take hold, or, even if they become embedded, fester rather than flourish.

Let me briefly say what I mean by "governance." I am less interested in the formal structures of government, such as national AIDS commissions or the "multisectoral" approaches to AIDS favored by UNAIDS and other donors (I agree with John Meyer and Brian Rowan's [1977] observation that such structures operate largely as "myth and ceremony"), than in how power and influence operate on the ground. The best formulation of this understanding of governance is Joel Migdal's "state in society" approach (see Migdal 1988, 2001). Migdal emphasizes that both states and other social actors such as clans, tribes, militias, and ethnic groups "seek predominance through binding rules" and that "[t]he major struggles in many societies, especially those with fairly new states, are struggles over who has the right and ability to make the countless rules that guide people's social behavior" (Migdal 2001, 65, 64). If one thinks about what AIDS NGOs seek to accomplish on the ground, they are certainly in the business of trying to remake "rules that guide people's social behavior."

Migdal warns that state-building faces often insuperable obstacles in the form of existing leaders and the forms of cooperation and dependence they enforce. His caution applies equally, or even more so, to international donor organizations, and it is worth quoting at length for its fundamental sociological realism:

> The literature on the Third World has paid scant attention to existing rule-making organizations outside the domain of the state and in conflict with the aims of state leaders. Yet, strategies offered to people through these structures may be quite complex and binding. During the last century, there has been a tremendous upsurge in the strength of many such organizations. In a large number of cases, colonial divide-and-rule policies injected vast new resources—most notably, wealth and force—into the hands of local and regional leaders, enabling them to strengthen the strategies of survival they could offer clients and followers. In turn, their ability to make and enforce binding rules of behavior also increased. Even where there was no direct colonialism, the expanding world economy funneled resources into societies quite selectively, allowing for the strengthening of . . . leaders or strongmen [who] fashioned viable strategies of survival for numerous peasants and workers. (Migdal 2001, 67)

Onto What Root Are Donor Practices Grafted? Patron-Client Ties and Personal Dependence

In their classic collection, *African Political Systems,* Meyer Fortes and E. E. Evans-Pritchard (1940) and their contributors describe a variety of African political systems, from formal kingdoms to loose kin groupings. Most of these African systems nonetheless had features in common, particularly the principle that material resources derive from and are converted into interdependencies among people. Traditional African economies meant that "wealth in people"—children, wives, clients, and other dependents—was also the key to increasing material wealth (see Miers and Kopytoff, 1977; Guyer, 1993). In bride-wealth systems, young men who needed cattle in order to marry had to borrow from their elders, so that older men converted their wealth into obligations from younger men (Collier, 1988). In chiefdoms, resources flowed upward to chiefs, whose sacred power made people and land fertile and whose material resources were redistributed in performance of ritual obligations (Collier, 2004). Clan and lineage groups indebted younger or more distant members of the lineage to clan elders or chiefs, who were responsible for the well-being of their followers. In the contemporary derivatives of these systems, in Daniel Jordan Smith's (2003) language, what matters is "having people"—the connections that give access to opportunities and resources (see also Smith 2006). The fundamental meaning of wealth in turn is that it can help meet one's obligations to the people who make up one's family, clan, tribe, or ethnic group. For Nigeria, Smith (2003, 707) notes that the political economy is "structured by patron-clientism. . . . Igbos, and Nigerians more generally use kinship and other social relationships of reciprocity to mobilize affective ties for instrumental political and economic purposes. Such relationships combine moral obligation and emotional attachment. They also serve to perpetuate an ethic of appropriate redistribution that fuels corruption."

Writing broadly about African politics, Chabal and Daloz (1999, 28) also point to the pervasiveness of "vertical" ties of personal interdependence:

> Most political actors are simultaneously dominant and dominated, one of the links in one of the many chains of dependence. Although there are strong inequalities within clientilistic relations, it is well to remember that patrons suffer considerable constraints. The maintenance of their status is entirely dependent on their ability to meet the expectations of their clients—clients who are, as it were, the material embodiment of their standing—and who in turn must placate their own clients.

This description of African political systems as organized around vertical ties of personal dependence, whether described as pervasive corruption (Bayart 1993; Smith 2006) or as responsive hierarchical rule (see Karlström 1996), gives us a basis from which to understand how external logics insert themselves into African contexts.

The NGO as Patron

The most obvious point is that in societies where everyone is searching for patrons and the resources patrons can provide, international NGOs and their local representatives are cast in the role of potential patrons. This means not only that locals are eager for whatever resources the foreign NGO may provide, though that is certainly the case. Even more, the foreign NGO creates resources and contacts that allow local actors to cast themselves as patrons in turn.

What are the cultural forms and social practices through which international donors and local participants actually meet? One of the most common, most recognizable, and easiest to describe is the "workshop" or "training" in which an international organization carries out its program by training or educating local staff. Daniel Smith's (2003) study of a Nigerian family-planning program is provocatively titled, "Patronage, Per Diems and 'The Workshop Mentality.'" What Smith names, anyone working in international philanthropy, and especially in the AIDS world, has noticed as well—the extraordinary interest in "training," workshops, the "training of trainers," and so forth (across the continent, Lwanda [2004, 37] refers in similar terms to "the Malawi 'seminar culture'"). And it does not take long to understand why. For local participants, training and workshops create opportunities for extra income—travel expenses and per diems—to supplement salaries far below the international standard (the very standard to which participants are exposed by interacting with international staff).

I interviewed a young American who had worked on a CDC project in Namibia, conducting "training of trainers" for Voluntary Counseling and Testing (VCT). The Americans had set up one-week training sessions lasting from Monday through Friday, but they rapidly discovered that local trainees were showing up a day late and leaving a day early. The Americans finally discovered that Namibian civil service rules wouldn't pay per diems for travel that occurred on weekends. In Malawi we were surprised at how many nurses, recently graduated from nursing school, turned down their first job assignments. Then one explained that if you weren't in the city, there were no opportunities for "workshops" and "training," and thus no opportunity for the travel expenses and per diems such activities allowed.

A Peace Corps volunteer I interviewed noted with distress that villagers she worked with in Burkina Faso expected to be "motivated" by some material reward when they participated as volunteers in an AIDS education project, a bike-a-thon to promote condoms, or a project in which groups competed to produce the best AIDS drama. She reported that "code words" had developed, so that if one called something a "project" or "training" one had to compensate people. Even middle school students, after creating maps of Burkina and Africa to paint on their school walls, angrily handed back the rulers she had given them. If she wasn't going to pay, she was told, she had to call the activity "community mobilization" or "community beautification," not a "project." "Very frustrating," she said, that "even thirteen-year-olds" had learned such expectations.

Daniel Jordan Smith (2003, 705), however, points to the much more general pattern in which "donor-funded programs involve complex and often unacknowledged accommodations between international sponsors and local implementing partners, with apparent contradictions overcome because each party is able to manipulate and interpret events, information, and the very models of what is happening to suit their own priorities." It is not only that donors and their local partners manage to get along. Rather, the same social practices operate as culturally appropriate, "successful" strategies for each party, even though the parties' understandings of those practices and their aspirations differ.

Workshops, for example, not only give local participants direct benefits—both educational and material. They also, Smith notes, allow participants to build up their own networks of clients and to reward their patrons. When a new approach to family planning was being promulgated, there was great enthusiasm about planning the workshops. "But the liveliest deliberations revolved around the selection of participants, trainers, and distinguished guests who would be invited to the opening and closing ceremonies. Such workshops were, after all, political events. At workshops, project staff could repay the patrons who installed them as officers in the 'dollar project' and build their own networks of clients by doling out the per diems and allowances that are paid to participants" (Smith 2003, 711). At the same time, workshops satisfy donors' desire to indoctrinate local people with the "correct" ideas and practices, and as Smith points out, workshops and training give donors a measurable "product"—people trained, workshops held, and information transmitted.[5]

Volunteers

Workshops and training are not the only cultural practices through which donors and local participants find common ground. Another meeting ground—one found at the village level, where international organizations seek to create programs for the actual people they hope to help—is the "voluntary group."

Particularly in AIDS work, where the question of what exactly constitutes prevention remains obscure, many organizations end up promoting the formation of clubs or other voluntary groups. In Malawi, the various NGOs such as Save the Children or World Vision, as well as a government AIDS project, all involved the creation of "clubs" in the villages. Sometimes these were clubs for youth ("AIDS Toto" ["Stop AIDS"] clubs), sometimes sports clubs that were also supposed to promote AIDS education; other activities involved groups of village youth or students who put on plays or skits to warn about the danger of AIDS. A Malawian government initiative, meant to reach rural villagers who might be illiterate and unlikely to encounter printed AIDS messages, involved creating a set of village AIDS clubs in which villagers, brought together to listen to a once-a-week radio broadcast about village life, would talk about their problems and possible solutions and then perhaps have the opportunity to broadcast their activities so that other villagers could learn from them. (In a very poor country like Malawi, radio is the means of mass communication with the greatest reach. Early on AIDS was sometimes called "the radio disease" since it appeared to exist only insofar as it had been described on the radio [see Lwanda 2004]).

Volunteering also characterizes two other common organizational strategies at the interface between donor organizations and local practices. The first is a "volunteer" management committee, often elected by other villagers. Frequently a donor, such as the Peace Corps or World Vision, requires some level of local commitment or local buy-in before the donor contributes to a project. Then a "volunteer" committee is set up, perhaps with an elected president, vice president, secretary, treasurer, and so forth, to manage the activity. This is the way health clinics were run both in Burkina Faso and in Kenya, according to interviews with Peace Corps volunteers who had worked in each place. This is also the structure World Vision uses in its development projects. An elected committee of local volunteers runs its Area Development Programmes (ADPs) in Tanzania and elsewhere. These committees of volunteers are often elected, although as one Peace Corps volunteer pointed out, those elected are often the same local influentials—a chief's brother or son, those from the wealthier end of the village—who usually run things.

In addition to volunteer groups or clubs and volunteer management committees, the actual work of donor-sponsored projects is often done by volunteers. When one interviews donors, they frequently describe, for example, having discovered or been put in touch with a village woman who had been using her own resources to feed and care for a number of orphans (some perhaps her own grandchildren) in her community. The Global AIDS Interfaith Alliance (GAIA), a small San Francisco–based AIDS organization, has such a story on its web page: Its founder, Rev. William Rankin, met a group of twenty-seven AIDS orphans, being cared for "in a tiny village at the end of a dirt road in southern Malawi. A wonderful woman, her elderly mother, and a few teenagers care for these kids. No funds come from outside. Every second day the children receive a cup of Nsima, a maize product that is a staple of Malawi. Otherwise they get only sugared tea or sugared water. . . . When I was there I saw no child in motion, nor did any of them speak" (Global AIDS Interfaith Alliance [GAIA] 2002). One hears very similar stories from orphan care projects in Zambia, Uganda, and elsewhere.

Volunteer workers are important not only in donor-financed initiatives, but in local African responses to AIDS as well. The remarkably successful Zambian organization, Society for Women and AIDS in Zambia (SWAAZ), claims about 10,000 members in chapters around the country. These volunteers undertake the task of educating their fellows about HIV and AIDS. A Zambian AIDS hospice, whose director I interviewed, was originally organized through a local Catholic parish to care for ill parishioners, and now serves as a clinic, hospice, and orphan-care center for ten villages and compounds. It has a small paid staff including a director, a few nurses and care-givers, and a part-time physician, but its activities depend largely on volunteers—those in the villages who keep watch over AIDS patients at home, alerting the clinic when they have fallen ill and need care, and widows of those who have died in the hospice who stay on caring for other patients.

Amy Kaler and Susan Watkins (2001) offer an analysis of the underlying logic of such "volunteer" activities. They found that the volunteer Community Based Distributors (CBD) in a German-funded Kenyan family planning project often used criteria other than those officially mandated to decide which women should be offered family planning services. Kaler and Watkins show that the volunteer family-planning workers had their own agendas. They treated the local women as their "clients" and sought to offer services only in situations where they could accumulate local prestige by seeming to support community values, not in situations where they could be blamed for subverting such values. Kaler and Watkins note that the women used their volunteer positions to create what amounted to patron-client ties with the women they assisted: "CBD work is a means for women to earn respect and obligation from other people, where earning money is difficult. The GTZ/MOH CBD program may enable these women to attain a measure of power and respect by giving them new ways to take advantage of one of the few avenues open to women. International and national agendas and resources are thus being drawn into a local, historically rooted dynamic" (261).

Opportunism

Kaler and Watkins (2001) point out that the Kenyan family-planning workers did not, at least so far as the interviewers could ascertain, receive direct material benefits from their family-planning clients (as in many such projects, they may receive small stipends for transportation or other expenses). Nonetheless, they speculate, "CBD agents may be storing up the goodwill of clients against some future time of need. Given that many people in South Nyanza regard the future as unpredictable, seeing the value of respect generated through CBD work as a kind of insurance is logical" (266).

The point is a much more general one. In many areas of Africa people are very poor and much of life is unpredictable (Johnson-Hanks 2005). In such circumstances, people are frequently on the lookout for possible opportunities—to earn income or other material benefits, but also simply to build up goodwill, to open avenues of possible exchange, or to seek patrons or the potential future benefits that may come from having clients.

In general, clients need not directly produce material benefits for their patrons. Indeed, in the kind of insecure world many Africans inhabit, especially for those who do not have jobs in the formal economy, a kind of generalized "opportunism," a willingness to do favors for others with only the loosest expectation that those favors will be returned in the future, is both rational and culturally appropriate (Johnson-Hanks 2005, 2006). From soliciting a foreigner as a "pen pal," to taking generalized pleasure in sociability, to willingly doing a favor for a stranger, one notices in Africa the peculiarity of our own, Western calculations about time, personal relationships, and hoarding our personal and conversational resources, but also the generalized openness of people in poor circumstances to any opportunity to expand the web of connections that might bring something unexpected their way.

The presence of outsiders (especially those whose standards about money are inevitably so out of sync with local realities) creates a potential bonanza unconstrained by local resources or obligations. This is the problem of "extraversion" (Bayart 2000; Callaghy et al. 2001) writ small as well as large. Contact with outsiders creates the possibility of resources that can lubricate local patron-client ties. Here NGOs act in contradictory ways, both encouraging universalism and becoming particularistic patrons. Let me describe two different sorts of examples, both from Kenya. I interviewed a young woman who worked as the local director for a small "mom-and-pop" NGO that sends international volunteers to Africa. She always checked what she was doing with the local district commissioner, who wanted, for example, to suggest families that her volunteers might live with during their stays. The amount the organization paid these families for the volunteers' upkeep was hardly enough to cover expenses, but she acknowledged that she had herself become so committed to the family she lived with that she decided to pay school fees for life for the youngest child, a girl, who otherwise would not have been sent to school. Another student volunteer on her project was able to arrange a full scholarship at an American university for the son of the family with whom he lived. This is, if you will, double-layered patron-clientelism—the district commissioner is a patron, sending opportunities the way of his clients, and the families themselves, no doubt genuinely attached to the volunteers they house, also recruit them as potential patrons.

The other case, perhaps more typical, is that of a Peace Corps worker, Neil Gagen,[6] who spent months of frustration hoping that someone in the Kenyan health center where he worked (in a semi-rural town) would begin to take initiative, following up on ideas they generated in meetings about what projects might benefit the local community. He was willing to help—even to help local health officials with fundraising—but only if they actually had commitment to the project sufficient to follow through. Each time, after enthusiastically developing ideas in meetings, they essentially waited for him to make the ideas happen. But then, miraculously, a local man, Moses Kimosop, walked into Neil's office and announced that he had AIDS—the first person to acknowledge this illness in a region with very high prevalence. Moses had come close to death, and now he felt that God had called him to use his remaining time to educate others. Armed with this local collaborator, the Peace Corps volunteer was suddenly energized. After Moses "went public," another HIV+ couple was introduced by a district HIV/AIDS control official. With the Peace Corps volunteer's help, Moses and his wife along with the other couple founded Tolosio, the first local group for HIV+ people, gradually attracting members until their organization had some seventy members. The Peace Corps volunteer arranged for Moses to speak at local schools, and the two men formed a fast friendship. When Moses fell desperately ill, Neil was able to get him antiretroviral drugs from a nearby hospital, initially paying for the drugs out of his own stipend:

> I first met Moses soon after his physical strength returned. Thin, frail and with little energy Moses began the awareness activities that would leave him exhausted afterwards. It was soon decided that Moses should be taken to a newly formed AIDS clinic at the Provincial Hospital about 2 hours outside the district. . . . With help Moses was able to afford the ARVs ($80 in Oct. 2002). . . . According to one of the American doctors at the clinic, Moses would have died in January. Instead he has been able to dedicate himself to truly improving his community. The Tolosio group would not

exist if it were not for the ARVs. Moses was the leader and the corner-
stone from the beginning and continues to be today as he solely manages
all the day to day operations 5 days a week. At the same time without his
leadership amongst the other PLWHA [people living with HIV/AIDS] it is
fairly certain that nobody else would have gone public at this time. (Gagen
2004, 6)

And of course it is the Peace Corps volunteer who helped the local group apply
for AIDS funding from the new National AIDS Control Council and who has
also raised funds through his friends back in the states to support antiretroviral drugs for Tolosio's members.[7]

In my interviews, in case after case, the critical breakthrough for an NGO is
finding the right intermediary, someone who is familiar with the local region
and can navigate local barriers for the NGO, but also someone the NGO workers can trust—someone who seems genuinely dedicated to the welfare of the
local community, who is honest, and who can serve as an extension of the
norms of participation and local involvement that the NGO shares. Sometimes
the local intermediary is an international who has been in the region for many
years: an Italian priest who had been in Guinea Bissau for thirty years facilitated a UN official's contact with a charismatic local woman who became the
key activist committed to guinea worm eradication; a Polish nun attached to
the local Catholic church founded the Zambian AIDS hospice. But more often
the key to success is simply stumbling on a local partner who provides the
access and local contacts the NGO is seeking. Sometimes a school principal
or the minister of a local church makes his organization an ally of the international NGO; and sometimes, as in Moses Kimosop's case, it is simply a key
individual. It is inevitable in such circumstances that the NGO (or the individual NGO worker) becomes a kind of patron to the local collaborator, who
may in turn have clients of his or her own.

Another example of such a strategy is GAIA's relationship with Jones
Leviwa. GAIA was created to take advantage of an African interfaith network
(and the fundraising prowess of its founder, Rev. William Rankin) to try to
intervene in Africa's AIDS epidemic. At first GAIA worked in Tanzania and
Kenya supporting various worthy projects—an orphanage, a self-help group,
and the like. But then they renewed their relationship with Jones Leviwa, a
religious leader who worked in Malawi. Through him, GAIA developed a new
"model," a "women's empowerment project funded by the Bill and Melinda
Gates Foundation. Working in 25 villages in Malawi's famine-stricken south,
the 125 community caregivers provide HIV prevention education, care for
orphans, and care for people who are ill" as well as encouraging VCT and

trying to overcome stigma.[8] After developing their successful connection to Mr. Leviwa, GAIA decided to focus all its energies on Malawi. There Mr. Leviwa decides what villages to enroll in the program, sets up the local programs (in which, after public meetings to explain the program, women are elected by their fellow villagers) and monitors their success. Donors and officials of GAIA visit these villages and various other projects their organization supports, writing to their supporters to report heart-rending suffering and heart-warming progress. The orphans who were so malnourished they didn't move during an earlier visit by Dr. Rankin were now playing happily:

> Two years ago, when Bill Rankin visited Tiyamike School he had come away greatly disturbed by the 27 three- and four-year old orphans. Their nutritional status rendered them virtually inert and mute. . . . But in May 2004 GAIA trustees Nancy Murray, Dr. Don Thomas, and International Programs Director Ellen Schell visited the little village in which the nursery school is operated, near Zomba, Malawi. They recorded a remarkable change that had taken place, owing to the generosity of many of you.
>
> This year 75 orphans receive two meals each day: a breakfast of porridge, and a lunch of corn meal, vegetables, and sometimes dried fish. There is a new outdoor house in which the children gather and play. Though the number of orphans continues to grow, the kids are full of life, bouncing around the yard and eager to have their pictures taken. (GAIA 2004)

Dialectics of Patronage: What Clients Do for Patrons

In this concluding section I bring together three lines of argument: Steve Cornell and Joseph Kalt's (2000) work on "cultural match," the role of patron-client ties in organizing the interactions between NGOs and their clients in Africa, and the problem of how Western donors seek accountability as they pour resources into the struggle against African AIDS.

I start with accountability. The World Bank and other donors have devoted resources and expertise to the effort to create Western-style bureaucratic accountability for donor-funded projects in sub-Saharan Africa. Malawi, the first African country to receive a GFATM grant to deliver antiretroviral drugs, the country that Stephen Lewis has described in glowing terms as a desperately poor country determined despite overwhelming odds to get ARVs to its people, and the only country permitted to pool donor funds rather than having them earmarked for specific programs, has a monitoring and evaluation plan created in a year of exhausting labor by a World Bank consultant working with

Malawi's National AIDS Commission. The consultant's job was to corral Malawian officials and stakeholders and to invent or adapt bureaucratic mechanisms to monitor the results of AIDS expenditures (Malawi National AIDS Commission, 2004). It will come as no surprise that finalizing the monitoring and evaluation system required many workshops and considerable "training" and "training of trainers" to perform the monitoring activities the plan requires.

The monitoring and evaluation plan calls for substantial grants to five "umbrella organizations" that are responsible for gathering and coordinating the information required for monitoring (the initial round of grants are announced in National AIDS Commission 2004): Action Aid Malawi, Canadian Physicians for Aid and Relief (CPAR), World Vision International, Plan International, and Save the Children (USA). Each of the umbrella organizations is responsible for coordinating data gathering and monitoring sub-grants to local NGOs and community organizations, with Malawi's twenty-eight administrative districts divided among them.[9]

Examining how these umbrella organizations actually work reintroduces the issue of patron-client ties. World Vision and Save the Children operate "child-sponsorship" programs in which donors give money to support a child and then, at least in theory, receive reports or letters from the child they have sponsored. Over time, however, these organizations have become more general development organizations. As we learned in a visit to one of their local offices, they support many families in a village, in part to prevent envy of particular children and families who are supported. And the chief has some influence over which families get support. Several organizations also support more general development projects, such as wells, health centers, and other improvements. Thus the organizations responsible for Malawi's formal monitoring and evaluation activities are themselves part of another very different and considerably less bureaucratic system. They are acting as patrons, both directly by providing financial support to families and villages and indirectly by allowing chiefs and other local influentials to direct their efforts to particular families and particular villages.

If patron-client ties organize the relationship between Malawi's bureaucratic monitors and local community members (additional patron-client ties—or at least additional opportunities for the benefits of myriad workshops and training sessions—are built into the monitoring and evaluation process itself), then we can ask what it is that clients do for their patrons. This is a question rarely asked about patron-client systems. Of course, where there are benefits to holding office and clients possess votes, as in the operation of big-city political machines, clients provide votes for their patrons. In the literature on African societies, there is an assumption that simply showing that one is a big man, that one is wealthy enough to attract numerous clients, is a source of prestige and influence. And of course where underlings have control over resources—as in invitations to workshops that can be directed back to patrons, or general favors, flattery, or information—patrons may benefit in important but hard-to-specify ways from having clients. But if clients are poor families in a village, people living with AIDS, caregivers, orphans, or other recipients of donor aid, one has to ask what these people might do for their patrons. The answer, of course, is that they can show up and be counted.

The value of NGO clients is both formal and informal. In Malawi the larger, more experienced NGOs such as Save the Children and World Vision keep formal records documenting their activities. Local staff fill out forms reporting the number of young people who participate in youth group meetings, the numbers who come to hear an AIDS theater presentation, the number who attend an AIDS club, and so forth. While the administrators of such programs acknowledge that they can't really verify the accuracy of such reports, forms are filled with very specific numbers—seventeen at this meeting, three children enrolled in vocational education, one who is in high school—and aggregated into monthly, quarterly, and annual reports. Their experience with such detailed record keeping makes the five umbrella organizations in Malawi good candidates to coordinate national record keeping and to train other NGOs to do the same thing. Malawi's NAC Activity Report System (NAC ARS) rests on such activity report forms.[10]

For most NGOs however, counting people on forms is not the major way they benefit from their clients. Rather, clients appear when donors, officials, or NGO administrators visit. It is the actual flesh and blood appearance of villagers—orphans playing, women meeting to discuss AIDS, teenagers performing, and so forth that directly demonstrates the organizations' effectiveness.

If one tracks AIDS organizations' self-presentation, one finds report after report in which NGOs and their donors recount visits with local people. Such visits are especially important for organizations, such as Save the Children and World Vision, that depend on child sponsorship by individual donors. At the local office of one such organization in rural Malawi, pictures of individual donors were displayed on the wall, and we heard reports about the visits of these donors. Indeed, one of the ways the local administrator assures himself that out in the field there really is a women's group, or a children's AIDS theater project, or an AIDS club is that the members of such groups assemble to meet groups of donors on tour. Hundreds, indeed thousands, of similar reports are found on the Internet. An excerpt from the second day's journal kept during a week-long visit to Malawi by a Save the Children delegation (board members, a development professional, staff, and several donors) in February 2002 gives a flavor of these visits:

> [After lunch] we drove further into the hills, to visit Ngowo VAC [Village AIDS Committee], at Chiumbangame Village. . . . The villagers were not only patiently waiting for us, but broke out into traditional song as we arrived. This was a COPE [program] village, and it showed.
>
> Chiumbangame Village has a population of 3200, with 50% under 15 years old, and 137 orphans. Like many others, the estimate was that there were 7 to 10 times more orphans than 10 years ago, and life expectancy was dropping for all.
>
> Whilst the death rate was depressing, and the orphan count high, the Village was taking its future into its own hands. There was lots of laughter as short speeches on progress were given by the VAC Chairman and Secretary—although with an even bigger smile we all realized that it was one of the mothers that is the critical player in driving the VAC forward. Whenever a question needed answering, she was the one to cover the issues in the most detail—even as she breast fed her baby. Later, she proudly introduced us to a terminal Aids patient who, through good home care, was at least enjoying a non-stigmatised life in her Community.

After photographing some of the children, provoking "Mob Scenes. Funny scenes. Poignant scenes. Life," the trip's diarist concludes:

> There is an active Youth Group, who sang us their songs about HIV, safe sex and helping others. We all wondered whether the kids at home could (or would) do that.[11]

Accountability, Patronage, and Cultural Match

Like many other scholars who have studied international development programs and the role of NGOs, I am skeptical that most development projects can live up to their lofty goals, or that many locals involved in the programs actually want them to. But perhaps the issue of accountability cannot really be solved, as the World Bank and the Global Fund are attempting to do, by developing the sort of tight, bureaucratic paper trail of accountability we see in the Malawi NAC monitoring and evaluation report. To understand what the alternative might be, I turn briefly to Steve Cornell and Joseph Kalt's (2000) concept of "cultural match." In a study of more than two hundred American Indian tribes, Cornell and Kalt found that a tribe's economic development was predicted by the quality of its governance and not by any other measures of natural resources, local labor market conditions, human capital, or other factors. They then asked what causes good governance, concluding that the degree to which a tribe is governed by a structure similar to the form of government it had before conquest—the degree of "cultural match" between its current government and its historical pattern—is the best predictor of current success in governance.

Of course, in Africa there was, historically, no single form of "government." Africa had an extraordinary diversity of political units, varying in size, complexity, and form of governance, from Bantu bureaucracy to kingdoms and empires like those of Benin or Ashanti to chiefdoms and acephalous bands. Furthermore, whatever the "traditional" configurations of governance, they were often destroyed or defeated, and when left intact were altered by incorporation or cooptation within systems of "indirect rule" (see the classic analysis in Mamdani 1996). Nonetheless, as I have argued above, what seem to survive are structures and cultural patterns resembling chiefdoms, in which power and resources flow to a chief, who redistributes resources "downward" to his people. Mamdani offers a powerful analysis of the way traditional chiefdoms were altered by colonial rule. Rather than the traditional pattern, in which chiefs were responsive because the people could always "run away" from a bad chief (Mamdani 1996; Herbst 2000; Collier 2004), colonial powers and postcolonial states imposed territorially defined rule, often backed with military force, and turned the chief into a tax collector, so that resources flowed upward to chiefs but failed to flow down again. The responsive chief whose sacred power and redistributive ritual actions guaranteed fecundity of people and animals was replaced by the corrupt chief who monopolized resources without redistributing them.

Despite this bleak picture, there is considerable evidence that ideals of "good" chieftaincy remain vital African cultural patterns. Mikael Karlström's (1996, 1999) work on cultural understandings of Ugandan politics suggests that the ideals of civil interaction within the clan, and of chiefs who are "democratic" because they "listen to" or "consult with" their people, remain persuasive. The pervasiveness of patron-client ties suggests a resilient set of cultural practices in which people seek security by embedding themselves within "vertical" relationships, in which support flows upward to patrons and resources flow downward to clients. As Chabal and Daloz (1999) repeatedly note, "bad" patrons are not those who are corrupt, but those who fail to redistribute their gains to their kin and clients. Therefore, they argue for "a properly grounded 'moral economy of corruption,'" in which the standard of accountability is not whether universalistic, neutral norms are applied, but whether leaders in fact "redistribute along lines that are judged to be socially desirable" (99–101).

Here again, Malawi is instructive. Dr. Hastings Kamuzu Banda, the dictatorial president who governed Malawi from before independence in 1966 to 1994, is now viewed with some nostalgia: he built roads; he had wells dug; and most important, he stored vast reserves of grain in silos outside the capital city, so that when famine came he could redistribute grain to the people. (Banda also portrayed himself as the "uncle" or mother's brother responsible for the children in a family.) The silos are still there, towering over the capital, but now they are empty—one is told because the new political leaders, no doubt under pressures for structural adjustment, sold off the grain to European traders. When famines came in 2001 and 2002, there was no grain to redistribute to keep the people alive. Both Banda and the new leaders are taken to be corrupt, but Banda did what good patrons do: he redistributed resources to his people, especially those in need. This image of Kamuzu Banda as the uncle who provided for his people in times of want is another piece of evidence testifying to the resilience of patron-client ties as a central way of understanding political relationships.

Recognizing patron-client ties as a pervasive cultural code suggests an alternative way to think about the export of cultural logics by NGOs and other philanthropic or nonprofit organizations. Perhaps what really matters is not whether NGOs enter, despite themselves, into patron-client relationships in which they are cast as patrons. Instead the question is whether NGOs institute social practices that make patrons more responsive to their clients. Those who administer NGOs should be asking whether the concrete social practices they put into effect give clients leverage to keep their patrons aware of their responsibilities to consult, to consider their clients' well being, and to redistribute resources, or whether local NGO staffs consider themselves the end of the patron-client chain, monopolizing access to those external agencies that provide the resources.[12]

George Collier (1994), in an analysis of the political and economic background of the Zapatista rebellion in Chiapas, Mexico, develops a contrast between what he calls "cooptative or remunerative" political strategies and "exclusionary" ones. He argues that as the flow of patronage resources through Mexico's political system decreased during the 1980s, the old system, in which local leaders put together large followings of potential voters to win public works projects or other benefits for their communities, was undermined by emerging class divisions and by a sharp constriction in the flow of government resources. Small cliques competed to monopolize what there was and exclude others. In an earlier period,

> Mexico's ruling party secured widespread support through redistributive
> state programs which successively bought the loyalty of one, then another

sector of society. Mid-century indigenous leaders consolidated followings by brokering such programs as land reform, road building, and schooling. But competition for the largesse of oil-fed development in the 1970s sharpened factional splits in communities like Zinacantán. Ambitious state projects drew rank and file into semiproletarian wage work, as elites competed to profit from trucking and commerce, and Zinacanteco stratification shifted and sharpened. Earlier politics of rank, in which generous leaders heralded the right to speak for followers on whose support they depended, gave way to relations of class in which elites' power no longer depends on followings. Leaders now sometimes disdain to drink with would-be followers. (1–2)

Collier's distinction between exclusionary and cooptative politics is useful for thinking about the relationship of NGOs to their constituencies in sub-Saharan Africa. We might pose the contrast as one between "exclusionary" politics, in which local elites try to capture the flow of resources from international NGOs by shutting others out, and a more redistributive patron-client system, in which patrons depend upon, and thus are responsive to, their clients.[13]

More generally, we might think about the relationship between NGOs and patterns of local governance by asking when NGO activities will increase or decrease the local accountability of both governmental and non-governmental activities (see Tsai 2007). We should ask how NGO interventions increase or decrease social trust, social capital, and the local rootedness of political institutions. Putting the matter this way focuses attention on the many ways in which international funders, however virtuous and well thought out their programs, inevitably turn the sights of local actors "upward" toward funders and their priorities, rather than "across" toward potential collaborators and allies on the one hand, and "downward" toward potential clients on the other.

Working inductively from interviewing and observing NGOs of various sizes working in a variety of ways on the ground, I have found that the usual rhetoric about including all "stakeholders" (see Campbell 2003) or adopting a "multisectoral" approach probably doesn't do much good. But practices that adapt culturally meaningful, local institutional forms to new purposes can have great value. A second discovery is the critical role played by certain "brokers" who mediate between local communities and international donor organizations. Sometimes, as in the case of the Peace Corps volunteer in Kenya, a donor organization finds a local ally who is public-spirited, honest, and committed to the goals of the international actor, and who provides a way to link up with the local community. In several other cases, an international—a priest, a missionary, or an NGO worker—with years of local experience, good local contacts, and the trust and respect of the local community can make all the difference in embedding an international program in the local institutional landscape. In such situations, even when foreign funding is involved, what Cornell and Kalt call cultural match can operate to "indigenize" the international organization and to help new institutional possibilities emerge.

One of the most important parts of such cultural match is the ability of international organizations to manage patron-client ties. The aspiration should be to stimulate and reinforce responsive patrons who seek to redistribute resources downward to their clients. Odd as it may seem, something as simple as having the donors show up to observe the clients may stimulate the sort of patron-client ties that can make programs responsive to the communities they serve.

Despite the many failures of African politics and the disruptions, distortions, and perversions of traditions of African chiefdom, these cultural patterns still have real vitality. Indeed they have remained resilient in the face of greater onslaughts than the current wave of NGO missionaries and transparency reformers from the World Bank (Collier 2004). In part this is because no new institutional order—such as a market economy with a reliable labor market—has emerged to provide alternative rules that could organize daily life (Migdal 2001). Insecurity encourages constant "opportunism"—the fluid quest for possible connections that could lead to economic opportunity, exchange and mutual help, or ties to a responsive patron (Johnson-Hanks 2006).

NGOs and other international donors enter this cultural terrain with their own agendas. But whatever their intentions, they are likely to be cast in the role of patrons, with willing clients. This is as true of missionaries or other religious organizations (Englund 2003) as of international NGOs. Waging direct assaults on local patterns of organization is not likely to prove successful. But attempting to build on and extend local patterns in more robust and productive forms can generate new institutional capacity, as when the Zambian hospice becomes a focal point for communal mobilization to watch out for those living with AIDS, to care for orphans, and to provide medical care. This is what Cornell and Kalt mean by "cultural match"—the preservation of notions of accountability, forms of micro-political practice, that can be reanimated to make a political system work.

Acknowledgments

The Canadian Institute for Advanced Research provided both release time and the intellectual impetus for this project. This research was also supported by the Center for Health Policy, the Center for African Studies, and the Committee on Research of the University of California, Berkeley. Fieldwork in Malawi was supported by grants NICHD RO1HD/MH41713 (P.I.: Watkins, Susan C.) 9/26/01–8/31/06 "Gender,

Conversational Networks and Dealing with STDs" and NICHD R01 HD044228 (P.I. Kohler, Hans-Peter) 7/1/03–6/30/08 "AIDS/HIV Risk, Marriage and Sexual Relations in Malawi." I am grateful to Rachel Sullivan and Keyvan Kashkooli for research assistance and to Dennis Altman, Jane Collier, George Collier, Arlie Hochschild, and Susan Watkins for advice and feedback. I also want to thank Lis Clemens and the other participants in the SSRC "Philanthropic Projections of Power" conference for valuable comments and suggestions.

Notes

1. There is a large literature on the ambiguity of the NGO concept and the conflicting evaluations of the role and effectiveness of NGOs. For examples, see Fisher (1997); Khagram et al. (2002); Keck and Sikkink (1998); Kassimir (2001); Sharma (2006).

2. Family planning (now framed as "child spacing" or "reproductive health") also attempts to alter fundamental aspects of sexual relations, interactions between women and men, and family life. But AIDS prevention and treatment have the added complexity of dealing with stigmatizing disease and death, addressing sexual practices seen by both local and international actors as "promiscuous" or immoral. For a picture of the political and social tensions that surrounded early family planning efforts in Zimbabwe see Kaler (2003).

3. The downward revision in numbers of infections is due to newer methods of estimating HIV prevalence based on surveys rather than testing pregnant women at antenatal clinics, not to a decline in the actual number infected (see UNAIDS/WHO 2007).

4. The core of the Malawi Diffusion and Ideational Change Project (MDICP) is a demographic survey of social networks, attitudes, and behaviors relevant to HIV/AIDS. The MDICP has conducted five surveys in rural Malawi, in 1998, 2001, 2004, 2006, and 2008. The initial sample consisted of approximately 1,500 ever-married women and their husbands; in 2004, a sample of approximately 1,500 adolescents (ages 15–24) was added. Semi-structured interviews with randomly selected sub-samples of the initial sample were also conducted. More detail is available at www.malawi.pop.upenn.edu.

5. Smith (2003, 712) also notes that "[f]or international donors, workshops and other training activities fit the dominant Western model of social change. This Western model assumes a Eurocentric perspective in which 'traditional' (Nigerian/African) cultural beliefs are viewed as inhibiting the kinds of practices that development agencies aim to encourage. It also privileges a construction of the individual as an autonomous rational decisionmaker. The working premise is: 'provide the target population with "the right information" and people will make "the right decisions" (i.e., adopt contraception to lower fertility).'"

6. All interviews were carried out with guarantees of anonymity and confidentiality; the informed-consent form offered interviewees the option of using their real names. This volunteer, Neil Gagen, wanted his name used. Moses Kimosop's name appears in the literature of Tolosio and in Mr. Gagen's written description of his experience, which he has circulated in an effort to raise funds to support antiretroviral therapy for members of the Tolosio group.

7. Vinh-Kim Nguyen (2005b) describes another case in which those who "came out" and participated actively in a self-help group attained privileged access to scarce antiretroviral drugs.

8. Available at: http://www.thegaia.org/news/archives/june2004.htm (accessed November 22, 2004).

9. The five umbrella organizations are assigned to divide up Malawi's 28 districts as follows. These organizations have received grants through Malawi's National AIDS Commission to carry out the training, the workshops with stakeholders, and the actual data collection their monitoring role requires (Malawi National AIDS Commission 2004, 45).

Action Aid: Chitipa, Chiradzulu, Zomba, Thyolo, Mulanje, Phalombe, Mwanza;
World Vision: Ntcheu, Ntchisi, Machinga, Dowa, Mchinji, Dedza, Nsanje,
    Chikwawa;
CPAR: Nkhata Bay, Rumphi, Likoma, Karonga;
PLAN: Kasungu, Mazimba;
Save the Children: Neno, Mangochi, Nkhotakhota, Balaka, Salima, Lilongwe,
    Blantyre.

10. Malawi's monitoring and evaluation system is enormously complex. There are many problems of coordination, both internally—for example, reading between the lines, one surmises that the Ministry of Health, with its own hospitals, clinics, and professional staff, is reluctant to become part of the NAC reporting system—and externally, where, for example, someone has to make sure that among Malawi's AIDS indicators the UNAIDS's Millennium Goals are included. Health indicators (such as sero-prevalence for pregnant women), information from surveys such as the DHS, and figures such as the number of people on antiretroviral drugs also have to be included. The planned role of the activity report forms is described as follows:

NAC ARS database: All NAC Activity Report Forms received from implementers
of HIV interventions on a monthly basis are recorded electronically by capturing
data onto the NAC ARS database. A draft database was developed in July 2003
for capturing all piloting information, and it was agreed during this first stage of
development that the FMA would develop a comprehensive and fully functional
database once it has taken over the administration of the NAC ARS. By the start of
the mission, the FMA has not yet developed this database. It should be noted that
events during the mission itself and some of the recommendations in this report
negates the need for this to be developed by the FMA—please refer to section 5.5
for more details. (Malawi National AIDS Commission 2004, 15)

11. Available at: http://www.yatesweb.com/Africa/Malawi%203.htm (accessed January 31, 2005).

12. In a fascinating article, Harri Englund (2003) develops a remarkably similar analysis of the theological and practical conflicts that arise within Pentecostal churches in Malawi about whether the religious leaders will share or seek to monopolize

the spiritual and material benefits that come from alliances with churches from abroad.

13. See Leonardi (2004) for others who are thinking about accountability in these terms.

References

Allen, Tim, and Suzette Heald. 2004. "HIV/AIDS Policy in Africa: What Has Worked in Uganda and What Has Failed in Botswana?" *Journal of International Development* 16: 1141–54.

Bayart, Jean François. 1993. *The State in Africa: The Politics of the Belly*. New York: Longmans.

———. 2000. "Africa in the World: A History of Extraversion." *African Affairs* 99: 217–67.

Callaghy, Thomas M., et al., eds. 2001. *Intervention and Transnationalism in Africa: Global-Local Networks of Power*. Cambridge: Cambridge University Press.

Campbell, Catherine. 2003. *"Letting Them Die": Why HIV/AIDS Prevention Programmes Fail*. Bloomington: Indiana University Press.

Chabal, Patrick, and Jean Paul Daloz. 1999. *Africa Works: Disorder as Political Instrument*. Bloomington: Indiana University Press.

Collier, George A. 1994. "The New Politics of Exclusion: Antecedents to the Rebellion in Mexico." *Dialectical Anthropology* 19, no. 1: 1–44.

Collier, Jane Fishburne. 1988. *Marriage and Inequality in Classless Societies*. Stanford, Calif.: Stanford University Press.

———. 2004. "A Chief Does Not Rule Land; He Rules People (Luganda Proverb)." In *Law and Empire in the Pacific: Fiji and Hawai'i*, ed. Sally Engle Merry and Donald Brenneis, 35–60. Santa Fe, N.M.: School of American Research Press.

Cornell, Stephen, and Joseph P. Kalt. 2000. "Where's the Glue? Institutional and Cultural Foundations of American Indian Economic Development." *Journal of Socio-Economics* 29: 443–70.

DiMaggio, Paul J., and Walter W. Powell. 1983. "The Iron Cage Revisited: Institutional Isomorphism and Collective Rationality in Organization Fields." *American Sociological Review* 48: 147–60.

Englund, Harri. 2003. "Christian Independency and Global Membership: Pentecostal Extraversions in Malawi." *Journal of Religion in Africa* 33, no. 1: 83–111.

Epstein, Steven. 1996. *Impure Science: AIDS, Activism, and the Politics of Knowledge*. Berkeley and Los Angeles: University of California Press.

Fisher, William F. 1997. "Doing Good: The Politics and Antipolitics of NGO Practices." *Annual Review of Anthropology* 26: 439–64.

Fortes, M., and E. E. Evans-Pritchard, eds. 1940. *African Political Systems*. London: Oxford University Press.

Gagen, Neil. (2004). Personal Communication.

Global AIDS Interfaith Alliance (GAIA) (2002). GAIA Update, July 2002. Available at: http://www.thegaia.org/news/archives/july1y2002.htm (accessed February 27, 2005).

Guthrie, Doug. 1999. *Dragon in a Three-Piece Suit: The Emergence of Capitalism in China.* Princeton, N.J.: Princeton University Press.

Guyer, Jane I. 1993. "Wealth in People and Self-Realization in Equatorial Africa." *Man,* new series 28, no. 2: 243–65.

Heimer, Carol A. 2007. "Old Inequalities, New Disease: HIV/AIDS in Sub-Saharan Africa." *Annual Review of Sociology* 33: 551–77.

Herbst, Jeffrey. 2000. *States and Power in Africa: Comparative Lessons in Authority and Control.* Princeton, N.J.: Princeton University Press.

Johnson-Hanks, Jennifer. 2005. "When the Future Decides: Uncertainty and Intentional Action in Contemporary Cameroon." *Current Anthropology* 46, no. 3: 363–85.

———. 2006. *Uncertain Honor: Modern Motherhood in an African Crisis.* Chicago: University of Chicago Press.

Kaler, Amy. 2003. *Running after Pills: Politics, Gender, and Contraception in Colonial Zimbabwe.* Portsmouth, N.H.: Heinemann.

Kaler, Amy, and Susan Cotts Watkins. 2001. "Disobedient Distributors: Street-Level Bureaucrats and Would-Be Patrons in Community-Based Family Planning Programs in Rural Kenya." *Studies in Family Planning* 32, no. 3: 254–69.

Karlström, Mikael. 1996. "Imagining Democracy: The Political Culture and Democratisation in Buganda." *Africa* 66, no. 4: 485–506.

———. 1999. "Civil Society and Its Presuppositions: Lessons from Uganda." In *Civil Society and the Political Imagination in Africa: Critical Perspectives,* ed. J. L. Comaroff and J. Comaroff, 104–23. Chicago: University of Chicago Press.

Kassimir, Ronald. 2001. "Producing Local Politics: Governance, Representation, and Non-State Organizations in Africa." In *Intervention and Transnationalism in Africa: Global-Local Networks of Power,* ed. T. M. Callaghy, R. Kassimir, and R. Latham, 93–112. Cambridge: Cambridge University Press.

Keck, Margaret, and Kathryn Sikkink. 1998. *Activists beyond Borders: Transnational Advocacy Networks in International Politics.* Ithaca, N.Y.: Cornell University Press.

Khagram, Sanjeev, et al., eds. 2002. *Restructuring World Politics: Transnational Social Movements, Networks and Norms.* Social Movements, Protest and Contention. Minneapolis: University of Minnesota Press.

Leonardi, Cherry. 2004. "Conference Report: 'Traditional' Accountability and 'Modern' Governance in Africa." *African Affairs* 103, no. 413: 661–63.

Luke, Nancy, and Susan Cotts Watkins. 2002. "Reactions of Developing-Country Elites to International Population Policy." *Population and Development Review* 28, 4: 707–33.

Lwanda, John Lloyd. 2004. "Politics, Culture, and Medicine: An Unholy Trinity? Historical Continuities and Ruptures in the HIV/AIDS Story in Malawi." In *HIV and AIDS in Africa: Beyond Epidemiology,* ed. E. Kalipeni, et al., 29–42. Malden, Mass.: Blackwell.

Malawi National AIDS Commission. 2004. Technical Support for Operationalisation of Malawi's M&E system: End of Mission Report.

Mamdani, Mahmood. 1996. *Citizen and Subject: Contemporary Africa and the Legacy of Late Colonialism.* Princeton, N.J.: Princeton University Press.

Meyer, John W. 1983. "Conclusion: Institutionalization and the Rationality of Formal Organizational Structure." In *Organizational Environments: Ritual and Rationality*, ed. J. W. Meyer and W. R. Scott, 261–82. Beverly Hills: Sage.

Meyer, John W. 1987. "The World Polity and the Authority of the Nation State." In *Constituting State, Society, and the Individual*, ed. G. M. Thomas, et al., 41–70. Beverly Hills: Sage.

Meyer, John W., and Brian Rowan. 1977. "Institutionalized Organizations: Formal Structure as Myth and Ceremony." *American Journal of Sociology* 83: 340–63.

Miers, Suzanne, and Igor Kopytoff, eds. 1977. *Slavery in Africa: Historical and Anthropological Perspectives*. Madison: University of Wisconsin Press.

Migdal, Joel S. 1988. *Strong Societies and Weak States: State-Society Relations and State Capabilities in the Third World*. Princeton, N.J.: Princeton University Press.

———. 2001. *State in Society: Studying How States and Societies Transform and Constitute One Another*. Cambridge: Cambridge University Press.

National AIDS Commission. 2004. Press Release: The National AIDS Commission Grants Awards to Organisations. *The Nation*. Malawi.

Nguyen, Vinh-Kim. 2005a. "Uses and Pleasures: Sexual Modernity, HIV/AIDS and Confessional Technologies in a West African Metropolis." In *Sex in Development: Science, Sexuality, and Morality in Global Perspective*, ed. V. Adams and S. L. Pigg, 245–67. Durham, N.C.: Duke University Press.

———. 2005b. "Antiretroviral Globalism, Biopolitics and Therapeutic Citizenship." In *Global Assemblages: Technology, Governmentality, and Ethics as Anthropological Problems*, ed. A. Ong and S. J. Collier, 124–44. Malden, Mass.: Blackwell.

Putzel, James. 2004. "The Global Fight against AIDS: How Adequate Are the National Commissions?" *Journal of International Development* 16, no. 8: 1129–40.

Resource Flows Project. 2004. Financial Resource Flows for Population Activities in 2002—Summary, UNFPA, UNAIDS, NIDI.

Sharma, Aradhana. 2006. "Crossbreeding Institutions, Breeding Struggle: Women's Empowerment, Neoliberal Governmentality, and State (Re)Formation in India." *Cultural Anthropology* 21, no. 1: 60–95.

Shiffman, Jeremy. 2008. "Has Donor Prioritization of HIV/AIDS Displaced Aid for Other Health Issues?" *Health Policy and Planning* 23: 95–100.

Smith, Daniel Jordan. 2003. "Patronage, Per Diems and 'The Workshop Mentality': The Practice of Family Planning Programs in Southeastern Nigeria." *World Development* 31, no. 4: 703–15.

———. 2006. *A Culture of Corruption: Everyday Deception and Popular Discontent in Nigeria*. Princeton, N.J.: Princeton University Press.

Tolbert, Pamela M., and Lynne G. Zucker. 1983. "Institutional Sources of Change in the Formal Structure of Organizations: The Diffusion of Civil Service Reform, 1880–1935." *Administrative Science Quarterly* 28: 22–39.

Tsai, Lily L. 2007. *Accountability without Democracy: Solidary Groups and Public Goods Provision in Rural China*. Cambridge: Cambridge University Press.

UNAIDS/WHO. (2002). AIDS Epidemic Update, December 2002. Joint United Nations

Programme on HIV/AIDS (UNAIDS) and World Health Organization (WHO) 2002. UNAIDS/WHO. (2004). AIDS Epidemic Update, December 2004. Joint United Nations Programme on HIV/AIDS (UNAIDS)/World Health Organization (WHO). Available at: http://www.unaids.org/wad2004/EPI_1204_pdf (accessed February 16, 2005).

UNAIDS/WHO. (2007). AIDS Epidemic Update, December 2007. Geneva, Switzerland, UNAIDS.

UNFPA. (n.d.). Financial Resource Flows for Population Activities in 2002.

WHO. (2004). "3×5" Progress Report. Released at 11 GMT January 26, 2005, World Health Organization.

PART 4.
Transnational Logics

9. The Political Logic of Institutional Adaptation

NGOs' Strategies Abroad

← ———————————————————————————————— →

ELIZABETH BLOODGOOD

The means by which nongovernmental organizations (NGOs) seek to influence governments' policies and practices are at the heart of their ability to exert power in international politics. These tactics and strategies are crafted to maximize their limited resources and, as a result, take careful account of the institutional frameworks in which they operate. The organization and operation of NGOs, at home and abroad, are strongly conditioned by the domestic political environments of their home countries, as well as the international forums in which they operate. Because effective tactics in one setting may be useless in another, the ability of NGOs to project power beyond their home country may be sharply curtailed by their organizational design and the "logic" of this design abroad. This chapter explores how differences in institutional context affect NGOs and their efforts to influence policy making and practice. When NGOs encounter problems with fit between their organization, strategies, and new national contexts, that is, institutional illogics, can they adapt to the new institutions? Or must NGOs apply standard operating procedures only to find themselves bound by their original designs?

This chapter examines key features of the institutional contexts within which NGOs operate, including formal political institutions and informal national norms, and the tactics available to NGOs to influence states' making of foreign policy. I examine both the logic of institutional design, that is, how NGOs operate within a given decision-making forum, and the effect of transplanting this logic when NGOs expand their operations abroad. To address questions of institutional design and adaptation, I examine the operations of Greenpeace and Friends of the Earth and their climate-change campaigns in the United States, Great Britain, Germany, and Japan.

Institutional constraints on NGOs come from the decision-making forums in which they operate, including formal rules about division of power and policy-making responsibilities, and longstanding customs regarding decision makers' relationships with private actors and popular engagement with politics. NGOs must work within available channels in the policy-making process, according to their ability to target the actors who ultimately decide policy, given regulations enumerating civil and political rights, lobbying, and campaign contributions. The transparency of decision making and the openness of the political system also shape NGO campaigns as NGOs take into account the independence of information outlets, including newspapers, radio, and the Internet; the interest and involvement of citizens in public affairs; and the acceptability of contentious political action.

NGOs have a broad repertoire of tactics developed to cope with varying national institutions and political cultures. Although not all NGOs engage in all tactics, at least some use all of the following: informational lobbying, campaign contributions, elections work, service provision, and normative persuasion. Alternatively, NGOs attempt to influence policy and practices indirectly via mass mobilization, public protest, economic boycotts, and civil disobedience.[1] International NGOs can also use their international networks to persuade sympathetic governments to put pressure on resistant home governments, squeezing decision makers from above and below.[2] Most NGOs do not find all of these tactics acceptable. Indeed, the organization and ethos of an NGO shape the policy changes it seeks, as well as the means by which it seeks them. While some see government engagement as cooptation, and lean toward contentious politics, others condemn direct action as violence and prefer direct involvement in the political process.

I argue that variations in formal and informal government institutions shape the means by which NGOs access policy making in different countries, narrow their options, and limit the efficacy of one international strategy traveling across institutional contexts. However, variations in national institutions are small, and NGOs already operate within relatively narrow bounds. While NGOs have a choice among tactics in any given campaign, the constraints imposed by the availability of resources and their principled commitments narrow the options. I find little evidence that NGOs become trapped by their organizing principles when they attempt to take a set of strategies designed for one institutional context into another context. This is likely due to the high degree of isomorphism already present across states' institutional contexts and NGOs' formal organization, making both NGOs and state decision-making institutions increasingly similar. To the extent that NGOs face constraints on their operations moving across institutional contexts, these come from informal customs shaping state and non-state relations rather than formal rules constraining NGO behavior.

Greenpeace and Friends of the Earth, the cases examined here, have similar resource endowments, name recognition, and status at the United Nations, but very different ways of organizing their operations. Greenpeace is a highly centralized, corporate body, while Friends of the Earth is a loose network of independent franchises. These two organizations also favor different tactics. Friends of the Earth takes a more conservative insider approach as opposed to Greenpeace's spectacular direct actions. The United States, Britain, Germany, and Japan were selected as representatives of different mixes of formal and informal political institutions. All are powerful democracies, but they have different political cultures and state-society relations.[3] Despite these differences, Greenpeace and Friends of the Earth work on the issue of climate change in each of these countries. Studying these organizations in different national contexts allows me to address organizational fit and campaign tactics across different institutional contexts in order to assess the institutional logic of NGO expansion internationally.

There are several caveats. First, I examine the tactics NGOs use to gain access to decision making across institutional contexts, but I beg the question of whether they can influence outcomes once they gain access. Second, the category of organizations considered here, NGOs, is a broad one. I limit my analysis to international nongovernmental organizations in order to examine the international spread of NGOs working in different countries on the same issue. International NGOs are commonly defined as formally organized bodies independent of government representation, with international aims and projects in and funding and members from at least three countries, a permanent headquarters, and a governing body.[4]

Institutional Isomorphism, Diffusion, and NGO Efficacy

In line with other chapters in this volume, I examine the extent of institutional adaptation as NGOs travel abroad—both the extent to which NGOs have adapted strategically to new contexts and the extent to which they need to adapt (the degree of institutional variation across countries). There are prima facie reasons to believe NGOs' need to adapt is limited by institutional isomorphism and the historical evolution of governing institutions, even as the ability of international NGOs to adapt is limited by their principled commitments and organizational underpinnings. In this chapter, I focus on the constraints national political institutions impose on NGOs and the degree to which NGOs have adapted or have innovated new techniques and tactics (both operational and organizational) to maneuver within these constraints.

Sidney Tarrow argues that social movements seize upon openings in political structures in order to engage individuals in collective action against political authorities and the status quo. Successful movements draw upon known repertoires of contention, built upon culturally specific symbols and local networks, with innovations at the margins to allow the movement ideas to spread and take root in new locations.[5] "Both challenge and response are nested in a complex social and policy system in which the interests and actions of other participants come into play, and traditions and experiences of contention and conflict become the resources of both challenges and their opponents."[6] In order to succeed on a global scale, NGOs, like social movements, must develop modular forms of collective action, which transcend sociopolitical contexts, but can innovate to fit the elements of their repertoire to the particulars of each national context. "[P]articular structures give rise to characteristic forms of collective action."[7]

While the expansion of a social movement can occur through direct and indirect means, including media coverage, relational networking, and coalitional campaigns,[8] international NGOs adopt a more controlled form of expansion involving the formal establishment and linking of branches. "The resource needs of an SMO [social movement organization] influence the internal structure of the organization. In contrast to the possibly amorphous nature of the underlying social movement, the [resource mobilization approach] maintains that [social movement organizations] are inclined to adopt a hierarchical and highly routinized structure to maximize their efficiency in collecting money, activating members, and achieving policy success."[9] Incentives driving NGOs toward hierarchical, bureaucratic structures are reinforced by competitive pressures between NGOs. As DiMaggio and Powell argue, "highly structured organizational fields provide a context in which individual efforts to deal rationally with uncertainty and constraint often lead, in the aggregate, to homogeneity in structure, culture, and output."[10]

The state in particular drives organizational isomorphism by setting the "structural determinants of the range of choices that actors perceive as rational or prudent," including rules for incorporation, financial reporting requirements, protected civil liberties, and criminal codes.[11] "[O]rganizational success depends on factors other than efficient coordination and control of productive activities . . . it depends on the ability of given organizations to conform to, and become legitimated by, environmental institutions."[12] Pressures for conformity come from society as well as formal state institutions. "Many of the positions, policies, programs, and procedures of modern organizations are enforced by public opinion, by the views of important constituents, by knowledge legitimated by the educational system, by social prestige, by the laws, and by the definitions of negligence and prudence used by the courts."[13]

But scholars debate how bureaucratic, hierarchical, and centralized an organization must be to succeed. Strang and Meyer argue that when "diffusion involves the social construction of identity [as might be the case with the establishment of a new NGO], whether and when intensified relations promote homogeneity rather than differentiation seems unclear."[14] In particular, the way in which the organization conceives of itself, its mission, and its operations (its "theorization" in Strang and Meyer's terminology) will affect the nature of its diffusion (the speed of growth and geographic expanse) and the extent to which diffusion produces homogeneity or differentiation.[15] Indeed, in his comprehensive survey of European environmental organizations, Dalton finds "sectors of the environmental movement seemingly prefer a decentralized structure that reflects the participatory tendencies of their members. . . . [T]he ethos within [new social movements] supposedly evokes an aversion to the elitism and hierarchy that [resource mobilization]/rational-choice theory maintains is a prerequisite for an effective SMO."[16] The anticorporatist, antistatist orientations of these organizations shape their tactical preferences, leading them toward unconventional and more highly contentious activities for the core of their repertoire.[17]

A key question emerges from these conflicting approaches: to what extent must international NGOs shape their organization and operations to the national institutions in order to expand successfully, or can international NGOs remain true to their principled commitments? Meyer and Rowan argue that "isomorphism with environmental institutions has some crucial consequences for organizations: they incorporate elements which are legitimated externally, rather than in terms of efficiency; they employ external or ceremonial assessment criteria to define the value of structural elements; and dependence on externally fixed institutions reduces turbulence and maintains stability."[18] Tarrow too argues that

> although movements almost always conceive of themselves as outside of and opposed to institutions, collective action inserts them into complex policy networks, and, thus, within the reach of the state. If nothing else, movements enunciate demands in terms of frames of meaning that are comprehensible to a wider society; they use forms of collective action drawn from an existing repertoire; and, they develop types of organization which often mimic the organizations they oppose.[19]

Boli confirms that by and large, international NGOs operate in most countries with a considerable degree of autonomy, but the importance of the state in national and international governance means international NGOs must work through and with the state to achieve their ends and thus enables institutional isomorphism among international NGOs and between international

NGOs and governing institutions.[20] But not all institutional environments are fully bureaucratized, providing some range of choice for organizations as they expand. Some organizations may gain leverage from their lack of conformity with "rational institutional myths,"[21] although Boli and Thomas argue these are the exception rather than the rule.[22]

The question of institutional adaptation by international NGOs may be becoming less relevant as national institutions also begin to converge. States are becoming more alike, in part due to the activities of international NGOs themselves. "Empirical studies of nation-states find striking structural homology across countries in, among other things, education, women's rights, social security programs, environmental policy, and constitutional arrangements."[23] World culture, "a set of fundamental principles and models . . . defining the nature and purposes of social actors and action," has driven homogenization via the actions of international NGOs serving as the embodiment of these values.[24] The diffusion of the idea of modernity has helped to construct and legitimize both international NGOs and nation states. "Modernity connotes the organization of society and the nation-state around universalized notions of progress and justice, as built up of rational organizations and associations, and as composed of autonomous, rational, and purposive individual citizens. And it implies the integrated functioning of these elements so that collective goods are enhanced by individual and organizational progress and contribute to such progress."[25] "The more modernized the society, the more extended the rationalized institutional structure in given domains, and the greater the number of domains containing rationalized institutions."[26] The expectation of these scholars is that as the modern bureaucratic state has become the common model, the institutional environments of states have become increasingly alike. International NGOs thus face increasingly similar operating environments, and expansion will require less adaptation to new cultural, institutional, social, and political environments.

The remainder of this paper examines empirically two questions arising from this literature. First, to what extent can and do NGOs alter their operations as they cross national boundaries and, second, what are the implications for their campaigns if they select not to adapt their practices to local conditions?

Nongovernmental Tactics and Strategies

In order to understand institutional constraints on NGO operation and the impact of transporting NGO institutional logics across political contexts, we first need to examine NGOs' available tactics and the formal and informal governmental constraints upon NGO operations. This section examines the options available to NGOs, which they choose, and why. The design of NGOs' campaigns and their strategic signatures cannot be attributed entirely to the institutional environment, as their organization culture, principled commitments, and interests shape activities they consider effective and appropriate. Nevertheless, if an NGO is to succeed in changing government policy, its operations must accommodate the political institutions it faces and available opportunities for influence.

NGOs engage in three broad categories of activities: field operations, political advocacy, and public education and motivation. They, as a result, have three primary classes of tactics: the provision of goods and services, education, and affective action.[27] Within these general categories is a much longer list of particular behaviors, as can be seen in Table 1.

NGO strategists consider three factors when designing their campaigns: available resources, possible tactics, and their principled beliefs.[28] In general, the provision of goods and services are more expensive than political advocacy via lobbying or attention seeking via affective actions. NGOs then select among available strategies based upon internal organizational principles and beliefs. The provision of goods, services, and information has fewer moral and reputational implications than direct action, civil disobedience, or political protest. While NGOs are driven by principled beliefs,[29] the individuals responsible for strategic planning realize they operate under stringent resource constraints and thus design international campaigns to maximize their influence.[30] The social and political, formal and informal institutions NGOs face determine the logic or illogic of NGO project planning across political contexts.

TABLE 1. NGO TACTICS BY CATEGORY

Goods and Services	Information	Affective Actions
Relief and development	Public education	Mass demonstrations
Local provision of social services	Media contacts and briefings	Public protests
Campaign contributions	Meetings with government officials	Civil disobedience
Environmental cleanup	Participation in legislative process	Direct action
Management of local resources	Problem assessment	Economic boycotts
Legal services and representation	Scientific research	Judicial action
Economic boycotts	Report writing and distribution	
	Preparing legal briefs	
	Op-eds and exposés	

Source: Dalton, *The Green Rainbow* (Yale University Press, 1994); Bloodgood, "Influential Information" (Ph.D. diss., Princeton, 2002).

Domestic Institutional Framework

I limit the number of factors considered in order to include formal institutions, informal practices, and norms of national governance, but examine more variables than past cross-national studies of the interaction between nongovernmental actors and domestic political institutions. This analysis is stylized to increase its tractability.[31] This section examines formal institutions, contained in national constitutions and laws, followed by informal norms and past practices which shape the interaction of government decision makers and NGOs.

Formal Institutions of Foreign Policy

The United States, Great Britain, Germany, and Japan are often differentiated according to the effect of their formal political institutions on the access and influence of non-state actors, in particular the ability of government to resist societal demands.[32] The United States and Germany have decentralized national governments which create multiple points of access and multiple veto points where influence can be exerted on foreign policy. The governments of the United States and Germany are argued to be connected to social interests via a wide range of rights and regulations that provide at least select groups access to the governing process. Japan is commonly portrayed as a centralized governing system in which access to government is structured along corporatist lines and strongly constrained, while in Britain, government holds society at arm's length.[33] Five formal institutional characteristics summarize these differences: the distribution of power and responsibilities for foreign policy across branches of government; civil and political rights accorded citizens; regulations regarding campaign contributions and lobbying by interest groups; and specific regulations for nonprofits, including registration requirements and consultative status. Decentralized institutions should impose fewer restrictions on NGOs' operations, enable a variety of strategies to access decision making, and create fewer difficulties for the importation of an institutional logic from a different national context. NGOs moving from decentralized to centralized governing systems are more likely to encounter problems transferring their operations and have ill-fitting strategies for the new context.

THE UNITED STATES

The presidential system of the United States, with its well institutionalized and respected system of checks and balances between branches of government, provides interested parties with a number of points of access to the decision-making process. While power and responsibilities for making foreign policy lie with the president, treaties, declarations of war, and appropriations require legislative approval. Thus the United States is characterized by an independent legislature with a powerful set of checks and balances on the authority and power of the president, leading to a competitive, open political system.[34] Key members of Congress (those at the heads of committees) play an important role in challenging and changing foreign policy. Access is available for interested groups to agencies within the executive, which are responsible for drafting policies for the president and implementing legislation passed by Congress.

The U.S. political system, with its transparent policy-making process, is extremely open to outside actors. The system is critiqued as being overly parochial, and decision makers are said to be within the pockets of powerful interest groups.[35] Because of this perception, a number of specific regulations constrain interest group behavior, in particular lobbying and campaign contributions. Campaign contributions have been defended as a form of constitutionally protected free speech, but recent legislation has limited campaign spending to prevent undue influence by private interests. Corporations, labor unions, and federal contractors may not make contributions to candidates, but U.S. entities can establish political action committees (PACs) to pool voluntary contributions.[36] Nonprofit organizations' contributions to issue-advocacy groups are not limited, but foreign nationals and entities may not make campaign contributions of any kind, including to PACs.[37] Similarly, U.S. organizations may not contribute to foreign officials in order to "obtain or retain business."[38] A special class of regulations apply to organizations seeking charitable status. These 501c and 527 organizations can register for tax-exempt status as charitable organizations. Such organizations face limitations on the range of activities in which they can engage; in particular they cannot support political candidates or partisan positions, although they may engage in issue advocacy.[39]

The transparency of the political process within the United States, a result of liberal freedom-of-information laws and the right of the media to cover the political process, enable interested parties to become informed about policy and target their advocacy efforts. Individuals and group representatives may also be called upon by the government to give testimony, serve on expert panels, and otherwise participate in policy making in their official capacities.

Protections on freedoms of speech, press, and assembly are enshrined within the Constitution. These protections aid advocacy efforts by interest groups of all persuasions. Freedom House maintains a well-known record of countries' civil and political rights and regularly gives the United States top marks for its civil and political liberties.[40] Private groups can print, publish, and speak their issue positions freely and without fear of legal retribution, allowing them to use a range of advocacy strategies, such as informational lobbying, mass mailings, and public protests, without fear of legal retribution.

THE UNITED KINGDOM

The United Kingdom is also a liberal democracy, with strong commitments to limited government, a free and fair political process, and individual rights. As a parliamentary system, it divides power more effectively between political parties (the Government and the opposition) than branches of government, which are traditionally in the control of the same party or coalition of parties (with the exception of a strong and independent judiciary). The prime minister, selected from the House of Commons, has the right to form a government by filling cabinet posts, nominally at the pleasure of the monarch, but effectively at the pleasure of the Parliament. Short of a no-confidence vote, strict party loyalty keeps members of Parliament (MPs) in line with Government policy, allowing little opportunity to pass alternative policies.[41] NGOs thus have limited channels into the policy-making process. Parliament plays a watchdog role as legislators demand Government accountability, in particular via institutionalized Question Hours held weekly in the House of Commons. Debate is often heated on issues of foreign affairs, and private experts and interested individuals are invited to testify on legislation under consideration. Members can introduce private bills, although these usually concern localized constituent issues. Judicial review, another potential check to executive authority, was instituted only in 1998.[42]

The British political process is less transparent than the American, as a result of the overlapping responsibilities of members of Parliament and members of Government, overlapping jurisdictions of the British and European Union governments, and the unclear role of the House of Lords. Much is done by tradition rather than regulation, including protections for speech, press, and assembly.

While there are proposals being circulated in Parliament to institute a register of lobbyists and code of conduct, this has not come to pass. There are strong reservations against regulating informal lobbying and lobbying by nonprofessionals.[43] By tradition, MPs hold regular office hours in their constituencies, during which they can be approached by any interested group.

The giving of campaign contributions is unrestrained, but expenditure limits are placed upon candidates.[44] Corporations are subject to additional regulations under the Department of Trade and Industry. The Electoral Commission was created only in 2000 to administer electoral laws, although the candidate spending-limit formula dates from the Representation of the People Act of 1983.[45]

The Charities Acts of 1960 and 1992 provide for the identification, registration, and management of charitable organizations in Britain. In order to be defined as charitable, an organization's purpose must be exclusively charitable (thus apolitical). Once registered as a charity, organizations "at once have the protection of the Crown, the Courts, and the [Charity] Commission for their purpose."[46] In particular, charities receive constitutional protection, tax exemptions, and legal protections from lawsuits. Voluntary agencies, a second designation, may have for-profit or political objectives and may get discretionary tax relief.[47]

GERMANY

The formal political institutions enshrined in the German Constitution, like in Japan, are much newer than in the United States or Britain. The government is characterized by cooperative federalism. Decision making is decentralized by virtue of the interdependent nature of federal and state policy making.[48] Fragmentation comes from the diversity of jurisdictions. The variety of actors involved in making foreign policy does not increase access for interest groups, however, as the executive is inaccessible, the legislature is weak, and the party system produces centripetal rather than centrifugal forces.[49] This institutional design was deliberate, via an electoral system which combines proportional representation and single-member districts, in order to limit competition between parties and avoid a collapse like the Weimar Republic's.[50]

The German executive (chancellor) has greater control over foreign policy than does the U.S. president and is stronger than either the legislature or the bureaucracy. The legislature is quite weak—the lower house, the Bundesrat, requires localities' support for policies to pass.[51] The federal bureaucracy in Germany is very small, and most tasks are delegated to the localities, but localities have rival jurisdictions over a number of federal policy areas, complicating and obscuring policy making and implementation.

Designed to provide long-term strategic vision and political and economic stability, in part by preventing activist politicians, the German political system is corporatist, privileging and networking a few large actors, including labor groups, corporations, and public agencies.[52] "The role of the state and of public authority within Germany is one of regulation, facilitation and delegation by public agencies, rather than direction."[53] The main exception is the German Federal Constitutional Court, which has the power of judicial review, providing a powerful check on the executive.[54]

The German constitution provides protections for speech, press, and assembly, and the media are free and independent. While freedom of association is guaranteed, political parties must be democratic to receive federal funding.

Public rallies and marches require official permits, often denied to right-wing radicals. Right-wing propaganda, particularly Nazism, is also illegal.[55]

German political parties are funded by state grants based on past electoral performance as well as membership dues. All donations over 20,000DM must be publicized, but there are no limitations on the amount an individual or group can donate. Nonprofit, charitable, and church organizations may not donate to political parties, and campaign contributions are defined broadly to include the donation of services to the party.[56]

Registration procedures for lobbyists exist within Germany, and registration is necessary to access federal buildings and participate in the policy-making process. Informal lobbying, however, does not require registration, and interest groups are commonly involved in the preparation of legislation.[57] Government-society relations are structured along a democratic-corporatist model. The political party system helps to act as mediator between the government and interest groups, and all significant interest groups have found political representation within a party.[58] "This neo-corporatist style of policy making, which seeks to establish consensus prior to parliamentary decisions, bypasses the constitutional order and weakens the power of parliament."[59]

German law differentiates between member and nonmember organizations, and thus the category NGO crosses types of institutions German law treats as separate, including differentiations according to legal personality (private versus public), taxation status, and financial structure.[60] There are thus complicated regulations regarding NGOs' treatment under law and strategic incentives, in terms of taxation advantages and legal treatment, to certain institutional designs.

JAPAN

The government of Japan is the prototypical example of a strong, centralized state, one capable of governing with limited societal involvement.[61] While it is formally a competitive system, the Liberal Democratic Party (LDP) has been in power since the establishment of a democracy (with a brief exception in 1993–94). "The strength of the Japanese state derives from the intimate relations between the governing Liberal Democratic Party (LDP)" and "a prestigious and cohesive state bureaucracy."[62] The unified nature of the executive and legislature typical of parliamentary systems means that there is no rivalry for control of the bureaucracy, and thus few incentives to limit its power over tasks delegated to it.[63] "Despite recent reforms aimed at curbing the power of the bureaucracy, policy is still generally shaped by senior civil servants rather than elected politicians."[64]

The government operates with little pressure for transparency. The judiciary is independent, but without the right to judicial review. Strict party loyalty, as well as dependence upon the party for campaign funding, limits legislator independence. The nature of the political party system, namely multimember districts, creates incentives for candidates to focus on particularistic interests. Because the party must run competing candidates in each district, no candidate can win on broad policy issues, as members of the same party will undercut each other within the district. Candidates win by constructing minority voting blocs around campaign spending, special interests, and patronage politics.[65] This practice provides an opportunity for outside influence. Party leaders and members of the Diet use *zoku,* or study groups, for policy expertise and advice, in a loose parallel to congressional subcommittees.[66] Unlike in Germany or Britain, however, parties are limited in power, particularly relative to the bureaucracy, because individual Diet members can lure local supporters with small favors.[67]

Corruption scandals, which caused the LDP to lose majority control of the Diet, led to a series of reforms, including provisions on campaign finance. As of 2005, political donations to individual politicians are illegal. Donations go to the parties, which distribute funds from private sources and government subsidies. There are no limits on the size of donations to party organizations, however.[68]

The Japanese press is formally free and independent, but not assertive or outspoken. Membership in press clubs gives media outlets privileged access to government. Journalists who belong to these clubs often do not report sensitive stories in order to maintain their privileged access.[69]

Charitable organizations are defined within the Civil Code as "associations or foundations . . . relating to the public interest and not having for its objective the acquisition of gain."[70] In order to establish a charitable organization, a group needs approval from the "competent governmental agency" in each prefecture in which they operate and must demonstrate sufficient financial assets to sustain operations, currently 300 million yen (US$2.3 million). Once established, however, charitable organizations enjoy tax benefits, including the right to give tax deductions to donors.[71] Charitable organizations in Japan do not have universal prohibitions on political activity as in the United States and Britain.

CROSS-NATIONAL COMPARISON
Table 2 compares the main institutional features of each country. This chart helps to clarify key differences that should shape NGOs' organization, operation, and programs.

Formal government type—presidential or parliamentary—is less important than the devolution of power as a result of electoral rules and provisions regarding the responsibilities of government agencies in determining foreign policy. The United States and Germany are relatively open to interest groups

TABLE 2. FORMAL POLITICAL INSTITUTIONS

	United States	Germany	Japan	Great Britain
Government type	Presidential	Parliamentary	Parliamentary	Parliamentary
Nature of Electoral System	Single member districts	Mixed, PR and direct representation	direct representation	Single member districts
Number of Political Parties	4	6	5	9
Independence of Legislature	Yes	No	No	No
Judicial Review	Yes	Yes	No	Yes (1998)
Campaign Contribution Regulations	$5,000 candidate $20,000 party	Nonprofit, charitable, and and religious groups may not donate to parties	No contributions to individual candidates	None
Registration of Lobbyists	Yes	Yes	No	No
Registration of Nonprofits	Yes	Yes	Yes	Yes
Political and Civil Rights	Yes 1, 1	Yes 1, 2	Yes 1, 2	Yes 1, 2

with access to veto points in the legislature and the executive. Britain and Japan are centralized hierarchies with limited access for all but a few interest groups. The judiciary also gains independence in the United States and Germany from judicial review, contributing to increased fragmentation within the government. Although party loyalty is strong in Germany, there are more viable parties and so more interests represented than in Britain or Japan.

In terms of means of gaining access, campaign contribution laws are more restrictive in the United States and Germany. Political parties are all-important in Britain and Japan, and it is not surprising they distribute campaign contributions. Similarly, formal requirements to register lobbyists are found where lobbyists are most active and influential—the United States and Germany. Decision makers are less concerned about lobbying in Japan and Britain, where consultation is local and informal or within corporatist structures.

There are clear differences in the legal requirements for an NGO, although registration procedures for nonprofit organizations give tax advantages in all four countries. While it is more difficult to be recognized as a nonprofit in

Japan and Germany, once an organization is identified as a nonprofit, it is more difficult to engage in political activity in the United States and Britain. The more important variation is in the nature of NGO oversight—one central body in the United States and Britain versus corporatist linkages with government agencies in Japan and Germany.

As a result of institutional variations, I expect to find informational lobbying by NGOs to influence policy making in the United States (via the legislature) and Germany (via political parties) and the use of campaign contributions for access in Britain and Japan. High degrees of government transparency, fragmented decision making, and strongly guarded civil and political rights enable active formal participation in all levels of the political process in the United States. The German government is less transparent, but has strong regulations protecting most civil and political rights, and strong, formal institutions for interest representation at all levels of government. The appeal of monetary mechanisms for influence in Britain and Japan is increased by the many institutional barriers to participation in the formal political process.[72] There are no limitations on campaign contributions in the United Kingdom and Japan, while the use of campaign contributions to influence policy making is impossible in Germany and increasingly difficult in the United States.

Affective politics provide another means to influence policy making, which might be used to compensate for the lack of direct access. The success of affective politics, however, depends on the domestic political culture and norms of appropriate behavior.

Informal Norms and Structures of Political Advocacy

Often historical practice and social norms have more effect on the relations between state decision makers and NGOs than formal political institutions.[73] "Rather than emphasizing state structures, one should analyze the coalition-building processes . . . that is, the mechanisms and processes of interest representation by political parties and interest groups that link the societal environment to the political systems."[74] In this section, I examine commonly held perceptions in each country about legitimate forms of political action and the awareness and involvement of each public in politics to assess the efficacy of NGO strategies to educate and mobilize social groups. Groups which share a common interest or objective with the society in which they operate, which understand the principles of political action there, and which use an appropriate strategy given these norms are more likely to have success.[75]

Policy networks in each country provide societal groups with access to decision makers.[76] While the degree of government centralization has a strong impact on access, fragmentation in the nonprofit sector can limit the amount of influence social groups can have by blurring lines of communication, sowing confusion about the intentions of groups, and creating competition between groups for influence. Social fragmentation also limits the control government exerts on society, because there are many social levers and competing representatives of interests.[77]

In the United States, many different groups within a heterogeneous, internally differentiated society can access government. "The character of the American bureaucracy and regulatory commissions encourages in practice a symbiosis between public and private actors which is widely condemned in theory."[78] Shifting coalitions of social interests as well as shifting power configurations among government actors produce changeable policy outcomes. Economic interests, in particular, enjoy easy access to congressmen in need of electoral support and lacking strong national parties to protect them.[79]

In Britain, on the other hand, the range of active societal groups and interests is narrower than in the United States, and society is carefully held at an arm's distance from the government.[80] "The sharing of information, consultation, and bargaining distinctive of Britain's 'collectivist politics' take place at a table which separates public from private sectors."[81] The exceptions to this are historically determined special privileges for certain interest groups, in particular labor and the Campaign for Nuclear Disarmament (CND).[82]

In Japan, state-society relations are organized vertically using peak associations. "In contrast to Britain and, to a lesser degree, America, relations between business and the state are so symbiotic that it is virtually impossible to determine where one stops and the other begins."[83] Relationships built in university are reinforced throughout subsequent careers in bureaucracy, business, and government. Advising committees allow business representatives to help draft government policy. "This unified structure does not encourage infiltration from the bottom but rather invites accommodation at the top."[84] Tight links between business groups and government crowd out other groups with competing interests, and environmental and human rights organizations naturally compete with business interests. Japanese society is also marked by a relative lack of differentiation and thus reduced demand by social groups for accommodation.[85]

Germany is a middle case. German society is varied, as in the United States, but the connections between state and society are more closely organized than in the United States or Britain. Ties between state and society in Germany are neither as organized nor as close as in Japan, and the political system is open to outside influence.[86] "Business is organized in a number of powerful peak associations, uniformly dominated by its largest members, which offer an institutional mechanism for articulating the views of business and, very occasionally, affording the government an additional instrument in the pursuit of its policies."[87] Germany is distinctive with its powerful Green Party. While business interests are dominant, ecological values and the Green Party are competitive.

Table 3 summarizes the nature of the policy networks in each country. This chart provides information on three other variables: information availability, the interest and involvement of citizens in political affairs, and ideas about acceptable political behavior.

TABLE 3. INFORMAL NORMS OF STATE–SOCIETY INTERACTION

	United States	Germany	Japan	Great Britain
Policy Networks	Open system, close state-society relations	Democratic-corporatist; open system, limited state-society relations	Quasi-corporatist; closed system, close state-society relations	Closed system, distant state-society relations
Newspapers (per 1,000 people)	219	313	574	342
Televisions (per 1,000 people)	835	660	891	891
Telephone mainlines (per 1,000 people)	645	650	558	590
Internet use (per 1,000)	551	411	448	423
Legitimate forms of political action				
Public Meetings				
Petitions	79%			89%
Boycotts				54%
Demonstrations			62%	72%
Direct Action			33.2%	32%
Violent Action	0.4%			2%
Citizen involvement in political action				
Letter Campaign	30%			
Public Event	23%			11%
Donation	22.8%	20.8%	9.1%	24.2%
Petition	55%			3%
Boycott	15%		3%	
Protest Action	3.2%	6.7%	2.1%	3%

Source: World Bank, World Development Indicators, 1995, 1998, 2002; The Roper Center for Public Opinion Research, General Social Survey, 1994, 1996, 2001; *Times Mirror,* Los Angeles, Calif., 1988; NHK Broadcasting Culture Research Institute, April 1993; Market and Opinion Research International, 1995, 2001.

While all four share similar patterns of political participation and popular views of acceptable political tactics, there are historically determined differences regarding the legitimacy of challenges to authority and citizens' willingness to engage in political activities. As political activity becomes more extreme, public support drops in all countries. Public meetings, petitions, and letter-writing campaigns are seen as legitimate political tactics, and are supported by more than two-thirds of the population in each of these countries. Direct action tactics are seen as legitimate but supported by only one-third of citizens. The use of illegal or violent tactics is seen as illegitimate and supported by less than 2 percent of the populations. Many fewer individuals participate than hold opinions about the acceptable bounds of the political process. The more effort-intensive the activity and the greater the risk, the fewer people who are involved. Monetary donations are the most common means of political involvement, although less so in Japan. Petitions are also popular in the United States, although not in Britain.

Within these trends, there are some noticeable national variations. In Germany, participation in protest was more than twice the average across the four countries (6.7% compared to 3%), while participation in protest in Japan was markedly lower (2% compared to 3%). Overall, the populations of the United States, Britain, and Germany seem more activist than in Japan, although German data are incomplete.

These countries are similar in terms of the ability of NGOs to use popular media to communicate. It is not surprising to find a high density of information available, given these are advanced industrial liberal states. There are several differences that might prove important, however. First, there is a preference in the United States for TV and the Internet over newspapers. These media are better able to capture affective action, but have a hard time providing nuanced analysis of issues. In Germany, there is a weak preference for print media over more visual forms. Great Britain has the least connected public, as it ranks third or fourth on all indicators.

This admittedly sparse analysis of the formal and informal political and social institutions that NGOs face raises several strategic issues. The closer the match to prevailing views of acceptable behavior, the more success a campaign will have. As a result, NGOs are more likely to have political influence via insider tactics (lobbying and campaign contributions) in places where state-society networks are close, namely the United States and Germany. Nonprofit organizations may have trouble gaining access, however, given weak interest in their issues compared to economic interests. Affective politics may be a solution to distant state-society relations in Britain and weak institutions in Germany. While the use of extreme protest tactics is not condoned anywhere, protest tactics fare better in Britain and Germany than Japan. Monetary means of influence, via campaign contributions and economic boycotts, may be the best means for outsiders to influence policy in Japan.

This analysis demonstrates several reasons for NGOs to adapt their operations as they enter new countries, although the formal and informal political and social institutions in these countries may vary less than would be expected. It thus raises the question of whether this really happens. I examine the climate-change campaigns of Friends of the Earth and Greenpeace across all four countries to assess the extent to which these organizations can and do alter their campaigns and the significance of national variations for NGO efficacy.

Friends of the Earth and the Climate-Change Campaign

Friends of the Earth (FoE), initially founded in radical protest against the Sierra Club, has become one of the oldest, and most established, of the international environmental organizations. With a 1,782,035 euro budget, a staff of 1,200, a network of sixty-eight member groups, and more than a million individual supporters, Friends of the Earth has a global reach. Nevertheless, individual national campaigns on particular issues must accommodate domestic political and social institutions if Friends of the Earth is to succeed at its stated goals of sustainable development, democratization of international environmental politics, and environmental protection. The informal motto of FoE—"think globally, act locally"—is apt.[88] The directive is for individuals to act locally and directly upon environmental problems. As founder David Brower says, "We made it a point not to be clearly organized or directed by some old tired formula from the top. Find good people with the right ideas and let them move ahead their way."[89]

Founded in 1969, Friends of the Earth is an explicitly federated organization of autonomous member groups.[90] Member groups are given a great deal of freedom to select the issues they target as well as the means by which they address these issues. Members of FoE need not even adopt the Friends of the Earth name, and in fact the German organization BUND, which serves as FoE Germany, predated FoE by fifty years.[91] Members must agree to only the following: independence from political parties and other particularistic interest groups, national and grassroots activism, a focus on the main environmental issues of their countries, and open and democratic structures.[92] General meetings are held biannually, at which federation policies and guidelines for campaigns are decided. FoE has only a small international headquarters, based in Amsterdam, which is responsible for international networking and coordination. The day-to-day organization and operation is at the national level, producing a highly decentralized organization.

FoE operating principles include a dedication to grassroots activism and the belief that change must be local to be sustainable.[93] This stems from the conviction that humans must take responsibility for environmental deterioration and work to preserve resources.[94] FoE also stresses collaboration in order to mobilize the broadest range of resources to focus on the same goal.[95] In this vein, FoE seeks to "increase public participation and democratic decision-making."[96]

In their literature on global warming, FoE singles out Japan and the United States for their resistance to efforts to stop climate change.[97] FoE focuses on greenhouse gases, in particular carbon dioxide, from "the burning of fossil fuels for cars, industry, and electricity generation."[98] "Climate change brings enormous risks and human costs. Rising sea levels, droughts, flooding and extreme weather as a result of global warming will result in massive human suffering and disruption of food and water supplies."[99] FoE's solutions of choice focus on public awareness and international agreements to control the emissions of greenhouse gases, although they oppose the Kyoto Protocol for its granting of emission credits, the formula by which reduction obligations are derived, the creation of carbon sinks, and slow implementation.[100]

Although the campaign strategies used varied by country, the same three elements can be seen in each national advocacy campaign. FoE sought first, to win governments' commitment to reduce their emissions of greenhouse gases, in part via court cases against polluters; second, to move beyond emissions restrictions in Kyoto to a more intense agreement; and third, to change the behavior of international institutions and corporations whose practices currently enable climate change, for example investments in oil, mining, or gas industries.[101] National organizations combined individuality in their campaigns with collaboration internationally to take advantage of opportunities and constraints across political contexts. The rest of this section examines the main outlines of the campaign in each member group.

Friends of the Earth Japan (FoE Japan) relied on collaboration with other NGOs, such as the Kilko Network, and public information in its campaign against climate change. FoE Japan sponsored the International Conference on the Long Term Prospects of International Climate Change Policy in 2004 for experts and advocates to discuss political, ecological, and environmental issues concerning global warming.[102] FoE Japan also produced investigative reports on the problem of climate change, in order to recommend policy changes to business and government and educate the Japanese public.[103] FoE Japan has also researched the use of solar power as a substitute for burning fossil fuels.

While not a highly visible member, FoE Japan has a decent record of accessing government officials, including face-to-face meetings with the minister of finance and director of the Environmental Agency in 1993 and 1994. There is only affective campaign action publicized on the FoE Japan website. In 2001, FoE Japan cosponsored the "Stop Global Warming Family Parade" to publicize global warming.[104] Its public activities consist largely of leisure not politics, including Sunday hikes and eco-tours.[105]

Friends of the Earth Germany, or Bund für Umwelt und Naturschutz Deutschland, joined FoEI in 1989 as a preexisting federation of regional German environmental groups.[106] BUND organized one of the largest FoE direct action campaigns when more than 4,000 activists from more than thirty countries built a giant lifeboat in Bonn during 2001 climate talks.[107] BUND also organized a direct action campaign for youth in which 150 schools reduced CO_2 emissions more in eight months than the government had committed to reducing in eight years.[108] As part of FoE Europe, BUND was involved in the Carbon Dinosaurs campaign in 2004, using a giant inflated Carbon Dinosaur in European capitals, coal mining sites, and oil companies to identify and shame those responsible for continued greenhouse gas emissions.[109] An individual letter-writing campaign was part of the purpose of the Carbon Dinosaurs tour.[110] In general, the German FoE campaign for climate change is an outsider strategy geared toward using public involvement to press the government to change. "With spectacular public action we have consistently managed to bring the urgency of the climate problem to the media and increase pressure on politicians."[111]

Friends of the Earth UK is also a participant in FoE Europe and thus the Carbon Dinosaur campaign. FoE UK, however, pairs affective action to grab public interest with insider lobbying to limit emissions trading allowances, encourage cuts in emissions goals, and change the funding practices of international institutions such as the World Bank and the European Bank for Reconstruction and Development.[112] Over four thousand letters from FoE supporters were collected, calling on the secretary of state for international development to ensure that UK votes in multilateral institutions are against oil projects. These letters were delivered to the Department for International Development in the midst of a spectacle including a naked businessman, a model gas pump, and a rally led by activist/comedian Mark Thomas.[113] FoE UK targeted its mixed informational/direct action campaigns at Shell and BP and government support for the development of new oil projects.[114]

Friends of the Earth US combines direct action at the local level and informational lobbying at the national level with money politics and lawsuits in national courts. FoE US has Friends of the Earth Action PAC, a nonpartisan, non-philanthropic political action committee geared toward electing environmentally friendly candidates.[115] The FoE US Green Scissors campaign carefully monitors U.S. government spending for wasteful or environmentally damaging spending or tax provisions, including benefits given to corporations whose practices contribute to global warming.[116] This campaign combines media exposure, electoral pressure, and careful research into the opaque U.S. budget and tax code, voting records, and lobbying connections of individual legislators. In 2001, for instance, FoE US ran ads against Representatives Bishop, Thune, and Sununu in their local papers for their votes in support of tax breaks for the oil, coal, and automobile industries.[117] FoE US is working in particular to protect the Arctic National Wildlife Refuge from oil and gas exploration. While the climate-change campaign in the United States is detail oriented and information rich, most publicity, and the FoE US website, is devoted to the more spectacular aspects.

True to its principles, FoE also encourages citizens of these countries to take individual action to reduce their production of greenhouse gases by reducing personal energy consumption. FoEI publications advise: "Here are some simple ideas to get you started: ride a bike, take the train, car pool, and if you must buy a car, buy an energy-efficient one. Hang the washing out to dry instead of using a clothes dryer, and put on a sweater instead of raising the thermostat."[118]

Some of FoE's campaign strategies are dictated by the principles of the organization, independent of any institutional logic. These features of FoE operations are constant across national campaigns. First, FoE's commitment to grassroots activism and democratic decision making requires a degree of decentralization regardless of context. Second, public information and education are required by the philosophy "think globally, act locally."

An emphasis on effectiveness indicates concern for the fit between national organizations' tactics and domestic political context. "Friends of the Earth member groups . . . see Friends of the Earth International as a unique and diverse forum to pursue international initiatives, taking advantage of the varied backgrounds and perspectives of its members. By sharing information, knowledge, skills and resources on both the bilateral and multilateral levels, Friends of the Earth groups support each other's development and strengthen their international campaigns."[119] There is evidence of decentralization in the diversity of national campaign activities united by FoEI's requirement to serve "as a pressure group (as far as possible within the national context), they should campaign, educate, and research."[120]

This brief examination of the national FoE campaigns in the United States, Britain, Germany, and Japan demonstrates a mix of information tactics and affective action, with relatively little service provision (except in the category of information provision); a heavy reliance on attention getting, naming, and shaming; and public mobilization across countries. There are national differences, however. Information exchange and collaboration with other environmental organizations were dominant in Japan, public education and direct action topped the list in Germany and Britain, and informational lobbying and media blitzes popularized by affective politics were predominant in the United States. There was marked avoidance of affective tactics in Japan. There was some contact between FoE campaigners and members of the executive in Japan and the legislature in United States, while there was little direct contact with the governments in Germany or Britain, leading to lawsuits, letter writing, and spectacular displays to put indirect pressure on government. Friends of the Earth chapters have brought suits again the government in courts in Germany and the United States in order to acquire information, more effective regulation, or economic restitution.[121]

Greenpeace Climate-Change Campaign

Greenpeace has also become an established fixture in the international environmental movement, with branches in forty-one countries, a staff of more than 1,000, 2.8 million supporters, and a 163,439,000 euro budget, although it maintains the image of ardent activists working on the front lines.[122] Its mission statement reflects this self-image: "Greenpeace is an independent campaigning organization that uses non-violent, creative confrontation to expose global environmental problems, and force solutions for a green and peaceful future."[123]

Greenpeace is "committed to the principles of non-violence, political independence and internationalism. In exposing threats to the environment and in working to find solutions, Greenpeace has no permanent allies or enemies."[124] Greenpeace accepts no funding from governments, corporations, or political parties nor donations that could compromise its independence or integrity. These two principled positions—no government funding and no permanent friends—likely have a strong constraining effect on Greenpeace's access to policy making, as friendship and money are key for insider strategies. Campaigning is based upon the Quaker practice of "bearing witness" to abuses and the use of media outlets and Greenpeace publications to publicize these acts as a means of bringing pressure for change.[125]

Greenpeace is centrally managed as a nonprofit corporation. The main outlines of campaign strategy are set by central offices in Amsterdam, with general meetings held annually. Member groups are not members but field offices of the central organization. Regional offices have the responsibility to enact campaigns, manage local media coverage, and distribute information about Greenpeace's activities and policy proposals as they relate to the campaign. Campaign organizers see Greenpeace as "multimedia," combining traditional tactics such as lobbying, litigation, and research with grassroots activism and more radical direct actions.[126] Greenpeace's campaign seeks to end practices which contribute to global warming, such as burning fossil fuels and driving inefficient cars, and to promote alternative energy technologies.[127] While Greenpeace is committed to its principles, "we want to take on General Motors and the Pentagon and Dow and Du Pont and Exxon. You cannot do that by being a rugged individualist that remains true to some mythical standard of purity but remains as tiny and impoverished as possible."[128] There is a sense that rational considerations for efficacy may supersede principle.

Greenpeace USA was the founding "chapter" and is still dominant within the organization due to its financial weight. The Greenpeace USA campaign focuses on popularizing (even sensationalizing) the effects of global warming and encouraging increased use of renewable energy sources. Using the plight of polar bears, unusual climatological events (recent hurricanes and typhoons), the convenient release of "The Day after Tomorrow," and the Winter Olympics, Greenpeace USA publicizes global warming through press releases to local media, public demonstrations and direct actions, and its website. For instance, Greenpeace USA blocked the Texas headquarters of ExxonMobil during their annual general meeting in 2004 and projected scenes of tidal waves and floods on the ExxonMobil building during a shareholders meeting.[129] Greenpeace USA also focused efforts on publicizing misinformation released by the Bush administration regarding energy policies and relations with energy interest groups. In particular, Greenpeace USA investigates connections between Exxon-Mobil, the Bush administration, and think tank reports commissioned by Exxon to undermine environmental organizations and prevent greenhouse gas regulations.[130] Greenpeace USA also developed the "Rolling Sunlight" solar truck to showcase clean-energy technologies. The truck can generate enough energy to power three energy-efficient houses or be used to power outdoor events such as concerts.[131] Greenpeace supporters assisted the campaign by donating computer CPU time to help calculate global warming models and sending messages to major oil and auto companies to support lower emissions standards.[132] In 1987, Greenpeace USA spun off Greenpeace Action to lobby decision makers in Washington, using professional lobbyists and amateurs going door to door. "Our effective work for new laws and policies, has precluded contributions to Greenpeace from being tax-deductible," although their success makes a good advertising message.[133]

Greenpeace UK also has a two-pronged climate-change campaign directed at actions to stop the production of greenhouse gases and efforts to support alternative energy use, in particular "clean" forms such as wind, solar, and wave power.[134] Efforts to stop the production of greenhouses gases include economic boycotts of Esso and Land Rover (Ford), public shaming of "climate criminals" who block efforts to confront the problem, and direct actions to call attention to corporations and governments engaged in producing CO_2 emissions, such as party crashing an annual corporate party of the Shell oil company.[135] Greenpeace UK also uses public information laws to gather information about government policy and practice regarding global warming.[136] This information is used to publicize the gap between government rhetoric and action on climate change.[137] The Greenpeace UK climate-change campaign shows all the hallmarks of an outsider's campaign, including its own calls for the British PM Tony Blair to "drop his pro-business bias."[138] Greenpeace UK also uses its website to organize the modern-day equivalent of letter campaigns, asking supporters to email or fax Tony Blair, Esso, and Ford.[139] While the main focus rests on public pressure generated by direct action and public mobilization, Greenpeace UK also operates a political unit. The political unit is responsible for "communication with a wide range of those in the political arena—from Cabinet Ministers to backbenchers—using quality supporting materials produced by highly experienced campaigners and our science unit."[140]

Greenpeace Japan primarily engages in information campaigning, via press releases detailing dangerous practices and calling for government action. Greenpeace Japan also staged public rallies, for example, holding a press conference during a typhoon to draw attention to the threat of climate change and demand alternative energy sources or leafleting ExxonMobil Ltd. headquarters in Tokyo in conjunction with similar efforts in the United States.[141] While Greenpeace Japan is actively engaged, in particular in pushing Koizumi to adhere to Kyoto restrictions, it adds little new to the campaign. While Greenpeace Japan campaigners met with company and government spokesmen and PR people, they have had little luck accessing actual decision makers.[142]

Greenpeace's mix of informational lobbying and public protest tactics does not always sit easily within one organization, which may explain the need to spin off separate political units in Britain and the United States. "While we are best known for hanging banners and chasing whalers, much of our work is done behind the scenes in areas such as research and consultation. Our expertise has earned us attendance at major international environmental policy and treaty meetings and we maintain consultative status to the United Nations."[143] Greenpeace protests, while generating press and attention, also tend to generate arrest records. For instance, eighty campaigners were arrested in Britain and twenty-six in the United States during ExxonMobil protests in 2003.[144]

There is a great degree of homology in Greenpeace campaigns across countries. Each local campaign mixes anti–global warming and pro–alternative energy content while combining the tactics of public education and constituent lobbying with spectacular actions to generate interest and gain media attention to disseminate their message. There is little innovation across the different institutional contexts. Each campaign draws upon the same activities (protests with banners, direct action to halt business as usual, local letter writing, and media coverage) and targets the same "climate criminals"—Bush and Blair as well as ExxonMobil (Esso) and Ford/Land Rover.

Power Projection and Institutional Logic

While the adaptability of NGO campaigns is limited by their principled commitments, this chapter examines the room they have to adjust strategy to institutional constraints, and thus NGO power projection within different institutional contexts. My argument here is that the closer the fit between an NGO's strategy and national institutions, the greater its influence. Furthermore, the more decentralized and flexible an organization, the better its chances of adaptation. Table 4 summarizes and compares Friends of the Earth and Greenpeace. Greenpeace is a highly centralized corporation in which operations are conducted from the top down, while Friends of the Earth is a decentralized network of equal organizations with freedom to pursue independent campaigns within bounds set democratically at the center.

TABLE 4. FRIENDS OF THE EARTH AND GREENPEACE COMPARED

	Friends of the Earth (1971)	Greenpeace (1969)
Structure	Federation of autonomous organizations	Centrally managed corporate hierarchy
Country of Origin	United States	United States
Country of HQ	The Netherlands	
Budget	$1,782,035	163,439,000 euro
Staff	1,200	1,000
Membership	68 member groups 1 million individual members	41 regional offices 2.8 million supporters
Degree of Centralization	Highly decentralized	Highly centralized
Locus of Planning	Local	International
General Meetings	Biannual	Annual
Operating Procedures	Democratic, consensus	Top-down management by international board

I expected that the flexibility of FoE and its attention to the local would enable it to adapt to local institutions and adopt a greater variety of tactics, thus producing more successful campaigns. I expected the rigid, centralized planning of Greenpeace would hinder its operations as each campaign was conducted according to the same model regardless of institutional variations.

Before addressing the central question—can NGOs adjust to accommodate different institutions or are they bound by one institutional logic—it is important to consider the similarities between organizations set up to be opposites. Both Friends of the Earth and Greenpeace were founded in the United States, but with the intention to spread quickly. Both organizations were founded as antiestablishmentarian alternatives and yet have become established mainstays. Lastly, both organizations are large, well funded, multi-issue, multi-national advocacy groups. Greenpeace and Friends of the Earth thus compete for recognition and resources. This competition likely affects their operations alongside their unique political philosophies and the domestic political institutions within which they function.

I have found that while FoE seems to have a large degree of flexibility, principled commitments to democracy and public education require a good deal of commonality in campaigns across institutional settings. Similarly, Greenpeace's principled commitment to independence of action and the avoidance of political entanglements constrains their actions, although this is particularly problematic in corporatist settings such as Germany and Japan.

I find a surprising propensity to affective action in Germany via both public protests (ExxonMobil blockade) and direct action (Bonn lifeboat, Esso boycott) by both FoE and Greenpeace. While affective politics are a better fit to German political culture than others examined, its decentralized political system raises the prospects for using informational mechanisms instead. While information campaigns were undertaken by both FoE and Greenpeace, affective actions seemed to receive more attention and energy.

In Japan, FoE engaged in information campaigns as well as attempts to collaborate with other environmental groups to obtain access, which accords well with the corporatist nature of interest representation in Japan and societal bias against protest. Greenpeace Japan, on the other hand, engaged in the economic boycott of Esso and demonstrations against ExxonMobil, despite public sentiment that protest is inappropriate.

In the United States, both organizations attempted several variations of lobbying, including traditional approaches to decision makers by specialized political units as well as letter-writing campaigns. With little success in the prevailing political climate in Washington, D.C., FoE turned to creative economic lobbying via its Green Scissors campaign, while Greenpeace turned to its more traditional affective politics. This shows adaptability in a limited sense by FoE, but a return to basics for Greenpeace.

In Britain, FoE and Greenpeace engaged in affective politics to publicize climate killers. While Friends of the Earth also engaged in lobbying to change British votes in international institutions, Greenpeace UK used public information laws to demonstrate contradictions in officials' rhetoric and issue demands for change. Friends of the Earth appeared to have better access to government officials than Greenpeace in this case, although both used outsider strategies as well insider strategies.

In conclusion, FoE demonstrated a greater variety of tactics in their campaign and a slightly greater ability or willingness to fit campaign strategy to institutional context. That being said, both organizations used a relatively narrow and consistent set of tactics in all four cases. I also found a high degree of collaboration between the two organizations. Friends of the Earth and Greenpeace have filed a lawsuit in U.S. District Court in San Francisco on behalf of victims of global warming against the Export Import Bank and Overseas Private Investment Corporation over funding for environmentally destructive projects abroad.[145] Both FoE and Greenpeace were also involved in the Yes2wind project to publicize renewable energy sources, the Esso (ExxonMobil) boycott campaign, and the Bonn lifeboat.[146]

The similarities between campaigns across national settings, and between the campaigns of Greenpeace and FoE, may be explained in part by growing isomorphism on the part of government institutions presenting a similar set of constraints to NGOs across national contexts. Although there were institutional differences across the countries examined, these were neither as numerous nor as large as their similarities. There may also be a significant amount of learning between NGOs as they encounter one another more frequently in different national contexts and collaborate. The problem of NGO power projection across different institutional logics may thus be one of choice within increasingly common constraints. NGOs may find some adjustment necessary as they cross national boundaries, but the extent may be growing increasingly smaller.

Notes

1. Russell Dalton, *The Green Rainbow* (New Haven, Conn.: Yale University Press, 1994).

2. Margaret Keck and Kathryn Sikkink, *Activists beyond Borders: Advocacy Networks in International Politics* (Ithaca, N.Y.: Cornell University Press, 1998); Thomas Risse, Stephen C. Ropp, and Kathryn Sikkink, eds., *The Power of Human Rights: International Norms and Domestic Change* (New York: Cambridge University Press, 1999); Thomas

Risse, "The Power of Norms versus the Norms of Power: Transnational Civil Society and Human Rights," in *The Third Force: The Rise of Transnational Civil Society*, ed. Ann Florini (Washington, D.C.: Carnegie Endowment for International Peace, 2000).

3. Peter Katzenstein, ed., *Between Power and Plenty: Foreign Economic Policies of Advanced Industrial States* (Madison: University of Wisconsin Press, 1978); Dana Fisher, *National Governance and the Global Climate Change Regime* (Lanham, Md.: Rowman and Littlefield, 2004).

4. Union of International Associations, "Types of International Organization in the Yearbook," available at: http://www.uia.org/uiadocs/orgtyped.htm; UIA, *Yearbook of International Organizations* (Brussels: Union of International Associations, 1997/8); ECOSOC, "Consultative Relationship Between the ECOSOC and NGOs," available at: http://www.un.org/esa/coordination/ngo/.

5. Sidney Tarrow, *Power in Movement: Social Movements, Collective Action and Politics* (Cambridge: Cambridge University Press, 1994).

6. Ibid., 25.

7. Ibid., 35.

8. Ibid., 60.

9. Dalton, *Green Rainbow*, 7; William Gamson, *The Strategy of Social Protest* (Homewood, Ill.: Dorsey Press, 1975).

10. Paul J. DiMaggio and Walter W. Powell, "The Iron Cage Revisited: Institutional Isomorphism and Collective Rationality in Organizational Fields," *American Sociological Review* 48 (April 1983): 147.

11. Ibid., 149.

12. John W. Meyer and Brian Rowan, "Institutionalized Organizations: Formal Structure as Myth and Ceremony," *American Journal of Sociology* 83 (1977): 352.

13. Ibid., 343.

14. David Strang and John W. Meyer, "Institutional Conditions for Diffusion," *Theory and Society* 22 (1993): 490.

15. Ibid., 493.

16. Dalton, *Green Rainbow*, 9.

17. Ibid., 10.

18. Meyer and Rowan, "Institutionalized Organizations," 348–49.

19. Tarrow, *Power in Movement*, 25.

20. John Boli, "Conclusion," in *Constructing World Culture: International Nongovernmental Organizations Since 1875*, ed. John Boli and George M. Thomas (Stanford, Calif.: Stanford University Press, 1999), 269.

21. Meyer and Rowan, "Institutionalized Organizations," 347.

22. John Boli and George M. Thomas, eds. *Constructing World Culture: International Nongovernmental Organizations Since 1875* (Stanford, Calif.: Stanford University Press, 1999), 37–39.

23. Ibid., 14.

24. Ibid., 15.

25. Strang and Meyer, "Institutional Conditions for Diffusion," 501.

26. Meyer and Rowan, "Institutionalized Organizations," 345.

27. Other taxonomies use other means of categorizing NGOs, including membership, issue area, geographic interests, and resources. See UIA, *Yearbook of International Organizations*; Robert Keohane and Joseph Nye, *Power and Interdependence*, 3rd ed. (New York: Longman, 2001); Cheryl Shanks Harold K. Jacobson, and Jeffrey H. Kaplan, "Inertia and Change in the Constellation of International Governmental Organizations, 1981–1992," *International Organization* 50, no. 4 (1996): 593–627; and Werner J. Feld, *Nongovernmental Forces and World Politics* (New York: Praeger, 1972). Because I am concerned with NGOs' ability to affect policy making and the match between institutions and tactics, I prioritize the nature of their activities above their goals or the nature of the organization itself.

28. For examples of campaigning guides, see International Campaign to Ban Landmines, "Campaign 101," available at: http://www.icbl.org/tools/faq/campaign; Friends of the Earth, *How to Win* (London: Friends of the Earth, 2000); Greenpeace, "Take Action," available at: http://members.greenpeace.org/action/index.php; Clare Watson, Michael O'Cadhla, and Cristiona Ni Dhurcain, *Campaigns and How to Win Them* (Dublin: Wolfhound Press, 1997); Amanda Sussman, *The Art of the Possible* (Toronto: McClelland and Stewart, 2007).

29. For more on this point, see Keck and Sikkink, *Activists beyond Borders*; Risse, Ropp, and Sikkink, *The Power of Human Rights*; Ann Marie Clark, *Diplomacy of Conscience: Amnesty International and Changing Human Rights Norms* (Princeton, N.J.: Princeton University Press, 2001).

30. Herbert Kitschelt, "Political Opportunity Structures and Political Protest: Anti-Nuclear Movement in Four Democracies," *British Journal of Political Science* 16 (1986): 57–86; William Gamson, *The Strategy of Social Protest* (Homewood, Ill.: Dorsey, 1975); John McCarthy and Mayer Zald, "Resource Mobilization and Social Movements: A Partial Theory," *American Journal of Sociology* 82, no. 6 (1977):1212–41.

31. The work builds upon the important contributions made by Thomas Risse-Kappen, ed., *Bringing Transnational Actors Back In* (New York: Cambridge University Press, 1995) as well as Kitschelt, "Political Opportunity Structures and Political Protest"; Katzenstein, *Between Power and Plenty*; and Matthew Evangelista, *Unarmed Forces: The Transnational Movement to End the Cold War* (Ithaca, N.Y.: Cornell University Press, 1999).

32. See Michael Mastanduno, G. John Ikenberry, and David Lake, *The State and American Foreign Economic Policy* (Ithaca, N.Y.: Cornell University Press, 1988); Thomas Risse-Kappen, ed., *Bringing Transnational Relations Back In* (New York: Cambridge University Press, 1995); and Katzenstein, *Between Power and Plenty*.

33. Katzenstein, *Between Power and Plenty*, 604–605; Thomas Risse-Kappen, "Public Opinion, Domestic Initiative, and Foreign Policy in Liberal Democracies," *World Politics* 43, no. 3 (1991): 479–512; Helmut Anheier and Wolfgang Seibel, "Defining the Nonprofit Sector: Germany," Working Papers of the Johns Hopkins Comparative Nonprofit Sector Project, no. 6, ed. Lester M. Salamon and Helmut K. Anheier, 5 (Baltimore: Johns Hopkins Institute for Policy Studies, 1993).

34. Freedom House, "United States of America," available at: http://www.freedom house.org/research/freeworld/2003/countryratings/usa.html (accessed February 26, 2005); CIA, *The World Factbook,* United States, available at: http://www.cia.gov/cia/publications/factbook/print/us.html; Peter Cowhey, "Elect Locally–Order Globally," in John Gerard Ruggie, ed. *Multilateralism Matters* (New York: Columbia University Press, 1993), 164–65.

35. E. E. Schnattschneider, *The Semi-Sovereign People* (New York: Collier, 1960); Raymond Bauer, Lewis Dexter, and Ithiel de Sola Pool, *American Business and Public Policy* (Chicago: Atherton, 1972). Friends of the Earth and Greenpeace activists have often repeated this claim.

36. Michael Johnston, "International Corruption Via Campaign Contributions, US Policies and Risks," Working Paper for Transparency International, October 2000, available at: http://www.transparency.org/working_papers/country/us_paper.html (accessed February 26, 2005).

37. Ibid., 6.

38. FCPA quoted in ibid., 8.

39. Center for Responsive Politics, available at: http://www.opensecrets.org/; Federal Election Commission, www.fec.gov.

40. Freedom House, "United States of America."

41. Katzenstein, *Between Power and Plenty,* 894.

42. CIA, *World Factbook;* Freedom House, "United States of America."

43. European Union Secretariat General, "Relations with the Interest Groups," available at: http://europa.eu.int/comm./secretariat_general/sgc/lobbies/communication.html (accessed February 26, 2005).

44. Electoral Commission website, available at: http://www.electoralcommission .org.uk (accessed February 25, 2005).

45. Electoral Commission, Fact Sheet Campaign Expenditure, available at: http://www .electoralcommission.org.uk/templates/search/document.cfm/6128 (accessed March 4, 2005).

46. Jeremy Kendall and Martin Knapp, "Defining the Nonprofit Sector: The United Kingdom," Working Papers of the Johns Hopkins Comparative Nonprofit Sector Project, no. 5, ed. Lester M. Salamon and Helmut K. Anheier, 6 (Baltimore: Johns Hopkins Institute for Policy Studies, 1993).

47. Ibid., 7.

48. Herbert Kitschelt and Wolfgang Streeck, "From Stability to Stagnation: Germany at the Beginning of the Twenty-First Century," *West European Politics* (2003): 4.

49. Kitschelt, "Political Opportunity Structures and Political Protest," 66.

50. Kitschelt and Streeck, 6; Risse-Kappen, "Public Opinion, Domestic Initiative," 488.

51. Kitschelt and Streeck, "From Stability to Stagnation," 7.

52. Ibid., 27.

53. Ibid., 6.

54. Ibid., 8.

55. Freedom House, "Germany," available at: http://www.freedomhouse.org/research/freeworld/2003/countryratings/ger.html (accessed February 26, 2005).

56. Ulrich von Alemann, "The German Case," Working Paper for Transparency International, October 2000, available at: http://www.transparency.org/working_papers/country/german_paper.html (accessed February 26, 2005).

57. European Union Secretariat General, "Relations with the Interest Groups," available at: http://europa.eu.int/comm./secretariat_general/sgc/lobbies/communication.html (accessed February 26, 2005).

58. Anheier and Seibel, "Defining the Nonprofit Sector," 5, 9.

59. Ibid., 8–9.

60. Ibid., 9–10.

61. Risse-Kappen, *Bringing Transnational Actors Back In*; Katzenstein, *Between Power and Plenty.*

62. Katzenstein, *Between Power and Plenty,* 897.

63. Cowhey, "Elect Locally—Order Globally," 176.

64. Freedom House, "Japan," available at: http://www.freedomhouse.org/research/freeworld/2003/countryratings/japan.html (accessed February 26, 2005)

65. Cowhey, "Elect Locally—Order Globally," 176.

66. Ibid., 178.

67. Ibid.

68. Verena Blechinger, "Corruption through Political Contributions in Japan," Working Paper, Transparency International, October 2000, available at: http://www.transparency.org/working_papers/country/japan_paper.html (accessed February 26, 2005).

69. Freedom House, "Japan."

70. Takayoshi Amenomori, "Defining the Nonprofit Sector: Japan," Working Papers of the Johns Hopkins Comparative Nonprofit Sector Project, no. 15, ed. Lester M. Salamon and Helmut K. Anheier, 7 (Baltimore: Johns Hopkins Institute for Policy Studies, 1993).

71. Ibid., 8.

72. The exception is organizations within corporatist networks in Japan, although as will be discussed, these are unlikely to be environmental groups.

73. Peter Katzenstein, "Introduction: Domestic and International Forces and Strategies of Foreign Economic Policy," *International Organization* 31, no. 4 (1977): 601.

74. Risse-Kappen, "Public Opinion, Domestic Structure," 485.

75. A claim made by Katzenstein, Kitschelt, and Tarrow.

76. Katzenstein, "Introduction: Domestic and International Forces"; Risse-Kappen, „Public Opinion, Domestic Structure."

77. Katzenstein, "Introduction: Domestic and International Forces," 894.

78. Ibid., 895.

79. E. E. Schnattschieder, *Semi-Sovereign People;* Bauer, Pool, and Dexter, *American Business and Public Policy.*

80. Katzenstein, "Introduction: Domestic and International Forces," 894–95; Jeremy

Kendall and Martin Knapp, "Defining the Nonprofit Sector: The United Kingdom," Working Papers of the Johns Hopkins Comparative Nonprofit Sector Project, no. 5, ed. Lester M. Salamon and Helmut K. Anheier (Baltimore: Johns Hopkins Institute for Policy Studies, 1993).

81. Katzenstein, "Introduction: Domestic and International Forces," 894–95.

82. CIA, *World Factbook*, "Britain," available at: https://www.cia.gov/library/publications/the-world-factbook/geos/uk.html.

83. Katzenstein, "Introduction: Domestic and International Forces," 899; Amenomori, "Defining the Nonprofit Sector."

84. Katzenstein, "Introduction: Domestic and International Forces," 898

85. Ibid., 898.

86. Ibid., 900–904; Risse-Kappen, "Public Opinion, Domestic Structure."

87. Katzenstein, "Introduction: Domestic and International Forces," 904.

88. Paul Wapner, *Environmental Activism and World Politics* (Albany: State University of New York Press, 1996.)

89. FoEI, "The Early Years," available at: http://www.foei.org/about/25years.html; Jonathan Porritt, *Saving the Earth* (London: Friends of the Earth, 1991); Robert Lamb, *Promising the Earth* (London: Routledge, 1996).

90. FoEI, "Structure," available at: http://www.foei.org/about/structure.html.

91. FoEI, "Friends of the Earth Germany," available at: http://www.foei.org/groups/members/germany.html (accessed March 5, 2005).

92. FoEI, "Membership Criteria," available at: http://www.foei.org/about/membercriteria.html (accessed March 5, 2005).

93. Wapner, *Environmental Activism and World Politics*.

94. FoEI, "Mission Statement," available at: http://www.foei.org/about/mission_statement.html.

95. FoEI, "Membership Criteria."

96. FoEI, "Mission Statement."

97. FoE, "Climate Change FAQs," available at: http://www.foei.org/climate/faq.html (accessed February 20, 2005).

98. Ibid.

99. Ibid.

100. Friends of the Earth, "The Politics of Climate Change" (FoEI, 2000); Friends of the Earth, "Can't See the Wood Through the Trees?" (FoEI, 1998); FoE, "Emissions Trading and Joint Implementation," (FoEI, 1998).

101. FoE, "Climate Change," available at: http://www.foei.org/climate/index/html (accessed February 20, 2005 and January 30, 2008).

102. FoE Japan, "The International Conference on Long Term Prospects of International Climate Change Policy," available at: http://www.foejapan.org/en/climate_evt_2e.html.

103. FoE Japan, "Our Philosophy," available at: http://www.foejapan.org/en/about/philosophy.html (accessed February 25, 2005).

104. FoE Japan, "History," available at: http://www.foejapan.org/en/about/history.

html (accessed February 25, 2005); FoE Japan, "The International Conference on Long Term Prospects of International Climate Change Policy."

105. FoE Japan, "Our Activities," available at: http://www.foejapan.org/en/about/ activity.html (accessed February 25, 2005 and January 30, 2008).

106. FoEI, "Friends of the Earth Germany," available at: http://www.foei.org/groups/ members/germany.html (accessed February 23, 2005).

107. Ibid.

108. Ibid. The kids won, and the bet then grew to a Europe-wide challenge.

109. Friends of the Earth Europe, "Carbon Dinosaurs," available at: http://www.foeeu rope.org/dinosaur/ (accessed March 4, 2005).

110. Friends of the Earth Europe, "Climate Change: The Biggest Threat Our Planet Is Facing," available at: http://www.foeeurope.org/climate/index.html.

111. BUND, "Climate Protection: Closing Loopholes in Climate Protection," available at: http://www.bund.net/lab/reddot2/klimashutz_1217.html.

112. FoE UK, "Climate and Energy Campaigners Update, July 2004," 4; September 2003, 6.

113. FoE UK, "Climate and Energy Campaigners Update, September 2003," 7.

114. FoE UK, "Climate and Energy Campaigners Update, July 2004," 5.

115. "Go With the FoE," *Grist*, available at: http://www.grist.org/comments/ interactivist/2004/09/20/blackwelder/.

116. FoE US, "Take Action!" available at: http://www.foe.org/act/.

117. FoE US, http://www.foe.org/act/.

118. FoE, "Climate Change FAQs."

119. FoEI, "Mission Statement."

120. FoEI, "Membership Criteria."

121. FoEI, "Cases," available at: http://www.foei.org/en/campaigns/climate/cases.html (accessed January 30, 2008).

122. Greenpeace, Annual Report 2004, available at: http://www.greenpeace.org/ international_en/multimedia/download/1/567579/0/ar2004.pdf (accessed February 26, 2005).

123. Greenpeace, "Our Mission," available at: http://www.greenpeace.org/internation al_en/?item_id=4265&language_id=en.

124. Ibid.

125. Robert Hunter, *Warriors of the Rainbow* (New York: Henry Holt, 1979); John May and Michael Brown, *The Greenpeace Story* (London: Dorling Kindersley, 1991); Wapner, *Environmental Activism and World Politics*; Greenpeace, "The History of Greenpeace," available at: http://www.greenpeace.org/international_en/history/; Greenpeace, "About Us," available at: http://www.greenpeace.org/international_en/aboutus/.

126. Rik Scarce, *Eco-Warriors: Understanding the Radical Environmental Movement* (Chicago: Noble Press, 1990), 51.

127. Greenpeace, "Choose Clean Energy," available at: http://www.greenpeace.co.uk/ climate/.

128. Peter Dykstra, Greenpeace spokesperson, in Scarce, *Eco-Warriors*, 52.

129. Greenpeace USA, "The Day before Shareholder Meeting, ExxonMobil Is

Confronted with 'The Day After Tomorrow,'" available at: http://www.greenpeaceusa .org/press/release?item_id=518433&campaign_id=.

130. Greenpeace, "Global Warming and Energy," available at: http://www.green peaceusa.org/campaigns/.

131. Greenpeace USA, "Greenpeace and Students Power Up Earth Day Events with 'Rolling Sunlight' Solar Truck," available at: http://www.greenpeaceusa.org/press/ release?item_id=519112&campaign_id=.

132. Greenpeace USA, "Global Warming and Energy," available at: http://www.green peaceusa.org/campaigns/.

133. Greenpeace USA, "About Us."

134. Greenpeace, "Choose Clean Energy," available at: http://www.greenpeace.co.uk/ climate/. The name of the alternative energy campaign is, rather catchily, Juice.

135. Ibid.

136. Ibid.

137. Greenpeace UK, "Only Action Will Clear the Air," August 12, 2004, available at: http://www.greenpeace.org.uk/climate/climate/.

138. Greenpeace UK, "You've Lost Your Credibility on Climate Change Blair," January 25, 2005, available at: http://www.greenpeace.org.uk/climate/.

139. Greenpeace UK, "What You Can Do," available at: http://www.greenpeace.org .uk/climate/takeaction/index.cfm.

140. Greenpeace UK, "Political Corner: Overview," available at: http:/www.green peace.org.uk/contentlookup.cfm?ucidparam=200111113182539&CFID=19.

141. Greenpeace Japan, "Welcome to Greenpeace Japan's Website," available at: http://www.greenpeace.or.jp/index_en.html.

142. Greenpeace Japan, "Stop Sabotaging the Efforts to Curb Global Warming," avail- able at: http://www.greenpeace.org.jp/press/2003/eng/.

143. Greenpeace USA, "About Us."

144. Greenpeace USA, "The Day Before Shareholder Meeting."

145. FoEI, "US Climate Victims File Suit," available at: http://www.foei.org/publica tions/link/rights/53.html (accessed February 20, 2005).

146. FoE UK, "Climate and Energy Campaigners Update, September 2003," 4, 9.

10. Exporting Institutional Logics into the Amazon?

American and German Efforts to Protect the Ecosystems and Traditional Peoples of the Amazon Basin

◄───►

SANDRA MOOG

Transnational efforts to save the Amazon rainforest have represented one of the longest-running and most intense campaigns in the history of global environmental politics. Beginning in the early 1980s and reaching a fevered pitch in the years running up to the UNCED "Rio Summit" in 1992, these efforts have maintained significant momentum even today, some thirty years later. Efforts to protect the Amazon Basin's ecosystems and indigenous peoples are often held up as a paradigmatic example of transnational politics in our current era of technical, economic, and political globalization (Keck and Sikkink 1998; Castells 1997, 129). Engaging a multitude of actors from dozens of different countries, not only in South and North America, but in Europe and Asia as well, the fight to save the Amazon represents precisely the kind of transnational effort that is often presented as a testament to the rise of what many have begun to call the new "global civil society" (see Lipschutz 1994; Wapner 1996, 2000; Smith 1998; Anheier, Glasius, and Kaldor, 1999).

As the case of transnational Amazon activism illustrates, the last few decades have indeed witnessed the development of increasingly intense and coordinated civil society efforts that transcend national borders and span the globe (Smith 1997; Keck and Sikkink 1998). However, as I hope to demonstrate here, there are important and enduring differences and discontinuities in the landscape of transnational activism—differences that have been overlooked in many recent studies precisely because this research has focused too exclusively on the global level.[1]

In the discussion that follows, I trace the development of Amazon advocacy in the United States and Germany since the mid-1980s, highlighting some interesting differences in the institutional development and political outlook of the movement in the two countries.[2] Applying insights derived from some recent literature that has been critical of the discourse of "global civil society," I suggest that U.S. organizations have engaged much more intensively than their counterparts in Germany in efforts that reach across the "civil society/market axis."[3] Availing themselves of significantly more financial resources, U.S. groups have been able to participate more directly in development and conservation projects in the Amazon Basin, and in the consolidation of new NGOs in the region. The U.S. groups, however, have failed to find a coherent "center of balance" in their Amazon efforts. Thus, in exporting their approaches abroad, they risk exporting conflict abroad as well. The movement in Germany, on the other hand, focusing more attention across the "civil society/state axis," has developed a more unified approach to Amazon advocacy and a more consistent message for the German public and for German state agencies. In comparison to the U.S. movement, the German movement has kept more distance from the corporate sector. Maintaining a focus on ecologically responsible behavior at home, and on the responsibility of German citizens *qua* citizens for the fate of the world's rainforests, this movement has managed to significantly reorient the development programs of the German state. Its efforts have helped to make Germany a leader in international efforts to support capacity building within the ministries and enforcement agencies of Amazon Basin governments. But the German movement has not played nearly as strong a role in directly shaping the development of civil society organizations in the Amazon over the last few decades. These enduring differences in the orientations and competencies of U.S. and German organizations, I suggest, have important implications for our understanding of the development of transnational civil society in the current era.

The Institutional Landscape of Transnational Civil Society

The rising number of social movements and nongovernmental organizations (NGOs) engaged in international and transnational politics represents one of the most important new developments in post–Cold War politics.[4] NGOs and other civil society organizations play ever more important roles in international negotiations and regime-building[5] and in the implementation of bilateral and multilateral development projects abroad.[6] In recent years, they have also come to constitute an increasingly autonomous arena for political agenda-setting on issues of global relevance.[7] The growing significance of transnationally engaged groups, especially in matters concerning human rights and the global environment, has led many observers to the conclusion that what we have been witnessing in recent decades represents, in essence, the development of a new kind of "global civil society" (see Lipschutz 1994; Wapner 1996, 2000; Anheier, Glasius, and Kaldor 2001–2004/5; Keane 2003). The early literature addressing these new forms of political activity has documented some important developments in post–Cold War politics. However, many scholars, in their enthusiasm for the possibilities suggested by the rise of a new "global civil society," "world polity,"[8] or "transnational public sphere," have tended to focus their attention too exclusively at the global level.[9]

Though their lines of communication and political activities may cross many borders, most of the NGOs and social movement groups that engage in new forms of transnational activism are still essentially nationally based phenomena. Groups' activists and funds are primarily drawn from within national borders. Even the member organizations that make up the large international NGOs like Greenpeace and Amnesty International are generally incorporated according to domestic laws.

Calling attention to the important role that national origin can play in shaping the outlook and activities of transnational actors, a number of critics have recently begun to question the universalizing bent of the global civil society literature. Thus, although scholars such as Ulrich Beck suggest that we turn our gaze *away* from the category of the nation state in favor of the "global" and the "globalized local," critics warn that such an approach obscures important power dynamics within the emerging transnational public sphere. For scholars such as Pasha and Blaney (1998); Howell and Pearce (2001), Chandhoke (2002), and Anderson and Rieff (2005), the dominant discourse on global civil society has failed to recognize the extent to which so many of the institutions engaged in transnational politics bear the imprint of particular political visions and the nationally based organizations that promote them. To phrase their concerns in the language of this volume: it results, they insist, not just from the diffusion and evolution of new cosmopolitan norms and institutions, but also, quite importantly, from the projection of particular ideologies and hegemonic institutional forms from *particular* centers of global power. Not surprisingly, in the current political climate, many of these authors are particularly concerned about American centers of power, and about the role of U.S. money, interests, and institutional pressure in the shaping of global civil society (see especially Howell and Pearce, 2001; Chandhoke 2002; and Anderson and Rieff, 2005).[10]

Admittedly, U.S. foundations are some of the most well-endowed in the world (Anheier and Toepler 1999, 11), and they have played an increasingly active role on the world stage in recent decades (Anheier, Glasius, and Kaldor 2001, 206). American NGOs have also been dominant within some particular spheres of transnational activity, such as wildlife conservation. But are there really particular kinds of institutional logic that we might label "American" logics? If so, how might we identify them? And what role do they play in transnational politics?

Surprisingly, despite the continued significance of national-level organizing for transnational politics, few studies in the new literature on global civil society pay significant attention to differences in the activities of networks and NGOs that arise from their origins in different national settings.[11] In the discussion that follows, I explore such questions with evidence from my research on a particular cross-section of transnationally active movements and NGOs based within two different national settings: the United States of America and the Federal Republic of Germany.[12] Looking comparatively at the efforts of U.S. and German groups that have addressed issues of environmental destruction, human rights abuses, and the need for new development models in the Amazon Basin, this research addresses empirically the kinds of questions raised in recent debates about global civil society. It explores whether there are, in fact, important differences in the bases of support, forms of organization, and kinds of political culture that are possible within different nation states.

Tracing the evolution of Amazon activism in the United States and Germany provides a particularly interesting comparison. The movement to save the Amazon has been unusually strong in these two particular countries. There has been, since the mid-1980s, significant cross-fertilization of ideas and strategies among German and U.S. activists. They have even engaged in a number of joint campaigns over the years. Nevertheless, though the general timing and broad ideological contours of the movement have been quite similar in the two countries, closer examination of what *kinds* of political orientations and organizational competencies have been fostered in these two national settings over the past few decades reveals some very interesting differences.

The Amazon as an Object of Global Public Concern in the 1980s

During the 1980s and 1990s the fate of the Amazon forest became one of the most highly publicized of a number of new global environmental problems.[13] One of the last great stretches of intact wilderness on the planet, the Amazon Basin not only provides a home to some of the last isolated indigenous groups on Earth, but also has been widely recognized as crucial for global climactic stability and for the maintenance of biological diversity.[14] As Latin American governments began in the 1970s and 1980s to pursue aggressive development schemes in the region, they set off processes of environmental degradation and escalated conflict among indigenous populations and various groups of settlers.[15] Alarm about the pace of deforestation and the precarious situation of indigenous peoples within the Amazon Basin was first expressed in the 1970s and early 1980s by a small number of Latin American and Northern scientists and anthropologists and by urban-based indigenous intellectuals in a number of Latin American countries. It was not until the second half of the 1980s, however, that problems in the Amazon became the object of widespread public concern and transnational mobilization.

In the mid-1980s the advocacy efforts of a number of human rights and environmental NGOs began calling attention to ecological and human rights problems in the Amazon Basin. As the international indigenous rights movement gained significant momentum through a series of UN processes, this provided an opportunity for Indians from throughout the Amazon Basin to come together, define common problems, and create new organizations.[16] Preparation for participation in the UN Working Group on Indigenous Populations, which met in Geneva in 1984, for example, led to the establishment of an umbrella organization for Amazon indigenous groups, the Coordinating Body of Indigenous Organizations of the Amazon Basin (COICA). Participation in these UN fora brought leaders from indigenous groups to the United States and Europe and provided them opportunities for collaboration with northern NGOs. Groups such as Oxfam, Survival International (United Kingdom), and Cultural Survival (United States) not only provided technical and financial support for indigenous participation in these events; they also became strong public advocates for Amazonian indigenous rights, attempting to raise awareness in the North of the threats indigenous peoples faced at home in the rainforest.

It was another development, however, a cleverly conceived "multilateral development bank" (MDB) campaign waged by new "international departments" within three established environmental NGOs in Washington that did the most to bring problems in the Amazon to the attention of Northern publics. In 1983 activists from the National Wildlife Federation (NWF), the National Resources Defense Council (NRDC) and the Environmental Policy Institute (EPI) began to lobby key decision makers in the U.S. Congress. Criticizing aggressive and uncontrolled colonization and extractive development programs in the Amazon, these activists highlighted the crucial role of World Bank and Inter-American Development Bank (IDB) loans in funding those ill-fated programs (Bramble and Porter 1992; Rich 1994). Working closely with Republican Senator Robert Kasten and the Senate Appropriations Committee on Foreign Operations, the environmentalists' efforts resulted in a series of congressional oversight hearings regarding World Bank and IDB financing of the Brazilian *Polonoroeste* development program.

The campaign was very successful. Not only did it accomplish its more specific goal of forcing through real policy changes within the World Bank, but it helped to disseminate a deeper critique of traditional approaches to development.[17] The campaign also succeeded in bringing the destruction of the tropical rainforests onto the political agenda of citizens' organizations throughout the world. By 1985, a surprising number of environmental and human rights organizations (among them, groups from Sweden, Australia, Germany, and the Netherlands) had joined the Washington-based MDB campaigners (Rich 1994, 137). In April of 1986, the World Rainforest Movement, a global coalition of advocates fighting to halt tropical forest destruction and to protect the livelihoods of traditional forest inhabitants, was founded in Penang, Malaysia.[18] And in September of 1986, advocacy organizations from all over the world converged in Washington to stage a joint protest action on the occasion of the annual World Bank/IMF meeting there, a performance which was to be repeated again in Berlin in 1988.

The fight to save the Amazon was a transnational effort: activists in Latin America, North America, and Europe communicated regularly and coordinated a number of transnational networks and joint campaigns (Keck and Sikkink, 1998; Brysk, 2000). Organizations collaborated intensively in international lobbying and protest efforts—at meetings of the International Tropical Timber Organization; at meetings of the United Nations and the Bretton Woods institutions; and at the summits of heads of states, such as the G7/G8 meetings (Kolk 1996). They conducted joint campaigns in support of the Brazilian Yanomami and other indigenous groups; and they waged transnational boycotts as well, targeting first McDonald's and Burger King's rainforest beef, in the mid-1980s, and then tropical hardwood imports in 1989/1990.

Not only were common repertoires developed and diffused through these joint campaigns,[19] but new kinds of political orientations and identities emerged in the process as well. In the earliest days of the movement, organizations and their activists had been drawn primarily from three pre-existing institutional milieux. Some, primarily concerned about the destruction of tropical ecosystems and forests, came from biology departments or from the environmental movement. Others came from a background in issues of social justice and development: these were activists engaged in the Third World Solidarity Movement, or professionals from humanitarian and development organizations.[20] A third group of activists were indigenous leaders, anthropologists, and NGO professionals involved in the global indigenous rights movement. In the course of the Amazon mobilization, however, a novel approach to advocacy developed in a number of Northern countries, one incorporating a more deeply integrated vision of environmental rights *as* human rights. In fact, a whole new generation of environmental groups was born in the course of the fight to save the Amazon, new "environmental justice" organizations dedicated to protecting natural ecosystems by supporting the livelihoods of traditional, subsistence-oriented populations who depended on those resources. This new generation of organizations—NGOs such as the Rainforest Foundation in the

United States, Norway, and the United Kingdom; and urgewald in Germany—flourished throughout both North America and Northern Europe in the early 1990s.[21]

The rainforest movement of the late 1980s was a truly transnational phenomenon. Nevertheless, as I will demonstrate in the following section, attention to what kinds of contributions to this transnational effort were able to take root within two very different national polities in the late 1980s can provide some interesting insights into the questions I opened with above: namely, what kind of institutional logics are at play in the new global civil society, and does the national origin of advocacy groups still matter in an era of transnational activism?

Rainforest Mobilization in the United States and Germany, 1986–1992

Public interest in the Amazon rainforest was especially pronounced in the United States and in the Federal Republic of Germany.[22] In both of these countries, by the end of the 1980s and beginning of the 1990s, diverse networks of environmental activists, solidarity groups, and professional NGOs were agitating to influence the course of development in the Amazon Basin. Activists in the United States and Germany frequently combined forces in joint campaigns, and the basic ideological contours of the struggle were similar in the two countries. However, what is particularly interesting is how substantially the campaigns in the two countries differed in terms of their institutional roots and political strategies. The movement took root in very different political and institutional milieux in the two countries. As a result, the kinds of organizations and orientations which dominated in each country were different as well.

In the United States established NGOs and foundation funding played a dominant role throughout the course of the mobilization. There, defense of the ecosystems and traditional peoples of the Amazon Basin was initially taken up by a few larger professional NGOs, all based in four major metropolitan areas: New York, Boston, Washington, D.C., and the San Francisco Bay Area. The indigenous cause, for example, was championed by established NGOs such as Oxfam America and Cultural Survival. And it was some of the larger environmental NGOs, such as NWF, EPI, and NRDC (later joined by EDF, the Environmental Defense Foundation), which spearheaded the MDB campaign. As the movement gained momentum in the United States, the strength of the private philanthropic and professionalized NGOs scene allowed a number of new rainforest NGOs to quickly establish themselves as formal organizations with substantial budgets. By 1992 organizations such as Rainforest Action Network in San Francisco and the Rainforest Foundation and Rainforest Alliance in New York, for example, were employing relatively large professional staffs, and presiding over substantial enough budgets to make grants to Amazon-based NGOs and grassroots groups.

In Germany, by contrast, a more geographically dispersed grassroots movement to save the Amazon and other tropical rainforests flourished initially. There, the environmental and human rights NGO scene was in general less centralized and professionalized, relying more on volunteers and local and regional action groups. Although some of the larger German NGOs took part in early international campaigns, it was a diverse set of smaller grassroots activist groups throughout Western Germany that carried the movement to save the Amazon forward. While a handful of these movement groups managed to persist in the fight to save the Amazon and other tropical rainforests well into the 1990s, these German groups remained smaller and more geographically dispersed. With smaller staffs and budgets, they had significantly fewer resources for independent participation in global-level politics or for financial transfers to groups in the South.

In Germany a few professional NGOs did get involved in early transnational campaigns. On the environmental side, the DNR (Deutsche Naturschutz Ring), a formal network of environmental organizations and BUND (the national Friends of the Earth affiliate in West Germany), played an early role in the MDB campaigns. On the human rights front, the Gesellschaft für Bedrohte Völker (GfbV) helped host indigenous leaders from the Amazon Basin in their efforts to lobby the German government and European Community. But these groups, though they were at that point long-established, formally registered *Verbände* (citizen's associations), relied primarily on volunteers and on local and regional chapters for most of their campaign work. This was certainly the case with their Amazon-oriented campaigns.[23]

The early efforts of these few established NGOs were joined in the course of the 1980s by the mobilization of a large number of smaller protest and solidarity groups, dispersed all over the country, from Munich to Hamburg, and in dozens of big cities and smaller towns in between. It was, in fact, these smaller groups that carried the movement for the Amazon rainforest forward in West Germany—local groups of environmentally concerned university students; small third-world solidarity groups associated with either local churches or the radical leftist parties;[24] and people involved in the citizens' *Bürgerinitiativen* initiatives, coordinating "alternative lists" for local and regional elections.

This mobilization grew out of a thriving social movement milieu in West Germany at the time. The United States had experienced similar waves of protest and movement activism around issues of civil rights, women's rights, and the environment throughout the 1970s. In the United States, however, these movements had, one after the other, fairly quickly institutionalized into a strong, professional NGO scene, based for the most part in Washington, D.C. In West Germany, however, mobilization on many of these issues was to reach its high point a bit later, and under quite different conditions. There, the 1980s represented a period of intense protest and movement activity, as thousands took to the streets in various towns and cities all over Western Germany in the unprecedented mobilization against the siting of nuclear weapons and nuclear power plants on German soil. The 1980s was a period of widespread mobilization on a number of different fronts—around issues of ecology, women's rights, local citizen's rights, peace, and third-world solidarity (Burns and van der Will 1988; Koopmans 1995).[25]

Activists and organizations from the various German movement sectors began to engage in intensive dialogue and coordinated effort during the eighties. Joining ranks to protest what many saw as an essentially undemocratic stranglehold on national politics on the part of big business and organized labor, in collaboration with both of the major political parties, activists in a variety of new social movements attempted to develop fundamentally new forms of politics. Local citizens' initiatives and leaders in the antinuclear movement elaborated new forms of *Basisdemokratie* (base, or grassroots, democracy), and encouraged dialogue among organizations with different popular bases and ideological bents. Groups from these different movement sectors engaged in intensive negotiation through their coordination of alternative candidate lists for local and *Land* (state) elections—a process that coalesced, as well, in the founding and consolidation of the German Green Party. Even large-scale actions and protests during this period, such as the antinuclear mobilizations, were generally coordinated as joint efforts by myriad local and regional movement organizations. In essence, there was a committed attempt within the movement scene in West Germany at the time to "act locally" and to keep organizations small and close to bases of activist support (*basisnah*).[26] German efforts to save the tropical rainforests were very much a part of this organizational milieu.

In the mid-1980s small volunteer protest and solidarity groups formed throughout the country to address the issue. One of the earliest was the all-volunteer, Hamburg-based Rainforest Center. With a total budget of a few hundred deutschmarks, Rainforest Center activists began a consumer campaign against tropical timber in 1986 that would eventually blossom into the most successful tropical timber boycott in the world (Behrend and Paczian 1990, 170). Later, in 1988, the annual World Bank/IMF meetings in Berlin provided an opportunity for the coordinated lobbying and protest efforts of many smaller groups from all over Germany. Highlighting tropical deforestation in the Amazon as a prominent theme, the Berlin protests brought together a wide spectrum of groups. Environmental activists, peace activists, left-wing unionists, small third-world solidarity groups, and human rights organizations joined efforts with elements of the Berlin *Autonomen* (autonomous leftist/anarchist) scene and with members of the Berlin Alternative Lists (Mayer-Ries, 1999: 2; Dissent! G8, 2005). In July of 1989, another Berlin event, the *Amazonientage* (Amazon Days), a five-day public informational event attended by five indigenous members of COICA, was organized by a loose network of activists from the universities, North-South solidarity and church-based development groups, and representatives of the Berlin Alternative Lists (Mayer-Ries 1999). In 1990, dozens of small, local, environmental and solidarity groups from throughout Germany joined efforts in the Regenwaldforum (Rainforest Forum), demanding action on the part of the German government for the protection of the tropical rainforests (Kuhlmann and Wolters 1994, 1). Gathering signatures around the country for a "Rainforest Appeal" that was signed by over 300,000 people and periodically presented by caravans of activists to Chancellor Kohl and the federal government, the campaign would eventually encompass over 124 groups throughout Germany (ibid., 26–29).

A number of small, professional environmental justice organizations evolved out of this activist scene, all advocating for environmental protection in the Amazon through the support of indigenous and traditional peoples and their livelihoods. Rettet-den-Regenwald (founded in Hamburg in 1986); Arbeitsgemeinschaft Regenwald und Artenschutz (ARA, founded in Bielefeld, 1987); pro-REGENWALD (founded in Munich, 1989/90), and urgewald (founded in Sassenberg, 1992) are, for example, four of these groups which are still engaged in advocacy and lobbying work in this area. They have continued their close collaboration over the years. Throughout the 1990s, they have met regularly as part of the Agenda 21 process in Germany, and they have regularly coordinated lobbying efforts and issued joint statements in relation to the German government's development and forestry policies. They have also frequently joined forces for consumer education campaigns, such as the "2000plus Initiative" a recent effort by urgewald, pro-REGENWALD, and ARA to get German school students to switch to recycled notebooks. Many of them are committed not only to lobbying the German and foreign governments on behalf of traditional forest dwellers, but to providing direct support for local populations' political campaigns and alternative development projects. Such efforts have been minimal, however, as these organizations have remained fairly small over the years, with, on average, four or five members of paid staff and fairly modest budgets, (none significantly over 300,000 euro in 2002).

In the United States a new generation of environmental organizations was born in the late eighties and early nineties as well, groups whose efforts combined a focus on politics, consumption, and markets at home in the North with support for forest dwellers in the South. In the United States, however, this development took on a quite different organizational character. There, an institutionalized environmental movement, backed by a well-established foundation scene and a strong tradition of private charitable giving, allowed for the rapid establishment of a number of larger, more professionalized nonprofit organizations. In the spring of 1985, for example, when a number of environmental and indigenous rights activists resolved to launch a broad-based tropical rainforest campaign, the Threshold Foundation hosted a weekend conference in West Virginia. The meeting was attended by activists from a number of professional NGOs, many of which had been active in the MDB campaigns and in support of indigenous organizing in the Amazon Basin (Cowell 1990, 134–35). One of these activists, Randy Hayes of Friends of the Earth, outlined there his plans to launch, together with Mike Roselle (co-founder and former director of Earthfirst!), a new organization, the Rainforest Action Network (RAN). Securing office space in the offices of Earth Island Institute with a budget of $13,000, he started to build his new NGO.

Raising significant funds through foundation sources, fundraising on the West Coast, and the support of celebrities such as the Grateful Dead, Hayes proceeded to develop an organization which was to become a strong presence in the U.S. environmental scene. A major part of RAN's strategy was the coordination and training of a nationwide network of direct action and protest groups, which they called Rainforest Action Groups, or RAGs. The RAGs, based mostly on college campuses, played a crucial role in the success of the group's first major campaign, a boycott of Burger King and its tropical beef hamburgers (Rosmarin 1995, 2). By 1995, RAN had twenty-four paid employees and a budget of over $2 million. It was training activists and coordinating the efforts of over 150 RAG groups throughout the country, and it was providing significant support to rainforest dwellers throughout the world through its Protect-an-Acre small grant program and its Amazon Program (ibid., 12).

Two parallel efforts in New York City resulted in the development of professional nonprofit groups with significant staff and relatively large budgets as well. In 1987, Daniel Katz, a young lawyer concerned about deforestation in the tropics, banded together with a group of like-minded professionals, some of whom he had met at a lecture on the topic, and founded a group called the Rainforest Alliance. Although this organization did not originate within the professional environmental or human rights NGO scene, Katz and his board were nonetheless able, through fundraising among wealthy New Yorkers, established foundations, and corporate donors, to develop quickly into a large, very professionally run organization. By 2002, the organization had twenty-four paid employees and revenues of over $6 million per year; it was making numerous small grants to remote rainforest communities throughout the world; and it was working with a large number of U.S.-based multinationals, providing eco-certification for products such as Chiquita bananas and Domtar Paper products (Rainforest Alliance 2002).

In 1989, another group was founded in New York, the U.S.-based affiliate of the Rainforest Foundation network.[27] This organization, founded by Sting in the wake of his incredibly successful publicity tour and fundraising concerts in the late 1980s, successfully tapped into elite charity networks in New York, as well, holding gala events as well as rock concerts to raise funds. The Rainforest Foundation managed to establish itself by the middle of the 1990s as a professional NGO, acting as a foundation providing funds to Southern (mostly Brazilian) NGOs, forest activists, and indigenous groups, from an annual budget of over $2 million (Rainforest Foundation 2002).

Thus, while both the United States and Germany experienced an upwelling of popular support for groups trying to address the issue of rainforest degradation in the late 1980s, and both countries witnessed the birth of a new generation of rainforest groups during this period, the different institutional roots of the rainforest movement in the two countries were formative in each case, helping to shape the organizational competencies and outlook of groups. I will explore these differences in more depth below, when I discuss further developments in the two countries in the years since 1992.

Conceptualizing National Differences in Transnational Activism

Differences in the institutional landscape of the rainforest movement in the United States and Germany can be seen as a particular expression of more systematic differences in how associational life is structured in Germany and the United States. The United States is a country with a strong liberal tradition, in which sovereign authority has traditionally been seen to reside more in the private institutions of civil society than in the state (Jepperson 2002; Schofer and Fourcade-Gourinchas 2001). There, a strong tradition of private philanthropy (both a culture of private giving and a strong foundation sector) has supported a diverse universe of well-institutionalized civil society organizations (Salamon and Anheier 1998). Germany, in contrast, has developed in accordance with a significantly different model of state-society relations, in which the state itself has been considered the center of sovereign authority, and a more corporate model of civil society organization has evolved (see Jepperson 2002). Although a rich network of nonprofit associations developed in

Germany throughout the nineteenth and twentieth centuries, the majority of these have tended to be service providers (i.e., hospitals, educational institutions, and semi-private insurance associations). The private foundation money that circulates within German society (relatively speaking, about half as much per capita as in the United States; see Anheier and Romo 1998, 86) has tended to be devoted to the support of these kinds of service organizations, rather than to organizations dedicated to politically oriented activity. Scholars categorize the German nonprofit sector as one which has traditionally played more of a "social service" role, rather than a "civil society" role (Anheier and Romo 1998, 87; Anheier and Seibel 2001).

In the United States rainforest activists were able to quickly consolidate new organizations by drawing upon financial resources afforded by the foundation scene, the charity circuit, and corporate donations. In Germany, however, groups had a harder time establishing financial security through such means. After the extraordinary events of the fall of the Berlin Wall and national reunification, and with the absorption of many movement elements into the Green Party throughout the eighties and early nineties (Mayer and Ely 1998), the heyday of the new social movements passed into an era of more established politics. As the mobilizational moment faded, however, those German groups that continued their efforts on behalf of the Amazon as professional NGOs found it challenging to secure sufficient financial resources. These groups continue to receive significant support through small donations from supportive citizens who frequent their websites, subscribe to their newsletters, pay annual membership fees, or send occasional donations. Nevertheless, many of these groups have been dependent on government money to support their activities—through reliance on the labor of state-paid interns, through grants for public educational projects, and in extreme cases through reliance on state unemployment benefits and back-to-work programs, which have allowed activists to continue working full-time despite being unable to cover their own personnel costs from their groups' budgets. In fact, of the German rainforest groups discussed above, only one has been able to secure funding levels sufficient to support a substantial full-time staff and strong lobbying efforts at the national and international levels, and this group has received a significant portion of its funding over the last decade from U.S. foundations, identified with the help of U.S. campaign partners.[28]

Some of the critics I discussed in the first section of this chapter point to just this kind of imbalance when they suggest that U.S. NGOs and U.S. money play a hegemonic role in transnational politics today. Kenneth Anderson and David Rieff insist, for example, that the legitimacy claimed by international NGOs and UN agencies is essentially illusory. What these organizations offer, they claim, is "legitimacy and cover—a sort of branding process, whereby money from various national sources, particularly from the U.S., is 're-branded' with the logo of some NGO or UN agency, or both" (Anderson and Rieff 2005, 38). But how far can such an analysis take us? Are there identifiably American ideologies or institutional logics being exported abroad through U.S. foundations and NGOs? Are particular American interests expressing themselves in hegemonic ways through these transnational channels?

As I will show in the following section of this chapter, in the years since the 1992 Earth Summit in Rio, the NGO scene in the United States has sustained a diverse array of nonprofit advocacy groups. These organizations pursue a diversity of approaches to issues of deforestation and human rights in the tropics—a broader diversity, in fact, than has been supported in the German national context over the last two decades. Thus, it would be difficult to identify a set of coherent American interests at play in the Amazon advocacy of U.S. NGOs.

Some of the theoretical insights offered by recent critics of the discourse of "global civil society" can, nevertheless, provide us with useful analytic tools, allowing us to see that there may, in fact, be distinctly American logics that are being "exported abroad" through the transnational efforts of U.S. NGOs. Chandhoke (2002) and Howell and Pearce (2001) have questioned the common adoption in the literature of a "three sector" model of society, whereby civil society is understood to be a sphere of social action possessing a fundamentally different logic from that of the state or the market. According to these authors this "three sector fallacy," (Chandhoke) or "tripartite model" (Howell and Pearce) has tended to obscure the fact that civil society organizations are, more often than not, dependent on financial resources deriving either from the state or from market actors. It has also led to an under-theorizing of the relationships between civil society organizations and institutions from these other two spheres, that is, along the "civil society/state" and "civil society/market" axes (see Howell and Pearce 2001, 76–80). In fact, it is precisely in terms of their relative dependencies on, and orientations toward, institutions of the national polity and of the market sector that the NGO scenes in the United States and Germany differ in quite interesting ways.

As shown in the brief history above, the rainforest groups which developed in Germany in the late 1980s were born in the final years of an important conjunctural moment in the development of German political culture. During this period, a number of different social movements, including, quite importantly, a number of the movements which had been central to the foundation of the German Green Party, were actively engaged not only in developing new forms of environmental consciousness, but in trying to reform notions of citizenship and modes of citizen participation at various levels of the political system. The German NGOs which grew out of the rainforest movement, as I have discussed above, have remained committed to a vision of an environmentally circumspect citizenry—committed to showing solidarity for struggles abroad by demanding responsible action on the part of their government, but accepting responsibility for the effects of their own consumption at home as well. Thus, throughout their history, the German rainforest NGOs have focused primarily on the role of the German government (be it local government's role as consumer of tropical hardwoods for public projects, or the national government's trade policies and development programs), and on the average German qua citizen. Thus, although they have occasionally engaged in hard-hitting boycotts against large corporations, such as the home improvement (DIY) stores which sell tropical hardwoods to consumers, their focus has been primarily on (1) widespread public education for "green consumption," at home, (2) stronger governmental regulation at home and abroad, and (3) increased bilateral and multilateral aid for anti-deforestation interests abroad (i.e., for beleaguered government enforcement agencies in tropical countries and for the organization of forest-dependent, traditional peoples). Thus, while they have targeted domestic corporations from time to time, their primary competency has remained engaging in public educational efforts, lobbying, and monitoring and advising on government policy in the tropics.

The U.S. groups, on the other hand, have been much more active along the civil society/market axis, both in terms of their fundraising and in terms of the targets of their activism. The U.S. rainforest groups mentioned above, though they have all embraced a commitment to defending traditional peoples in their environments and have participated in joint rainforest campaigns at the global level, nevertheless represent political ideologies that span a great spectrum. Thus, some of the East Coast groups, such as the Rainforest Alliance, are committed to market approaches to solving environmental problems and see themselves as reforming business practices by working from the inside out as advisors to corporations. A number of West Coast groups, such as Rainforest Action Network, on the other hand, have their roots in much more radical environmental politics. They take a more combative stance toward corporate targets, play a significant role in the anti-neoliberal globalization movement, and are much more critical of levels of consumption at home in the United States.

American NGOs from both ends of this political spectrum have been willing to accept funding from the corporate sector; they have also, however, spent the vast majority of their campaign energy targeting not the average American citizen, but rather key corporate actors. While none of the German rainforest groups mentioned above accepts significant funding from corporate sources, the majority of the U.S. groups do accept such funds. And while the most successful German campaigns have targeted various levels of government, or general consumer behavior (i.e., tropical hardwood garden furniture or recycled paper), the U.S. NGOs have consistently engaged the corporate sector in their campaigns. RAN, for example, has consecutively targeted Burger King, Weyerhaeuser, Mitsubishi, Home Depot, Bank of America, and most recently Ford. Their consistent strategy has been to choose a frontrunner in an industry with a bad record on tropical forest issues, to target it for a negative PR campaign, and then, increasingly, to bring it to the table to engage in joint standard-setting for the industry at large.[29] The Rainforest Alliance, on the other hand, has been at the forefront of efforts to develop positive PR for responsible industry leaders, for example through certification schemes for tropical timber products, coffee, bananas, and environmentally friendly tourism. The U.S. groups have also been able, through their more intense engagement with the corporate sector and wealthy individual donors, to leverage funding in order to pursue their own projects abroad, or to directly fund communities and NGOs abroad. Thus, the Rainforest Foundation has been able to send millions of dollars abroad to help finance the land demarcation struggles of Amazon Basin indigenous communities, and both RAN and the Rainforest Alliance have, though their small grants programs, been able to target local alternative development projects in the Amazon Basin as well.

As I discuss in the following section, which traces developments in U.S. and German Amazon activism in the years since the Earth Summit in 1992, these different orientations in the two countries have continued to shape the movement over the past fifteen years.

Amazon Activism in the United States and Germany, 1992–2006

International attention to the problems of ecology and human rights in the Amazon reached a peak in the years leading up to the UNCED "Earth Summit" in Rio in 1992. During this period, NGO and social movement mobilization in Europe and North America helped sustain a wave of media coverage and public concern. In the face of intense global scrutiny, an originally recalcitrant Brazilian government began to reorient its development policies for the Amazônia Legal, and to accept offers of multilateral assistance in order to begin trying to slow the pace of deforestation there (Hurrell 1992). Meanwhile, Northern governments set about trying to develop novel approaches to influence development in the region. By the end of the decade, the World Bank had reassessed its funding policies in the Amazon and the IDB had suspended payments on loans to the region.[30] The G7 nations, led by Germany's Chancellor Kohl, agreed to finance an unprecedented Pilot Program (PPG7) for the management of tropical rainforests in the Brazilian Amazon (Fatheuer 1994; Kolk 1996). Development assistance agencies from a number of countries, including the United States, Germany, and Britain, began to develop new, environmentally oriented programs in the region as well.

Despite this flurry of unprecedented international effort, however, the pace of deforestation has not slowed in the ensuing decade. Deforestation rates in 2004 in the Brazilian Amazon were the second highest annual rates ever recorded (Barreto et al. 2005). As destruction in the Amazon Basin has continued apace, so too have the efforts of activists and NGOs in the United States and Germany. However, in the years since 1992, they have had to contend with a very different public climate, in which it is relatively difficult to attract the attention of domestic politicians or the news media for such an "old" story, and hard to compete with newer environmental and political causes for the attention of supporters.

What kinds of institutional momentum has the movement to save the Amazon been able to maintain in the United States and in Germany under these conditions? In the discussion that follows, I examine some of the key differences that have developed in the institutional scene in the two countries since 1992 by means of three structured comparisons. First, I describe the development of two fascinating experiments in North-South network building, one in the United States and one in Germany, both inspired by a call for solidarity from COICA. Second, I discuss the relative capacity of the movement in the two countries to generate new organizations, both at home and abroad, in recent years. And third, I discuss the overall center of balance that has been achieved among different types of organizations within the movement in the two different countries. Although, due to space considerations, I am only able develop these three comparisons schematically here, I nevertheless hope to highlight through these comparisons the quite different orientations that have characterized the movement in the two countries in the years since Rio.

A Tale of Two Networks: The Climate Alliance and the Amazon Alliance

In 1989, COICA began reaching out to environmentalists in Europe and North America, looking for strategic alliances for their communities' struggles to secure title to their traditional lands and protect their local environments from the incursions of colonists, miners, loggers, and international oil interests.

The indigenous leaders were concerned that their communities were being left out of high-level negotiations among their national governments, extractive multinational industries, and international environmental organizations, in which their traditional lands were being negotiated as potential protected areas in some of the first "debt-for-nature" swaps.[31] In an open letter addressed to the "Community of Concerned Environmentalists," COICA warned: "We are concerned that you have left us, the Indigenous Peoples, out of your vision of the Amazonian Biosphere. The focus of concern of the environmental community has typically been the preservation of the tropical forest and its plant and animal inhabitants. You have shown little interest in its human inhabitants who are also part of that biosphere" (COICA 1989).

In the years following this initial plea, a series of meetings in Berlin, Frankfurt, Boston, New York, Washington, and Iquitos (Peru) between the leaders of COICA and Northern environmental and human rights organizations resulted in the founding of two innovative North-South networks, the Climate Alliance, based in Frankfurt, in 1992–93, and the Amazon Alliance, based in Washington, D.C., in 1994. While the history of each of these two networks is fascinating in its own right, it is the comparative history of the two organizations that is particularly interesting for our analysis here. Whereas each network was originally incorporated as a formal alliance to support COICA and its member organizations, the two networks are very different in terms of their basic structure, their political orientations, and their competencies.

The idea of a Climate Alliance *(Klimabündnis)* was first conceived at the *Amazonientage* (Amazon Days) meeting in Berlin in 1989. Representatives from Green Party lists had entered the governing coalitions in a number of key German municipalities, and were eager to develop new policies to concretely express their concerns for Northern environmental responsibility and their desires for new forms of solidarity with peoples in the South. In discussions in Berlin and Frankfurt, the idea of a formal alliance was born, in which European municipalities would pledge to reduce their own production of greenhouse gases, while simultaneously supporting the efforts of indigenous peoples in the Amazon Basin to secure and protect their native lands. Public education, political advocacy, and direct financial support for native Amazonian organizations would be financed through new municipal-level "foreign policy" budgets. By 2002, 1,119 municipalities across Europe,[32] representing over 47 million residents, had committed themselves to the Climate Alliance, and its coordinating office in Frankfurt am Main presided over an annual operating budget of more than 990,000 euro (Klimabündnis 2002). The Climate Alliance has provided European municipalities with an opportunity for the regular exchange of information about their public educational efforts and their municipal-level greenhouse gas-reduction policies (particularly in the realms of transportation and energy policy)—through newsletters, annual Climate Alliance meetings, and awards such as the Climate Star awards, given to municipalities each year for innovative approaches to climate policy. At the same time, the network has provided for the direct support of COICA and its programs in the Amazon Basin by channeling funds from the municipalities directly to COICA and its member organizations and by facilitating direct partnerships between particular municipalities and individual indigenous communities.

During the same period that COICA was working with activists in Berlin, Kassel, and Frankfurt to establish the Climate Alliance in Europe, a similar effort was underway in the United States to establish a formal network between COICA and North American environmental organizations. That effort culminated in the formal founding of the Amazon Alliance (originally named the Amazon Coalition) in Washington, D.C., in 1994. Forged in the course of a series of meetings and press conferences in the United States and Peru in 1989 and 1990, the Alliance brought together a large number of U.S. NGOs from many different areas: (1) larger U.S. conservation organizations (Conservation International, WWF-U.S., the National Wildlife Federation), (2) environmental advocacy groups (such as NRDC, Environmental Defense, and the Sierra Club), (3) human rights, development, and indigenous rights organizations (such as OxFAM America, Cultural Survival, and a number of smaller North American Indian organizations), and (4) the new generation of rainforest advocacy groups profiled above (RAN, the Rainforest Foundation, and the Rainforest Alliance, among others). It has been financed over the years through grants from major foundations, such as the Ford Foundation and the Goldman Fund, as well as through annual contributions from member NGOs.

The Amazon Alliance has, since its founding, served as an advocate and facilitator for COICA in Washington and in international negotiations and conferences. It has also, however, facilitated the creation of unique new forms of transnational political space, bringing NGOs from North and South America into contact with one another and with a large cross-section of the hundreds of indigenous member organizations of COICA. It has regularly organized annual meetings in South and North America and has held myriad seminars and exchanges organized in various Amazon Basin countries each year by its regional working groups (Pieck and Moog, 2006). By 2002, it had an annual operating budget of over $550,000, and included over ninety-five indigenous people's organizations and Northern and Southern NGOs in its formal membership. However, as I will discuss in more depth below, it has not been very successful at sustaining the active membership of the larger U.S.

environmental NGOs, and has, in fact, become more of a dedicated indigenous rights organization in recent years.[33]

Thus, in the development of these two networks throughout the 1990s, we again see some of the systematic national differences identified above. The Climate Alliance, true to the political orientations of the German Green movement, has oriented itself primarily across the civil society/state axis, securing funding for its work with COICA and other indigenous organizations of the Amazon Basin by tapping into municipal government funding and carrying out public educational campaigns through local government efforts. It has also focused a major part of its advocacy efforts on the public education of European citizens as ecologically conscious citizens and consumers. The Amazon Alliance, on the other hand, has been able to rely on the financial resources of its member organizations and on the strength of the American foundation sector, in order to finance its activities. It has used these resources not only to directly support COICA and its member organizations, but to actively organize civil society events (seminars, workshops, and community exchanges) throughout the Amazon Basin countries over the last decade.

Capacity-Building in the Amazon: Supporting Local Organizations versus Founding New Organizations Abroad

Since the peak of global Amazon mobilization 1992, German Amazon advocacy groups have continued to support a wide array of partner organizations in Latin America. This support has taken the form of political advocacy at home. It has also involved sporadic financial support for civil society groups abroad. In their efforts, Germans have tended to support already established civil society organizations in Amazon Basin countries: local rural unions and landless organizations; Amazonian indigenous organizations; church-based groups (such as CIMI, a missionary order within the Brazilian Catholic Church, dedicated to indigenous advocacy); local grassroots environmental efforts (such as the Campaña para la Vida en Amazonia in the Ecuadorian Oriente), and indigenous support groups (such as the Commissão Pro-Yanomami in Brazil). Generally they have not, however, engaged in efforts to found new organizations abroad.[34] Because the years since Rio have been a period of relative retrenchment for German Amazon advocacy, direct financial support for Amazon Basin groups has not been increasing in recent years, and has never represented an especially significant force in shaping the development of Amazon Basin civil society. The German groups, have, however, actively engaged in encouraging the German government to fund local civil society organizations and to include them in bilateral and multilateral development efforts.

In their lobbying and monitoring efforts, the German groups have maintained a strong focus on the importance of including the active participation of local Amazon Basin civil society groups in all regional development efforts. Throughout the 1990s, for example, a large group of German NGOs met regularly as part of an effort to follow and monitor the PPG7 (Pilot Project for the Brazilian Amazon), the multilateral development/conservation effort proposed by Chancellor Kohl to the G7 in 1990, and financed and administered in the following years primarily by the German government and its development agency, the GTZ. The German groups insisted throughout on the importance of including Brazilian civil society groups not only in impact assessment evaluation of the projects, but in the conception and design of PPG7 projects, and in their concrete implementation. As part of this approach, Amazon Basin groups were brought together into a coordinating umbrella group, the GTA (Grupo de Trabalho Amazônico), which facilitated the efforts of local indigenous groups and other grassroots community groups, environmental NGOs, and rural unions, helping them to take part in the PPG7 projects, coordinate their political advocacy, and seek funding for their own projects (see Fatheuer 1994).

The U.S. Amazon activist scene, on the other hand, has been more expansionist in the years since Rio. During this period, which one might have expected to represent a "post-mobilizational" time of retrenchment for Amazon groups worldwide, a number of successful new NGOs have managed to establish themselves at home in the United States. There, the 1990s witnessed the birth of a number of new Amazon advocacy organizations: the Amazon Conservation Team (Washington, 1995), Pachamama Alliance (San Francisco, 1995), Amazon Watch (Los Angeles, 1996), and Earthrights International (Washington, 1996), to name a few. Perhaps even more interesting, in terms of our orienting questions about institutional logics and their exportation, the U.S. NGO scene not only succeeded in expanding its institutional reach within the United States throughout the 1990s, but has also been quite actively engaged in helping to found new "partner" and "daughter" organizations abroad throughout this period.

Many U.S. NGOs, like their German counterparts, collaborate with strong Amazon Basin NGOs such as CIMI, ISA (the Brazilian Social-Environmental Institute), CIR (the Indigenous Council of Roraima state, Brazil), Acción Ecológica (an Ecuadorian environmental organization), or CEADES (Colectivo de Estudios Aplicados al Desarollo Social, in Bolivia). Today, however, the U.S. groups also find themselves working intensively with Latin American activists employed within a number of organizations which are essentially "spin-offs" of U.S. organizations—groups such as WWF-Brazil[35] and the

Nature Conservancy's Amazon Program, both based in Brazil; or CDES (the Centro para Desarollo Económico y Social) and Fundación Pachamama, both Ecuadorian-based partner organizations of U.S. NGOs.[36] These new daughter and partner organizations are staffed primarily by Latin American activists. They have significant autonomy from their North American counterparts, and have developed uniquely Southern perspectives in their work. They collaborate on a regular basis with U.S. organizations, however, and remain dependent on funding from Northern sources—from the World Bank or Global Environment Facility, from U.S. foundations, from USAID, or from their American mother/partner NGOs. U.S. NGOs have also influenced the development of new organizations in the Amazon region by influencing the agenda of USAID and large foundations such as the Ford and Moore foundations, which have become some of the most important sources of financing for new NGOs and grassroots organizations in the Amazon.

Centripetal and Centrifugal Forces: Finding a Center of Balance in the Movement

If U.S. organizations have been more prone to engage directly, not only in funding, but in *founding* projects and organizations in Amazon Basin countries, does this mean that the U.S. foundation and NGO scene has been actively exporting its own institutional logics abroad? Clearly, this could be the case only if the U.S. institutions share in common a set of organizing principles or political perspectives. In the discussion so far, we have identified some interesting commonalities across the political spectrum in the United States—the U.S. groups' willingness to engage the corporate sector, for example, and their tendency to directly engage in projects and institution-building abroad. In fact, I would argue that civil society organizations in the United States seem to operate according to an inherently pluralist or entrepreneurial model of citizen action. Groups actively identify social problems, find pragmatic courses of action which might address the problems identified, and implement those actions as they see fit—at home or abroad, and across the civil society/state axis or the civil society/market axis. In pursuing their plans, U.S. groups implicitly assume that they may meet with resistance from opposed civil organizations, either at home or abroad. In such entrepreneurial efforts, they requisition whatever resources they can find; the majority of them do not rule out donations from, or strategic alliances with, the corporate sector.

This model contrasts significantly with the German case, where groups within the rainforest movement has been more committed to trying to speak with one voice, waging joint consumer and public education campaigns, and unanimously signing joint letters to government officials. They have also been much more circumspect about intervening in the development of civil society in the Amazon region, insisting on supporting pre-existing Amazon region groups. They emphasize the importance of letting native civil organizations manage their own relations and forge common visions, through, for example, the coordination allowed by umbrella organizations such as the GTA. This approach, I would argue, stems from a fundamentally different vision of the role of civil society organizations, according to which such groups are seen primarily as *citizens'* groups, whose main role should be to influence the broad scope of political culture and government action. Thus, groups in Germany have maintained closer contact and coordination throughout the history of rainforest campaigning, and have managed over the years to solidify a fairly coherent ideological center of balance in their work—one committed to encouraging ecologically responsible consumption at home and to supporting indigenous and traditional peoples in their struggles abroad.

In the United States, on the other hand, a much larger and wealthier NGO scene, operating with more implicitly pluralistic assumptions about the role of nonprofit organizations at home and abroad, has not managed to forge as coherent an ideological center of balance in its efforts to address deforestation and human rights problems in the Amazon. In the United States, where various facets of the Amazon campaign were so quickly absorbed into a diversity of professionalized NGO sectors, much of the movement has actually come to be split in recent years between those pursuing a more conservation-oriented agenda and those pursuing a more exclusively indigenous rights angle. By the end of the 1990s, for example, most of the large environmental groups which had helped found the Amazon Alliance had fallen out of active participation in the network. This left the Alliance to pursue a more exclusively indigenous rights agenda over the years (Pieck 2006), and left indigenous leaders feeling that they had once again lost their capacity to influence the large American conservation organizations targeting their lands for new large-scale landscape level conservation schemes (Khare and Bray 2004; Pieck and Moog, 2008). The lack of communication and integration within the movement has resulted, in fact, in a significant amount of polarization within the U.S. NGO scene.

A recent exposé on the big American conservation groups' turn away from attempts to collaborate with native and traditional peoples, which was published in *World Watch* magazine in 2004 and which inspired an unprecedented sixteen pages of responses from both sides of the movement, is a testament to the depth of this divide in the U.S. context (see Chapin 2004, and responses in *World Watch Magazine* 2005). The U.S. environmental community had attempted in the late 1980s and early 1990s to integrate advocacy for indigenous land rights and alternative development with the international conservation agenda. Inspired by the idea of sustainable development, by calls such as COICA's from indigenous communities, and by increasing interest on the part of major donors such as USAID and the World Bank, environmental groups of a variety of different orientations had all attempted during this period to forge a new, more "people-oriented," approach to their efforts, especially in developing countries. However, according to Chapin, a long-time advocate of indigenous rights at the Center for Native Lands in Washington, D.C., by the late 1990s such approaches were already being abandoned by the large U.S.-based conservation organizations (WWF-U.S., Conservation International, and the Nature Conservancy, for example).

While this shift in priorities was inspired, in part, by the failure of a number of concrete efforts to develop integrated conservation and development programs (ICDPs) in the field, the turn away from working with indigenous and traditional peoples' communities has also been related to influence exerted by the financial dependencies of these powerful conservation organizations. Increasingly dependent on corporate sponsors and multilateral financing for their program costs, the large U.S. conservation organizations have been reluctant to involve themselves, for example, in political disputes concerning native land rights and extractive industries.[37] This has meant in practice that while local traditional populations are often supported in their struggles against extractive industries by the more politically aggressive wing of the U.S. rainforest movement (groups such as RAN, Amazon Watch, and the Rainforest Foundation–U.S., for example), as well as by American human rights and indigenous rights NGOs, this wing of the movement increasingly feels itself at odds with a conservation movement which has frequently shown a willingness to facilitate these same extractive industries. As Chapin points out: "Isn't it a bit odd that in 2003 Oxfam America supported an indigenous organization in the Amazon Basin against the depredations of Chevron Texaco, while the large conservationist NGOs were providing the same company with a green fig leaf in exchange for financial aid?" (Chapin 2004).

Thus, while the German rainforest movement has managed to maintain a more unified center of balance in its work, in the United States we find not only a much greater diversity of visions and approaches within the NGO sector, but significant tension and conflict as well, a situation which is not unrelated to its more complicated set of relations across the civil society/market axis.

Conclusions: U.S. Civil Society—Exporting Pluralism Abroad, or Exporting Conflict Abroad?

In 2003, reporter Tom Knudson ran an award-winning series in the *Sacramento Bee,* entitled "State of Denial," in which he documented the contradictions of California's strict environmental regulations and unremittingly high consumption patterns.[38] In the series, he highlighted the Ecuadorian Oriente, the site of intense struggles around issues of land rights and oil extraction, where oil exploitation has had toxic effects on the health and social integrity of indigenous and traditional communities. As Knudson notes, Californians are the ultimate source of much of the conflict, through their refusal to allow offshore drilling along their own coasts, combined with their unbridled consumption of Ecuadorian oil (Knudson 2003). The contradictions go even deeper, however, as California is also the source of some of the most successful transnational efforts to defend local communities in the Ecuadorian Oriente. Rainforest Action Network, the Earthjustice Legal Defense Fund (formerly the Sierra Club Legal Defense Fund), Amazon Watch, and the Pachamama Alliance have been some of the most important transnational allies strengthening civil society in local communities there, and helping to battle international oil concerns in both the U.S. and international courts of justice.

In the years since the 1992 Rio conference, the American foundation and NGO scene has been very successful at maintaining momentum in the transnational effort to protect the Amazon. Raising significant funding for alternative development projects and NGO capacity-building in Amazon Basin countries, U.S. activists have played an important role in shaping the battle against deforestation and cultural decimation there. But in its transnational efforts, U.S. civil society projects both its strengths and weaknesses abroad. It is not just American resource struggles and the conflict that they entail that are being exported abroad, after all. As I have argued here, specificities of American institutional logics have played an important role in recent decades in shaping civil society in the Amazon Basin as well.

The fate of the American environmental and human rights movement at home is likely to have a significant impact on ecological struggles in the Amazon region in the decades to come. While the last few decades have seen Greenpeace, with its relatively aggressive green politics, rise to prominence as the most powerful environmental organization in Germany[39] (and, recently, a frontline participant in transnational Amazonian politics as well), the situation in the United States is quite different. There, the environmental organizations that have been the most critical about the role of U.S. consumption, trade, and extractive industries abroad, groups such as Greenpeace and Friends of the

Earth (and to some extent the Sierra Club as well) have been losing members and facing reductions in their operating budgets (see Bosso and Gruber 2003). Meanwhile, the large conservation groups, which as Chapin points out, have often proven hesitant to address issues of American consumption and extractive industries in the tropics, have become by far the most powerful environmental organizations in the United States. How the current debates among different sectors of the U.S. NGO scene play out in the coming years is likely to have a significant impact on the power of transnational civil society to influence the fate of the Amazon forest.

Notes

1. Studies have addressed, for example: (1) the activities of international NGOs such as Greenpeace, Amnesty International, and the IUCN, which are truly multinational organizations, with base chapters in multiple countries (see Wapner 1996; Boli and Thomas 1999); (2) transnational campaigns launched by activist alliances from a wide array of different countries, (Smith, Chatfield, and Pagnucco 1997; Keck and Sikkink 1998); or, (3) participation of NGOs from a wide array of countries in processes of global governance (see Arts 1998; Walk and Brunnengräber 2000).

2. On the concept of "advocacy groups" and "transnational advocacy networks" see Keck and Sikkink 1998.

3. The concepts of the "civil society/state" and "civil society/market" axes, as elaborated in the work of Jude Howell and Jenny Pearce (Howell and Pearce 2001) are developed in further detail later in this chapter.

4. Following common usage in most of the literature now, I use the term "international" to refer to those arenas in which a number of different nation states interact, and dominate proceedings (i.e., the UN, WTO, and other bilateral and multilateral negotiations and institutions), whereas "transnational" refers to the cross-border engagement of *non-state* social actors, i.e., individuals, and organizations such as corporations, nongovernmental organizations, or social movements with entities based in different nation states.

5. On NGO participation in international negotiations and regime-building see Walk and Brunnengräber 2000; Khagram, Riker, and Sikkink 2002.

6. On the role of NGOs in bilateral and multilateral development projects see Hulme and Edwards 1997; Hudock 1999; Howell and Pearce 2001; and Anheier, Glasius, and Kaldor 2003.

7. On agenda-setting through transnational campaigning and lobbying efforts see Risse-Kappen 1995; Keck and Sikkink 1998; and Smith, Chatfield, and Pagnucco 1997. On agenda-setting in independently organized transnational movement events see Wood 2005 on the People's Global Action network, and Correa Leite 2005 on the World Social Forum process.

8. Since the early 1980s sociological "institutionalists" such as John Meyer and his colleagues have been asserting that the "world polity" has constituted a homogenizing

force for a world culture, diffusing universalistic, "standard scripts" or "rationalizing" discourses within national societies (Meyer et al. 1997; Boli and Thomas 1997). By the end of the 1990s, theorists within this tradition had identified the work of international NGOs (INGOs) as one of the most important mechanisms for the diffusion of this world culture, promoting ideals of universalism, individualism, scientific and economic "progress," rational voluntaristic authority, and "world citizenship" (Boli and Thomas 1999, 14). However, despite the fact that a number of theorists associated with the institutionalist school have developed nuanced explorations of differences in political culture and institutions within *national-level* polities (see Jepperson 2002; Soysal 1994), world polity scholars have only very recently begun to explore divergences in the political outlook and institutional constitution of different transnational NGOs (see for example Lechner and Boli's discussion of global "countercultural" movements, Lechner and Boli, 2005). Surprisingly, however, scholars within this tradition have not yet begun to explore differences arising from these organizations' national origins.

9. Some scholars central to this new literature have even insisted that in order to grasp conceptually the emergent phenomena which they group under such labels, we must first challenge some of the very foundations of mainstream social scientific thinking, such as its "methodological nationalism" (Anheier, Glasius, and Kaldor 2001; Beck 2002). Ulrich Beck, for example, insists that, in the face of new global realities, a sociology oriented toward nation states as bounded social realities is essentially a backward-looking sociology, one based on "zombie categories" (Beck 2002, 24)

10. While Chandhoke asserts that "the values of global civil society reflect those held by a narrow group of influential states in the international order (2002, 51), both Anderson and Rieff (2005) and Howell and Pearce (2001) explicitly discuss U.S. hegemony.

11. Increasing attention has been dedicated in recent years to problems arising from power asymmetries between NGOs from the "global North" and "global South" (see Pearce 1997; Hudock 1999; Wood 2005). Current research has paid significantly less attention, however, to the differences between, and relationships among, transnational NGOs of different Northern origins. See, however, some of the contributions to Joe Bandy and Jackie Smith's *Coalitions across Borders: Transnational Protest and the Neoliberal Order* for some of the first studies of this nature, including excellent chapters by Daniel Faber on transnational environmental justice movements and John W. Foster on the Trinational Alliance against NAFTA (Bandy and Smith, 2005).

12. When discussing the German case in this chapter, I refer primarily to the Federal Republic of Germany, as the German rainforest movement was, before the fall of the Berlin Wall and German reunification, predominantly a West German phenomenon. There was, however, some participation from activists within the GDR in the West German Rainforest campaign, even in the years before the fall of the Wall in 1999 (see Kuhlmann and Wolters 1994, on the participation of East German activists in the Regenwaldkampagne).

13. Concern about the Amazon was one of what Lester and Costain call the "third generation" of environmental problems: new issues like global warming, acid rain, and the loss of the ozone layer, which became key concerns in the 1980s and suggested

the need for a more international approach to regulation and a more transnational approach to activism (Lester and Costain 1995).

14. Some of the very strong claims first made in the 1980s about the central role of Amazon deforestation in processes of global warming have become the subject of scientific and political controversy in the ensuing years. However, though the exact level of contributions to global warming made by the Amazonian deforestation is still debated, they are generally held to be quite significant (see Rohter 2003 for an update on the state of this debate). Recent evidence indicates that the forests of the Amazon Basin have played a very significant role in maintaining stability of rainfall and air and ocean currents responsible for the maintenance of climactic patterns in places as far away as Africa and Europe (Branford 2005).

15. The Brazilian military government's colonization and development schemes were particularly aggressive. Beginning in the mid-1960s, they attempted to open a number of "development poles" in the heart of the Amazon for the establishment of extractive industry and for the resettlement of poor, landless farmers from the Northeast and South of Brazil. These poorly designed development plans led to intensified land speculation, violence, poverty, and high rates of deforestation in the Brazilian Amazon (Cowell 1990; Hecht and Cockburn 1989).

16. Reunions of the of the UN Working Group on Indigenous Populations, which began meeting in 1984, and the meetings leading up to the adoption of ILO Convention 169 in 1989, provided especially important opportunities in this regard (see Niezen 2003).

17. The campaign to increase the number of staff in the environmental departments of the multilateral banks, to ensure their influence on the early stages of project design and approval, and to improve the banks' transparency has been a protracted struggle, but much ground was gained throughout the 1990s. For a detailed history of this process see Rich 1994, chapters 5–7.

18. The 1986 meeting was hosted by the Penang Conservation Organization and Sahabat Alam Malaysia, the Malaysian Friends of the Earth affiliate. In 1985, Friends of the Earth International had turned its attention to the threat of tropical deforestation in its first truly global campaign, one which included the participation of many of the network's new southern partner organizations.

19. New lobbying strategies and new forms of markets campaigning were developed, for example.

20. Some of these humanitarian and development organizations were church-affiliated groups, such as Misereor and Brot für die Welt in Germany. Others were nonsectarian NGOs—Oxfam for example (a group which was particularly strong in Britain and the United States).

21. For a more detailed discussion of new forms of "indigenist-environmentalist" transnational politics see Brysk, 2000. For an excellent ethnography of Amazon activism and the different orientations of activists within the movement, see Andrea Zhouri's 1999 ethnography of the "trees," "people," and "trees and people" orientations within the British rainforest movement.

22. In the United States, a revalorization of Native American history and culture, inspired in part by new standards of cultural sensitivity achieved through the civil rights movement, had inspired a growing fascination with indigenous culture within the American middle classes. And deforestation had become, by the mid-1980s, a sensitive political issue in the United States as well, where struggles to protect old-growth forests, especially in the Pacific Northwest, had inspired a whole new generation of environmental activism. Forest issues had played a very important role in the German environmental movement as well, where the effects of acid rain on Northern European forests (*Waldsterben,* or "forest-death") was perhaps second to only the nuclear issue in terms of its centrality in awakening public environmental concern for ecology throughout the 1980s (see Lehmann 2004). A longstanding fascination in Germany with Native American culture, including the cult of Winnetou (the fictional Indian character invented by beloved childhood author Karl May), may have helped inspire particularly intense German interest in the plight of Indians in the Amazon as well.

23. Personal communication with activists from Bund and GfbV. GfbV, although it had been formally incorporated since 1973, was in fact during the 1980s a mostly volunteer organization, in which many students, in particular, were active. In the case of the larger environmental organizations, many of them, for example Bund and many of the groups within the DNR, were intentionally organized as associations of myriad local environmental groups. Though Bund, for example, had a national headquarters with professional paid staff, and conducted some centralized lobbying at the federal level, it relied on local volunteer activism for a great deal of its activity.

24. Though many of the most active solidarity groups were based in local church congregations, the development organizations of the two officially recognized German churches, Misereor (affiliated with the Catholic Church) and Brot für die Welt (affiliated with the Lutheran, or *evangelisch,* church) played important roles in funding and coordinating early rainforest mobilization as well.

25. For an excellent table depicting the peak of years of this mobilization, measured in terms of the relative number of protest events garnering attention in major German newspapers, see Koopmans 1995, 107.

26. On the German movement milieu see Rauprich 1985; Roth and Rucht 1987; Burns and van der Will 1988.

27. The Rainforest Foundation was originally a broad transnational network comprised of a multitude of Rainforest Foundation organizations around the world, in many of the countries where Sting had held his fundraising concerts in the late 1980s on behalf of the Kayapó and other threatened Amazonian indigenous groups. Though many of the Rainforest Foundations were short-lived, there are still strong organizations remaining in Norway, the United Kingdom, and the United States.

28. Information on these groups' sources of income was gathered through personal interviews with activists and review of groups' internal, sometimes confidential, documents. For this reason, I have not identified group names with their sources of funding here.

29. The "Equator Principles" for private lenders that RAN recently developed in conjunction with Bank of America is an example of this strategy.

30. The IDB, for example, suspended loan payments for construction of the Amazonian highway BR-164 (Bramble and Porter 1992; Rich 1994).

31. Conservation International had, for example, negotiated relief of $650,000 of Bolivia's debt in 1987, in exchange for creating a national park on the land of the Chimani Indians, who were not consulted in the negotiations (Day 1990). A similar incident was to occur in Ecuador in 1990, when the National Resources Defense Council, in negotiations with the Ecuadorian government, helped facilitate an oil-drilling concession for Conoco on the reserve of the Huaorani Indians, a concession which had been vigorously opposed by local citizens' groups and environmental NGOs (Dowie 1996).

32. By 2002, Climate Alliance municipalities hailed from: Germany, Italy, Austria, Spain, Luxemburg, the Netherlands, Greece, and Chechnya, among others (Klimabündnis 2002).

33. See Pieck 2006; Korten 2005.

34. One important exception to this generalization is the recent establishment of a new Greenpeace Amazon office in Manaus, Brazil, in 1994. The Greenpeace Amazon Program was established and financed by Greenpeace International, in which German funding and leadership are dominant today.

35. Although WWF is formally an multinational NGO with headquarters in Switzerland, WWF-Brazil grew out of a Brazil Program originally directed primarily from WWF's U.S. headquarters, where its Latin American Program is based.

36. Their American founding organizations are, respectively, the New York–based Center for Economic and Social Rights, and San Francisco–based Pachamama Alliance.

37. Among corporations channeling money to the big three U.S.-based conservation organizations, according to Chapin, are many of the multinational corporations which represent some of the biggest threats to tropical forest ecosystems, including multinational oil, pharmaceutical, and logging concerns such as Chevron Texaco, ExxonMobil, Shell International, Weyerhaeuser, Monsanto, Dow Chemical, and Duke Energy (Chapin 2004).

38. Knudson was awarded a Global 2004 Reuters-IUCN Award for Excellence in Environmental reporting for the series at the Bangkok IUCN congress in November 2004.

39. On the relative strength of various environmental groups in Germany see Öko-Test 2002.

References

Anderson, Kenneth, and David Rieff. 2005. "'Global Civil Society': A Sceptical View." In *Global Civil Society 2004/5*, ed. Helmut K. Anheier, Mary H. Kaldor, and Marlies Glasius, 26–39. Oxford: Oxford University Press.

Anheier, Helmut, Marlies Glasius, and Mary Kaldor, eds. 2001–2005. *Global Civil Society Yearbook, 2001–2004/5*. Oxford: Oxford University Press.

Anheier, Helmut K., and Frank Romo. 1998. "Foundations in Germany and the United

States: A Comparative Analysis." In *Private Funds, Public Purposes: Philanthropic Foundations in International Perspective,* ed. Helmut K. Anheier and Stefan Toepler, 79–118. New York: Kluwer Academic/Plenum Publishers.

Anheier, Helmut K., and Wolfgang Seibel. 2001. *The Non-Profit Sector in Germany: Between State, Economy and Society.* Manchester, UK: Manchester University Press.

Anheier, Helmut K., and Stefan Toepler, eds. 1999. *Private Funds, Public Purpose: Philanthropic Foundations in International Perspective.* New York: Kluwer Academic/Plenum Publishers.

Arts, Bas. 1998. *The Political Influence of Global NGOs: Case Studies on the Climate and Biodiversity Conventions.* Utrecht: International Books.

Bandy, Joe, and Jackie Smith. 2005. *Coalitions across Borders: Transnational Protest and the Neoliberal Order.* Lanham, Md.: Rowman and Littlefield.

Barreto, Paulo, et al. 2005. "Human Pressure in the Amazon." *IMAZON: State of the Amazon,* no. 3 (May).

Beck, Ulrich. 2002. "The Cosmopolitan Society and Its Enemies." *Theory, Culture and Society* 19, no. 1–2: 17–44.

Behrend, Reinhard, and Werner Paczian. 1990. *Raubmord am Regenwald: Vom Kampf gegen das Sterben der Erde.* Reinbeck bei Hamburg: Rowohlt Taschenbuch Verlag.

Boli, John, and George M. Thomas. 1997. "World Culture in the World Polity: A Century of International Non-governmental Organization." *American Sociological Review* 62: 171–90.

———. 1999. *Constructing World Culture.* Stanford, Calif.: Stanford University Press.

Bosso, Christopher J., and Deborah Lynn Gruber. 2003. "The Boundaries and contours of American Environmental Activism." In *Environmental Policy: New Directions for the Twenty-First Century, Edition,* ed. Norman J. Vig and Michael E. Kraft, 79–101. Washington, D.C.: CQ Press.

Bramble, Barbara, and Gareth Porter. 1992. "Non-governmental Organizations and the Making of U.S. International Environmental Policy." In *The International Politics of the Environment: Actors, Interests, Institutions,* ed. Andrew Hurrell and Benedict Kingsbury, 313–53. Oxford: Clarendon Press.

Branford, Sue. 2005. "Running on Empty." *Guardian,* November 2.

Brundtland, Gro Harlem, et al. 1987. *Our Common Future.* Oxford: Oxford University Press.

Brysk, Alison. 2000. *From Tribal Village to Global Village: Indian Rights and International Relations in Latin America.* Stanford, Calif.: Stanford University Press.

Burns, Rob, and Wilfried van der Will. 1988. *Protest and Democracy in West Germany: Extra-Parliamentary Opposition and the Democratic Agenda.* London: Macmillan Press.

Castels, Manuel. 1997. *The Power of Identity.* Oxford: Blackwell.

Chandhoke, Neera. 2002. "The Limits of Global Civil Society." In *Global Civil Society Yearbook, 2002,* ed. Marlies Glasius, Mary Kaldor, and Helmut Anheier, 35–53. Oxford: Oxford University Press.

Chapin, Mac. 2004. "A Challenge to Conservationists." *World Watch Magazine,* November/December, 17–31.

COICA, 1989. "To the Community of Concerned Environmentalists." Reprinted in Alberto Chirif, Pedro García Hierro, and Richard Chase Smith. 1991. *El indígena y su territorio son uno solo:estratégias para la defensa de los pueblos y territorios indígenas en la Cuenca Amazónica.* Lima, Perú: Oxfam America and Coordinadora de las Organizacones Indígenas de la Cuenca Amazónica, COICA.

Correa Leite, Jose. 2005. *The World Social Forum: Strategies of Resistance.* Chicago: Haymarket Books.

Cowell, Adrian. 1990. *The Decade of Destruction: The Crusade to Save the Amazon Rainforest,* New York: Henry Hold.

Day, Mark R. 1990. "Indians, Environmentalists Meet." *Christian Science Monitor,* May 21, 6.

Dissent! Network of Resistance against the G-8. "We Will Disrupt this Conference! Resistance to the 1988 IMF and World Bank Conference in West Berlin." In *Days of Dissent: Reflections on Summit Mobilizations.* Nottingham, UK: Days of Dissent Magazine. (Captured on December 24, 2005 from www.daysofdissent.org.uk. Text translated and edited from: A.G. Grauwacke, *Autonome in Bewegung: aus der ersten 23 Jahren,* available at http://autonx.nadir.org).

Dowie, Mark. 1996. *Losing Ground: The Crisis of American Environmentalism.* Cambridge, Mass.: MIT Press.

Fatheuer, Thomas W. 1994. *Novos Caminhos para a Amazonia? O Programa Piloto do G-7: Amazonia no Context Internacional.* Rio de Janeiro: FASE/SACTES.

Hecht, Susanna, and Alexander Cockburn. 1989. *The Fate of the Forest: Developers, Destroyers, and Defenders of the Amazon.* London: Verso.

Howell, Jude, and Jenny Pearce. 2001. *Civil Society and Development: A Critical Exploration.* Boulder, Colo.: Lynne Rienner.

Hudock, Ann C. 1999. *NGOs and Civil Society: Democracy by Proxy?* Cambridge: Polity Press.

Hulme, David, and Michael Edwards, eds. 1997. *NGOs, States and Donors: Too Close for Comfort?* New York: St. Martin's Press.

Hurrell, Andrew. 1992. "Brazil and the International Politics of Amazonian Deforestation." In *The International Politics of the Emvironment,* ed. Andrew Hurrell and Benedict Kingsbury, 398–429. Oxford: Oxford University Press.

Jepperson, Ronald L. 2002. "Political Modernities: Disentangling Two Underlying Dimensions of Institutional Differentiation." *Sociological Theory* 20, no. 1: 61–85.

Keane, John. 2003. *Global Civil Society?* Cambridge: Cambridge University Press.

Keck, Margaret E., and Kathryn Sikkink. 1998. *Activists beyond Borders.* Ithaca, N.Y.: Cornell University Press.

Khagram, Sanjeev, James V. Riker, and Kathryn Sikkink, eds. 2002. *Restructuring World Politics: Transnational Social Movements, Networks and Norms.* Minneapolis: University of Minnesota Press.

Khare, Arvind, and David Barton Bray. 2004. "Study of Critical New Forest Conservation

Issues in the Global South: Final report Submitted to the Ford Foundation, June 2004." Unpublished manuscript.

Klimabündnis. 2002. *Klimabündnis 2002 Jahresbericht.* Frankfurt am Main: Klimabündnis.

Knudson, Tom. 2003. "Staining the Amazon: The Tropics Suffer to Satisfy State's Thirst." Chapter 1 of "State of Denial" special report in the *Sacramento Bee,* April 27. Available at: www.sacbee.com/static/live/news/projects/denial.

Kolk, Ans. 1996. *Forests in International Environmental Politics: International Organizations, NGOs and the Brazilian Amazon.* Utrecht: International Books.

Koopmans, Ruud. 1995. *Democracy from Below: New Social Movements and the Political System in West Germany.* Boulder, Colo.: Westview Press.

Korten, Alicia. 2005. *Amazon Alliance Evaluation Report.* Renewal Resources Group. June, 2005.

Kuhlmann, Wolfgang, and Jürgen Wolters. 1994. *Das Regenwald-Memorandum, ARA Konkret 1.* Bielefeld, Germany: Arbeitsgemeinschaft Regenwald und Artenschutz, e.V. (ARA).

Lechner, Frank J., and John Boli. 2005. *World Culture: Origins and Consequences.* Maldon, Mass.: Blackwell.

Lehmann, Albrecht. 2004. "Mythos Wald: Was unser Waldbewusstsein und Waldwissen beeinflusst." *politische ökologie 89* (June): 12–16.

Lester, James P., and W. Douglas Costain. 1995. "The Evolution of Envrionmentalism: From Elitism to Participatory Democracy?" In *The New American Politics: Reflections on Politics Change and the Clinton Administration,* ed. Bryan D. Jones, 231–56. Boulder, Colo.: Westview Press.

Lipschutz, Ronnie D. 1994. "Reconstructing World Politics: The Emergence of Global Civil Society." *Millenium: Journal of International Studies* 21, no. 3: 389–420.

Mayer, Margit, and John Ely, 1998. *The German Greens: Paradox between Movement and Party.* Philadelphia: Temple University Press.

Mayer-Ries, Jörg. 1999. *Globalisierung lokaler Politik: Das Klima-Bündnis europäischer Städte mit den indigenen Völker Amazoniens.* Wiesbaden: Deutscher Universitäts-Verlag.

Meyer, John, et al. 1997. "World Society and the Nation-State." *American Journal of Sociology* 103, no. 1: 144–81.

Niezen, Ronald. 2003. *The Origins of Indigenism: Human Rights and the Politics of Identity.* Berkeley and Los Angeles: University of California Press.

Öko-Test. 2002. "Ökospenden." *Öko-Test,* November.

Pasha, Mustapha Kamal, and David L. Blaney. 1998. "Elusive Paradise: The Promises and Perils of Global Civil Society." *Alternatives: Societal Transformation and Human Governance* 23, no. 4: 417–50.

Pearce, Jenny. 1997. "Between Co-optation and Irrelevance? Latin American NGOs in the 1990s." In *NGOs, States, and Donors: Too Close for Comfort?* ed. David Hulme and Michael Edwards, 257–74. New York: St. Martin's Press.

Pieck, Sonja. 2006. "Crossed Paths to Eden: NGO Conflicts over Amazonian Nature." Ph.D. diss., Geography Department, Clark University.

Pieck, Sonja, and Sandra Moog. 2008. "Competing Entanglements in the Struggle to Save the Amazon: The Shifting Terrain of Transnational Civil Society." Paper presented to the American Sociological Society Meeting, Boston, Mass., August 4.

Rainforest Alliance. 2002. *Rainforest Alliance 2002 Annual Report.* New York: Rainforest Alliance.

Rainforest Foundation. 2002. *Rainforest Foundation 2002 Annual Report.* New York: Rainforest Foundation.

Rauprich, Nina. 1985. *Erst wenn der letzte Baum gestorben ist! Alternative Organizationen im Umweltschutz.* Frankfurt: Fischer.

Rich, Bruce. 1994. *Mortgaging the Earth: The World Bank, Environmental Impoverishment, and the Crisis of Development.* Boston: Beacon Press Books.

Risse-Kappen, Thomas, ed. 1995. *Bringing Transnational Relations Back In: Non-state Actors, Domestic Structures and International Institutions.* New York: Cambridge University Press.

Rohter, Larry. 2003. "Deep in the Amazon Forest, Vast Questions about Global Climate Change." *New York Times,* November 4.

Rosmarin, Heather, ed. 1995. *Ten Years of Rainforest Action Network.* San Francisco: Rainforest Action Network.

Roth, Roland, and Dieter Rucht, eds. 1987. *Neue soziale Bewegungen in der Bundesrepublik Deutschland.* Frankfurt: Campus Verlag.

Salamon, Lester M., and Helmut K. Anheier. 1998. "The Social Origins of Civil Society: Explaining the Nonprofit Sector Cross-Nationally." *Voluntas* 9, no. 3: 213–48.

Schofer, Evan, and Marion Fourcade-Gourinchas. 2001. "The Structural Contexts of Civic Engagement: Voluntary Association Membership in Comparative Perspective." *American Sociological Review* 66: 806–28.

Smith, Jackie. 1997. "Characteristics of the Modern Transnational Social Movement Sector." In *Transnational Social Movements and Global Politics: Solidarity Beyond the State,* ed. Jackie Smith, Charles Chatfield, and Ron Pagnucco, 42–58. Syracuse, N.Y.: Syracuse University Press.

———. 1998. "Global Civil Society? Transnational Social Movement Organizations and Social Capital." *American Behavioral Scientist* 42, no. 1: 93–107.

Smith, Jackie, Charles Chatfield, and Ron Pagnucco, eds. 1997. *Transnational Social Movements and Global Politics: Solidarity Beyond the State.* Syracuse, N.Y.: Syracuse University Press.

Soysal, Yasemin Nuhoglu. 1994. *Limits of Citizenship: Migrants and Postnational Membership in Europe.* Chicago: University of Chicago Press.

USAID. 1978. Proceedings of the U.S. Strategy Conference on Tropical Deforestation. Sponsored by U.S. Agency for International Development, Washington, D.C.

Walk, Heike, and Achim Brunnengräber. 2000. *Die Globalisierungswächter: NGOs und ihre transnationalen Netze im Konfliktfeld Klima.* Münster: Verlag Westfälisches Dampfboot.

Wapner, Paul. 1996. *Environmental Activism and World Civic Politics.* Albany: State University of New York Press.

———. 2000. "The Normative Promise of Non-state Actors: A Theoretical Account of

Global Civil Society." In *Principled World Politics: The Challenge of Normative International Relations,* ed. Paul Wapner and E. J. Ruiz. Lanham, 268–74. Lanham, Md.: Rowman and Littlefield.

Wood, Lesley J. 2005. "Bridging the Chasms: The Case of Peoples' Global Action." In *Coalitions across Borders: Transnational Protest and the Neoliberal Order,* ed. Joe Bandy and Jackie Smith, 95–117. Lanham, Md.: Rowman and Littlefield.

World Watch Magazine. 2005. "Reader Response," January/February.

Zhouri, Andrea. 1999. "Trees and People: An Anthropology of British Campaigners for the Amazon Rainforest." Ph.D. thesis, Department of Sociology, University of Essex.

Contributors

Sada Aksartova: Postdoctoral Research Fellow at the Center for Global Studies, George Mason University; Ph.D., sociology, Princeton University, 2005.

Elizabeth Bloodgood: Assistant Professor of Political Science, Concordia University, Montreal, Canada; Ph.D., politics, Princeton University, 2002.

Brendan Goff: Visiting Assistant Professor and Postdoctoral Fellow at the Eisenberg Institute for Historical Studies, University of Michigan; Ph.D., history, University of Michigan, 2008.

David C. Hammack: Haydn Professor of History and Mandel Center for Nonprofit Organizations, Case Western Reserve University.

Steven Heydemann: Vice President, Grants and Fellowships Program, and Special Adviser, Muslim World Initiative, United States Institute for Peace; Director, Center for Democracy and Civil Society at Georgetown University, 2003–2007.

Akira Iriye: Charles Warren Professor of American History, Harvard University.

Michael Lounsbury: Professor, School of Business, University of Alberta, Canada.

Sandra Moog: Lecturer in sociology, University of Essex, United Kingdom; Ph.D. candidate in sociology, University of California, Berkeley.

Kenneth Prewitt: Carnegie Professor of Public Affairs, School of International and Public Affairs at Columbia University.

John W. Slocum: Director, Initiative on Global Migration and Human Mobility, and Co-Chair, Higher Education Initiative in Russia, MacArthur Foundation.

David Strang: Professor of sociology, Cornell University.

Ann Swidler: Professor of sociology, University of California, Berkeley.

Jonathan VanAntwerpen: Research Fellow and Program Officer, Social Science Research Council; Ph.D. candidate in sociology, University of California, Berkeley.

Index

Boli, John, xi, 227–228
Boraine, Alex, 113–114
Borer, Tristan, 105
Borlaug, Norman, ix
Botha, P. W., 104
Boy Scouts, 50, 56, 60
Brazil, 28; development programs, 262, 273–274; social entrepreneurship, 85. *See also* Amazon Basin
Bretton Woods, 263
Bridgespan Group, 78
British Petroleum, 243
Brody, Reed, 98–99
Brower, David, 241
Bund für Umwelt und Naturschutz Deutschland (BUND), 241, 243, 265
Burger King Corporation, 263, 268, 273
Burt, Martin, 86
Bush, George W., 42, 246, 248

Cadet Corps Charity Foundation, 154n27
CAF-Russia, 143, 146, 147, 154n31, 155n37, 156n40, 187n31
Cairo agenda, 197
Calhoun, Craig, xii
CAMBIA, 90
Campaign for Nuclear Disarmament, 238
Canadian International Development Agency, 144, 194
Canadian Physicians for Aid and Relief, 208
Cárdenes, Stella, 88, 90
Cardoso, Henrique Fernandez, 7
CARE, 39, 194, 196
Carnegie Corporation, 40, 144
Catholic Charities, 32
Catholic Church, 14, 194, 277
Catholic Relief Services, 37
Central Asia, and Western grant economy, 23, 24, 160–191
Central Intelligence Agency, 40
Centro Mexicano para la Filantropía (CEMEFI), 11
Chabal, Patrick, 211
Chapin, Mac, 280–281, 283
Charities Aid Foundation, 141, 143, 146, 154n27, 170. *See also* CAF-Russia

Charles Stewart Mott Foundation, 144, 146, 147, 154n27, 187n31
Chernyshkova, Elena, 145
Chevron Corporation, 281, 287n37
Chikane, Frank, 105
child protection, 87, 88, 90. *See also* youth, at-risk
Childline, 85
China, ix, 9, 12, 42, 51, 89
Church World Service, 32, 37
Cissé, Garba Hamadoun, 88
civil rights movement, 10, 14, 286n22
civil society: in Eastern Europe, viii–ix, 9; and globalization, ix, 3–4, 12–13, 258, 259–261, 271; institutional characteristics, vii–viii, 259–261; Russian, 137–159; transnational, 258–292
Climate Alliance, 275–276, 277
climate-change campaigns, 241–250. *See also* Amazon Basin
Clinton, William Jefferson, 75
Clinton Foundation, 195
COICA. *See* Coordinating Body of Indigenous Organizations of the Amazon Basin
Cold War, 19, 23, 33, 34, 37–38, 41, 42
Collier, George, 212–213
Commission for Civil Society and Human Rights (Russia), 165
Committee to Democratize Information Technology, 85
Communist Party, 140, 180
Community Action Network, 81–82
Community Development Venture Capital Alliance, 79
conflict resolution, 9, 22
Congress of Vienna, 35
Conservation International, 276, 281, 287n31
Cooperative for American Remittances to Europe. *See* CARE
Coordinating Body of Indigenous Organizations of the Amazon Basin, 262, 267, 274–277, 281
Cornell, Stephen, 207, 210–211, 214
cosmopolitan discourse, 96–97, 124
cultural exchange, 37, 40–41, 171

cultural match, 207, 210–211, 214
Cultural Survival, 262, 264, 276

Daloz, Jean Paul, 211
Daly, Erin, 116
David, Andrea, 88
Dees, Gregory, 73–74, 79–80
democracy promotion, viii, 13, 18, 23–24, 39, 144, 171
Dengi i blagotvoritel'nost' (journal), 143
Detskii fond (Children's Fund), 140
Deutsch Naturschutz Ring (DNR), 265
developmental assistance, 37, 38–39, 208
diffusion of ideas, 3–7, 11, 12–13, 16–17, 21, 72, 73, 91–92, 100–102, 168–172, 179, 223–226
DiMaggio, Paul, xi, 100, 195, 226
disaster relief. *See* humanitarian relief
Dow Chemical Company, 287n37
Doxtader, Erik, 116–117
Drayton, Bill, 83
Drucker, Peter, 78
Du Pont, 87
du Toit, André, 110, 111
Duck Revolution, 85
Duke Energy Corporation, 287n37
Durón, Jorge Fidel, 64
Dynasty Foundation, 141, 145, 147, 154n27

Earthjustice Legal Defense Fund, 282
Earthrights International, 278
Eastern Europe, viii–ix, 23–24; civil society, 19; social entrepreneurship, 82; truth and reconciliation, 111
Echoing Green, 79
Ecologic, 86
Emerson, Jed, 80
Endeavor Global, 90
Englund, Harri, 216n12
Environmental Defense Foundation, 264, 276
Environmental Policy Institute, 262, 264
environmentalism, 4, 9, 18, 27–28, 37, 86, 144, 182, 227, 241–250, 258–283. *See also* Amazon Basin; Friends of the Earth; Greenpeace
Escobar, Arturo, xi

Escobar, Enrique, 7
Eurasia Foundation, 146, 147, 161, 163, 170, 171
Europe: HIV/AIDS programs, 194; individual rights expansion, 12; international community making, 34–36; NGO diffusion, 14–15
European Bank for Reconstruction and Development, 243
European Commission, 144
European Foundation Centre, 11, 145–146
European Union, 42
Evans-Pritchard, E. E., 198–199
Export Import Bank, 250
ExxonMobil Corporation, 246, 247, 248, 249, 250, 287n37

fair trade, 86
Family Health International, 194
Federation of Atomic Scientists, 37–38
Ferguson, James, 7
Fisher, Jesse C., 57–60, 61, 62, 66
Fisher, Martin, 85, 87
Foote, William, 86
Ford Foundation, ix, 11, 19, 38, 40–41, 144, 154n27, 161, 276, 279
Ford Motor Company, 247, 248, 273
foreign policy, 223–257
forgiveness, 95, 100, 103–104, 106, 108–111, 114–115, 118–124
Fortes, Meyer, 198–199
foundations. *See* philanthropic foundations
4-H clubs, 56, 60
Frances, Nic, 86
Freedom House, 231
FreePlay, 86, 87
Friends of the Earth, 27, 224–225, 241–245, 248–250, 282–283, 285n18
Fukushima, Kisoji ("Bill"), 47, 48, 49, 54, 57, 66
Fulbright program, 40
Fundacion Paraguaya, 86, 90
Furniture Resource Center, 86
Furuno, Takao, 85, 86, 87, 90

Gabriel, Peter, 88

Iacocca, Lee, 76
Ignatieff, Michael, 98, 100, 111
Immigration Act (1924), 48–49
India, 13, 42, 66, 82, 85, 88
innovativeness, 73–74
Institute for Justice and Reconciliation, 99, 102, 103, 112, 114–115, 123
Institute for OneWorld Health, 88, 90
Institute for Social Entrepreneurship, 79
Institute of Pacific Relations, 50
institutional logics: Amazon Basin, exporting into the, 258–292; contesting, 23–27, 137–220; defined, 7–9; and NGOs, 8–9, 258–292; and philanthropy, 8–9, 137–159; projection of, viii–ix, 3–31, 47–134, 248–250, 258–292; of reconciliation, 95–134; of social entrepreneurship, 71–74, 90–92; success stories and, 73, 82–85, 91–92; of transitional justice, 95–134; transnational, 5, 27–28, 41–43, 47–70, 223–292
Inter-American Development Bank, 262, 273–274
Inter-American Foundation, 11
International Center for Transitional Justice, 99, 102, 112, 113–114
International Committee of the Red Cross, 35. See also Red Cross
International Foundation for Civil Liberties, 153n17
International Monetary Fund, 165, 186n13, 263, 266–267
International Research and Exchanges Board (IREX), 145, 154n27, 170
International Tropical Timber Organization, 263
International Union for Conservation of Nature (IUCN), 283n1
Interregional Siberian Center for Social Initiative Support, 154n27
Irvine, E. L., 53
isomorphism: buzz words, 195–197; coercive, 19–20, 24–25, 148, 149, 150, 181–184; in the former Soviet Union, 137, 148–150, 160–191; and HIV/AIDS programs, 195–198; institutional, 4, 16, 100–101, 225–228; and legitimacy,

148–150; and local governance, 197–198; mimetic, 24, 195; and reconciliation, 124–125, 126; and social entrepreneurship, 22

Japan: climate-change campaigns, 242–243, 245, 247, 249; government system, 234–235, 236–237; political advocacy, 238, 239, 240–241; post-WWII, 19, 32–34, 65–66; Rotary clubs, 17, 20–21, 47–70; social entrepreneurship, 85
job training, 88
John D. and Catherine T. MacArthur Foundation, 144, 151n1, 154n27, 170, 184n3
John Snow Inc., 194
Johns Hopkins University, 194
Johnson, Lyndon, 75
Johnstone, Walter L., 48, 49
Jordan, Alexis, 154n27
Journal of Voluntary Action Research, 76, 77
justice. *See* restorative justice; transitional justice

Kairos Document, 104, 105
Kaiser Family Foundation, 194
Kaler, Amy, 203, 204
Kalt, Joseph, 207, 210–211, 214
Kaminarskaya, Natalya, 155n31
Karlström, Mikael, 211
Katz, Daniel, 268–269
Kauffman Foundation, 79
Keck, Margaret E., xi, 35
Kellogg Foundation. *See* W. K. Kellogg Foundation
Khodorkovsky, Mikhail, 142, 146
KickStart, 85, 86, 87, 90
Kilko Network, 242
King, Charles, 78
Kitashima, Watari ("Kitty"), 53, 65, 66
Knudson, Tom, 282
Kohl, Helmut, 267, 274, 278
Koizumi, Junichiro, 247
Komatsu, Takashi, 62–64, 65–66
Korean War, 38
Krog, Antjie, 95, 96, 109, 111

Kyoto Protocol, 242
Kyrgyzstan, and Western grant economy, 160–191

Law on Endowments (Russia), 141, 143, 150, 153n22
League of Nations, 49
Lebedev, Platon, 142
legitimacy, and isomorphism, 148–150
Leviwa, Jones, 206–207
Lewis, Richard, 81
Lewis, Sinclair, 58
Lewis, Stephen, 207–208
Liberal Democratic Party, 234, 235
logics, institutional. *See* institutional logics
Lutheran World Relief, 37
Lyons, F. L. S., 35

Mabaso, Lybon, 129n72
MacArthur, Douglas, 32, 65–66
MacArthur Foundation. *See* John D. and Catherine T. MacArthur Foundation
Madariaga European Foundation, 147
Malan, Wynand, 128n50
Malawi, 26, 194, 196, 202, 203, 206–210, 212
Malawi Diffusion and Ideational Change Project, 215n4
Manchester Craftsmen's Guild, 76, 78, 81
Mandel, Ruth, 188n41
markets, and social services, 4
Mauss, Marcel, xi, 8
Maynes, Bill, 146
Mbeki, Thabo, 106
McCarthyism, 33
McDonald's Corporation, 263
McKinsey & Company, 78, 84
Means, George, 65–66
Megata, Baron, 47
Méndez, Juan E., 113
Merck, 87
Metsenat (journal), 143
Mexican Center for Philanthropy, 11
Meyer, John W., xi, 100, 101, 102, 124, 226–227, 283n1
Migdal, Joel, 198

Mitsubishi Motors, 273
Mkhatshwa, Smangaliso, 105
Monsanto, 287n37
Moon, Nick, 85, 87
Moore Foundation. *See* Gordon and Betty Moore Foundation
moral globalization, 98, 100–103, 111
Moscow State Institute of International Relations, 143
Mott Foundation. *See* Charles Stewart Mott Foundation
Muslim migration, 14
Mxenge, Griffiths, 129n72

Napoleonic Wars, 34–35
nation building, 38, 72, 115, 121–122, 123, 129n73
National AIDS Commission (Malawi), 208
National AIDS Control Council (Kenya), 206
National Business Plan Competition for Nonprofit Organizations, 81
National Gathering of Social Entrepreneurs, 80
National Resources Defense Council, 262, 264, 276, 287n31
National Social Venture Competition, 80–81
National Wildlife Federation, 262, 264, 276
Nature Conservancy, 278–279, 281
Naudé, Beyers, 105
New Eurasia Foundation, 146, 147, 154n27
New Profit, 79
Nguyen, Vinh-Kim, 196–197
nongovernmental organizations (NGOs): Africa, 192–220; Brazil, 85, 269, 277–279; China, 9, 12; Europe, 35–36; and foreign policy, 223–257; Germany, 233–234, 238–241, 265–267, 269–283; and institutional logics, 8–9; and international community making, 32–43; Japan, 234–235, 238, 239, 240–241; Kyrgyzstan, 160–191; Mali, 88; Mexico, 11; Russia, 137–191; tactics and strategies, 228–229; United Kingdom, 232–233,

238, 239, 240–241; United States, 9, 32–34, 36–42, 230–232, 238, 239, 240, 260, 264–265, 267–283

nonprofit academic programs and associations: Association for Research on Nonprofits and Voluntary Action (ARNOVA), 77; Association of Voluntary Action Scholars, 76, 77; Case Western Reserve University, 77; City University of New York, 77; Columbia University, 77, 79, 80–81; Cornell University, 77, 79; Duke University, 77, 79; Haas School of Business, 80; Harvard University, 77, 79–80, 81, 194; Independent Sector, 77, 78; Indiana University, 77; London Business School, 79; Maryland Association of Nonprofits, 78; Minnesota Council of Nonprofits, 78; New School for Social Research, 77; Nonprofit Academic Centers Council, 77; Northwestern University, 77; Oxford University, 79, 83; Program on NonProfit Organizations (PONPO), 76, 77; Stanford University, 77, 79; SUNY/Stony Brook, 77; University of California/Berkeley, 79; University of Colorado/Denver, 77; University of Missouri/Kansas City, 76–77; University of Pennsylvania, 77; University of San Francisco, 77; Yale University, 76, 77, 81

Nonprofit and Voluntary Sector Quarterly, 77

nonprofit organizations. *See* nongovernmental organizations (NGOs)

North America Free Trade Area, 42

North American Aerospace Defense Command (NORAD), 194

Novica.com, 87, 90

Ohtani, Noboru, 53

Open Russia, 141, 142

Open Society Institute, 142, 144, 147, 154n27, 160, 170, 171, 185n9

Open World Program, 171

Organization for Security and Co-operation in Europe, 165

Ovation Entertainment, 81

Overseas Private Investment Corporation, 250

Oxfam, 262, 264, 276, 281, 285n20

Pachamama Alliance, 278, 282

Parsons, Talcott, 8

Partnership of Russian Community Foundations, 146–147, 155n31

Partnership on Nonprofit Ventures, 81

Paul, Saint, 103

peace and arms control, 37–38, 40–41, 43, 60–61

Peace Corps, 194, 200–201, 202, 205–206

Pearson, Kristine, 86

Penang Conservation Organization, 285n18

People Tree, 89–90

perestroika, 180, 187n28

Perry, Chelsea, 55

Personal Responsibility and Work Opportunity Reconciliation Act (1996), 75

Peters, Thomas, 76

Pew Charitable Trusts, 81

philanthropic foundations: American, viii, 12, 13–14, 16–17, 19, 40–42, 160–191, 243–244, 245, 246, 249–250, 258–259, 260, 264–265, 267–283; defined, 151–152n5; European, 11, 12, 14–15; German, 241, 243, 245, 249, 258–259, 265–267, 269–283; in Russia, 137–159

philanthropic projection, viii–ix, 3–31; African AIDS programs, 192–220; in the Amazon Basin, 258–292; climate-change campaigns, 223–257; defined, 6, 7; and international community making, 32–43; in Russia, 137–159; and social entrepreneurship, 71–74, 90–92

Pinneo, Roger D., 48

Pinochet, Augusto, 104

Plan International, 208

PMTCT+ (Prevention of Mother-to-Child Transmission Plus), 195

political action committees, 231, 243–244

political reconciliation, 115, 117. *See also* reconciliation; truth and reconciliation

Population Services International, 194

Skoll, Jeff, 17, 81, 83, 91
Skoll Foundation, 79, 82–89, 91
Skoll World Forum on Social Entrepreneurship, 84
slavery abolition, 35
Smith, Adam, 71, 91
Smith, Daniel Jordan, 199, 201
Smith, David Horton, 76
Social Enterprise Alliance, 78, 79, 80
Social Enterprise Initiative, 79–80
social entrepreneurs, characteristics of,
   89–90, 92
social entrepreneurship: academic programs, 76–77, 79, 80–81; Australia, 86;
   Bangladesh, 82; Brazil, 85; business
   models, 80–81; case studies, 73, 82–90;
   Chile, 89; China, 89; Colombia, 88;
   defined, 71–74, 87–88; Egypt, 86, 88;
   foundation support, 79, 82–85; France,
   82; Hungary, 88; India, 82, 85, 88; international spread of, 81–82; Japan, 85;
   Kenya, 85; Mali, 88; Paraguay, 88; Philippines, 88; project examples, 85–89;
   projection of, 17, 21–22, 71–74, 90–92;
   success story model, 21–22, 82–85; U.S.
   origins, 71–72, 75–81
social science, and philanthropic studies,
   vii–ix
Social Venture Partners, 79
Society for Women and AIDS in Zambia,
   203
Solana, Javier, 147
Soros, George, 142, 144, 147, 160, 181. *See
   also* Open Society Institute
South Africa, Truth and Reconciliation
   Commission, 17, 18, 22–23, 95–134
Soviet Union, vii, viii. *See also* post-Soviet
   era; Russia
State Department. *See* U.S. Department
   of State
Stear, Rory, 86
Stefan Batory Foundation, 147
Stewart, Potter, 71, 73, 87
Sting (Gordon Sumner), 269
Strang, David, 226–227
Strickland, Bill, 76, 78, 81
Survival International, 262

SWAAZ. *See* Society for Women and
   AIDS in Zambia
Synergos, 11

Takata, Masakazu, 57
Tarrow, Sidney, 225–226, 227
technology training, 85
technology transfer, 17
terrorism, 41–42
Third World Solidarity Movement, 263
Thomas, George M., xi, 228
Thomas, Mark, 243
Thompson, Dennis, 110, 117–121, 124
Threshold Foundation, 268
Tilly, Charles, 101, 102
Tokugawa, Marquis, 50, 58, 59
Tolosio, 205–206
TransFair, U.S.A., 86, 87, 90
transitional justice, 22–23, 95–134
transnational logics, 5, 27–28, 41–43,
   47–70, 223–292
Trauma Center for Victims of Violence
   and Torture (South Africa), 118
Trump, Donald, 76
truth and reconciliation: Australia, 111;
   Burma, 111; Chile, 106, 107, 109, 111; East
   Timor, 111, 112; Eastern Europe, 111;
   Ghana, 112, 113; Guatemala, 122; Latin
   America, 18, 125; Northern Ireland,
   111; Peru, 96, 111, 112, 113; Sierra Leone,
   96, 112, 113; South Africa, 17, 18, 22–23,
   95–134
Tulane University, 194
Tutu, Desmond, 22, 95, 96, 103, 104, 105,
   106, 107, 108, 109, 111, 118–119, 120, 122

ubuntu, 95, 109, 111, 122, 126n2
UNAIDS, 194, 198, 216n10
UNESCO, 43
Union of Charitable Organizations of
   Russia, 143
United Kingdom: climate-change cam-
   paigns, 243, 245, 246–247, 250; govern-
   ment system, 232–233, 236–237; politi-
   cal advocacy, 238, 239, 240–241; social
   entrepreneurship, 81–82, 90
United Nations: AIDS funding study,

David C. Hammack is Hiram C. Haydn Professor of History at Case Western Reserve University. His most recent books include *Identity, Conflict, and Cooperation: Central Europeans in Cleveland, 1870–1930* (edited with John Grabowski and Diane Ewart Grabowski) and *Making the Nonprofit Sector in the United States: A Reader* (Indiana University Press, 1998).

Steven Heydemann is Director and Research Associate Professor at the Center for Democracy and Civil Society at Georgetown University. A political scientist whose research focuses on democratization and economic reform in the Middle East, and on the relationship between institutions and economic development more broadly, Heydemann has edited *Networks of Privilege in the Middle East: The Politics of Economic Reform Revisited* and *War, Institutions, and Social Change in the Middle East.* He is author of *Authoritarianism in Syria: Institutions and Social Conflict, 1946–1970.*

* 9 7 8 0 2 5 3 3 5 3 0 3 0 *